Trance and Treatment

TRANCE
and
TREATMENT

Clinical Uses of
Hypnosis

HERBERT SPIEGEL, M.D.
DAVID SPIEGEL, M.D.

Basic Books, Inc., Publishers   New York

Library of Congress Cataloging in Publication Data

Spiegel, Herbert   1914–
  Trance and treatment.

   Bibliographic References: p. 357
   Includes index.
   1. Hypnotism—Therapeutic use. I. Spiegel,
David, 1945–   joint author. II. Title.
[DNLM: 1. Hypnosis. WM415.3 S755t]
RC495.S67   616.8′916′2   77–20420
ISBN: 0–465–08687–X

To our patients, students, teachers,

and colleagues,

who share with us the excitement

of learning

CONTENTS

PART III

Using Hypnosis in Treatment

PREFACE

A few weeks after Pearl Harbor, one of us (H.S.) was transformed from a psychiatric resident at St. Elizabeths Hospital in Washington, D.C., into an Army psychiatrist at Ft. Meade, Maryland. Lewis B. Hill, my analyst at the time, introduced me to Professor Gustave Aschaffenburg who gave me informal instructions on hypnosis, which I found extremely useful in the Army, especially while in combat in North Africa. After returning to the States, the Army assigned me to teach at the School of Military Psychiatry at Mason General Hospital, where I was able to develop my interest and research in hypnosis.

A senior analyst advised me to be careful regarding this interest because it could "tarnish" my reputation as a serious psychiatrist and psychoanalyst. After all, Freud had abandoned hypnosis! At the time I resumed analytic supervision with Frieda Fromm-Reichman, Harry Stack Sullivan, and Erich Fromm, I mentioned to Clara Thompson, my new analyst, that I was considering dropping my work with hypnosis. She obviously informed Fromm-Reichman about this because at my next supervisory session Frieda berated me for succumbing to such conventional thinking, and she wondered why I felt so fragile that I had to worry about such nonsense as being "tarnished." Furthermore, in her persuasive manner she arranged in 1947 to have me give a seminar on hypnosis at the White Institute in New York and she enrolled as the first student. To my surprise, she was fascinated by hypnotic phenomena, although she claimed she herself did not feel comfortable using hypnosis in therapy.

One of the issues which emerged during our seminars dealt with the relationship between hypnotizability and mental illness. At that time, fresh from combat experience, I assumed that hypnotizability was a direct function of emotional stress and illness; for example, to be hypnotizable meant being psychologically weak or fragile. Frieda challenged this notion. She felt that although hypnotizability was *identified* in stressed persons, it could also be identified in secure, trusting, non-stressed, mentally healthy persons as well. She proposed that I expand my data base to explore this proposal. At first I dismissed this notion. After all, she admitted that she herself did not use hypnosis, whereas

I did. But as my work continued I did indeed learn that not only were secure and healthy people hypnotizable, but the severely mentally ill were not hypnotizable at all. Thus, as I gained more experience and knowledge over the years, I discovered that Frieda's insight in 1947 had been right and I had been wrong.

This realization sparked interest in other issues, especially the need to find a practical clinical measurement for trance capacity. By the 1960s experimental psychologists working in the laboratory had developed assessment tests, but these tests had serious shortcomings for clinical use. What I had in mind, on the other hand, was the aphorism: If you can measure it, it is science; everything else is poetry. The challenge was to develop a clinical measurement that could transform much of the rich body of clinical intuition, observations, and anecdotal data into more fruitful and systematic information.

I was further encouraged by pressure from students in the hypnosis courses (which I have conducted yearly since 1962) at Columbia University College of Physicians and Surgeons. This ultimately led to the development of the Hypnotic Induction Profile.

Once the assessment of trance capacity became possible, we were able to distinguish between trance capacity and treatment strategy. The ambiguous fusion of the two has been typical of most of the classical literature on hypnosis to date. This fusion has also unfortunately accounted for illusions of power on the part of many therapists using hypnosis. There are still some therapists who even today believe, overtly or covertly, that they have some God-given power to impose trance upon others. Mesmer believed this two hundred years ago, but modern therapists have learned a more appropriate humility.

The separation and the interaction between trance assessment and relevant treatment strategy emerged in my own thinking at the same time that my son and coauthor emerged as an inquiring student and ultimately a stimulating colleague. Over the past fifteen years we have spent countless hours mulling over what has become the thesis of this book.

Except for the early development of the eye roll and the Hypnotic Induction Profile, I would, if pressed, find it impossible to separate with any clarity or fairness what is clearly his or my contribution. This work developed out of our dialectical relationship. One of the delights and rewards of being a father is to experience creative moments with a son. We have had many and I hope we have more.

The other of us (D.S.) was fortunate enough to have had an inherited rather than an acquired exposure to hypnosis. I was profoundly influenced by watching and learning from my father's work with patients. The rapidity with which he established clinical rapport and the effectiveness of the brief therapy techniques along with the pleasure he derives from his work impressed me. During my medical and psychiatric training, I discovered that the use of hypnosis often counted among those rare times when I felt that what I had done made a real difference for the patient. The experience of helping a young asthmatic master her attacks and avoid hospitalization provided confirmation of my developing belief that the mind had an important role to play in the maintenance of health in the body. My existential orientation was tempered but not overwhelmed by the study of medicine.

I was greatly stimulated by attending the hypnosis course at Columbia University, first as a student, and in later years as a teacher. The atmosphere of excitement, the predictability with which the unexpected happened, and the shared enthusiasm of teacher and students infected me. We have tried to capture some of this spirit in the written word.

We have been intrigued by hypnotic phenomena throughout our professional careers. Attempting to utilize hypnosis has enriched our clinical experience in both understanding and treating patients. This book has been written to make available to clinicians a brief, disciplined technique for mobilizing and learning from an individual's capacity to concentrate. In the past there have been exaggerated fears about hypnosis and overblown statements of its efficacy. Our effort has been to bring scientific discipline to bear on the subject and to systematically explore its clinical use and limitations. The first rule of medicine is: Do no harm. Those of us who intervene in the lives of others can best obey this rule by knowing our instruments well. We have written *Trance and Treatment* as an introduction for someone new to the subject of hypnosis, but we have also included material in sufficient depth so that therapists with wide experience in the field can acquire new perspectives. Our approach differs from the current clinical literature in emphasizing the importance of performing a systematic assessment of hypnotizability; our method is described in detail along with data relating performance on our Hypnotic Induction Profile to personality style, psychopathology, and treatment outcome.

The book will have special interest for the psychiatrist, psychologist, and psychotherapist. It is also meant to be of use to physicians, dentists, and other clinicians who are interested in learning to use hypnotic techniques for problems such as pain control, habit control, and the differential diagnosis of functional from organic disease. We hope that our data are sufficiently systematic to provoke controversy and interest among scientific students of hypnosis.

Although immersed in a psychiatric tradition that carries considerable respect for objectivity and precise description, we describe human behavior phenomenologically as it relates to hypnosis in a probable rather than an absolute fashion. In this spirit we present our experience with hypnosis in a clinical setting. We have not exhaustively reviewed the considerable literature in the field, although we have reviewed certain portions that seem particularly relevant to the important themes in the book. Where possible, we have applied statistical methods to test our hypotheses. Much of this work continues; at this stage we are as much engaged in hypothesis generation as in hypothesis confirmation.

The realm of investigation encompassing hypnosis and psychological dysfunction is a comparatively new one. We are only beginning to see the results of studying trance capacity in relation to a variety of psychological and neurobiological dimensions. We look forward with particular excitement to the day when there will be greater convergence of knowledge regarding hypnosis and brain function.

We also gratefully acknowledge use of excerpts from the following sources:

From *International Journal of Clinical and Experimental Hypnosis:* Spiegel, Herbert, "A Single Treatment Method to Stop Smoking Using Ancillary Self-Hypnosis," 1970, vol. 18, pp. 235–250; Spiegel, Herbert, "The Grade 5 Syndrome: The Highly Hypnotizable Person," 1974, vol. 22, pp. 303–319; Spiegel, Herbert, "Hypnotic Intervention As an Adjunct for Rapid Clinical Relief," 1963, vol. 11, pp. 23–29. All copyright by The Society for Clinical and Experimental Hypnosis. Reproduced by permission of the publisher.

Irwin M. Greenberg, "General Systems Theory of Trance State." Used by permission of the author.

Herbert Spiegel, *Manual for Hypnotic Induction Profile: Eye-roll Levitation Method*, rev. ed. (New York: Soni Medica), 1973.

"Dream Existence," in *Being in the World: Selected Papers of Ludwig Binswanger*, translated and with a Critical Introduction to his existential psychoanalysis by Jacob Needleman. © 1963 by Basic Books, Inc., Publishers, New York.

"The Evil Seekers" by Anne Sexton in *The Awful Rowing Toward God*. Copyright © 1975 by Loring Conant, Jr., Executor of the estate of Anne Sexton. Reprinted by permission of Houghton Mifflin Company.

From "The Love Song of J. Alfred Prufrock" in *Collected Poems 1909–1962* by T. S. Eliot, copyright © 1936 by Harcourt Brace Jovanovich, Inc., copyright © 1963, 1964 by T. S. Eliot. Reprinted by permission of the publishers.

HERBERT SPIEGEL
DAVID SPIEGEL

New York City
January 5, 1978

ACKNOWLEDGMENTS

We are grateful to many people who kindly lent support and encouragement, provided technical assistance, shared case material, critically discussed ideas, or reviewed the manuscript. We wish to thank in particular the following individuals.

The late William A. Horwitz, M.D., Lawrence C. Kolb, M.D. of the College of Physicians and Surgeons, Columbia University, Bernard Holland, M.D., Nicholas Avery, M.D., Leonard Friedman, M.D., Gary Aamodt, Ph.D., Thomas P. Hackett, M.D., Christian von Doepp, M.D., and Farrell Phillips, all provided early suggestions, encouragement, and support. Professor Hope Jensen Leichter of Teachers College, Columbia University was especially helpful with advice in developing the first draft.

Bert S. Kopell, M.D. and the staff of the Psychiatry Service at the Palo Alto Veterans Administration Hospital and the Department of Psychiatry and Behavioral Sciences at Stanford were generous in their support as the book was being completed.

The psychodiagnostic work of Florence Schumer, Ph.D., Florence Halpern, Ph.D., and Rose Wolfson, Ph.D. was a rich resource for our research relating psychiatric diagnosis to hypnotizability. Donnel B. Stern, Ph.D. provided formal and informal methodological consultation and has been a patient and constructive critic. Joseph L. Fleiss, Ph.D. offered invaluable statistical consultation which was later implemented by John Nee, Ph.D. Brian Maruffi, Laurie Lipman, and Marc Aronson provided thoughtful and diligent technical assistance. Edward Detrick, Ph.D. and Donald Farber were helpful in our literature review.

The following individuals shared important aspects of their clinical experience with us: Barbara H. DeBetz, M.D., Ernest E. Rockey, M.D., Burton Nackenson, M.D., John T. Janics, M.D., Jerome Haber, M.D., and Sandra Marcowitz Behrman.

Doris and Robert A. Magowan and the Charles E. Merrill Trust, Audrey Sheldon, and the Merlin Foundation provided generous financial support for the research studies reported in this book.

We are especially grateful to Irvin Yalom, M.D. for taking the time to read the manuscript carefully and offer many helpful critical suggestions. Herb Reich of Basic Books provided a series of necessary but gentle pushes in the direction of completion and many useful suggestions regarding the manuscript. Helen Blau, Ph.D. provided support, criticism, and encouragement throughout.

H.S.

D.S.

Trance and Treatment

Prologue

L'intelligence est caracterisée par
une incomprehension naturelle de
la vie.
*Intellect is characterized by a
natural inability to understand life.*
Henri Bergson
Creative Evolution

In these few sardonic words the French philosopher Bergson posed a
fundamental problem faced by anyone attempting to study the human
mind and human behavior. Our fixed concepts invariably distort what
we study. Yet the data available are so rich and diverse that some order
must be imposed to make our perception of human behavior possible
and to some degree more meaningful. Philosophically we begin with a
recognition that our undertaking is paradoxical; we cannot help but
impose certain constructs upon the phenomena we observe, yet we
know that we are influencing and in some ways distorting what we
study. We will record and simplify our presumptions so that their impact
can be evaluated.

A particular problem confronts us as therapists in discussing the
clinical uses of hypnosis. Hypnosis is commonly viewed as something
"done to" a person and it is widely considered a therapy. From our perspective, hypnosis is not in itself a therapy, yet it can tremendously
facilitate a therapeutic strategy. Thus it makes good sense to present
hypnosis in the context of treatment, although in itself it is not a treatment. Furthermore, it is strictly speaking not something done to a person, it is rather a capacity for a certain style of concentration which can
be evoked either alone or in the presence of others.

We present hypnosis not as an isolated phenomenon, but in the context of its occurrence. One must examine alternative types of human

consciousness to understand hypnosis; to make the best use of it in psychotherapy, one must consider alternative personality styles, diagnoses, and therapeutic strategies.

The following propositions are fundamental to our work:

1. The balance between focal and peripheral awareness is the fundamental parameter of the trance experience.
2. As an isolated phenomenon, hypnosis has no significant meaning. It attains significance only in relation to the individual's innate perceptive and cognitive capacities as they are utilized within the context of his environment.
3. Trance induction is a ceremony which facilitates a transformation from a customary to a special awareness.
4. Trance capacity, as measured by the Hypnotic Induction Profile, has a significant relationship to the total adult personality structure.
5. Except under special circumstances such as severe environmental stress, psychophysiological decompensation, and neurological deficit, an adult's style of transformation into the trance state (his trance capacity) tends to be stable over time.
6. Three overlapping characterological styles are related to the degree of trance capacity. Each style is composed of a cluster of distinctly identifiable, internally consistent cognitive and behavioral patterns. We identify these as Dionysian, Apollonian, and Odyssean.
7. The assessment of hypnotizability is a useful diagnostic aid that can facilitate the choice of an appropriate treatment modality along the entire spectrum of mental health and illness.
8. Hypnosis can facilitate and accelerate various primary treatment strategies.

We will attempt to demonstrate, amplify, and apply these points to the clinical use of hypnosis. By way of perspective on the thoughts and data to be presented, we will review briefly the "state of the art," first in clinical and experimental hypnosis, and then in psychiatry.

State of the Art

The literature on hypnosis is a fascinating amalgam of anecdotal assertions, mystical speculations, and extremely astute clinical observations. At the same time there have been remarkable advances in the laboratory in applying disciplined investigative procedures from the behavioral sciences to the field of hypnosis. Unfortunately, comparatively little fruitful integration has occurred between clinicians and researchers, a situation sometimes referred to as a "cross sterilization" of disciplines.

A major problem in integrating clinical experience with the more disciplined but remote laboratory experience has been the absence of an adequate clinical probe, a means of assessing hypnotic capacity which would be appropriate to the clinical setting. Measures such as the Stanford Hypnotic Susceptibility Scale (Weitzenhoffer and Hilgard

1959), the Harvard Group Scales of Hypnotic Susceptibility (Shor and Orne 1962), the Barber Suggestibility Scale (Barber and Glass 1962), and others were developed in the laboratory, usually using college student populations. These tests proved to be time consuming and were in some ways inappropriate to the atmosphere of urgency for problem resolution which typifies the clinical setting. A clinical probe was needed which would represent some of the discipline of the laboratory measures and would also be clinically appropriate.

This book is an effort to synthesize laboratory discipline and an appropriate respect for the observations and intuitive judgments of the clinician. It is hardly a final product but it does represent an approach to making clinical experience with hypnosis more systematic by using measurements that have evolved during the past decade.

In reviewing the past decades in the field of psychiatry there appears to be a tendency by therapists to employ the treatment modality which they are trained to use without carefully scrutinizing the relevance of that treatment for a given patient. For example, we have gone through phases where electroconvulsive therapy, insulin shock therapy, and prefrontal lobotomy have been used rather freely and indiscriminately. Of the three, only ECT is still used and only then with clinicians obliged to define a subpopulation who really benefit from the procedure. Among the currently popular forms of treatment are drug therapy, behavior modification, and psychoanalytic psychotherapy. These very often have been applied without examining the relevance of a given therapy for a patient and that patient's capacity to make good use of the treatment experience.

Sometimes it is easier to gain perspective by taking examples from other disciplines. Let us take the hypothetical example of a young surgeon training under a master surgeon who teaches him to perform the best possible cholecystectomy. The young surgeon realizes that with this skill he now has an edge on his colleagues. He goes into private practice and reasons in the following manner: "Since I spent the best years of my life learning how to do this cholecystectomy I now have good reason to use it." As a result, each patient appearing in his office with abdominal pain is very likely to undergo a cholecystectomy whether the indications for it are clear or not. It is easy to condemn his approach, but is there not something like it going on in the field of psychiatry? Do we not tend to specialize in treatments rather than in treating patient's needs? We attempt to cope with this problem in psychiatry by making as clear as possible those situations in which hypnosis is not relevant to a given clinical situation. The clinical assessment of hypnotizability is particularly useful in making this distinction. It is perhaps more important to inform clinicians when the use of hypnosis is not relevant than to tell them when it is.

Another phenomenon apparent in the recent history of psychiatry has been a preoccupation with labeling the various disease syndromes in detail. We employ labels only to the extent that they are operationally useful. Nosology is necessary insofar as it helps the therapist and the patient make appropriate treatment decisions. It is not absolute; it is rather a means to an end.

Freud's continuing presence in the psychiatric scene is undeniable. His work has left us with something of a polarization between the psychodynamic therapies and the descriptive organic school of psychiatry. Disagreements between these schools have taken the form of emphasizing theoretical detail and psychotherapeutic process versus precise empirical description of disease states and outcome evaluation. Our quest for certainty in the face of the ambiguities and complexities of human behavior has led to a kind of either/or thinking in which one approach is exalted at the expense of all others.

We have drawn on concepts from various schools within psychiatry— psychoanalytic, biological, interpersonal, and existential among others —and have tried to avoid condemning any of the various approaches. In a sense, almost any modality may be helpful to somebody, somehow, under certain conditions. We are proposing the assessment of hypnotizability as one rational means for classifying the various schools of psychotherapy, and for helping the clinician make a better match between patient and treatment. Our approach represents a systematic attempt to identify, measure, and utilize a given patient's optimal therapeutic potential. This process, which has in the past been relegated to clinical intuition, is subject to more precise study and consensual validation.

Theory and Practice: Philosophical Background

These problems of reconciling theory with empirical data have troubled philosophers for centuries and several philosophical concepts have been helpful to us.

Ortega y Gasset provides a valuable characterization of the dialectical interplay between the observer and that which is observed (Marias 1970). In a series of elegantly sweeping generalizations regarding the development of the theory of knowledge, he poses three metaphors of knowing. The first is "the seal which leaves its delicate imprint on the wax." In this "realist" or empiricist view, man's mind is the wax, reality is inherent in objects, and man approximates to it. Ortega considers this metaphor unsatisfactory; objective reality is not so simple, nor is the observer so insignificant.

Emerging from the first is his second metaphor: "the container and its contents." In terms of this "idealist" metaphor, observed events are mere contents of the container which is ultimate reality. In order for something to be perceived, the container must be there; and the structure of the container determines the reality of its contents. Ortega then moves beyond this metaphor and thereby abandons both the realist and the idealist portions in favor of his third, the metaphor of light: "Man has a mission of clarity upon the earth." He is in this way suggesting an interplay between man and his world. The act of shedding light is inseparable from what is observed. Truth and the act of exploration cannot be separated.

This third metaphor is consistent with our existential orientation. The relationship between the observer and that which is observed must never be taken for granted. Our approach is dialectical in that we emphasize the relationship between things rather than the things in themselves: hypnosis in the context of states of consciousness; hypnosis as a facilitator of a therapeutic strategy rather than as a treatment in itself. The dialectical frame of reference provides a perspective from which we can comprehend the significance of behavior which at first may seem contradictory. In this context apparent paradoxes of thought and behavior become relevantly opposed. For example, it is as important to study what information the person in trance is ignoring, as it is to describe the information to which he is paying attention.

Our thinking and the structure of our presentation is influenced by the existentialist and structuralist descendants of the philosopher Hegel. His emphasis on dialectics, a study of process and relatedness rather than objecthood, led to the existentialist emphasis on man's capacity to relate to himself in an infinite variety of ways. Philosophers such as Kierkegaard, Heidegger, and Sartre emphasize the importance of choice in human experience. This approach is compatible with the hypnotic experience which for many people becomes a lesson in alternative ways of relating to themselves and to their bodies. We have incorporated this emphasis on choice into our treatment strategy.

Structuralists such as Piaget and Levi-Straus emphasize the importance of studying the relationship between events rather than the events in themselves. We have borrowed from their approach in studying trance capacity—for example, in comparing the characteristics of high in relation to low hypnotizability, rather than studying trances as disparate events.

Organization of the Book

The structure of the book parallels the sequence of treatment in an encounter with a patient. In the first chapter, the phenomenon of hypnosis is defined and discussed in some detail. Then the method for administering and scoring the Hypnotic Induction Profile (HIP), a ten-minute clinical assessment procedure, is presented. This procedure is crucial in our evaluation of a patient for treatment.

In the third section we present hypotheses and data relating performance on the HIP to personality style and psychopathology, along with a review of the pertinent literature and our own supporting research data. At this stage in the treatment session the clinician is formulating hypotheses regarding the patient's characteristics and problems. He then can proceed to define a problem area suitable for intervention. This process is discussed in detail in the fourth section of the book, from both a theoretical and a practical viewpoint. Following an exploration of the thinking behind the construction of a treatment strategy employing hypnosis are a series of strategies with clinical examples.

Some patients require more than brief treatment, or are interested in undertaking intensive psychotherapy. We present a method for utilizing the assessment of hypnotizability in selecting among the various types of treatment. Finally, special considerations in the psychotherapy of the highly hypnotizable individual are discussed.

It is our hope that the flow of a typical evaluation and treatment session will be experienced in the process of reading the book. In structuring the book this way, we wish to emphasize the assessment of hypnotizability in clinical work, and the possibilities for constructing a treatment strategy which excites involvement and thereby employs hypnosis but is not limited by its use.

PART I

Trance:
The Phenomenon
and Its Measurement

1

Naturally Occurring Trance Phenomena and Related Myths

Oh, do not ask "what is it?"
Let us go and make our visit.
T. S. Eliot
"The Love Song of
J. Alfred Prufrock"

Alterations of human awareness occur all the time. For example, there is the diurnal rhythm of sleep and wakefulness and the many stages of transition. Our contact with repressed and unconscious aspects of ourselves varies as well (Spiegel 1963b). Often in the course of the day we may enter and leave various meditative states or states of intensely excited activity, apathy, and exhilaration. Many of these states have in common the constant shifting back and forth between peripheral awareness and focal attention.

No absolute dividing line exists between nonhypnotic and hypnotic alterations in consciousness, but altered, dissociated or hypnotic-like experiences clearly occur in everyday life and provide a useful backdrop for understanding the hypnotic experience.

1. Daydreaming commonly occurs in almost everyone's experience. For defensive purposes, for relaxation, or for numerous other reasons, an individual can indulge in vivid imagery in such a concentrated way that his usual awareness of the surrounding world is suspended.

2. Intense concentration in either work or play maximizes focal awareness so that events may occur around a person and be entirely outside his awareness; whereas ordinarily the signals from the periphery would be consciously perceived.

3. Many individuals have had the experience of listening to an important talk or watching an absorbing play, only to discover after it was over that they had been so involved in the experience that they required a moment of reorientation back to their temporal and spatial setting.

4. It is frequently observed that the most boring people to be with are two people who are "in love with each other." They are so intensely involved with one another that they are unaware of the usual cues or counter-cues that go on in relation to the other people around them.

5. Natural childbirth, the work of Grantly Dick Read (1944), and the Lamaze Method provide us with another example of a hypnotic-like experience occurring in everyday life. Although the term "hypnosis" is not employed when a woman uses these relaxation methods to deliver with minimal pain or discomfort, whatever the actual phenomenon is, the experience of it must be something akin to hypnosis.

6. The placebo effect deserves attention in this regard. It is often dismissed as a triviality of medicine. Careful critical study, however, suggests that spontaneous trance may well be a part of it, and that the placebo phenomenon is quite complex, powerful, and tantalizing, though not yet well understood. Shapiro and Morris (1978) emphasize this with a thorough review of the literature along with their own investigations.

The placebo effect often occurs in response to situational context. For example, Beecher (1959) became interested in the problem of pain after serving as an anesthesiologist with the hospital unit at the Anzio Beachhead in World War II. He was impressed with the difference in pain reaction among soldiers at the battlefront, compared to civilians in a Boston hospital who had suffered the same degree of tissue damage. The soldiers reported far less pain and demanded considerably less pain medication than civilian surgical patients with comparable trauma. In general, when a soldier received a wound which was not severe enough to interfere with his awareness that he had been wounded, he was happy. He had received an honorable exit from combat and, in this state of euphoria and gratitude for being alive, the pain was minimally important. Further, unclouded consciousness and alertness were often necessary to remain alive during evacuation. For the postoperative surgical patients in Boston, the pain did not represent a statement of being alive; rather, it was an interference with their on-going process of living.

My (H.S.) personal experience as a combat battalion surgeon in North Africa during World War II confirmed the Beecher study. Our general use of morphine with combat casualties was much less than we had anticipated. Furthermore, on the last day of the battle in Tunisia, I was wounded. A shell fragment hit my right ankle, seared my boot, and broke my lower tibia. After the explosive noise, I felt general pain, but could not identify its source until I saw the steel fragment, like an arrow, sticking into my leg. My immediate concern was that if I had to see the wound to localize my pain, where else was I hit? When the aid man arrived, I turned over and asked him to examine my back. I felt elated when no other wounds were found. I certainly needed no morphine. This was a "dream wound" for an infantryman—bad enough to get out of the infantry, but not bad enough to make a serious difference in living. During the jarring four-mile ride on a litter to the mobile hospital, I held my leg to minimize the pain but it was an almost welcome and agreeable sensation, given what else could have happened.

7. There are thousands of people who have experienced the so-called "miracle cures" at Lourdes or similar shrines. It is undeniable that some people come there handicapped in their own way, and as the result of their inspirational experience or enlightenment leave improved or no longer handicapped. The walls of such shrines are decorated with crutches abandoned by many of the disabled pilgrims.

8. Some individuals spontaneously undergo fugue states during waking hours in which they experience "islands of time" or dissociative states that are inaccessible to them by conscious recall, even after they have been reoriented to their usual state of awareness. During these times such a person may act as though he were a different person with no conscious awareness of his normal identity, friendships, and occupation. He may even believe that he is experiencing a different place and time.

The following example illustrates this point. The military police brought to the hospital a perplexed, bewildered young woman who had been picked up nearby and was unable to identify herself. She knew that she was at Fort Meade but did not know her name or where she came from. As officer of the day I (H.S.) wanted her admitted to the hopsital. However, the registrar of the hospital was oriented along strictly military lines and he reminded me that the regulations made no allowances for the treatment or admission of nonmilitary personnel. Yet this was the middle of the night, the woman was in a serious predicament, and he refused to shoulder the responsibility of sending her away. He went back to the office and searched the Army regulations to see how he could legally admit this unfortunate woman as an emergency patient.

While his research was going on I succeeded in putting the woman into a trance, in which she was able to identify herself and give in detail the whole sequence of her dilemma.

She had come from her home in Florida when a friend wrote her that her husband was dating a woman near the camp. She decided to surprise her husband, a sergeant on the post, and planned to exert her influence to break up the affair. As she approached the camp gate her conflict became intense as to whether she really wanted to face what she was afraid she would see, or whether she would be better off not seeing what she feared. She resolved the conflict in an irrational manner by developing an amnesia and divorcing herself from her own identity as a protection against the impending crisis. With the hypnotic trance it was possible to help her restore some of her former self-regard; then it was possible to contact her husband. After the mediation of some common sense and understanding, she was able to meet him and within a matter of a half hour they embraced, reaffirmed their love for each other, and her amnesia was obliterated.

Just as this dramatic scene took place the registrar returned from his office with a triumphant smile on his face: he had found an Army regulation that sanctioned the admission of this woman to the hospital. When he saw that she had recovered from her symptoms it was so difficult for him to reorient himself to this entirely new situation that he found himself saying, "But she must be admitted, we've already made out the papers."

9. There are also sleep-walking experiences or somnambulism in which a person wakes up during or after a dream and may get out of bed, walk around and even perform complicated tasks and may or may not reorient himself before being awakened.

10. Traumatic interpersonal interactions may occur which are clearly hypnotic-like but in which hypnosis is never formally considered or employed. A woman in her late forties suffered from hiccups which were so severe that they interfered with her ability to eat or retain food or fluids. She lost considerable weight and was hospitalized to receive intravenous nourishment. In that setting she was seen and proved to be hypnotizable. Her hiccups ceased within an hour after the trance induction and treatment instructions. The next day she was removed from the critical list and discharged.

The drama of this response was clearly related to an experience of the patient fifteen years earlier, when she had had a similar attack of hiccups. Her general physician, who had just recovered from a myo-cardial infarction and was about to retire, heard about her dilemma and had a final consultation with her before he moved to Florida. In this dramatic setting, with the doctor still convalescing but concerned enough to see her, she came into his home and from his bedside he said to her: "I'm going to teach you some breathing exercises." With these breathing exercises her hiccups stopped for fifteen years, which is an impressive clinical result. But there was nothing said about hyp-nosis at that time and the doctor himself later denied any knowledge of it.

All of these illustrations, from different points of view and with varying degrees of alteration of awareness and dissociation, involve an increase in focal attention to one aspect of the total situation and a concomitant constriction of peripheral awareness of other aspects. Missing in many of these illustrations is the presence of a knowledgeable professional who says that he is using hypnosis with the individual, but his absence by no means implies that hypnosis has not occurred. Rather, the trance state exists on a continuum of everyday life experience. When we formalize its occurrence and exactly define its essence, we simplify things for ourselves but are not necessarily doing justice to this ubiquitous human phenomenon.

Prevalent Misconceptions

It has been said that myths are beliefs which never were true and always will be. Numerous myths about hypnosis exist among both professionals and lay persons. We have selected ten of the most prevalent myths for discussion and clarification.

Hypnosis is Sleep. This misconception is in part related to the rather unfortunate choice of the term "hypnosis" by Braid from the Greek root "hypnos," meaning sleep. The fact that a subject in a trance more often than not has his eyes closed, seems to be breathing quietly and regularly, and has some alteration in consciousness, often misleads people into thinking that he is asleep. Many clinicians and others who work with hypnosis still utilize sleep terminology: "You are going into a deep, deep sleep," or "wake up from that trance," or they think in terms of the awake versus the hypnotized state. Perhaps the term "poetic sleep" would apply to some trance experiences.

In fact, the subject, if he is to enter the trance state, becomes more alert and awake than usual. He is entering a state of intense concentration. The trance state and sleep do share a relative diminution of peripheral awareness. But when one is asleep, focal awareness is dissolved; in the trance state, it is intensified. This clinical observation has been reinforced by EEG studies which indicate a high incidence of alpha activity during the trance state (London et al. 1969). Alpha is most often described as the noise that the brain makes when it is alert and resting. It is inconsistent with the EEG patterns observed during sleep.

Hypnosis is Projected Onto the Patient. This myth that the hypnotist exudes some force or energy onto the patient may well derive from Mesmer's ideas about magnetic force in relation to the trance state. He felt that the trance was elicited by exposing subjects to some sort of electromagnetic force, and he would gather patients around a large magnet to experience the effect of this force. From this practice we have retained both the term "induction" in eliciting the trance state and the misconception that some force is exerted on the hypnotic subject which results in the trance experience. As we explained earlier, trance capacity is inherent in an individual. The operator merely provides an appropriate occasion for the subject to explore his own trance capacity if he wishes.

This distinction is absolutely critical for clinical work because it puts what happens in perspective. Many clinicians have had some experience with hypnosis in their training but have given it up, often for one of two reasons: either they are frightened by their "success" or discouraged by their "failures." Believing that eliciting a trance state involves projecting some quality of authority or control, a clinician will often be frightened when he meets an extremely compliant subject who seems almost ceaselessly plastic in responsiveness. Eventually this clinician is bound to run across a number of nonhypnotizable subjects and he would then assume that he had failed in some way. Either extreme implies taking more responsibility for what occurs in the trance condition than any operator has a right to do, and it confuses the diagnostic assessment.

Freud himself reported this alarmed reaction:

And one day I had an experience which showed me in the crudest light what I have long suspected. One of my most acquiescent patients, with whom hypnotism had enabled me to bring about the most marvellous results, and whom I was engaged in relieving of her suffering by tracing back her attacks of pain to their origins, as she woke up on one occasion, threw her arms round my neck. The unexpected entrance of a servant relieved us from the discussion. From that time onwards there was a tacit understanding between us that the hypnotic treatment should be discontinued. I was modest enough not to attribute the event to my own irresistible personal attractions, and I felt that I had now grasped the nature of the mysterious element that was at work behind hypnotism. In order to exclude it, or at all events to isolate it, it was necessary to abandon hypnotism. (Freud 1935, p. 27)

Performed with appropriate clinical measurements, no trance induction is either a success or failure for the tester; it is rather simply another clinical test. No neurologist takes credit for the result of a Babinski test he performs, be it positive or negative. And this attitude of dispassionate observation is also appropriate for inducing and assessing the trance state. It is knowing how to test and how to use the test data that reflects the tester's competence.

Only Weak or Sick People are Hypnotizable. This myth emerged from the famous debate between Charcot and Bernheim concerning the best subjects for hypnosis. Charcot, the great French neurologist, was hypnotizing his patients, especially those who were hysterics. He considered the capacity to be hypnotized a sign of mental dysfunction with a neurological basis. Bernheim, on the other hand, was hypnotizing his staff and was at least somewhat constrained to argue that the capacity to be hypnotized was not indicative of psychopathology (Ellenberger 1970). He also held that there was no physiological basis to hypnotic capacity. In terms of the relationship between hypnotizability and psychopathology, it seems that history favors Bernheim's position. Data we will present in subsequent chapters indicate that, if anything, the capacity to be hypnotized is a sign of relative mental health and that the most severely disturbed patients are in general incapable of hypnotic trance. While some perfectly normal people are not hypnotizable, in general the capacity to be hypnotized is a sign of relatively intact mental functioning.

Hypnosis Occurs Only When the Doctor Decides to Use It. The trance state is on a continuum with our normal waking consciousness. Individuals with trance capacity commonly slip in and out of trance states. Thus it is naive for a clinician to assume that if he is not formally employing hypnosis, it does not occur.

At the beginning of World War II, I (H.S.) had the occasion to spend some time with Dr. Gustave Aschaffenburg, who had been Professor of Forensic Psychiatry at the University of Cologne and was in this country as a political refugee. In those days he was distressed that as an alien he could not help directly in our war effort, but he did what he could to train young army psychiatrists in the use of hypnotic techniques. It was my good fortune to meet him in Baltimore. In several informal sessions he was able to tell us a great deal about his own early experience with hypnosis in Germany over the course of many years. When he was a boy he had chicken pox, and an infection of one of the lesions left a rather deep scar right in the center of his forehead. Years later, when he was studying criminals at the prison in Cologne, he observed that on many occasions during his psychiatric interview, the prisoner would tend to focus on this scar and become almost transfixed. At first he did not know what to make of it, but then it occurred to him that the men were experiencing a trance state. This attracted his interest to hypnosis, and from that time on he did much research in the field.

Patients respond to suggestions constantly. For example, many surgeons have learned that they get a much better response from their postoperative patients when they approach them in the morning with the question, "How are you feeling?" rather than "How is your pain?" The latter question becomes for some patients a subtle suggestion that to be in tune with their surgeon they must be experiencing pain. This is a special problem with highly hypnotizable individuals who are very prone to slip into trance states, especially under duress. Clinicians often see people at a time of stress, when spontaneous trance states are most likely to occur. Many hysterical symptoms are in fact spontaneous trance states, for example hysterical fugue states. They can be manipulated by the use of hypnotic techniques and are an example of spontaneous hypnotic phenomena which the astute clinician should recognize.

Symptom Removal Means a New Symptom. The symptom substitution argument arose from orthodox psychoanalytic principles. It was argued that to remove a psychologically determined symptom early in psychoanalytic treatment would ally the therapist with those parts of the patient's unconscious which were seeking to defeat resolution of the unconscious conflict instigating the symptom. In addition, the therapist who intervened in this matter might be playing into certain transference wishes of the patient. The rapid resolution of the symptom would either diffuse the patient's desire for understanding and mastery or would force the conflict to emerge in another way with a different symptom, perhaps a more serious one (Reider, 1976).

This notion derives from what is commonly termed Freud's "hydraulic" model—a closed energy system of a rather fixed relationship between the frustration of unconscious desires and the elaboration of a symptom. As he understood it, any neurotic symptom had its roots in unconscious conflict:

. . . people fall ill of a neurosis if they are deprived of the possibility of satisfying their libido—that they fall ill owing to 'frustration,' as I put it—and that their symptoms are precisely a substitute for their frustrated satisfaction. This is not supposed to mean, of course, that every frustration of a libidinal satisfaction makes the person it affects neurotic, but merely that the factor of frustration could be discerned in every case of neurosis that has been examined. (Freud 1917, p. 344)

It followed from this formulation that in order to effectively relieve a neurotic symptom one must disentangle the unconscious conflict— hence psychoanalysis as the treatment of choice.

However, this aspect of Freud's theories has been widely questioned. The connection seems more a theoretical nicety than an empirical fact. The most persuasive argument in our experience against this position is that we simply have not observed it happen. Certainly there has been enough successful symptom-oriented treatment via a variety of nonanalytic techniques (i.e., behavior modification, biofeedback, hypnosis) without the emergence of a substitute symptom to call this theoretical formulation into serious question. Patients who master symptoms in general feel better rather than discover new symptoms. In fact, we have observed what we have called a ripple effect.* (Spiegel and Linn 1969), that is, patients who master a troubling symptom in one area of their lives find themselves overcoming other problems in other aspects of their lives. They have a sense of mastery and accomplishment which, if anything, frees them to take a look at the unconscious significance of their symptoms when no longer humiliated and victimized by them.

Although a given unconscious conflict may give rise to the development of the symptom, it is not clear that that same conflict is operative in the perpetuation of the symptom. Often secondary factors such as social embarrassment, secondary loss, and habit may keep a symptom in operation long after the original conflict has receded in importance or been resolved. Finally, if long-term intensive psychotherapy is appropriate, there may be no better way to cement the working alliance in Greenson's sense of the term (Greenson 1965) than to utilize a technique such as hypnosis to help the patient master a difficult problem in his life. However, it is important to note that the way in which hypnosis is employed is critical. If the therapist employs it in a coercive or unpleasant way which denies the patient mastery rather than enhances his sense of mastery, it may indeed prove mischievous. It should be added that if the therapist has a conviction that the removal of one symptom will lead to another, this conviction may find its expression in the behavior of the patient (Spiegel 1967).

Hypnosis is Dangerous. There is simply no evidence to support the idea that hypnosis in itself is dangerous. In one study at a midwestern university this hypothesis was tested by doing a simple induction on one group of college students and allowing a control group to sit by themselves in a room for a similar period of time. The researchers expected a number of psychological problems to emerge in the hypnotized group. In contrast they found that the students who were hypnotized found it a rewarding and helpful experience, wanted to undergo it again, and

---

° We are indebted to Prof. H. J. Leichter of Teachers College, College University, for proposing the term "ripple effect" for this phenomenon.

as a group seemed more psychologically healthy than the control group (Faw et al. 1968). Further, the use of hypnosis in a professional setting has been officially sanctioned by the American Psychiatric Association and the American Medical Association (Group for the Advancement of Psychiatry 1962).

There have been occasional reports of a psychotic reaction in a patient who has been hypnotized (Joseph et al. 1949; Wineburg and Straker 1973). We are not aware of any report of harm to a patient as the result of hypnosis itself. These above reports did not include clinical details demonstrating causation or information about the therapist's expectancy regarding hypnosis or symptom removal. In our experience of using hypnosis with thousands of patients, we have had no case of a patient who became psychotic as a result of hypnosis. However, any form of coercion or intimidation, whether hypnosis is overtly employed or not, can have adverse consequences, particularly in a patient whose psychological status is fragile. Thus hypnosis should never be employed in a manner which is coercive or involves deception.

Some paranoid patients may attribute excessive powers to a hypnotist and may become angry or more psychotic at what they perceive as a loss of control. This problem can be handled easily by making the situation clear, explaining to the patient that all hypnosis is really self-hypnosis, and allowing the patient to make his own decision. Surprisingly, we have tested many frankly paranoid patients for hypnotizability with no adverse effect. One patient who had a delusion that he had been placed in a trance by his brother-in-law and was having his mind controlled in this manner eagerly cooperated with the Hypnotic Induction Profile, saying that he wanted to learn more about how his mind was being controlled.

Some depressed patients may place unrealistic hopes in the trance experience as a way of ending their depression. Their magical wishes should be explored and defused before the induction is performed, to avoid having yet another hope dashed in a situation which could provoke a suicide attempt.

If a responsible therapist takes the simple precautions of clearly explaining to the patient what the trance state is and what will be done, and if he avoids any coercive or deceptive uses of hypnosis, it can be stated without reservation that the trance state in and of itself is not at all dangerous. However, it is worth keeping in mind that good hypnotic subjects are especially sensitive to subtle cues, both conscious and unconscious, conveyed by the operator. Should an inexperienced hypnotist begin to panic, for example, at a patient's profound trance state—wondering whether the patient will "come out of it"—or should he become frightened at the intensity of an abreaction during an hypnotic regression, the subject may sense this anxiety and in turn become anxious. This back and forth reinforcement of anxiety can escalate to the point where it becomes a *folie à deux*. The main thing to keep in mind is that firm, quiet reassurance always works, even if a good hypnotic subject is quite upset. The very depth of the response indicates that the subject expects some structuring of the experience. The following clinical example demonstrates how sensitive a good hypnotic subject is even to subtle cues from the operator.

A few years ago I (H.S.) was asked to see a 24-year-old woman suffering with severe, chronic, generalized, postoperative abdominal pain. The diagnosis of Hodgkin's disease was confirmed during the abdominal exploration, and although her life span was limited, it was estimated that she had a number of years to live. Meanwhile, she built up her demand for meperidine hydrochloride (Demerol hydrochloride) to the point where addiction was feared. In this context I was asked to explore the use of hypnosis to contain her pain experience. In the presence of several medical students and residents, and as she was telling me that she could not possibly be hypnotized, she went into a trance intense enough to experience no cutaneous pain sensation when pricked with a pin. A program for controlling this pain was developed with posthypnotic signals. It was so effective that within twenty-four hours she was free of pain without any meperidine hydrochloride.

Because of the patient's persistent skepticism, the resident on the case accepted the responsibility of reinforcing this hypnotic control. This program went well for a few days until the resident, for personal reasons, became fearful about using hypnosis. The next day, with hesitation and conflict, he again gave the signal to the patient to reinforce the anesthesia to pain, but this time the patient was unable to go into a trance state, and the pain recurred. When I came the following day, she told me how sorry she was that she could no longer go into hypnosis and thanked me for trying to help her. But while saying this in my presence, she again went into a trance state as intense as any she had had before and was able to re-establish control of her pain without any medication.

Thus this patient, in spite of her high capacity for hypnosis, respected the resident's unconscious plea for her not to enter the trance state. He had in fact been "forbidden" to use hypnosis by his orthodox analyst, so her entering a trance would have placed him in a more than uncomfortable position.

Hypnosis is Therapy.   This is an equally troublesome myth. We avoid the use of the term "hypnotherapist" because by itself hypnosis is not therapy. The hypnotic state is a capacity; it is a certain type of attentive, receptive concentration and it can be used to create a receptive matrix for a therapeutic strategy. It may enhance therapeutic leverage but by itself it is not a treatment. In the service of a good therapeutic strategy it can accelerate and facilitate treatment; in the service of a bad therapeutic strategy it can accelerate and enhance deterioration.

Thus a clinician who is to use hypnosis must be well versed in the various clinical strategies which make up his discipline, be it psychotherapy or pain relief. He must also have that most valuable of professional attributes, the knowledge and willingness to seek appropriate help when he is unable to cope with a situation. An occasional patient who comes seeking help with hypnosis for weight control, for example, may in reality be suffering from anorexia nervosa, a life-threatening illness. If a naive therapist employs hypnosis to help the patient eat less, he may be providing professional sanction for the patient's thought disorder in regard to eating. To make good use of hypnosis one must first be a good clinician.

A Hypnotist Must Be Charismatic, Unique, or Weird. For every successful hypnotist with a reputation for eccentricity or who wears purple, there are ten whom one would never identify as such in a crowd. This myth is really a corollary to the earlier myth that hypnosis is something projected onto a patient. The good hypnotist can create an appropriate atmosphere in which the patient may explore his or her own trance capacity. The hypnotist's eccentricities may be tolerated so long as they do not interfere with that atmosphere. If the hypnotist does or says something which is aesthetically offensive to the patient, he may hamper the patient's performance. It is incumbent on the hypnotist that he establish sufficient rapport and trust with the patient that they can proceed to assess hypnotizability. In general, the respectful demeanor which is appropriate to any clinical setting provides the best atmosphere for the use of hypnosis.

Women are More Hypnotizable than Men. Our data on several thousand cases indicate no difference in hypnotizability of women as compared with men. This myth grows out of the same sex role stereotyping that implies that women are more passive and dependent and less assertive than men. It is simply another discredited stereotype.

Hypnosis is Only a Superficial Psychological Phenomenon. Referring back to the debate between Charcot and Bernheim, in which Charcot held that hypnosis was a neurological phenomenon with psychological overlay and Bernheim that it was solely a psychological one, it would seem that Charcot prevailed in this part of the argument. There is growing evidence relating the capacity for hypnosis to certain neurophysiological substrates and this evidence will be reviewed in later chapters.

Our finding of an interesting relationship between the eye roll—that is, the capacity to look up while closing one's eyes—and trance performance, along with other presumed neurophysiological phenomena, suggests to us that the capacity for hypnosis may well be a biological rather than a strictly psychological capacity. If good subjects are not born, then perhaps they are endowed in some way with the capacity at a very early age. In any event the Hypnotic Induction Profile is clinically useful because it relates a biological prediction of hypnotizability to behavioral and phenomenological measures. Some individuals live up to their presumed biological capacity while others do not, and this we think has clinical significance. In any event, there is growing evidence that hypnosis is as much a neurophysiological as a psychological phenomenon.

2

Formally Induced Trance Phenomena

Seeking and learning is all remembrance.

Socrates in *Meno* (Plato)

We define what we believe to be the most important aspects of the hypnotic experience bearing in mind that any definition is bound to do injustice to its subject. This experience is characterized by an ability to sustain in response to a signal a state of attentive, receptive, intense focal concentration with diminished peripheral awareness. It is a function of the alert individual who utilizes his capacity for maximal involvement with one point in space and time and thereby minimizes his involvement with other points in space and time. The hypnotized person is not asleep, but awake and alert.

The crux of the trance state is the dialectic between focal and peripheral awareness. Any intensification of focal attention necessitates the elimination of distracting or irrelevant stimuli. Likewise, a position of diffuse and scanning awareness requires a relinquishing of focal attentiveness. In fact, the one type of awareness implies the existence of the other. We not only pay attention to our given task, we also ward off distractions. The metaphor of our visual system may help to fix this concept. Our macular, or central visual field, encompasses a comparatively small arc of 5° to 7° in the visual field. We can see with good detail only a small part of the world that surrounds us. Our nonmacular or peripheral vision is rather diffuse and contains very few color receptors. A realistic view of our visual perception at any moment in time consists of a rather small circular area of detailed and color-filled vision surrounded by a rather hazy area, devoid of any details and color. Yet we assemble for ourselves a relatively stable, colorful, and detailed visual environment based on the presumptions that everything more or less stays where it is, and that the sum of our individual perceptions equals the total visual field. A temporal and spatial picture is assembled out of a series of momentary glimpses. It is our option to focus on an individual detail or to assemble the broader picture. The hypnotic state is analogous to macular vision; it is intense and detailed but constricted. It is perhaps no accident that tunnel vision, characteristic of certain kinds of hysteria, is associated with the high hypnotizability of hysterics. One responsive hypnotic subject informed us that she experienced tunnel vision every time she entered the trance state.

Thus, the trance state is a form of intense focal concentration which maximizes involvement with one sensory percept at a time. The process of weaving these percepts into the fabric of our total consciousness requires a kind of scanning awareness typified in the nontrance alert state. Our overall consciousness is a product of dialectical tension between intense focal experience and less intense, more balanced integration of various focal and peripheral experiences. We conceive of the hypnotic trance as a part of the everyday experience of any individual who has hypnotic capacity. We would expect that this capacity for intense trance experience would influence the general nature of a good hypnotic subject's consciousness, without the subject ever having had formal induction.

This position is supported by several research studies. Hilgard (1970) documented a tendency for imaginative involvement among highly hypnotizable individuals. Tellegen and Atkinson (1974) found that high hypnotizability was correlated with a trait that they labeled "absorption." This trait comprised a positive response to written questions about unusual and intense absorption in such experiences as reading a good book or watching a play. In fact, the trance experience is often best explained to new patients who have questions about it as being very much like being absorbed in a good novel: one loses awareness of noises and distractions in the immediate environment and, when the novel is finished, requires a moment of reorientation to the surrounding world.

Trance Induction and the Role of the Operator

Although the hypnotic experience may occur spontaneously in an individual with the requisite capacity, the experience is influenced by the presence of an operator whose goal is to elicit the trance state in a disciplined way. We disagree with the archaic notion that hypnosis is "projected" onto a subject by a charismatic and authoritarian figure. Nonetheless, the interpersonal aspects of the trance state are complex and, in the minds of patients seeking help with hypnosis, raise the question of who is controlling whom.

The hypnotic situation does not involve control of one person by another in an absolute sense; rather, it consists of someone more willing than many others to suspend his critical judgment. He is capable of employing critical judgment at any time, but is less prone to do so. We address the common question about whether someone in a trance state can be made to do something against his will in the following manner. Those who are highly hypnotizable, especially when in trance states (with or without a formal induction ceremony), are more prone to stretch the limits of their usual array of responses at the suggestion of someone else. They retain at all times the capability of breaking with the trance command, but are less likely to do so than a nonhypnotizable person. The more the command is in conflict with a person's customary beliefs and activities, the more likely the person is to break with the command. Time is another crucial factor in this equation; it is easier for a highly hypnotizable individual to correct outside premises according to his own judgment if he has several hours alone to do so. A persistently coercive atmosphere maximizes an individual's tendency to dissociate from his own critical judgment and to adopt the premises of another person.

There are essentially three major styles for evoking or inducing the trance state:

1. One can be frightened into a trance state by the use of fear and coercion.

2. Under appropriate conditions a subject can be seduced into a trance state. This seduction can be sexual, nonsexual, or a combination of both.

3. A subject can be simply guided or instructed to shift into the trance state. Obviously, the latter is the appropriate method in the therapeutic field and is the basis for our later discussion of trance induction procedures.

Case Example: Coercion. Even though there is no legitimate or ethical place for the first two styles in the therapeutic arts, it is useful for the student of hypnosis to know that these styles can be used and are certainly effective. The following experience that I (H.S.) had in the army during World War II illustrates the use of coercion. One day I received a phone message from the military police that there was a soldier in the emergency room who wanted to kill me. This was an alarming and attention-getting message, and I immediately proceeded down to the emergency room. As I opened the door in the small room in which this soldier was isolated, he lunged at me and tried to choke me. Fortunately for me, I was strong enough to grab him and to have my left hand on the back of his neck and my right hand twisting his right extended arm. In this awkward position his face was by coincidence toward the desk on which there was an ink bottle. I said to him on the spur of the moment while holding him tightly: "Look at that ink bottle and keep looking at it!" To my amazement I could feel his tense muscles relax and within seconds he became limp and collapsed to the floor. As he lay on the floor I talked with him and recognized him as a soldier with whom I had been involved the week before. It turned out that his rage was due to a clerical error reassigning him to active duty rather than assigning a medical discharge that I had promised him.

Having discovered how readily he could be frightened into a trance state, I readmitted him to the hospital for further treatment. It turned out that he was what we now identify as a grade 5 and I was able to do a number of research studies with him using hypnotic age regression, some of which has been reported (Spiegel et al. 1945).

Although I am not especially proud of demonstrating that a person can be frightened into a trance state, it seemed warranted under the circumstances and was not as aberrant as it would have been in a civilian setting. We suspect that this kind of induction goes on often in authoritarian settings such as schools, prisons, court rooms, and some families.

Case Example: Seduction. The seduction method also occurs over and over again, but it is usually not reported as such. The following case demonstrates how readily seduction can induce trance. An actress in Las Vegas attended a show which featured a stage hypnotist. She volunteered to be a subject for one of his demonstrations and discovered that she was not only highly hypnotizable but that the experience was erotically exciting for her. She returned the next day and volunteered again. After several similar experiences a serious personal relationship developed between the actress and the hypnotist, leading to an active sexual relationship. Her family was wealthy and the hypnotist soon found that out. He, at the time, was a married man with children but he suddenly decided to divorce. She was much younger and just getting over a divorce from a brief marriage. Upon learning of their plans to marry, the actress' father actively intervened to the point of persuading his daughter to come to New York to be examined psychiatrically. She complied with her father's wishes because "I love my Daddy and this is the least I could do to please him." When examined in New York, it was found that she was highly hypnotizable (grade 5) and was being coerced into marriage with hypnosis and deception. While in trance she was urged to delay her decision and consider alternatives. She came out of the trance state with an almost total amnesia for what had transpired and said that she did not know why but thought she would call off her planned marriage. She phoned her father, who was pleased to hear the news. She also phoned the hypnotist, who immediately flew to New York and, on the following day, managed to sequester her in a hotel bedroom and re-hypnotize her while engaging in sex. The next morning she phoned her father to say that she had made a terrible mistake in calling off her marriage, and had decided to marry that day. It became apparent that she was being used as a pawn between two hypnotists, one employing seduction and the other in essence acting as an agent for her father. This was an untenable treatment situation and the psychiatric intervention was terminated. In fact, she did marry this man, and within a year not only divorced him but agreed to pay alimony as part of the divorce settlement.

There is no doubt that, in one of the many variations of man's inhumanity to man, much abuse has occurred by enhancing fear or seduction with the extra leverage of hypnosis. Most of these events go unrecorded because the people who have mastered hypnotic techniques for exploitation do not write about their achievements. This is not the place to deal with the ethical, legal, and moral implications. We acknowledge that exploitation does occur and we point out that certain highly hypnotizable individuals are especially vulnerable.

Some good hypnotic subjects actively seek situations in which they feel they can place themselves under someone else's control. This may happen unconsciously, in spite of conscious protest. For example, some years back I (H.S.) conducted a study of hypnosis using sixteen of the twenty patients on a ward. During my absence from the ward, there was apparently much discussion about what went on in the examining room. One day one of the patients not involved in the study appeared in my office and said: "Sir, you could not hypnotize me even if you wanted to." I noticed that as he was saying this his right eye fixed on a pencil dot used for the trance induction, and then closed. I challenged him with: "Then why can't you open your right eye?" He struggled to open his right eye but was unable to. At the same time, in a mildly defiant way, he told me that he left eye was open. He was actually begging for the signal to enter the trance just as the other men had described it. I then said, "All right. Now both your eyes will close." They did, and he went into a deep trance state. This experience is not unusual; people with significant trance capacity manage to get themselves into trance states as long as the hypnotist does not interfere with the process.

Dependency and the Role of Self-Hypnosis

Unconscious expectations play into a transference problem common to many forms of psychotherapy—dependency. The patient is prone to attribute great powers of good and evil to the therapist and will expect him to take responsibility for the outcome of the treatment. Such expectations tend to shift the focus from a collaborative to a dependent and vertical relationship. Rather than being disappointed with himself, the patient can then convert failure into anger at the therapist.

The hypnotic situation can intensify dependency problems if conducted in an authoritarian manner. The approach recommended here defuses dependency by first evaluating trance capacity and then teaching self-hypnosis. Taking cognizance of dependency factors, an attempt is made to deal with them indirectly and by example, rather than by verbal exploration of the possible unconscious significance of the patient's expectations. The notion of a test of the patient's hypnotizability is explained briefly at the beginning of an evaluation. This explanation immediately sets the patient on notice that the therapist defines his role as evaluator. Thus the "responsibility" for the nature of the trance state rests with the patient. The implication is that fearful or angry feelings will affect his performance, but not that of the operator. Questions about the nature of the trance experience are answered briefly, and the patient is urged to observe for himself what the trance experience is like.

Dependent expectations are further countered by the incorporation of instructions for self-hypnosis within the Hypnotic Induction Profile. All hypnosis is in reality self-hypnosis, and the patient is taught from the beginning to master his own trance capacity. Furthermore, the treatment exercises which are taught incorporate the notion that the patient may hypnotize himself to reinforce a particular strategy. Unlike many other therapists who employ hypnosis, we do not encourage patients to return for repeated sessions of formally induced hypnosis.

Rather, we urge patients to practice hypnotizing themselves, usually every one or two hours during the first weeks. There are occasional situations when we ask a patient to return for further reinforcement. But in general, when treatment extends beyond one session, we utilize the time to discuss problems and reflect upon the trance experience. We will employ hypnosis repeatedly only if clarification of the induction procedure is needed, or if help is requested with a different problem.

Additional sessions are also employed to deal with problems which arise in the patient's life in relation to his change in behavior. Sometimes friends and family are surprised or even displeased by marked change. A person's altered view of himself relating to his mastery of a particular problem may lead him to question other assumptions in his life, and he may want to discuss them. For example, a young woman who entered treatment because of habitual hair pulling which had left the back of her head bare in spots decided to move on to other issues after overcoming her habit in a few weeks. She began to lose weight, and shifted the focus of the therapy to a discussion of her personal relationships. After several months of weekly sessions, she ended a long relationship with a disturbed man. Several other changes also occurred in her life. This brief illustration is an example of what has been described as the "ripple effect" (Spiegel and Linn 1969). Change in one area often leads to change in other areas, as an individual develops a sense of mastery over his or her life. If the need for extended therapy sessions arises, the sessions proceed along more conventional lines and usually do not involve repeated trance induction.

Occasionally patients who have not found the initial treatment strategy useful will want to continue in psychotherapy and pursue a more extended process of reasoning and perhaps transference exploration. For example, a woman in her thirties came for help with weight control, frigidity, and a feeling that she was unkind to people close to her. She was taught an exercise for help with the frigidity, which she felt was her primary problem. At first she noticed that there was no particular change in her sexual problem, but wanted to review her life situation, particularly as it related to an episode of sexual assault at age four which she had recalled prior to coming to the therapy. Thus the focus shifted from symptom treatment to personality exploration, utilizing the woman's extreme hypnotizability as one organizing theme. Her primary defense against her fear of being exploited was a kind of stony withdrawal, and she often adopted the attitude that people like her husband were "bothering" her. She spent long periods of each day in reverie, imagining that she was something other than what she was. The therapy took the direction of helping her control and limit these trance experiences, and of providing her with guidelines for asserting herself in interpersonal situations. Gradually she became less isolated and defensive, and began to enjoy her sexuality more and to feel she was becoming a warmer person. Surprised feedback from her husband confirmed this impression. After a year of weekly therapy she spontaneously overcame some old phobic problems and began to lose weight.

In this case, a brief symptom-oriented approach did not elicit a response, which occurred in relation to subsequent personality exploration helping this woman master her trance capacity and change her relationships with important people in her life. Her early expectation that something would be "done to" her was reinforced by an earlier experience with hypnosis in which the operator repeatedly induced a trance for weight control but did not teach her self-hypnosis. Her dissatisfaction with the early part of treatment shifted from criticism of the therapy to an evaluation of her tendency to keep people at a distance. With recognition of this, she made several important changes in her life.

Thus, whether the treatment consists of one session or extended psychotherapy, the emphasis on utilizing self-hypnosis deals by example with dependent expectations. It impels the patient in the direction of collaboration with the therapist and of mastery over life circumstances.

By using a standardized induction procedure, which involves systematic questioning regarding physiological, behavioral, and phenomenological responses, the variable influence of different operators on the trance performance is minimized and the trance capacity of a subject can be systematically documented. This approach is intrinsic to our method and will be described in later chapters. However, any hypnotic induction carries with it certain features which are worth noting: the aura, the psychophysiological enhancement, and the plunge.

Aura, Enhancement, Plunge

THE AURA

The aura is a series of expectancies and anxieties that the subject brings to the hypnotic situation. It can serve to enhance or maximize the hypnotic experience, as in a situation where the subject has been led to believe that this hypnotic encounter will result in the successful resolution of a major life problem. Or it can hamper the hypnotic experience as in a situation where the subject suspects that the operator will employ this trusting posture to exploit him.

As an example of the former, the senior author was invited, while he was visiting another university, to see a patient with hysterical paraplegia. This woman had been through a series of other approaches which had failed to help her and she was eagerly anticipating the meeting. She had agreed to be seen in front of a large audience of physicians, but the meeting was scheduled for a Sunday and she was a fundamentalist Baptist. She consulted her minister, who concluded that it would be "to the greater glory of God" were she to be healed on the Sabbath. With this background of expectation, she was wheeled into the auditorium and her wheelchair was stopped some twenty feet from the author. With no more than the introduction, she rose from the wheelchair to which she had been confined and walked over to introduce herself to him. In this case the aura was so profound and overwhelming that the formalities of hypnotic induction were unnecessary. The aura alone not only propelled the patient into a spontaneous trance, but evoked the desired therapeutic response.

In contrast, when a young doctor with little experience and appropriate anticipatory anxiety approaches a ward patient and announces: "I'm going to hypnotize you," and the unprepared patient responds with, "Doc, are you out of your mind?" we can conclude that the aura is minimal or nonexistent.

As an example of the kind of interference in trance capacity which a more negative set of expectancies can produce, we have encountered a number of subjects who thought they were not at all hypnotizable because of unsuccessful efforts by stage hypnotists. However, they proved to be quite hypnotizable with utilization of the Hypnotic Induction Profile in the less coercive and more respectful atmosphere of the doctor's office.

ENHANCEMENT

The set that is structured for the trance experience has inevitable physiological components which can be identified and enhanced. The operator can make use of naturally occurring physiological phenomena to create an atmosphere which will heighten the subject's receptivity. For example, if the subject is asked to focus on a pencil dot, it is predictable that after some time he will develop diplopia and see two dots, then one dot again, then two again, and so on. This process induces fatigue and gives the operator the opportunity to introduce the next instruction—fatigue of the eyelids—by saying: "As you look at the dots your eyelids will get heavier and heavier and it will be more difficult to keep them open until eventually they become so heavy that you let them close." The operator is simply using natural physiological sequences and allowing the person to identify with them and accept the plausible interpretation that these events are occurring because of the message from the operator.*

This induction technique, only one of the many practiced by clinicians, is an example of how the therapist can utilize physiological phenomena in the service of both getting the subject to pay attention to his own body and helping him discover his own flexibility in altering somatic sensations. Milton Erickson in particular is a master at subtly mobilizing psychological expectancy and physiological phenomena for the purpose of maximizing hypnotic compliance (1976). At some point in this process of exploration the subject will take the plunge into the formal trance state.

PLUNGE

This is the actual transition from ordinary scanning awareness to our maximal trance capacity. It can be used to characterize any technique which gets the subject to direct attention to the best of his ability. In maximally focusing on a specific sensation, he cuts loose from the usual mixture of somatic and environmental percepts which occupy part of his attention. Thus, in the dialectical relationship between focal and peripheral awareness, the plunge represents the individual's optimal shift toward focal attention, with a necessary and concomitant constriction of peripheral awareness. The plunge may take the form of paying attention to a sense of floating into the chair, to a sense of lightness in one's arm, or to a sense of heaviness in one's limbs. This guided experience involves maximizing focal attention with a relinquishing of peripheral distractions.

Overwhelming evidence in the literature indicates that some people consistently perform better than others as measured in a number of ways (Hilgard 1965; Morgan et al. 1974; Perry 1977). In virtually identical settings, with the same aura and psychophysiological enhancement, the nature of the plunge for each individual will be different. Hence our reference to Socrates that "seeking and learning is all remembrance." What we discover when we formally elicit the trance is an inherent capacity in the individual. This capacity is expressed in conjunction with the nature of the induction and thus may vary somewhat from time to time. As a generalization, however, it is clinically most useful to assume that the majority of the variations in response are

---

* These are old techniques of induction associated with the 'sleep' model of hypnosis. The induction which is part of the Hypnotic Induction Profile (Part II) is much more rapid.

related to the capacity of the individual. What the individual discovers when he takes the plunge is not some totally new experience, as he often expects, but the rediscovery of his own capacity—he learns what he already knew. The hope is that, in the service of a good therapeutic strategy, the subject will be able to make better use of his existing trance capacity. Any individual is capable of experiencing a shift in the interaction between focal and peripheral attention. However, the hypnotic experience is uniquely characterized by a sustained shift toward focal attention in response to a signal.

The Relationship Between Hypnosis and Imprint Learning

Both the capacity for hypnosis and the phenomena associated with it seem to have such a fixed and determined quality that metaphors which involve neurophysiological functioning or very early learning are most appropriate to explain them. Some studies indicate a significant heritability of hypnotizability (Morgan 1973; Duke 1969). A number of features of the trance state are reminiscent of imprint learning as described by Hess (1959). Imprint learning is different from associative learning in at least four distinct ways:

1. For associative learning of a specific discrimination, recency of experience is maximally effective. Primacy of experience is the most important factor in imprint learning.

2. In associative learning, painful or punitive stimulation results in avoidance. In imprint learning this stimulus increases the effectiveness of the imprint experience.

3. In associative learning visual discrimination develops more rapidly and is more stable when the training periods are interspersed with rest; imprint learning is more effective when the exposure is not interrupted by rest periods.

4. A drug such as meprobamate permits ducklings, for example, to learn color discrimination just as well as or better than they normally do, whereas the same drug reduced their imprint learning to almost nothing.

Thus these experimentally determined characteristics enable us to recognize two significantly different types of learning, each with its own set of rules. The difference is so fundamental that the imprint type of learning can be viewed as a foundation experience upon which subsequent learning and personality development are based. For our purposes imprint learning in humans cannot be viewed as an exact replication of the process observed in birds. But it is a useful concept in classifying a general category of learning that is not explained by the usual associative learning concepts.

It is apparent that all living animals learn by means of imprinting as

well as by associative processes. Even behavior that has been tradition-
ally regarded as innate or instinctive may now be understood in terms
of the species-specific kinds of learning acquired at critical and appropriate times early in the life cycle. The acculturation process that occurs
in the child prior to his mastery of language may well be predominantly
in the imprint mode. It is intriguing to speculate whether certain characteristics, such as receptiveness to the trance experience, may not be
the result of certain early imprint-like experiences.

In particular, the sensorimotor alterations which characterize the
trance state constitute a specific kind of language of action that makes
sense to certain individuals and seems like a foreign language to others.
This language is characterized by primitive, archaic, or paleological
thinking (that is, predicate–predicate rather than normal subject–
predicate identification as described by Von Domarus and later by Arieti)
(Arieti 1962). This language is rather like unconscious or dream language. In such thinking, temporal or spatial relatedness implies causation. Feelings are not distinguished from acts. One value of identifying
this mode of thinking, as distinct from the conventional and more
sophisticated mode, is that it may help in ascertaining the appropriate
type of treatment intervention (discussed in Chapter 21). The trance
state may indicate a capacity of an individual to return to an early
foundation-experience type of learning, to a logic of experience and
sensation rather than thought.

AGE REGRESSION

Some highly hypnotizable individuals are capable of age regression
in the trance state in which they relive parts of their life as though
they were at that age. When tested they will respond to vocabulary
questions like a two-year old, deny knowledge of the current president,
giggle when tickled as though they were a child. Some even become
nonverbal when regressed to the age of six months, and may without
specific instruction develop a grasp and a rooting reflex which characterize the partially developed nervous system of the infant. Many such
individuals seem to retain layers of memories analogous to the layers
of a city uncovered by archeologists. These primitive reflexes and
childish emotional responses remain stored in the unconscious, and in
some individuals they may be tapped using hypnosis (Spiegel et al.
1945).

A twenty-five-year-old man was hypnotized in a demonstration of
hypnotic age regression. When he was regressed to various ages, he
responded without difficulty, until he was signaled to place himself
back to his twelfth birthday. When asked for his name (as was done
previously at older age levels), he responded with some confusion and
tension but did not answer. When pressed for an answer, he looked
about and inquiringly uttered a word that sounded like: "Vas?" It then
became apparent that he did not understand English, and he had been
saying what ("was") in German. A third person who spoke German

served as translator. The subject seemed quite relieved and the interview and planned test program continued. The interpreter was subsequently necessary for every age level up to and including the thirteenth birthday. It turned out that at the age of 13½ he had escaped from Vienna to the United States, and by the time he was twenty-five years old his fluent English showed no trace of his native German tongue— a language he had learned to despise, so that he had difficulty with both speaking and understanding it. Even his handwriting reverted to German script at any age level under thirteen. From the ages of thirteen to eighteen, while under hypnotic regression, his spoken English revealed a gradually disappearing German accent.

Yet, despite this need to use an interpreter when interviewing him at ages under thirteen, he could understand and did respond without evidence of confusion to instruction related to his state of trance. For example, while being interviewed at the ten-year level, he was told: "When I touch your forehead, your eyes will close," or "You are now going back into the years; you are now six years old—this is your sixth birthday." His response was so clear that there was no doubt whatever that he understood exactly what was said. Again, at the age of six years, when asked: "How old are you?" he looked around with confusion and asked "Vas?"

This case illustrates both the layering of memories which are later tapped by the trance regression and the dual focus which characterizes the trance. The subject relived the world as he had experienced it at age twelve in German, and at the same time understood trance instructions in English as a twenty-five-year-old adult. This rather strange situation seemed to provoke little tension or puzzlement for the subject.

For reasons that are not clear, some individuals may retain their precognitive capacity to relate in an intense way to sensorimotor experience, and others lose or so thoroughly transform it into cognitive terms and functioning that it becomes more or less inaccessible. Influences that occur at an imprint-like level may in part be responsible. In any event, the experiential intensity of the trance experience suggests an individual's capacity to get in touch with early foundation experience. The importance of primacy of experience (rather than recency) for imprint learning, along with factors which make for a profound experience—such as pain and massive sensory input—combine to suggest that trance experience taps some earlier developmental experience. The ability to do this seems to change relatively little over the adult life span except where psychological or neurological dysfunction is involved.

It is becoming clearer, as will be discussed later, that the trance mode involves a different kind of language from our usual cognitive verbal functioning.

SUMMARY

Hypnosis is essentially a psychophysiological state of aroused, attentive, receptive focal concentration with a corresponding diminution in peripheral awareness. The capacity for this state varies among individuals and is relatively fixed throughout the adult life cycle. This capacity may be genetically determined or perhaps learned early in life, and it can be tapped and invoked in three ways: spontaneously; in response to a signal from another person (formal hypnosis); and in response to a self-induced signal (self-hypnosis).

A spontaneous trance can either be internally aroused (e.g., daydreaming, fugue state) or instigated by external cues (fear, seduction, intense concentration). The individual is generally unaware of his shifting into and out of this kind of trance experience and hence it is unstructured and undisciplined. For example, a person can become so absorbed in watching a movie that he is surprised to discover where he is when the show comes to an end.

Formal hypnosis differs from spontaneous trance in that it is contextually an interpersonal mode of communication. The subject maintains a sensitive, attentive responsiveness to an operator during the trance state. Technically, the authentic hypnotic experience can be defined as formal hypnosis only when it is knowingly induced by the operator; responded to by the subject in a sensitive, disciplined way; and terminated by the operator's signal. Using the Hypnotic Induction Profile, one ceremony for signaling trance, the operator actually tests for trance capacity and while measuring it simultaneously enables the subject to identify this special state of attention as hypnosis. When relevant, the operator can instruct the subject to shift knowingly into the hypnotic state (self-hypnosis), which differs from spontaneous trance in that it is effected by the individual's conscious design. It can be learned by instruction or discovered intuitively. It is instigated and terminated by the subject himself instead of by another person.

In reality all hypnosis is a form of self-hypnosis. In the formal induction of a trance, an individual enters a state of sustained, attentive–receptive concentration, either in response to an inner signal or to a signal from another person which activates this capacity for a shift of awareness and permits more intensive concentration in a designated direction.

We will now describe the Hypnotic Induction Profile, a clinically useful method for rapidly inducing the trance experience and measuring systematically the individual's response to it.

THE HYPNOTIC INDUCTION PROFILE (HIP)

3

Rationale for a Clinical Test

Ceremony versus Measurement

CEREMONIES

There are literally hundreds, perhaps thousands, of more or less acceptable induction techniques that have been used over the past two centuries to elicit trance compliance, e.g., eye fixation on fixed or moving targets, eye closure, body sway, touch by the hypnotist, evoking numbness, paresthesias or paralysis, etc. Most of the traditional induction ceremonies are thoroughly documented and described by Weitzenhoffer (1957) and Wolberg (1948), and require no further elaboration here.

What is relevant here is a clarification of the difference between the phenomenon of hypnosis itself and the ceremony that presumably elicits it. Trance phenomema may occur spontaneously, or in response to a myriad of ceremonies of induction, as long as the subject has trance capacity and is not aesthetically offended by the ceremony.

By definition, a ceremony is an action usually performed with some formality but lacking in deep significance. If the subject interprets the cues properly and conforms to what is expected, the trance ensues. The three overlapping phases described earlier—the aura, the psychophysiological enhancement, and the plunge—are, in effect, the common denominator usually apparent in all induction ceremonies.

There are large numbers of ceremonies for trance induction from different cultures that attract attention in the West, and deserve mention here. Our hypothesis is that these ceremonies elicit trance concentration in people who have trance capacity. For example, Chinese acupuncture employs a needle; Japanese acupuncture, Shiatsu, employs finger pressure. Transcendental meditation, Zen meditation, the relaxation response (Benson 1975), some forms of bio-feedback, yoga, primal therapy (Janov 1970), religious conversion, faith healing, laying on of hands, voodoo, are just some of the many other occasions that can elicit trance experience. Although we have not been able to make careful comparative studies, we do have some data on the hypnotic component of acupuncture, which is reported in Chapter 17. Until recently the clinical literature has largely ignored the assessment of hypnotizability. In its place there frequently has been reference to so-called "deepening techniques" (Erickson 1967), under the assumption that everyone is hypnotizable. These "deepening techniques" have, in our experience, been of little value. In general, if the setting is appropriate for both the patient and the therapist, the transformation into trance occurs quickly and to the person's optimal capacity. Repetition as a learning factor is usually of minor importance (Perry 1977).

What appears to be a "deeper" trance elicited by alleged methods is better understood as: clarifying the patient's motivation or the relevance of hypnosis in the first place; correcting misunderstandings or aesthetic preferences of the patient; altering expectations of the patient, the therapist, or both. Ceremonial repetitions provide a face-saving way to make these readjustments, and the trance then seems "deeper," although it is the same when measured. In other words, the secondary issues which influence the context of the trance experience are clarified, but the patient's actual trance capacity remains essentially the same. "Clarifying the context" is probably a more precise label than "deepening techniques."

From one point of view, the Hypnotic Induction Profile (HIP) can be regarded as another ceremony. But it is also more than just that: It is a measurement of hypnotizability in which a systematized sequence of instructions, responses, and observations are recorded with a uniform momentum in a standardized way, as the subject shifts into trance to the exent of his ability, maintains it, and then exits in a prescribed manner. It differs from traditional clinical induction techniques in that it is a measurement procedure and, in effect, the hypnotist is the measuring instrument. It differs from the research scales in being brief and clinically appropriate.

Once a Profile score is determined, the disciplined HIP procedure is no longer necessary. In general, subsequent inductions can be self-generated by the patient, or signaled by the therapist. The time for the shift into trance is a matter of a few seconds. The HIP is briefer and better standardized on a clinical psychiatric population than any other clinical scale.

MEASUREMENTS

What makes hypnosis a useful organizing concept in understanding its various ceremonies is the development of techniques for measuring a relatively stable trait—the capacity for hypnosis or hypnotizability. There are clinicians (Erickson 1967) and researchers (Barber 1956; Sarbin and Slagle 1972) who maintain that there are no reliable differences in hypnotic capacity. However, the preponderance of research in the last two decades, including our own, indicates that hypnotizability is a stable and measurable trait (Hilgard, E.R. 1965; Orne 1959; Morgan et al. 1974; Perry 1977; Spiegel, H. 1976). This evidence provides an opportunity for the clinician to use the phenomenon in a more disciplined and knowledgeable manner.

Several well-standardized scales of hypnotizability, hypnotic capacity, or hypnotic susceptibility have been developed (Weitzenhoffer and Hilgard 1959; Shor and Orne 1962; Barber and Glass 1962) with statistical reliability in mind. They were constructed as the summation score of a number of independent items which on testing proved highly intercorrelated (Hilgard, E.R. 1965). The Harvard Group Scales (Shor and Orne 1962) were designed so that the subjects themselves could score them, allowing for group administration, but they correlate highly with scores obtained on the same subjects using the Stanford Hypnotic Susceptibility Scale. These measures are lengthy to administer, requiring approximately one hour.

There was a need for a briefer measure of hypnotizability which would be practical and appropriate to the pressures of clinical work, and yet reliable and valid as a measure of the hypnotizability trait. Given the growing recognition among researchers that trance capacity is an important concept, it became imperative to introduce this kind of thinking into the field of clinical practice, which was still dominated by the concept of altering hypnotic "depth" or considering all patients to be good candidates for hypnosis. One such clinical measurement has been introduced as an adaptation of the Stanford Hypnotic Susceptibility Scales (Weitzenhoffer and Hilgard 1963). It requires approximately twenty minutes for administration. Like the parent scale, this is an additive measure with a series of ideomotor and challenge items.

From a clinical point of view there remained a need for an even shorter test of hypnotizability which would provide systematic information and at the same time facilitate the therapeutic atmosphere. The longer laboratory measures were not employed by busy clinicians and raised the additional problem of the development of fatigue during the testing. Context and motivation are critical factors in any psychological measurement. Tests standardized with subjects volunteering for the sole purpose of hypnotic experimentation measure different dimensions than those standardized on people presenting themselves for treatment (Frankel and Orne 1976). In this clinical context the assessment of hypnotizability is incidental to the treatment encounter and motivation is likely to be greater because the patient is seeking help with a personal problem rather than exercising curiosity. In this sense, paid volunteers for experimentation have a significantly different motivational set. Tests standardized on college student populations often reflect concern with only a limited sample of age and education, whereas the concern of the clinician must relate to the wide range characteristics of a patient population. Some earlier tests identified hypnotizability as "susceptibility," a description which offended many patients and hampered their cooperation. Presenting hypnotizability as a capacity or talent serves to avoid this impediment to patient acceptance. The traditional use of sleep terminology in earlier tests was also misleading and did not convey the therapeutically useful mobilization of concentration which characterizes trance. Some of the challenge items, such as hallucinating an insect, at times proved to be aesthetically disturbing to patients seeking relief from symptoms. Since hypnosis is an expression of integrated concentration, factors which impair concentration such as drugs, psychopathology, and neurological deficits should be taken into account, and were not in the standardization of the laboratory measures.

A chemical analysis of food, no matter how accurate, in no way identifies and differentiates gourmet from institutional cooking. The unique gourmet quality is missed by the analytic measurement, yet it is a quality identified by the trained palate. No measurement of hypnotizability is the same as the entire phenomenon itself, and any test will reflect the context of the experience and have inherent limitations and advantages. Given the fact that any test is at best a sampling and imposes distortions on the data it measures, and given the above considerations, it seemed necessary to develop and standardize a test within the clinical context.

The Hypnotic Induction Profile was developed during the past decade in an effort to resolve these difficulties. It consists of three major components: a biological measurement, the eye roll (Spiegel, H. 1972), which records presumed biological trance capacity; an ideomotor item, hand levitation; and a subjective discovery experience, the control differential between hands. The test yields information regarding a subject's hypnotizability sufficient to make a clinical decision regarding the role of hypnosis in treatment.

The HIP was developed in the hopes of creating a scale with rich relationships to treatment outcome and psychopathology factors as well as hypnotizability per se. We will present data regarding relationships between performance on the test and such factors as personality traits and degree of psychopathology.

The relationship between the HIP and the Stanford Hypnotic Susceptibility Scale is currently being studied in a college student population. The association appears to be a mild one. In due course, these findings will be published.

Introduction to the Hypnotic Induction Profile

The Hypnotic Induction Profile was developed to provide a useful measure in the clinical setting. It evolved out of a need for a rapid induction and testing procedure which could be easily integrated into the clinical diagnostic interview, so that trance capacity might then be quickly employed in treatment.

The HIP postulates that hypnosis is a subtle perceptual alteration involving a capacity for attentive, responsive concentration which is inherent in the person and which can be *tapped* by the examiner. A rapid procedure, the HIP takes five to ten minutes to administer. It is both a procedure for trance induction and a disciplined measure of hypnotic capacity standardized on a patient population in a clinical setting.

The HIP assesses a single trance experience as it flows through the phases of entering, experiencing, and exiting. The test also establishes a structure for this sequence. The specific point in time at which the shift from customary awareness into trance takes place varies from person to person. However, the trance experience is punctuated, tapped, and divided into phases by the ten individual items lettered A through L on the HIP score sheet (Figure 3–1). Six of these items (D, G, H, I, J, L) are used for rating the subject's trance capacity and for scoring the HIP according to the induction or profile-scoring method. Item D is the sum of items B and C. The remaining four items (A, E, F, K) round out the clinical picture and establish the procedures for entering and exiting trance and for subsequent self-reporting. Scoring these four items is optional, since they are not part of the HIP summary scores.

This technique induces the subject to enter the hypnotic trance quickly under observed, specified conditions, and then to shift out of trance on signal. At the same time, the HIP teaches the subject to use his own cuing system for entering and exiting trance. Thus, as the examiner observes and measures trance capacity, the subject can learn to identify the trance experience in order to initiate and use it independently (self-hypnosis) in the service of relevant goals.

The trance experience can be divided into four phases for measurement (see Table 3–1). The first is a pretrance or preinduction phase which lasts until eye closure. The second is the induction or entering phase in which instructions are given for the individual to shift into formal hypnosis. The shift may take place in response to the examiner's directions and, as part of this induction ceremony, instructions are given for induction responsivity. The induction ceremony and formal trance are terminated with the opening of the eyes, but hypnotic trance persists and the third phase begins. Phase three is a postinduction or postceremonial phase in which the person may actually experience five responses to the instructions given as part of the ceremony: dissociation, signalled

Hypnotic Induction Profile
Score Sheet

Name_____ Date_____

Sequence □ Initial_____ Previous_____ When_____

Position of Subject □ Standing_____ Supine_____ Chair_____ Chair-Stool_____

Item		
A	Up-Gaze	0 - 1 - 2 - 3 - 4

B		Roll:	0 - 1 - 2 - 3 - 4
C		Squint:	0 - 1 - 2 - 3 - 4
D	Eye-Roll Sign (roll and squint)		0 - 1 - 2 - 3 - 4

E   Arm (R-L) Levitation Instruction   0 - 1 - 2 - 3 - 4

F   Tingle   0 -   - 1 - 2

G_____   Dissociation   0 -   - 1 - 2

H_____   Levitation
(postinduction)
> no reinforcement   3 - 4
> 1st   "   2 - 3
> 2nd   "   1 - 2
> 3rd   "   1 -   Smile_____
> 4th   "   0 -   Surprise _____

I_____   Control Differential   0 -   - 1 - 2

J_____   Cut-Off   0 -   - 1 - 2

K   Amnesia to Cut-off   0 -   - 1 - 2
or No-Test_____

L_____   Floating Sensation   0 -   - 1 - 2

Summary Scores

_____ Induction Score   Profile Score   0 - 1 - 2 - 3 - 4 - 5

_____Soft   _____Zero   _____Intact

_____ Minutes   _____Decrement   _____Special Zero   _____Special Intact

Figure 3–1

TABLE 3-1

Four Phases for Measurement of the HIP.

The 4 phases		Items that tap the 4 phases	
1. Preinduction	—Pretrance or preceremonial; state of customary awareness	Up-Gaze*	(Item A)
2. Induction	—Ceremony for entering formal trance with eye closure —instructions for postceremonial responsivity; exit the formal trance with eye opening	Eye-Roll Sign Instructional Arm Levitation*	(Items B, C & D) (Item E)
3. Postinduction	—Postceremonial trance with open eyes; postceremonial responsiveness or experience tapped by Items F-J	Tingle* Dissociation Signaled Arm Levitation Control Differential	(Item F) (Item G) (Item H) (Item I)
	—Exit total program with examiner's touching of subject's elbow	Cut-Off	(Item J)
4. Postinduction	—After trance; state of customary awareness; retrospective aspects of the trance experience	Amnesia* Float	(Item K) (Item L)

*Denotes that recording a score for this item is optional.

arm levitation, control differential, cut-off, and float. It is important to note that what are often called posthypnotic phenomena actually represent the experience of hypnosis. "Posthypnotic" is a traditional label which can be confusing. A more appropriate label may be "postceremonial" or "postinduction."

Item J (cut-off) of phase three is the exiting procedure. Although the subject is out of formal trance and his eyes are already open, this period of postceremonial trance response must be terminated by the examiner touching the subject's elbow. A fourth postexperiential, nontrance phase is comprised of self-reports by the subject.

Measurements of up-gaze (Item A), the eye-roll sign (Items B, C, and D), and instructed arm levitation (Item E) supply an evaluation of inherent potential or capacity for success in initiating and sustaining the trance experience. They also comprise the induction procedure. Actual success in maintaining the trance experience, once it has been effected through specific instructions, is tapped by dissociation (Item G), signalled arm levitation (Item H), control differential (Item I), cut-off (Item J), and float (Item L). These five measurements, taken together, rate the degree to which the subject can attentively focus: they comprise the induction score (see Table 3–2).

The profile score is a statement of the relationship between a person's potential for trance and his ability to experience and maintain it. Ex-

TABLE 3-2

The Items of the HIP Induction Scale.

Dissociation	"Spontaneous," uninstructed. Score positive (1 or 2) if subject reports that the arm used in the preparatory levitation task feels "less a part" of the body than the other arm, or if that hand feels "less connected to the wrist" than the other hand.
Signaled Arm Levitation (Lev)	Score positive if, on the instructed signal, the arm rises to upright position. Positive scores vary from 1-4, depending on the number of verbal reinforcements necessary.
Control Differential (CD)	"Spontaneous," uninstructed. Score positive (1 or 2) if subject feels less control over the arm used in the Lev item. The examiner's questions do not indicate which arm is expected to be less controllable.
Cut-Off	Score positive (1 or 2) if, on instructed signal, subject reports normal sensation and control returning to arm used in Lev item.
Float	Score positive (1 or 2) if subject reports having felt the instructed floating sensation during the administration of the Lev item.

actly what this relationship means and how it is determined is discussed in the scoring and interpretation sections of this manual.

GENERAL CONSIDERATIONS

The HIP is best described as an objectively scorable, interpersonal hypnotic interaction which also serves as an induction technique. In order to obtain results comparable to the standardization data, *momentum* or *rhythm* must be established and maintained during the interaction; there should be no long silences or pauses during test administration, nor should the pace be so rapid that the subject does not have a chance to attend to his experience. If administered correctly, the test requires five to ten minutes.

The HIP requires of the operator a degree of expertise and familiarity with the test which is not required by other tests of hypnotizability. *The examiner himself is the instrument*, and if he is not finely tuned the HIP will not be valid. Persons new to the HIP should not expect to be able to master the technique immediately. They should be aware that several—perhaps many—practice administrations are a requisite to valid clinical or experimental application.

These qualities of the HIP have been preserved because the test is primarily a clinical instrument and was developed in the course of clinical practice. In the clinical setting, especially during the initial encounter in which the HIP is usually used, rapport must be encouraged and nurtured. Although the HIP items and even the wording of the test (insofar as this is possible) should be the same in each case, the particular responses of the subject must be acknowledged and woven into the fabric of the interchange.

In the following two sections the administration and scoring of the HIP are presented. Read the instructions given by the examiner for a single HIP item, and then the accompanying directions. To learn what it is the hypnotist observes and scores at this point, look up the item in the following section on scoring. When the connections are clear between the administration of the test and the behaviors and experiences to be observed, read the administration section from beginning to end without interruption. With the concurrent scoring by the examiner in mind, this uninterrupted reading should begin to communicate a sense of the rhythm of administration.

The physical setting can enhance the psychological one. Shifting into a state of peak responsiveness is in a sense "shifting gears" and the physical arrangement may reflect this. For example, during an initial clinical interview, the clinician may be seated in his customary place across the desk from the patient (or subject), or in an armchair across the room. But at the time of induction the clinician shifts his position, moving to another seat slightly forward and to the left of the patient. During the induction procedure he should be close enough to establish comfortable physical contact with the patient, as shown in Figure 3–2. After completing the procedure, the examiner may return to his customary seat if he wishes.

Throughout these instructions it is presumed that the subject's left hand will levitate. If the examiner sits to the right of the subject, right should be substituted for left in the examiner's instructions to the subject. In general, the subject should be seated comfortably, with a place to rest his arms and legs. Some testers find that the use of a footstool enhances the initial floating sensation which many subjects experience

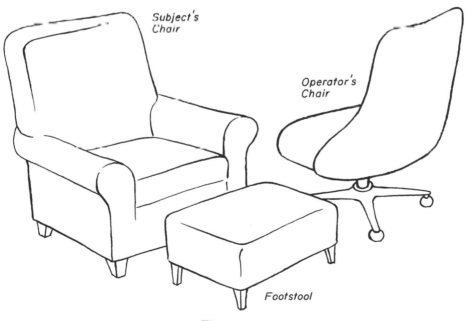

Figure 3–2

during hypnosis. If an armchair is not available, have the subject sit next to a table—placing his arms on the table, legs relaxed, and feet flat on the floor. Or ask the subject to imagine that his elbow is resting on an imaginary air cushion.

Until the examiner is comfortable with the procedure, he may find it helpful to keep the book open to the How to Administer section and next to the scoring form. Since this is an interpersonal interaction, eye-to-eye contact helps sustain the subject's attention even though the examiner may be referring to the instruction manual.

4

Administration and Scoring

Invite the subject to be seated. Your manner and tone of voice should be gentle and matter-of-fact. You may have noted already the subject's name, sequence (whether or not the subject has been hypnotized or taken the HIP previously, and if so, when), and position before "shifting gears."

All instructions given by the examiner to the subject are printed in italics. Directions and remarks meant for the examiner are in regular type. The spatial divisions between the two types of print do not imply pauses in the procedure.

Instruct the subject to: *Get as comfortable as possible with your arms resting on the arm of the chair and both feet up.*

This is an excellent opportunity to touch the subject's left arm by actually placing it on the arm of the chair gently, but firmly. Touching as you begin immediately establishes touching as a standard part of the procedure so that it will not startle the subject later. Touch is used by the examiner to focus the subject's attention on the physical sensations which may occur in response to verbal instructions. Touching also gives the tester the opportunity to actually measure the subject's physical response to some items on the test. For example, how light, heavy, stiff, or flexible the subject's left arm feels to the examiner is essential to measuring Item E, the instructional arm levitation. Touching encourages a trend toward regression and atavism. Remember that too soft and indefinite a touch may be seductive and distract the subject's attention rather than help focus it. Be firm and definite.

Item A: Up-Gaze. *Now look toward me. As you hold your head in that position, look up toward your eyebrows—now, toward the top of your head.*

The subject should be on an equal level with you (face to face). Otherwise, the upward gaze will appear to be greater if you are lower

than the subject, or lesser if you are slightly above him. Without paus-
ing, observe and perhaps measure the up-gaze according to instructions for Item A: Up-Gaze, pp. 52–53. This is a preparatory measure
for the eye-roll sign and is not a part of the induction or profile score,
so recording the score is optional.

Item B: Roll. *As you continue to look upward, close your eyelids slowly. That's
right . . . close. Close. Close. Close.*

Observe and score the roll according to the instructions for Item B:
Roll, pp. 53–54. This begins the induction procedure and is an important part of the profile score.

Item C: Squint. Occasionally, an inward "squint" or ophthalmological "A-
pattern" may occur as part of the up-gaze and/or eye-roll. It is not important
if it occurs with the up-gaze, but it adds to the score of the roll. See instructions under Item C: Squint, p. 104. You have to be quick to catch it if it occurs.

Item D: The Eye-Roll Sign. This item is part of scoring procedure only. It is
comprised of the procedures for Items B: Roll and C: Squint, p. 105.

Item E: Arm Levitation Instruction. *Keep your eyelids closed and continue to
hold your eyes upward. Take a deep breath, hold . . . . Now, exhale, let your
eyes relax while keeping the lids closed, and let your body float. Imagine a
feeling of floating, floating right down through the chair . . . . There will be
something pleasant and welcome about this sensation of floating.*

By instructing the subject to float downward instead of upward, you
contradict the usual expectations concerning the state of floating and
casually introduce a paradox, the acceptance of which may be a part
of the hypnotic experience. You also fix the subject's attention on your
voice and on your instruction to him. Often someone with a high trance
capacity (an intact grade 3 or 4) has already "floated away" and you
are refocusing his attention with the contradiction.

*As you concentrate on this floating, I am going to concentrate on your left
arm and hand.*

Gradually place your hand gently and firmly on the subject's wrist as
an indication that you are going to use touch next as an instruction. Be
careful not to startle the subject with a sudden touch which may jolt
him. If you find this awkward at first, verbally indicate that you are
going to touch him.

*In a while I am going to stroke the middle finger of your left hand. After I do,
you will develop movement sensations in that finger. Then the movements will
spread, causing your left hand to feel light and buoyant, and you will let it
float upward. Ready?*

Move your hand away from the subject's wrist and stroke the middle
finger of the left hand, beginning at the fingernail and moving along
the back or top of the hand and then up along the forearm until you
reach the elbow. Again, be firm but not hard or harsh. Pressing downward slightly may encourage the opposite response—rising upward—in
the subject's left hand and forearm. If there is an immediate response—

movements in the fingers and hand which spread so that the forearm rises into an upright position—proceed to: *Now I am going to position your arm in this manner so . . .* and continue from there. If there is no immediate indication of arm levitation in response to stroking of the arm, give this additional instruction as encouragement.

First one finger, then another. As these restless movements develop, your hand becomes light and buoyant, you elbow bends, your forearm floats into an upright position.

As you say this, gently and gradually encircle the subject's wrist with your thumb and forefinger, and give the arm a little lift. Note that this physical encouragement may be as effective an instruction for some subjects as the verbal instructions are for others. Both are integral means of teaching the subject what arm levitation is. If the subject takes over the upward movement by himself and sets his own momentum, you may either keep your hand around his wrist as a guide, or, once the subject gets started, you may let go. If the arm moves into position, proceed to: *Now I am going to position your arm in this manner so . . . .* If not, continue to lift the arm lightly upward as you give the further instructions.

Let your hand be a balloon. Just let it go. You have the power to let it float upward. That's right! Help it along! Just put it up there.

It is essential for the subject's hand and forearm to go into the upright position, even if you have to tell the subject to put it up, or if you have to guide it all the way. However, recording the score for Item E is optional. (See pp. 55–56.) When the forearm reaches the upright position, say:

Now I am going to position your arm in this manner, so . . . . And let it remain in this upright position.

Establish the position now by gently cupping the subject's elbow with both hands, positioning it in comfortable alignment with the chair arm, and flexing the hand forward (Figure 4–1). It is essential to present the following instructions verbatim, because scores on the remaining items depend on the extent to which the phenomena described in these instructions are actually experienced and reported by the subject. Note that you are instructing the subject to: 1) allow his arm to remain in an upright position; 2) allow the arm to levitate after you pull it down; and 3) feel "usual" sensation return in response to touching the left elbow. Earlier you instructed the subject to feel a "lightness or buoyancy," a sensation which will also be tested later. All of these instructions are for postinduction (or postceremonial) responsivity; they are given during formal trance and eye-closure, and while the arm is in the instructed upright position.

In fact, it will remain in that position even after I give you the signal for your eyes to open. When your eyes are open, even when I put your hand down, it will float right back up to where it is now. You will find something amusing about this sensation. Later, when I touch your left elbow, your usual sensa-

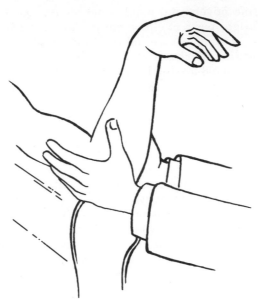

Figure 4–1

tion and control will return. In the future, each time you give yourself the signal for self-hypnosis, at the count of one your eyes will roll upward and by the count of three your eyelids will close and you will feel in a relaxed trance state. Each time you will find the experience easier and easier. Now I am going to count backwards. At two, your eyes will again roll upward with your eyelids closed. At one, let them open very slowly. Ready . . . . Three, two, with your eyelids closed roll up your eyes and one, let them open slowly. All right, stay in this position and describe what physical sensations you are aware of now in your left arm and hand.

These are the instructions for exiting from the formal trance ceremony. Note that just the induction ceremony is cut off, not the trance itself. The subject may now shift into a phase of postceremonial trance. Eye-opening marks the end of the trance ceremony and beginning of the postinduction phase. Introduce the following items by first asking: *Is it comfortable?*

Item F: Tingle. *Are you aware of any tingling sensations?*

You may substitute "pins and needles" for "tingling" if you wish. This item is not used in the induction or profile scores, and recording the score is optional. (See p. 56.)

Item G: Dissociation. *Does your left hand feel as if it is not as much a part of your body as your right hand?*

If the subject gives a definite "yes," go on the Item H. If he says "no" or gives a qualified "yes," say:

Does your left hand feel as connected to the wrist as your right hand feels connected to the wrist? Is there a difference?

This item is part of the Induction Score. (See pp. 56–57.)

Item H: Signalled Arm Levitation. *Now note this.*

Take the subject's left hand in yours, touch his palm, and gently lower the subject's hand until it rests on the arm of the chair. Let go and quietly observe, as you look pointedly at the subject's left hand for response. The method of administering this item is dependent on maintaining a *rhythm* in the hypnotic interaction. All the instructions that follow are simply a detailed, standardized description of the method to be used in the maintenance of this rhythm. Remember that you are trying to get an estimate of the subject's degree of responsivity to hypnotic instruction.

Item H is broken down into five parts, the initial presentation of the signal and the four verbal reinforcements. You need only go as far as necessary for the subject to show complete arm levitation (as depicted in Figure 4–1). At that point, move on to control differential. Different subjects require a different number of reinforcements, varying from none to the maximum of four. There are three rules to use in deciding when to give another reinforcement.

1. Give a reinforcement if there has been no arm movement in the five seconds following the previous reinforcement (or the initial signal).
2. Give a reinforcement if movement began within five seconds of the previous reinforcement (or the initial signal), but halted prior to achievement of the instructed upright position.
3. Give a reinforcement when the subject has shown continuous arm movement since the last reinforcement (or initial signal), but the movement has been so slow that the upright arm position has not been achieved after ten seconds. This rule has one exception: one waits only *five* seconds after the third reinforcement before giving the fourth.

Make sure to keep a close estimate of the time elapsed after each reinforcement; this will be one criterion for scoring. You may wish to turn to the instructions for scoring *Lcv* after you have read these instructions, because scoring and administration must be carried out simultaneously. (See pp. 57–59.)

(First reinforcement.) *Now turn your head, look at your left hand, and watch what is going to happen.*

This is the first reinforcement for signalled arm levitation. Although touching was used as part of the reinforcement for instructional arm levitation, do not use touch here.

(Second reinforcement.) *While concentrating on your left hand, imagine it to be a huge, buoyant balloon.*

(Third reinforcement.) *Now, while imagining it to be a balloon, permit it to act out as if it were a balloon. That's right. Be "big" about it.*

(Fourth reinforcement.) *This is your chance to be a method actor or a ballet dancer. Think of your hand as a balloon or as the arm of a ballet dancer and permit it to act as if it were a balloon. That's right, just put it up there, just the way a ballet dancer would.*

Request the subject to put his arm up, even if he has to "fake it." You may even have to say, *Pretend*. It is not necessary for the examiner to touch or to put the subject's arm in position at this point.

Item I: Control Differential. *While it remains in the upright position, by way of comparison raise your right hand. Now put your right arm down. Are you aware of a difference in sensation in your right arm going up, compared to your left? For example, does one arm feel lighter or heavier than the other?*

The difference in sense of control over one arm as compared to the other emerges as part of the trance experience. The subject was not instructed beforehand to feel this difference. It is *discovered* in this context. These first few instructions are preparatory. The subject's answers are not significant. Only the following question is scorable:

Are you aware of any relative difference in your sense of control in one arm compared to the other as it goes up? (Optional: *On a more or less basis, do you feel a difference in control?*)

If the subject answers "yes," the operator asks: *In which arm do you feel more control?* If the subject still says "no," say: *Let's try it again.* Give him a second chance by taking your thumb and forefinger and drawing the hand down onto the arm of the chair just as you did in Item H. Then ask the subject to: *Let it rise like a balloon or ballet dancer's hand. Just let it go up as it did before.* Now ask: *This time, do you have more or less control in one arm going up compared to the other?*

See p. 59 for scoring Item I, part of the induction and profile scores.

Item J: Cut-Off. *Now, note this.*

At this point give the cut-off signal: it is both verbal and physical. You cup the subject's left elbow with your right hand, touching both the inside and outside of the elbow. At the same time gently grasp the subject's left wrist with your left hand, slowly lower the subject's forearm and hand onto the arm of the chair, and say:

Make a tight fist, real tight, and now open it.

Let go of the elbow with your right hand. With your left hand stroke the subject's left forearm by pressing down firmly, starting at the elbow and moving towards the fingertips, and say:

Before there was a difference between the two forearms. Are you aware of any change in sensation now?

At the word "now," press the subject's left hand as a way of punctuating the end of stroking his left arm. The point of this procedure is to cut off the sense of less control in the subject's left "hypnotized" arm and to exit the postinduction trance program. Remember that in Item E you told the subject the cut-off signal—that you would touch the left elbow and the usual sensation would return. Note that touching the elbow is part of several other motions you carry out. The subject may continue to feel "pins and needles," tingling in the arm, or relative lightness or heaviness; however, these sensations are irrelevant to a difference in sense of control. A score of zero on control differential strongly suggests a score of zero on cut-off. However, the cut-off signal is always administered because of the rare circumstance in which the subject who scored zero on control differential does experience cut-off. In this event, control differential is rescored. When giving the cut-off, under these conditions, of course, the operator does not refer to a prior difference in the feeling of control over the two arms. The cut-off may be complete and the sense of control back to normal after this first signal. If so, go ahead to Amnesia. If not, tell the subject to: *Let your arm go again.* Give the cut-off signal again at this point.

Make a fist a few times. That's right. Open your fist and now put your hand down. Now, make fists with both hands at the same time. Lift your forearms up a few times and tell me when you feel that your control is equal.

Demonstrate this arm movement as you give these instructions to the subject. See pp. 59–60 for scoring Item J. Cut-off is part of the induction score.

Item K: Amnesia. *You see that the relative difference in control that was in your arms is gone. Do you have any idea why?*

You may need to specify by saying: *Is there anything I did that might account for it?* If the subject has scored zero on control differential, there is no test for amnesia to the cut-off signal. Check "no test" on the score sheet.

See p. 60 for scoring Item K, which is neither a part of the induction score nor the profile score. Scoring is optional.

Item L: Float. *When your left arm went up before, did you feel a physical sensation that you can describe as a lightness, floating, or "buoyancy" in your left arm or hand? Were you aware of similar sensations in any other part of your body—such as your head, neck, chest, abdomen, thighs, legs, or all over— or just in your left hand or arm?*

In the event that the subject claims that the left arm felt heavier, say: *Keep in mind that a boat can be heavy, but because of the buoyancy pressure from below it floats upward.* This helps to describe buoyancy and to define the sensation.

See p. 60 for scoring this item, which is part of the induction score. The float item concludes the HIP.

How to Score Each Item

Figure 3–1 (on p. 40) is a reproduction of the HIP score sheet on which observations are recorded during the test administration.

    Item A: Up-Gaze. This item is preparation for the eye roll and is not part of the profile or induction summary scores. Up-gaze received a score until it was found that it had only a small correlation with the remainder of the scale. Although it is not necessary to score it, it is essential for you to administer the procedure. The eye roll is awkward for some subjects, and separating it into the steps of up-gaze and then rolling down the eyelids clarifies and simplifies the instruction.

    Up-gaze is a measure of the distance, or amount of sclera relative to the size and shape of the eye, between the lower border of the iris and the lower eyelid as the subject is gazing upward. You are *not* measuring how much of the cornea disappears under the upper eyelid, but rather the amount of sclera rising from below.

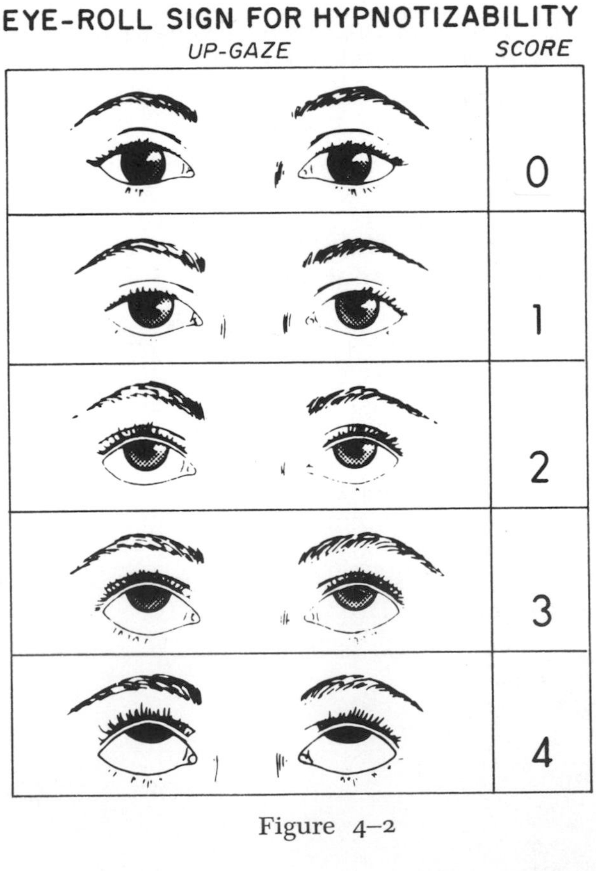

EYE-ROLL SIGN FOR HYPNOTIZABILITY

Figure 4–2

Up-gaze can be scored o, 1, 2, 3, or 4, according to Figure 4–2. Score o when there is no sclera between the two borders. Score 1 for any amount of sclera, however small, between the two borders. Score 2 when the distance falls below or approximately on the midline of the eye. *Midline* is an imaginary horizontal center that runs between the inner and outer corners of the eye, or canthi. Score 3 when the amount of sclera reaches a little above the imaginary midline. Score 4 when the amount of sclera rises far above the midline.

Record your measurement on the score sheet by circling o, 1, 2, 3, or 4 under Item A. Since the amount of up-gaze is not always clear-cut, two numbers may be circled to represent the measurement, o - 1 - 2 - 3 - 4, instead of o - 1 - 2 - 3 - 4, for example. However, it would not be correct to circle o - 1 because any sclera showing between the two borders would be recorded as o - 1.

As some subjects attempt to gaze directly upward, both irises may slant inward. See Item C: Squint.

Item B: Roll. The eye roll is a measure of the distance—or amount of visible sclera between the lower border of the iris and the lower eyelid—exhibited when the subject simultaneously gazes upward as high as possible and slowly closes the eyelids (Figure 4–3).

As the eyes are closing, score o, 1, 2, 3, or 4, according to Figure 4–4. Score o when there is no sclera apparent between the two borders. Score 1 for any amount of sclera visible, however small. Score 2 when the amount of sclera approaches the imaginary midline of the eye. Score 3 when the amount of sclera rises a little above the midline. Score 4 when the amount of sclera rises far above the midline and the iris disappears immediately under the upper eyelid. Record the measurement on the score sheet as described for up-gaze.

It is not unusual for a subject's eye roll to measure naturally lower or higher than his up-gaze. However, the potential capacity for eye roll, up-gaze, and squint may be misrepresented by myopia or previous eye operations that limit extra-ocular mobility. Always ask the subject about these possibilities when the score for eye roll is zero or markedly lower than the signalled arm levitation score. Also, contact lenses make up-gaze and simultaneous eye closure uncomfortable. Be sure the subject removes them before the induction procedure.

Item C: Squint. Occasionally, as a subject attempts to gaze upward and/or close his eyelids, both eyes may veer inward, thus causing an

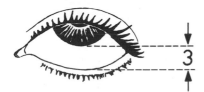

EYE-ROLL MEASUREMENT

Figure 4–3

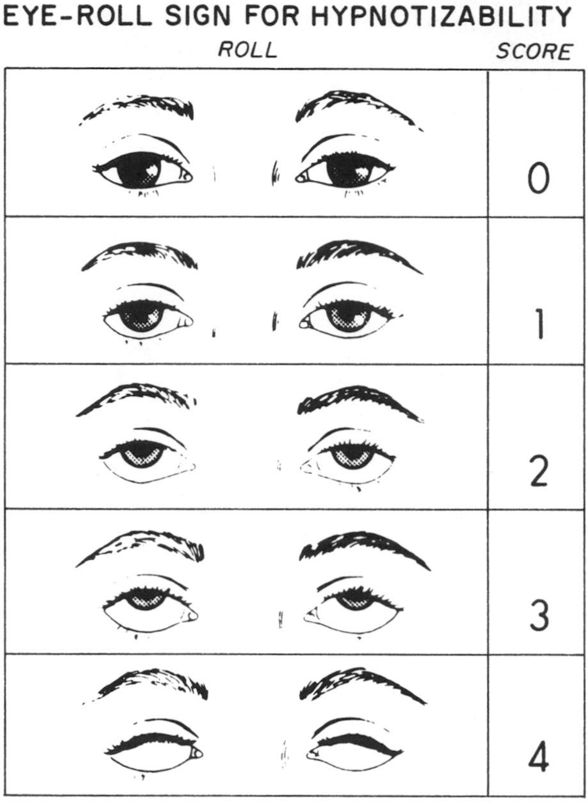

EYE-ROLL SIGN FOR HYPNOTIZABILITY

ROLL	SCORE
	0
	1
	2
	3
	4

Figure 4–4

internal squint or what ophthalmologists call an "A-pattern." Note and score a squint 1, 2, or 3, according to Figure 4–5.

Normally both eyes must veer inward simultaneously to constitute a squint. If one eye squints and the other (presumably not myopic) does not, only the amount of the higher roll of the two eyes is recorded. It is not unusual for a subject to squint internally as part of the up-gaze and not as part of the eye roll, or vice versa. However, it is only important to record as part of the eye-roll sign.

Item D: The Eye-Roll Sign. Our hypothesis is that the eye-roll sign, a measurement of mobility in extra-ocular eye movements, taps inherent potential capacity for experiencing hypnosis. It is part of the profile score. The sign consists of the roll and squint measurements added together. For example, a roll of 1 and a squint of 1 comprise an eye-roll sign of 2. A subject's eye-roll sign of 2 also may be comprised of no observable squint and a score of 2 on the roll, or a roll of 0 and a squint of 2. Most often, though, a roll with no squint is found. It is sometimes

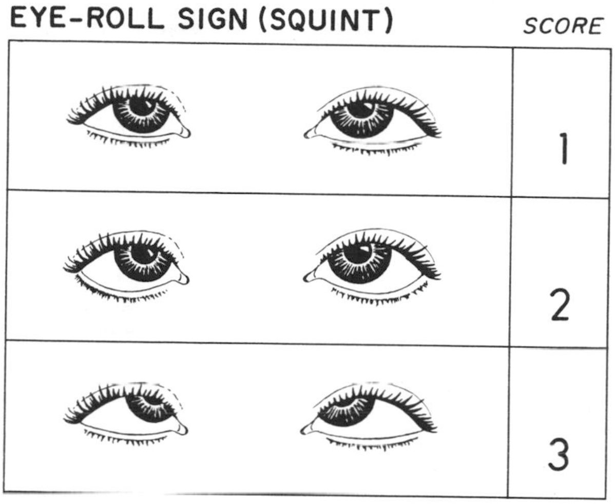

EYE-ROLL SIGN (SQUINT) *SCORE*

Figure 4–5

observed that the score for the eye-roll sign will remain stable, and the scores for its two components vary—e.g., on the first examination a subject shows a 2 roll and a 1 squint; on the next examination he shows a 1 roll and a 2 squint.

The eye-roll sign does not change over time for a given subject. You may choose to go through the procedure of eye roll during induction without scoring the sign. After completing the HIP, you may observe the eye-roll sign again as many times as you need to in order to obtain a score. Accurately rating eye-roll signs takes a great deal of practice. You may not feel confident in judging them until you have seen fifty to a hundred.

Item E: Arm Levitation Instruction. This item does not correlate strongly enough with other items (Table A–4, p. 341) to be part of either summary score, so scoring it is optional. However, it is a necessary procedure to administer.

Many clinicians find the item useful to rate because arm levitation tends to be a clinical indicator of a person's potential for initiating and sustaining the hypnotic trance experience. The subject's movement may start in the fingers, and spread to the hand and the wrist; then the whole forearm may rise into upright position. Both the operator's objective measurement (noting the amount of verbal encouragement) and his subjective one (feeling the weight and resistance of the subject's arm) are equally important.

Score 4 if there is immediate response to stroking the subject's arm. That is, the subject begins the movement upward into an upright position and sets the momentum of rising in immediate response to being stroked. The arm probably looks weightless and rises easily and smoothly. The movement should be completed without further instruction. The subject may be very surprised or even afraid of what the arm has just done.

Score 3 if the subject's forearm begins and sets the momentum for rising into the upright position within a few seconds of giving the first additional instruction. Completing the movement into position may take longer, but, after being given a boost by the operator, the momentum must be set by the subject. The subject usually sets the momentum for the upward movement without difficulty, but the examiner may continue to encircle the subject's wrist. The subject's arm may feel light, even weightless, and not resistant to the operator.

Score 2 if the operator gives further verbal instruction and more of a boost before the subject takes over. The subject's arm may feel heavy and perhaps at first be somewhat resistant to the tester. Score 1 if the subject's arm is even more resistant and if the examiner actually must place the subject's forearm into the upright position. Score 0 if the subject is so adamant that movement is resisted, even with help from the examiner. No further testing is then possible. Score the profile by recording the eye-roll score and zero, and by noting this abrupt end point. This occurs rarely.

The measurement is not clear-cut, but on a continuum. For example, the movement may begin in the subject's fingers and spread to his hand after the first additional verbal instruction, but then stop, requiring more encouragement in order to complete the movement into the upright position. Such a measurement would be recorded as: 0 -(2 - 3)- 4. Or a subject may complete the movement without being told to "just put it up," but take approximately ten to fifteen seconds. The measurement would be recorded in the same way—by circling 2 and 3. Be loose about it; the "soft focus" approach is best. Use your clinical judgment and remember that it takes time and practice to get a feel for this measurement.

Item F: Tingle. This is a clinical postinduction indicator of the subject's sensory experience, that is, of how much of a "tingling" or "pins and needles" sensation the subject reports that he is experiencing. Scoring this item is optional. The procedure is included because some subjects mistake a tingling sensation for a control differential (Item I). By asking about tingle now, it is clear to the subject later that a sensation of "pins and needles" does not indicate a sensation of control differential.

Score 2 if the subject answers definitely "yes." Score 1 if the subject spontaneously qualifies by answering "a little bit," "slightly"; or indicates that tingle is experienced in only one part of the body, such as his hand and forearm; or if you have to ask a second time and the subject reports tingling sensations. Score 0 if the subject indicates that he does not experience tingle.

Item G: Dissociation. Dissociation is a postinduction measure of the relative difference in the degree of connectedness which the subject may feel between the hand and wrist of the "hynotized" arm, versus the hand and wrist of the "nonhypnotized" arm. If the "hypnotized" hand feels disconnected from the wrist, the score is high; if the sense of connection is the same in both arms, the score is low. This item contributes to the induction score. Score 0, or 1, or 2—never 1 - 2 or 0 - 1. Because dissociation is not an everyday experience, it is important to phrase the questions about it exactly as they are written.

Score 2 if the subject answers definitely "yes" to your first inquiry; that is, if the left hand does not feel as connected to the body as the right hand does. Score 1 if the subject spontaneously qualifies his answer to the first inquiry (e.g., "a little bit"), or if the subject answers "no" to the second inquiry. Score 0 if the answer is "no" to the first and "yes" to the second inquiry, indicating that the hands feel equally connected to the wrists.

Item H: Signalled Arm Levitation. First study the grid on which Lev scores are recorded, reproduced below from the score sheet.

```
Levitation        ⎡ no reinforcement ⎤                    3 _ 4
(postinduction)   ⎢ 1 st      "      ⎢              2 _ 3
                  ⎨ 2 nd      "      ⎬           1 _ 2
                  ⎢ 3 rd      "      ⎢           1 _
                  ⎣ 4 th      "      ⎦    0 _
```

Two aspects of the subject's Lev performance may contribute to the Lev score: number of reinforcements necessary for achievement of the instructed upright arm position, and time elapsed. Number of reinforcements is represented by the single number on the far right of each row. The number 4 refers to the initial signal, 3 refers to the first reinforcement, and so on. The tester circles the reinforcement after which he sees the first arm movement, and he continues to circle reinforcements until he has circled the last one necessary for complete levitation. A simple example: a subject shows no movement until the second reinforcement and then completes levitation within five seconds. Circle the 2 in the third row, like so:

```
Levitation        ⎡ no reinforcement ⎤                    3 _ 4
(postinduction)   ⎢ 1 st      "      ⎢              2 _ 3
                  ⎨ 2 nd      "      ⎬           1 _ ②
                  ⎢ 3 rd      "      ⎢           1 _
                  ⎣ 4 th      "      ⎦    0 _
```

A second example of this type is: if the subject shows complete levitation within five seconds of the signal, you would circle 4.

More common is the situation in which movement begins after one reinforcement, but at least one more reinforcement is required for complete levitation.* In this case the examiner circles all the relevant numbers. For instance: a subject shows no movement until the first reinforcement and his response is slow enough to require a second reinforcement. Within five seconds of the second reinforcement, the response is complete. This sequence is recorded:

The horizontal dimension on the scoring grid represents time. If levitation is completed within five seconds of the last reinforcement, then no more than one number per row is circled, as in the previous example. If full levitation requires five to ten seconds, the tester circles both numbers on the line. For instance, if levitation began within five seconds of the signal but was not completed until ten seconds had passed, the score would be:

Levitation (postinduction) — no reinforcement; 1 st "; 2 nd "; 3 rd "; 4 th "

(3 - 4)
2 - 3
1 - 2
1 -
0 -

Another example: Levitation begins after the second reinforcement but is not complete until ten seconds have elapsed. Score as:

Note that a score of 0-1 is possible because the fourth reinforcement is mandatory after five seconds have elapsed since the third reinforcement. The fourth reinforcement is significant because it identifies a possible break in concentration. (See p. 58 and p. 59.)

The final Lev score is a joint function of time elapsed and number of reinforcements given. It might happen, for instance, that arm movement began after the first reinforcement but was slow enough to require the second reinforcement. However, levitation was not completed until

---

* See instructions for administration of this item on pp. 57–59 for criteria to be used in deciding when to give another reinforcement.

8 to 10 seconds after the secondary reinforcement. The reinforcements and the time are represented on the score sheet:

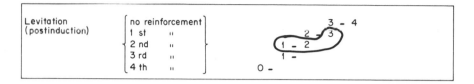

It may help in understanding these rules to think about Lev score as a process of subtraction: every subject begins with a score of 4 and loses parts of it as reinforcements and time are used.

The final Lev score is the arithmetic mean of the circled numbers. Each column, though, may only contribute a single number.

The Lev score is part of the profile and induction scores.

I: Control Differential. This is a posthypnotic measure of a difference in sense of control which the subject experiences between the "hypnotized" and "nonhypnotized" arms. The subject must feel *relatively* less control in the "hypnotized" arm than in the "nonhypnotized" arm for a positive score (1 or 2). The only scorable element is the subject's response to the questions concerning the relative difference in control. All other questions are preparatory and not scorable.

Item I is: *Are you aware of any difference in your sense of control in one arm going up, compared to the other?* Score 2 if the subject definitely answers "yes" to the scorable question and reports less control in the arm which levitated. Score 1 if the subject spontaneously qualifies a "yes" (e.g., "a little bit") and reports less control in the arm which levitated. If the subject says "no" or does not understand the question, record this first response, ask the question in the second way, and score 1 for a positive response. If the subject still says "no" give him a second chance by taking your thumb and forefinger and drawing the hand down onto the arm of the chair as you did in Item H. Then ask the subject to: *Let it rise like a balloon or ballet dancer's hand. Just let it go up as it did before.* Now ask; *This time do you have relatively more or less control in one arm going up compared to the other?* If the response is positive, put a square (denoting a second confirmation test) around 1. Score 0 if the response to this question is still negative.

The final score for control differential is part of the profile and induction scores.

Item J. Cut-Off. This is the postinduction-trance measure of the subject's capacity to end the hypnotic experience on signal. It is part of the induction score.

Score 2 if after you give the cut-off signal the subject indicates that his sense of control has returned to normal. If it has not returned to normal, give the cut-off signal again and score 1 if the subject then reports normal control. Score 0 only if the subject scored 1 for Item I; Control Differential. That is, if the subject had no sense of difference in control, the cut-off item is superfluous. However, as described in the instructions for administration of cut-off, the signal is always given because of the rare case in which control differential is actually discovered during the cut-off time.

Item K: Amnesia. This is a measure of amnesia to the cut-off signal. It has been found that amnesia, like instructed arm levitation, does not correlate with the remainder of the scale (Table A–4, p. 341). Thus the item is no longer necessary to score and is not part of the profile or induction scores derived from the HIP. It is included in the test because of its clinical utility; when someone with low hypnotizability experiences the amnesia, which frequently occurs, the experience can be used to deal with any skepticism concerning hypnosis. When the amnesia does not occur, the operator has the opportunity, if it seems appropriate, of dispelling myths about hypnosis—for example, the myth that one who has been hypnotized remembers nothing about the experience.

If you choose to score the item, score 2 when the subject does not remember both being touched on the elbow and being told that he will be touched in order to return to a state of usual awareness. Score 1 if the subject remembers one of the operator's two signals to him—either the touch or the verbal instructions. Score 0 if the subject remembers being told that the operator will *do* something and remembers having his elbow touched.

Check "No Test" if the subject scored 0 for Items I: Control Differential and J: Cut-Off.

Item L: Float. This is a postexperiential self-report measure of the amount of buoyancy that the subject remembers experiencing in the trance. It is part of the induction score.

Score 2 if the subject experienced the sensation of lightness, floating, or buoyancy in his left arm or hand *and* in at least one other part of his body. Score 1 if the subject experienced the sensations in only one part of his body. Score 0 if the subject did not experience the sensation in any part of his body.

HIP Summary Scores

Two summary scores, the profile and induction scores, are derived from the six scored HIP items:

Item D; The Eye-roll Sign (ER)
Item G; Dissociation (Di)

Item H; Signalled Arm Levitation (Lev)
Item I; Control Differential (CD)
Item J; Cut-Off (CO)
Item L; Float (Fl).

The profile score is the more clinically relevant of the two. It compares the level of biological, hypnotic potential (which is apparently tapped by ER) with the level of utilizable hypnotic capacity (measured by Lev and CD). The resulting score gives only a hint about the most appropriate therapeutic strategy but, if usable or experienced capacity is significantly lower than biological potential, it also gives an indication of the presence of severe psychopathology. (These topics will be covered in detail in Part II and in the Appendix.)

The induction score is a more traditional, purely quantitative scale of hypnotizability. It is the sum of scores of five hypnotic performance items (Di, Lev, CD, CO, Fl).

The following sections will explain the mechanics of deriving the profile and induction scores and some generally associated hypotheses.

THE PROFILE SCORE

The profile score is a qualitative score (nominal scale). It describes the hypnotic response pattern of the patient and is derived from three central components of the HIP: the eye-roll sign (ER), control differential (CD), and signalled arm levitation (Lev). Each profile score represents a specific relationship between the level of a person's inherent potential for hypnosis (tapped by ER) and the trance level actually experienced (tapped by Lev and CD).

Six profile patterns comprise these three main categories: 1) two patterns (regular zero and special zero) which represent zero potential for hypnotizability; 2) two patterns (regular intact and special intact) which represent *intact* capacity for hypnosis; and 3) two patterns (soft and decrement) which represent *nonintact* capacities. An intact profile indicates that utilizable hypnotic capacity or experience of hypnosis is at least as high as biological potential for hypnosis. A nonintact profile indicates that utilizable capacity is significantly lower than biological potential.

For frequency distributions of the types of profiles, see the Appendix. Evidence for the validity of the various inferences offered here is also presented in the Appendix. A summary of the scoring criteria for profile types is presented in Table 4–1.

Zero Profile Scores. Criterion: ER = 0

1. The *regular zero profile*: ER = 0, Lev = 0, CD = 0. This is a relatively rare profile pattern which shows no testable potential for hypnosis (zero levitation and control differential). Figure 4–6 is an example of this type of profile pattern.
2. The *special zero profile*: ER = 0, but either Lev, or CD, or both are scored greater than zero (see Figure 4–7). No inherent capacity for hypnosis is indicated, but trance may be partially experienced.

TABLE 4-1

Summary of Scoring the HIP.

Profile Score		ER	Lev	CD
Intact		+	+	+
(Special Intact: Lev is greater than ER by exactly 2 or more.)				
Zero	Zero	0	0	0
	Special zero	0	+ or 0 or +	and + and + and 0
Nonintact	Soft	+	4th reinforcement	+
	Decrement	+	+ or 0	0

+ denotes a positive score
0 denotes zero score
INDUCTION SCORE = Di + 1/2 Lev + CD + CO + F1 (0 through 10 possible)

Intact Profile Scores. Criteria: ER and CD are scored greater than zero and on the Lev item the subject shows complete arm levitation after the third reinforcement or sooner—that is, the fourth reinforcement is not required.

3. The *special intact profile*: All three items score greater than zero and the Lev score is two or more units higher than the ER. This profile pattern shows significantly more experience of hypnosis than potential indicates, and is hypothesized to indicate strong motivation for hypnotic experience, clinical treatment, or both. See Figure 4–8 as an example.
4. The *regular intact profile*: All profiles that satisfy criteria for the intact profile but which do not fall within the range of the special intact profile are part of the large group of regular intact profile types. For examples of regular intact profiles, see Figures 4–9 to 4–15.

Nonintact Profile Scores. Criteria: ER is scored greater than zero, CD is scored zero, and/or the fourth reinforcement was given on the Lev item.

5. The *soft* profile: ER and CD are scored greater than zero and the fourth reinforcement was necessary for Lev. In practice, Lev is usually scored zero, but a score of .5 may also represent a soft profile. This can occur when the arm begins to levitate in response to the third reinforcement, but requires the fourth reinforcement for completion. For an example, see Figure 4–16. In general, the soft pattern indicates that the subject shows potential for experiencing trance (positive ER), but signalled arm levitation is not motivated by the signal. The new instruction in the fourth reinforcement, to "just put it up there, pretend," is necessary for complete levitation. Once the arm is in the instructed position, the subject experiences hypnosis as part of the next procedure, control differential. Hence, it means that the soft pattern represents a borderline or partial hypnotizability in which the subject is unable to experience all his hypnotic potential.
6. The *decrement* profile: ER is greater than zero and CD is always zero. Lev may receive any score. It is hypothesized that the decrement profile

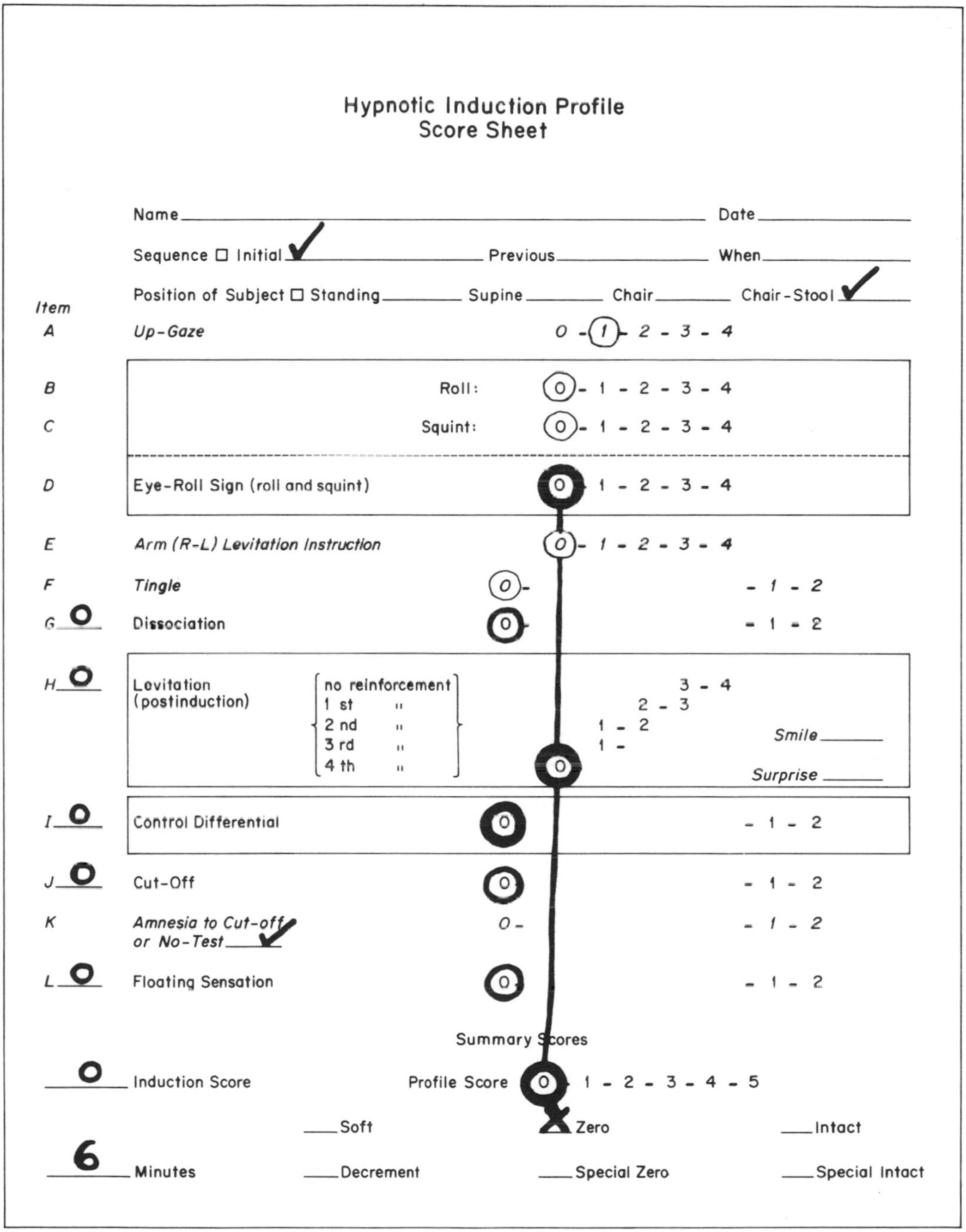

Hypnotic Induction Profile
Score Sheet

Name_____ Date_____

Sequence ☐ Initial ✓_____ Previous_____ When_____

Position of Subject ☐ Standing_____ Supine_____ Chair_____ Chair-Stool ✓

Item		
A	Up-Gaze	0 - (1) - 2 - 3 - 4
B	Roll:	(0) - 1 - 2 - 3 - 4
C	Squint:	(0) - 1 - 2 - 3 - 4
D	Eye-Roll Sign (roll and squint)	(0) - 1 - 2 - 3 - 4
E	Arm (R-L) Levitation Instruction	(0) - 1 - 2 - 3 - 4
F	Tingle	(0) - - 1 - 2
G ⊙	Dissociation	(0) - - 1 - 2

H ⊙	Levitation (postinduction)	no reinforcement 1 st " 2 nd " 3 rd " 4 th "	3 - 4 2 - 3 1 - 2 1 -	Smile_____ Surprise_____

I ⊙	Control Differential	(0) - 1 - 2
J ⊙	Cut-Off	(0) - 1 - 2
K	Amnesia to Cut-off or No-Test ✓	0 - - 1 - 2
L ⊙	Floating Sensation	(0) - 1 - 2

Summary Scores

____ ⊙ Induction Score   Profile Score (0) 1 - 2 - 3 - 4 - 5

____ Soft   ✗ Zero   ____Intact

6 ____ Minutes   ____Decrement   ____Special Zero   ____Special Intact

Figure 4–6:   Regular Zero Profile Configuration

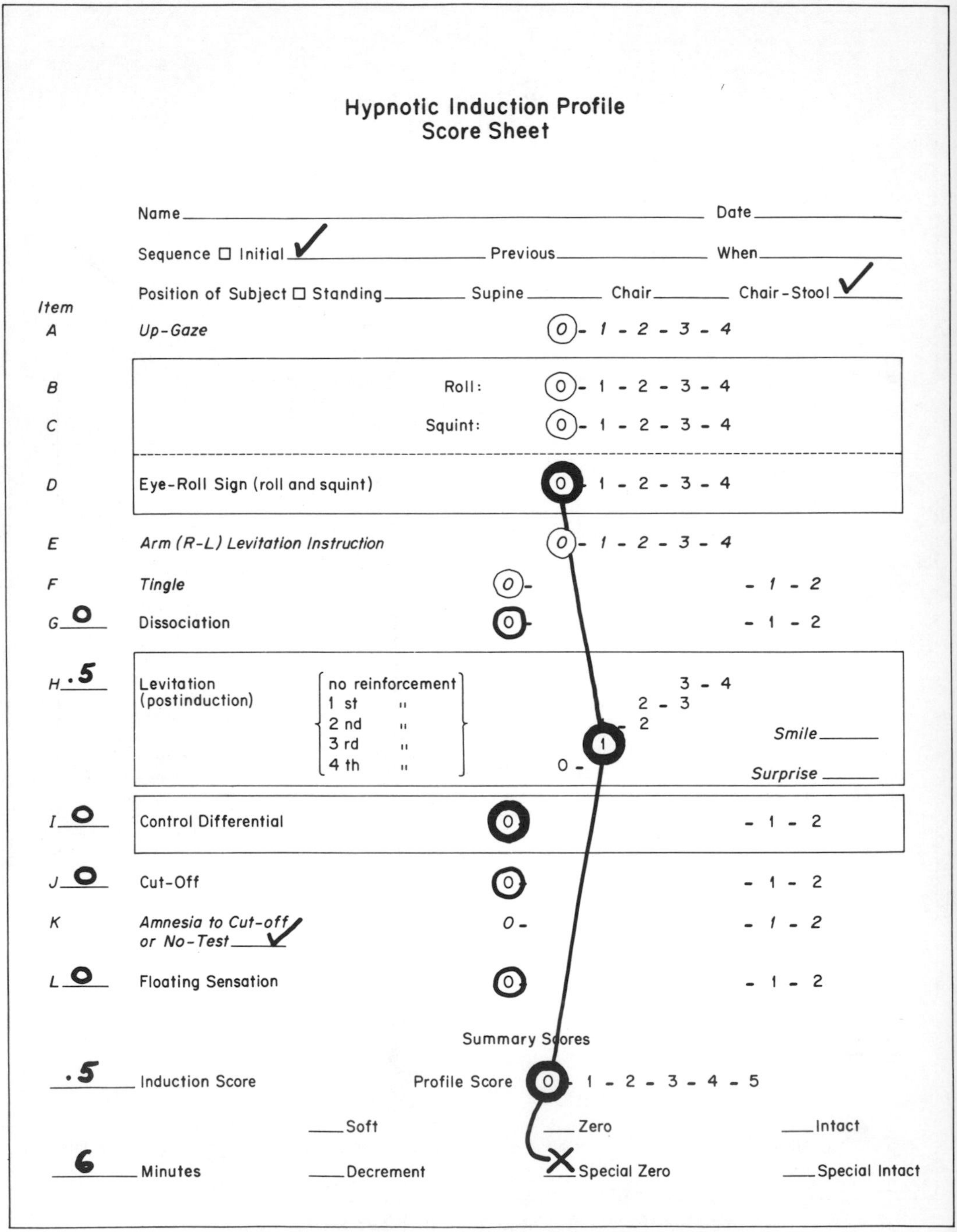

Hypnotic Induction Profile
Score Sheet

Name _____ Date _____

Sequence ☐ Initial ✔ _____ Previous _____ When _____

Position of Subject ☐ Standing _____ Supine _____ Chair _____ Chair-Stool ✔ _____

Item		
A	Up-Gaze	(0)- 1 - 2 - 3 - 4

B	Roll:	(0)- 1 - 2 - 3 - 4
C	Squint:	(0)- 1 - 2 - 3 - 4

D	Eye-Roll Sign (roll and squint)	**0** 1 - 2 - 3 - 4

E   *Arm (R-L) Levitation Instruction*   (0)- 1 - 2 - 3 - 4

F   *Tingle*   (0)-   - 1 - 2

G **0**   Dissociation   (0)-   - 1 - 2

H **.5**

	Levitation (postinduction)	no reinforcement 1 st " 2 nd " 3 rd " 4 th "		3 - 4 2 - 3 2 0 - **1**	Smile_____ Surprise _____

I **0**   Control Differential   **0**   - 1 - 2

J **0**   Cut-Off   (0)   - 1 - 2

K   *Amnesia to Cut-off* ✔ *or No-Test* _____   0 -   - 1 - 2

L **0**   Floating Sensation   (0)   - 1 - 2

Summary Scores

.5 _____ Induction Score   Profile Score   **0** 1 - 2 - 3 - 4 - 5

____Soft   ____Zero   ____Intact

6 _____ Minutes   ____Decrement   ✗ Special Zero   ____Special Intact

Figure 4–7:   Special Zero Profile Configuration

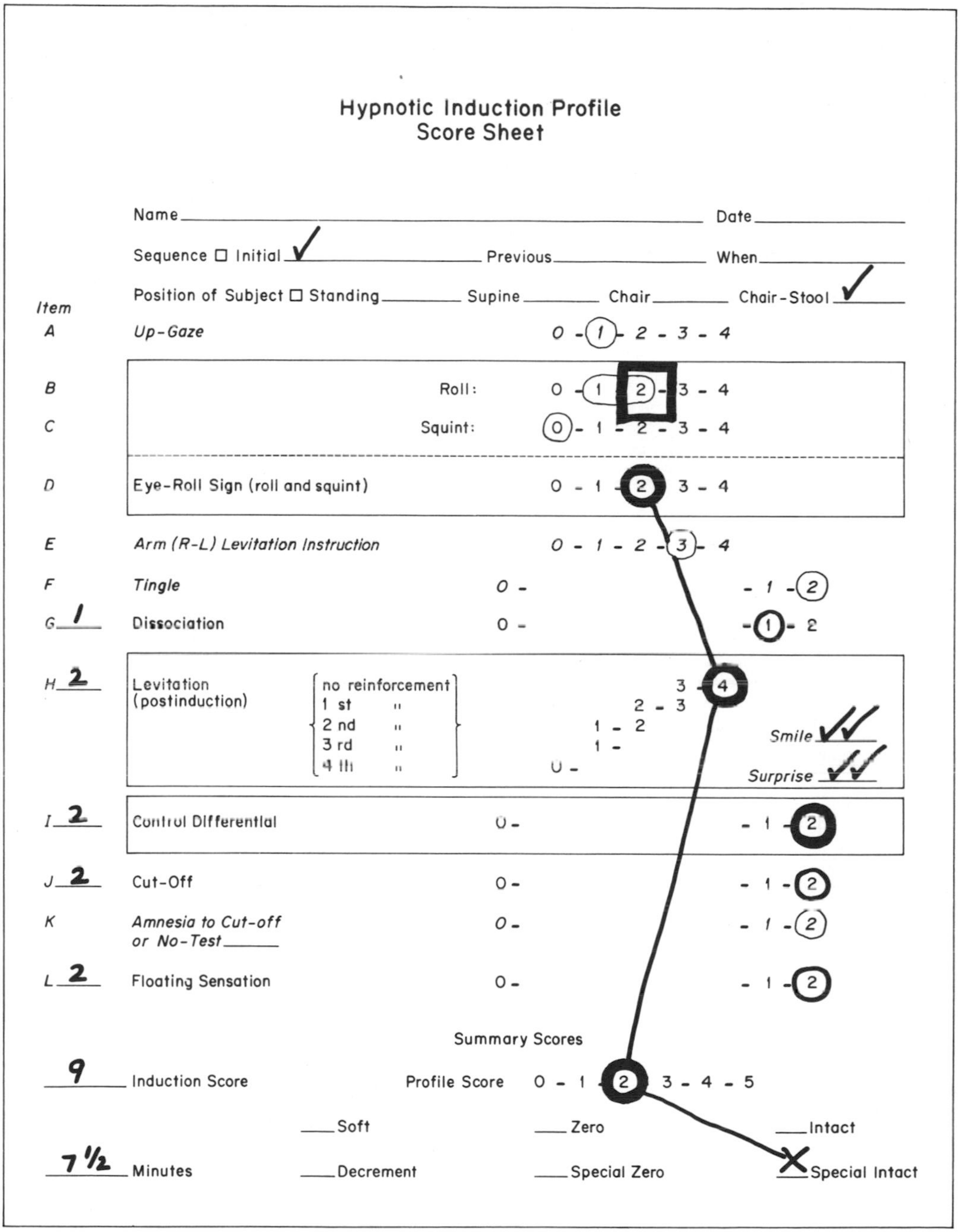

Hypnotic Induction Profile
Score Sheet

Name_____ Date_____

Sequence ☐ Initial ✓_____ Previous_____ When_____ ✓

Position of Subject ☐ Standing_____ Supine_____ Chair_____ Chair-Stool ✓

Item		
A	Up-Gaze	0 -①- 2 - 3 - 4

B	Roll:	0 -①- **2** - 3 - 4
C	Squint:	⓪- 1 - 2 - 3 - 4

D	Eye-Roll Sign (roll and squint)	0 - 1 -②- 3 - 4

E	Arm (R-L) Levitation Instruction	0 - 1 - 2 -③- 4
F	Tingle	0 - - 1 -②
G **1**	Dissociation	0 - -①- 2

H **2**	Levitation (postinduction)	no reinforcement / 1 st " / 2 nd " / 3 rd " / 4 th "

	3 -④
	2 - 3
	1 - 2
	1 - Smile ✓✓
	0 - Surprise ✓✓

I **2**	Control Differential	0 - - 1 -②

J **2**	Cut-Off	0 - - 1 -②
K	Amnesia to Cut-off or No-Test_____	0 - - 1 -②
L **2**	Floating Sensation	0 - - 1 -②

Summary Scores

9 Induction Score   Profile Score   0 - 1 -②- 3 - 4 - 5

_____ Soft   _____ Zero   _____ Intact

7 ½ Minutes   _____ Decrement   _____ Special Zero   ✗ Special Intact

Figure 4–8:   Special Intact Profile Configuration

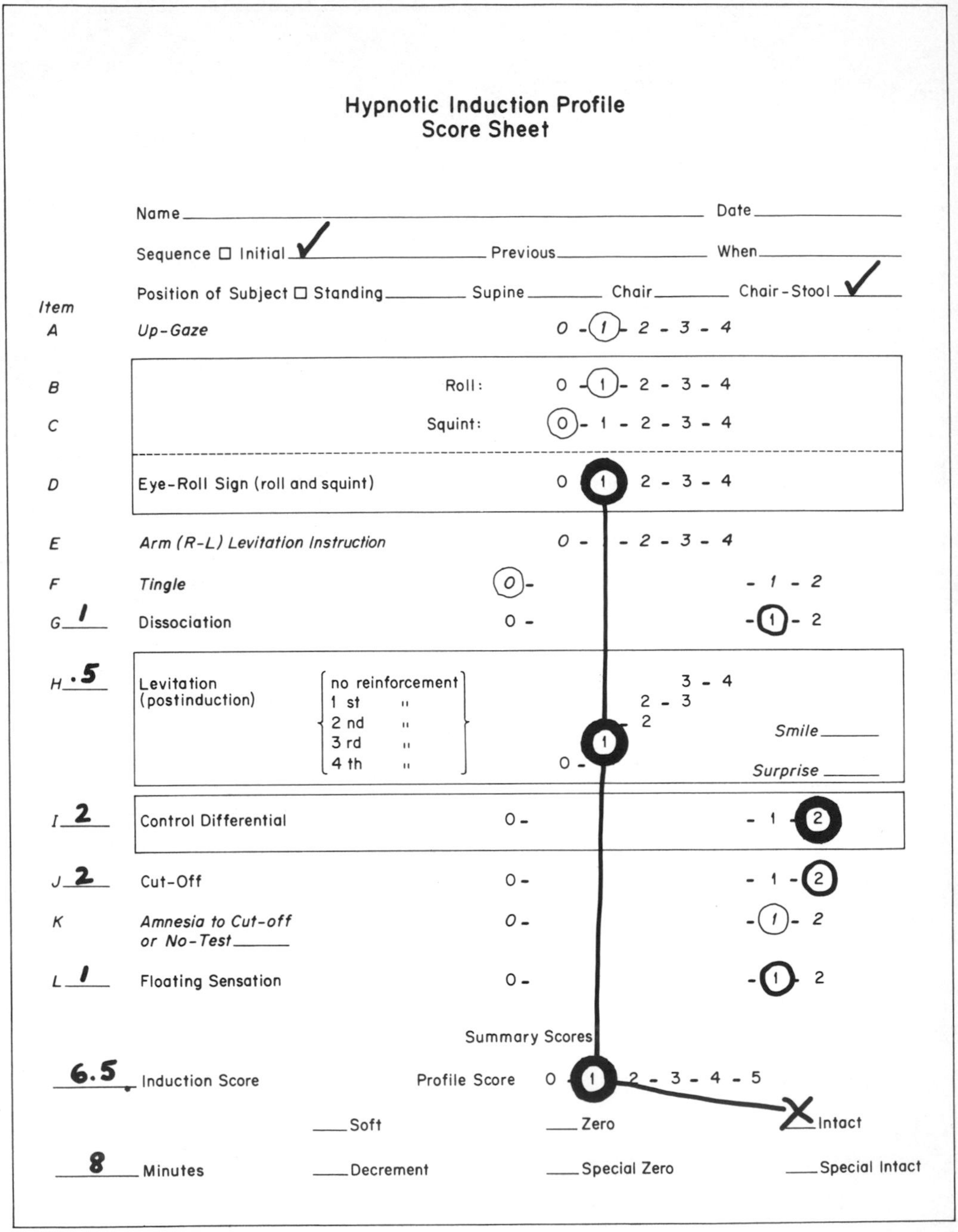

Hypnotic Induction Profile
Score Sheet

Name_____ Date_____

Sequence ☐ Initial ✓_____ Previous_____ When_____

Position of Subject ☐ Standing_____ Supine_____ Chair_____ Chair–Stool ✓

Item		
A	Up-Gaze	0 –(1)– 2 – 3 – 4

B	Roll:	0 –(1)– 2 – 3 – 4
C	Squint:	(0)– 1 – 2 – 3 – 4

D Eye-Roll Sign (roll and squint) 0 (1) 2 – 3 – 4

E Arm (R–L) Levitation Instruction 0 – _ – 2 – 3 – 4

F Tingle (0)– _ _ – 1 – 2

G **1** Dissociation 0 – _ –(1)– 2

H **.5** Levitation (postinduction)
  { no reinforcement }   3 – 4
  { 1 st " }   2 – 3
  { 2 nd " }   2
  { 3 rd " }   Smile_____
  { 4 th " }   0 –(1) Surprise_____

I **2** Control Differential 0 – _ – 1 –(2)

J **2** Cut-Off 0 – _ – 1 –(2)

K Amnesia to Cut-off or No-Test_____ 0 – _ –(1)– 2

L **1** Floating Sensation 0 – _ –(1)– 2

Summary Scores

6.5 Induction Score   Profile Score 0 –(1)– 2 – 3 – 4 – 5

____Soft   ____Zero   ✗ Intact

8 Minutes   ____Decrement   ____Special Zero   ____Special Intact

Figure 4–9:   Regular Intact Profile Configuration

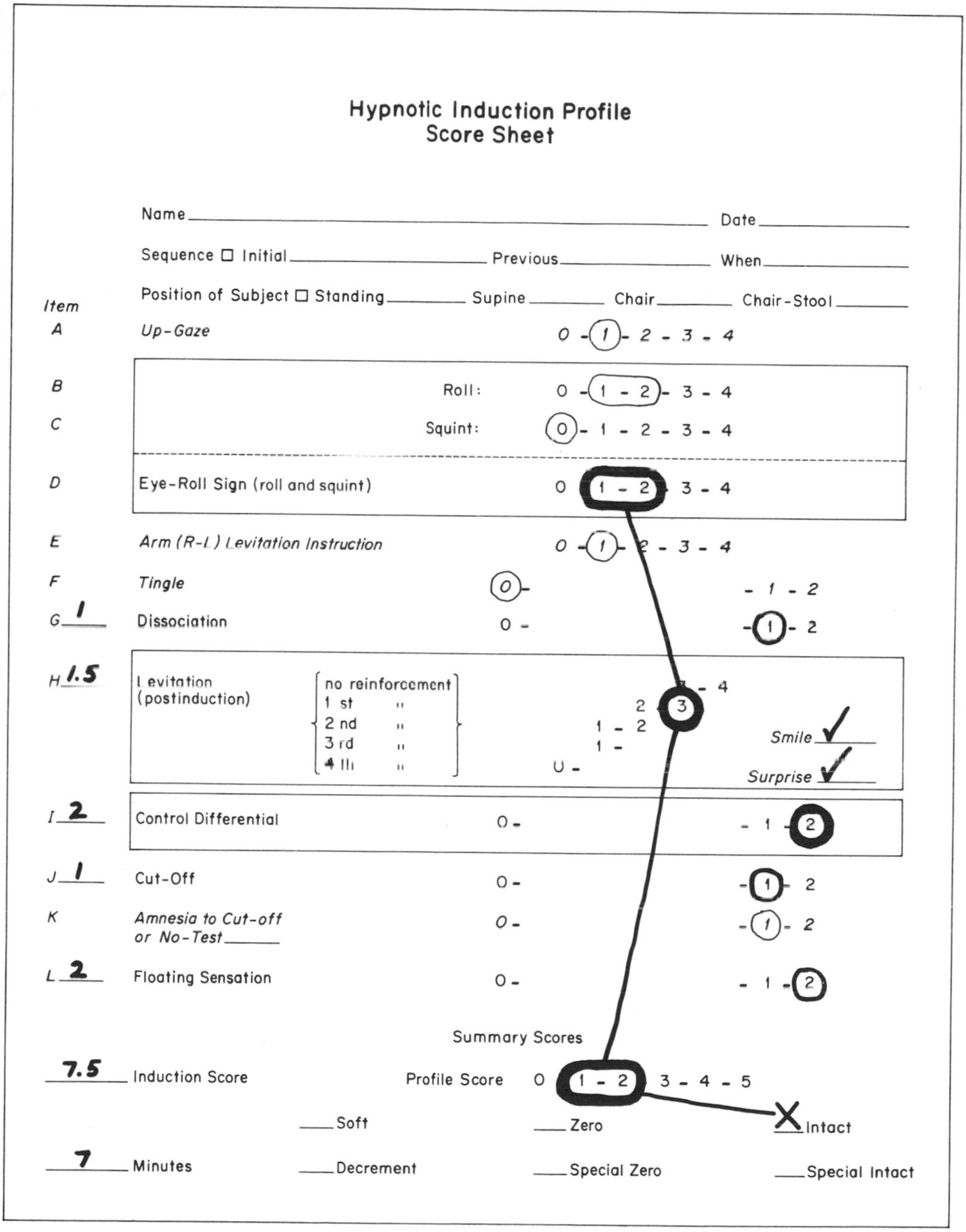

Hypnotic Induction Profile
Score Sheet

Name_____ Date_____

Sequence ☐ Initial_____ Previous_____ When_____

Position of Subject ☐ Standing_____ Supine_____ Chair_____ Chair-Stool_____

Item		
A	Up-Gaze	0 -①- 2 - 3 - 4

B	Roll:	0 -(1 - 2)- 3 - 4
C	Squint:	(0)- 1 - 2 - 3 - 4

D Eye-Roll Sign (roll and squint) 0 **1 - 2** 3 - 4

E Arm (R-L) Levitation Instruction 0 -①- 2 - 3 - 4

F Tingle (0)- - 1 - 2

G__*1*__ Dissociation 0 - -①- 2

H__*1.5*__ Levitation (postinduction)
[no reinforcement]
1 st   "
2 nd   "
3 rd   "
4 th   "

2 - 4
1 - 2   **3**
1 - 2
0 -

Smile ✓
Surprise ✓

I__*2*__ Control Differential 0 - - 1 -**2**

J__*1*__ Cut-Off 0 - -①- 2

K Amnesia to Cut-off or No-Test_____ 0 - -①- 2

L__*2*__ Floating Sensation 0 - - 1 -②

Summary Scores

__*7.5*__ Induction Score Profile Score 0 **1 - 2** 3 - 4 - 5

____Soft ____Zero **X**Intact

__*7*__ Minutes ____Decrement ____Special Zero ____Special Intact

Figure 4-10: Regular Intact Profile Configuration

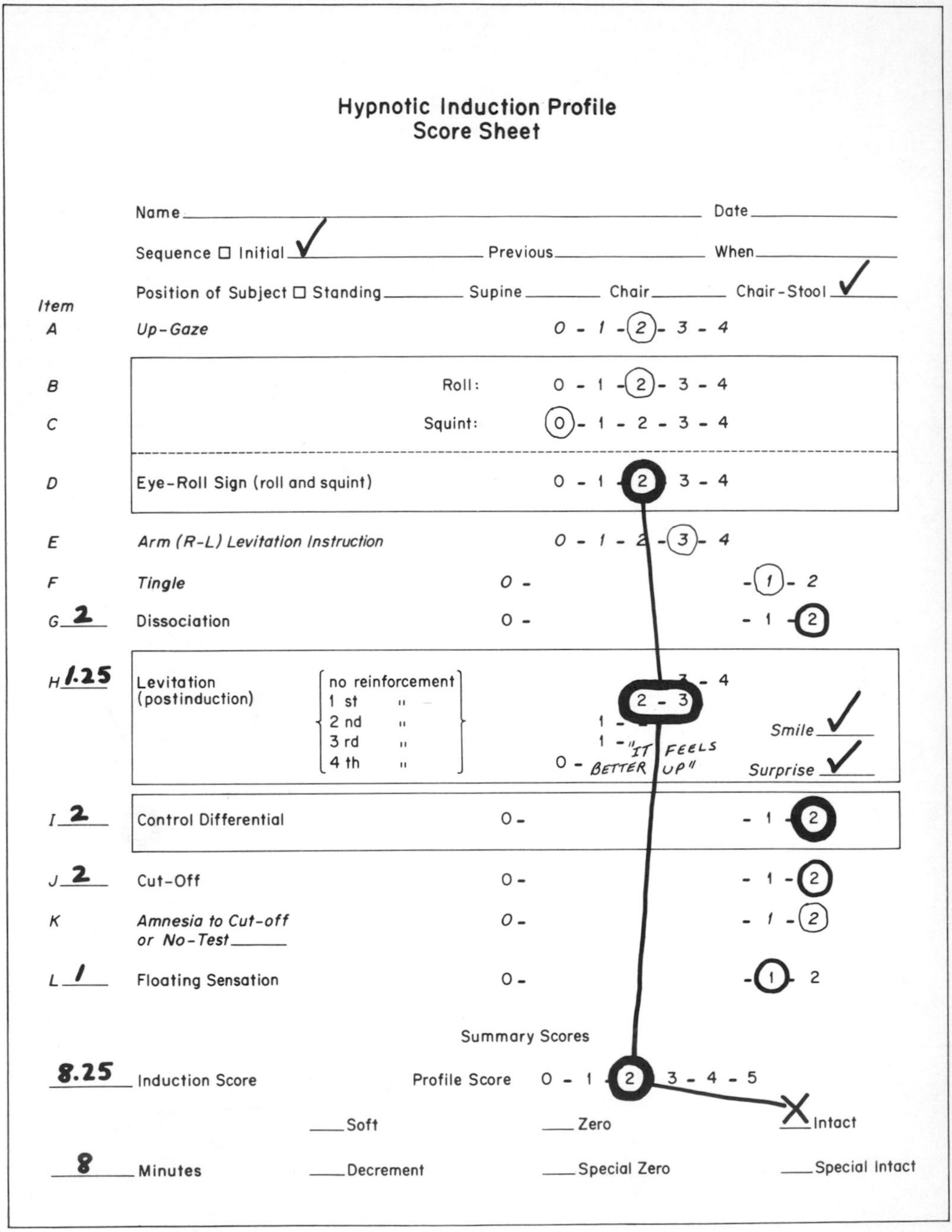

Hypnotic Induction Profile
Score Sheet

Name_____ Date_____

Sequence ☐ Initial ✓_____ Previous_____ When_____

Position of Subject ☐ Standing_____ Supine_____ Chair_____ Chair-Stool ✓

Item		
A	Up-Gaze	0 - 1 -②- 3 - 4

B	Roll:	0 - 1 -②- 3 - 4
C	Squint:	⓪- 1 - 2 - 3 - 4

D	Eye-Roll Sign (roll and squint)	0 - 1 - ② 3 - 4

E	Arm (R-L) Levitation Instruction	0 - 1 - 2 -③- 4
F	Tingle	0 - -①- 2
G **2**	Dissociation	0 - - 1 -②

H **1.25** Levitation (postinduction)

[no reinforcement]
1 st "
2 nd "
3 rd "
4 th "

3 - 4
② - ③
1 -
1 -"IT FEELS
0 - BETTER UP"

Smile ✓
Surprise ✓

I **2**	Control Differential	0 - - 1 -②

J **2**	Cut-Off	0 - - 1 -②
K	Amnesia to Cut-off or No-Test____	0 - - 1 -②
L **1**	Floating Sensation	0 - -①- 2

Summary Scores

8.25 Induction Score   Profile Score   0 - 1 -② 3 - 4 - 5

____Soft   ____Zero   ✗ Intact

8 Minutes   ____Decrement   ____Special Zero   ____Special Intact

Figure 4-11:   Regular Intact Profile Configuration

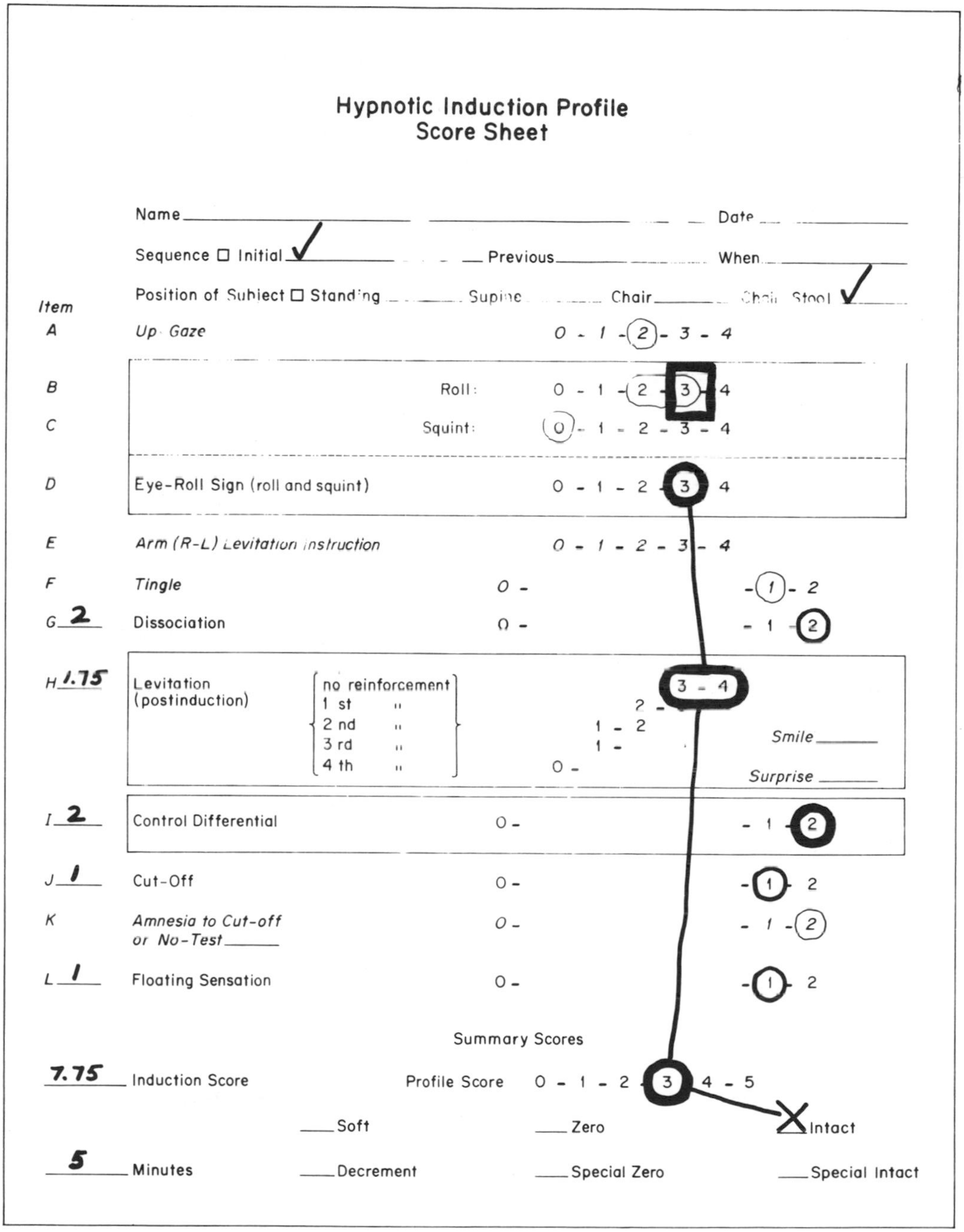

Hypnotic Induction Profile
Score Sheet

Name _____ _____ ___ Date ___ _____

Sequence ☐ Initial ✓ _____ ___ ___ Previous _____ _____ When ___ _____

Position of Subject ☐ Standing __ ____ Supine ____ Chair_____ Chair Stool ✓

Item		
A	Up Gaze	0 - 1 - ②- 3 - 4

B		Roll:	0 - 1 - 2 - **3** - 4
C		Squint:	⓪- 1 - 2 - 3 - 4

D	Eye-Roll Sign (roll and squint)	0 - 1 - 2 - ③ 4

E	Arm (R-L) Levitation instruction	0 - 1 - 2 - 3 - 4

F	Tingle	0 -	-①- 2
G **2**	Dissociation	0 -	- 1 -②

H **1.75**	Levitation (postinduction)	{ no reinforcement }	**3 - 4**
		1 st "	2 -
		2 nd "	1 - 2
		3 rd "	1 - Smile _____
		4 th "	0 - Surprise _____

I **2**	Control Differential	0 -	- 1 -②

J **1**	Cut-Off	0 -	-①- 2
K	Amnesia to Cut-off or No-Test _____	0 -	- 1 -②
L **1**	Floating Sensation	0 -	-①- 2

Summary Scores

7.75 Induction Score   Profile Score   0 - 1 - 2 - ③ 4 - 5

_____ Soft   _____ Zero   ✗ Intact

5 Minutes   _____ Decrement   _____ Special Zero   _____ Special Intact

Figure 4–12:   Regular Intact Profile Configuration

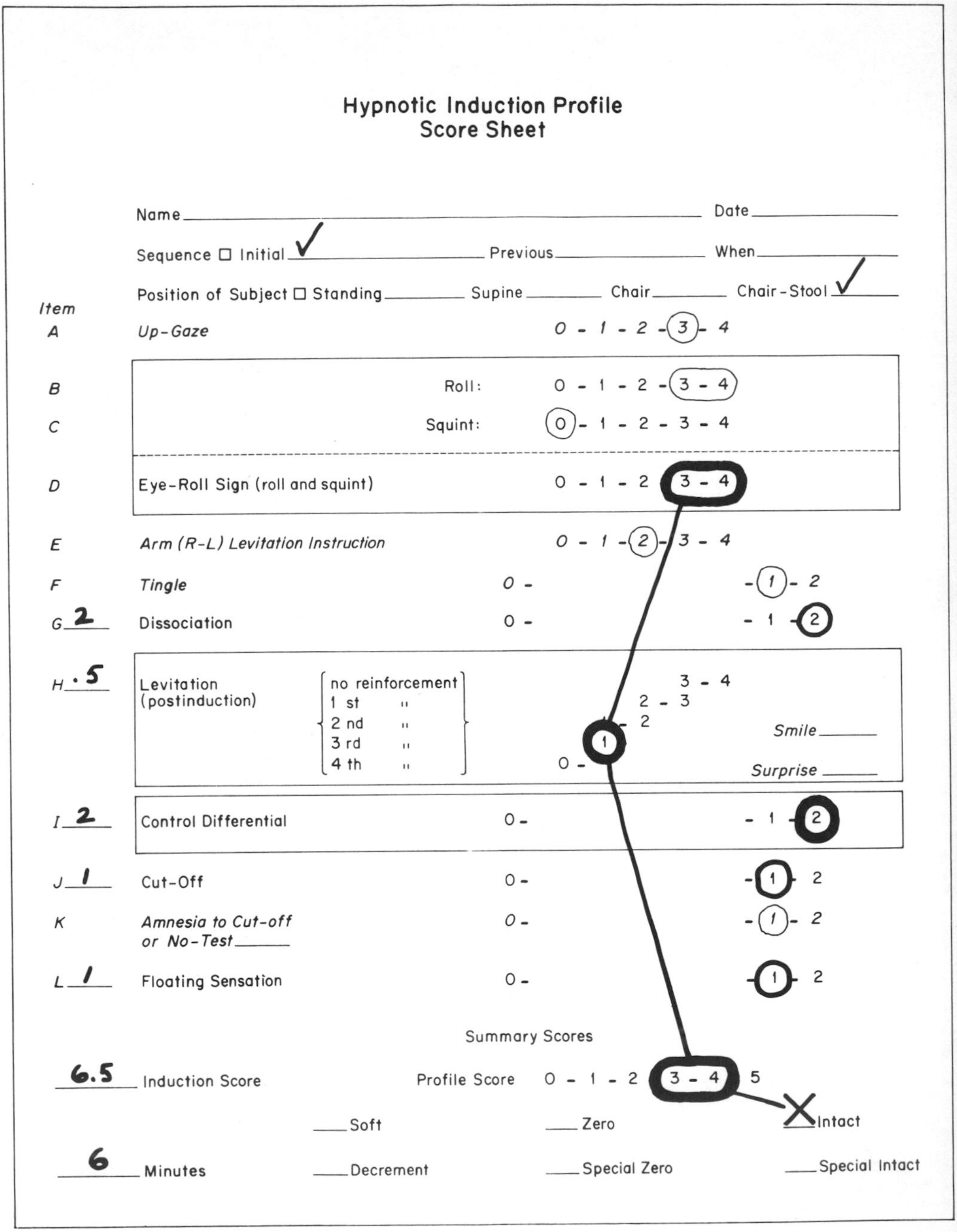

Hypnotic Induction Profile
Score Sheet

Name _____ Date _____

Sequence ☐ Initial ✓ _____ Previous _____ When _____

Position of Subject ☐ Standing _____ Supine _____ Chair _____ Chair-Stool ✓ _____

Item		
A	Up-Gaze	0 – 1 – 2 –(3)– 4

Roll: 0 – 1 – 2 –(3 – 4)

B

Squint: (0)– 1 – 2 – 3 – 4

C

D Eye-Roll Sign (roll and squint) 0 – 1 – 2 3 – 4

E Arm (R-L) Levitation Instruction 0 – 1 –(2)– 3 – 4

F Tingle 0 – –(1)– 2

G **2** Dissociation 0 – – 1 –(2)

H **.5** Levitation (postinduction)
  no reinforcement
  1 st "
  2 nd "
  3 rd "
  4 th "

  3 – 4
  2 – 3
  2
  0 –
  (1)
  Smile _____
  Surprise _____

I **2** Control Differential 0 – – 1 –(2)

J **1** Cut-Off 0 – –(1)– 2

K Amnesia to Cut-off or No-Test _____ 0 – –(1)– 2

L **1** Floating Sensation 0 – (1) 2

Summary Scores

6.5 Induction Score Profile Score 0 – 1 – 2 3 – 4 5

_____ Soft _____ Zero ☓ Intact

6 Minutes _____ Decrement _____ Special Zero _____ Special Intact

Figure 4–13: Regular Intact Profile Configuration

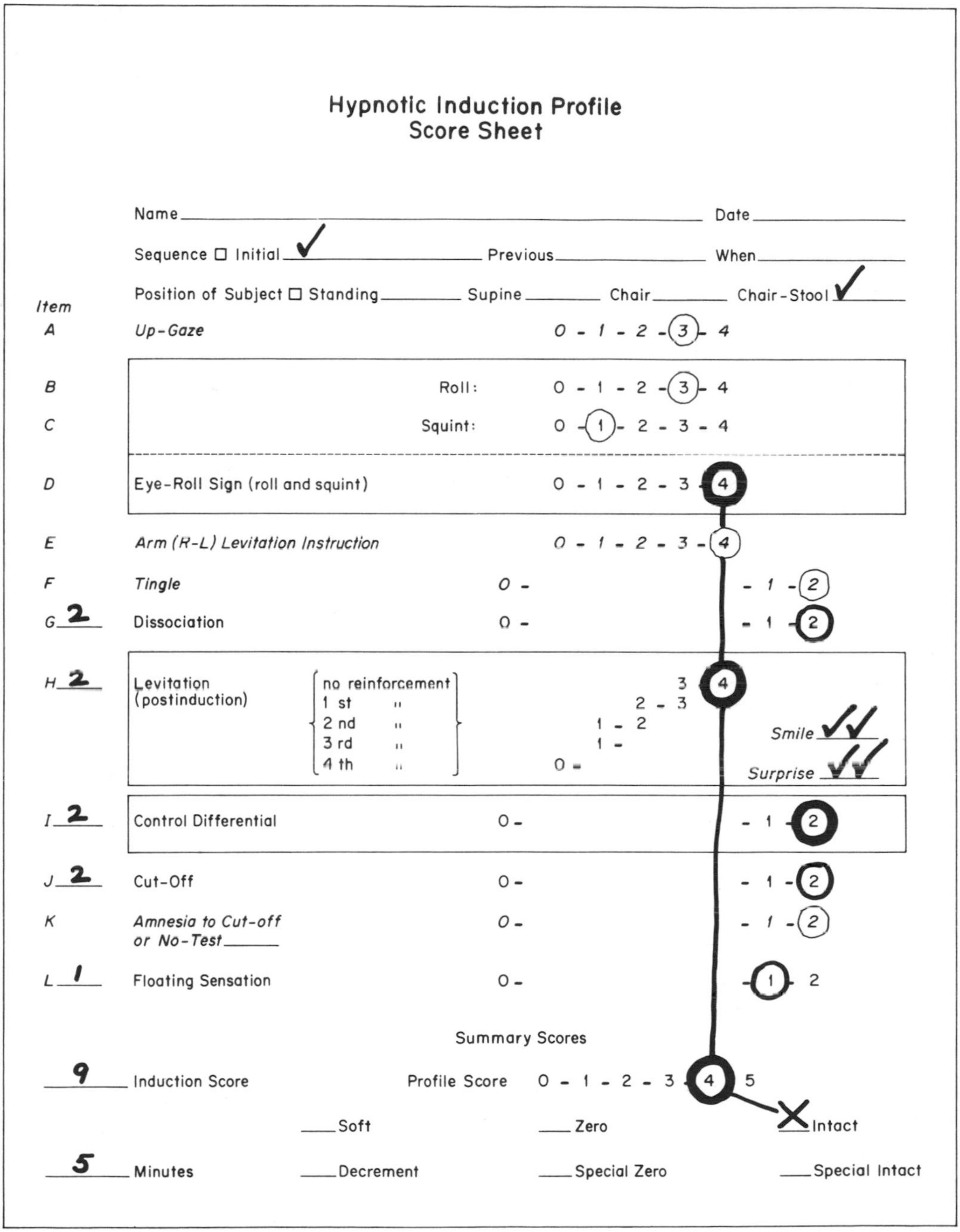

Hypnotic Induction Profile
Score Sheet

Name_____ Date_____

Sequence ☐ Initial ✓_____ Previous_____ When_____

Position of Subject ☐ Standing_____ Supine_____ Chair_____ Chair-Stool ✓

Item		
A	Up-Gaze	0 - 1 - 2 -③- 4

B		Roll:	0 - 1 - 2 -③- 4
C		Squint:	0 -①- 2 - 3 - 4

D	Eye-Roll Sign (roll and squint)	0 - 1 - 2 - 3 -④

E	Arm (R-L) Levitation Instruction	0 - 1 - 2 - 3 -④
F	Tingle	0 - - 1 -②
G **2**	Dissociation	0 - - 1 -②

H **2**	Levitation (postinduction)	no reinforcement — 3 ④
		1 st " — 2 - 3
		2 nd " — 1 - 2
		3 rd " — 1 -
		4 th " — 0 -

Smile ✓✓
Surprise ✓✓

I **2**	Control Differential	0 - - 1 -②
J **2**	Cut-Off	0 - - 1 -②
K	Amnesia to Cut-off or No-Test_____	0 - - 1 -②
L **1**	Floating Sensation	0 - -①- 2

Summary Scores

9 Induction Score   Profile Score   0 - 1 - 2 - 3 -④ 5

_____ Soft   _____ Zero   ✗ Intact

5 Minutes   _____ Decrement   _____ Special Zero   _____ Special Intact

Figure 4-14:   Regular Intact Profile Configuration

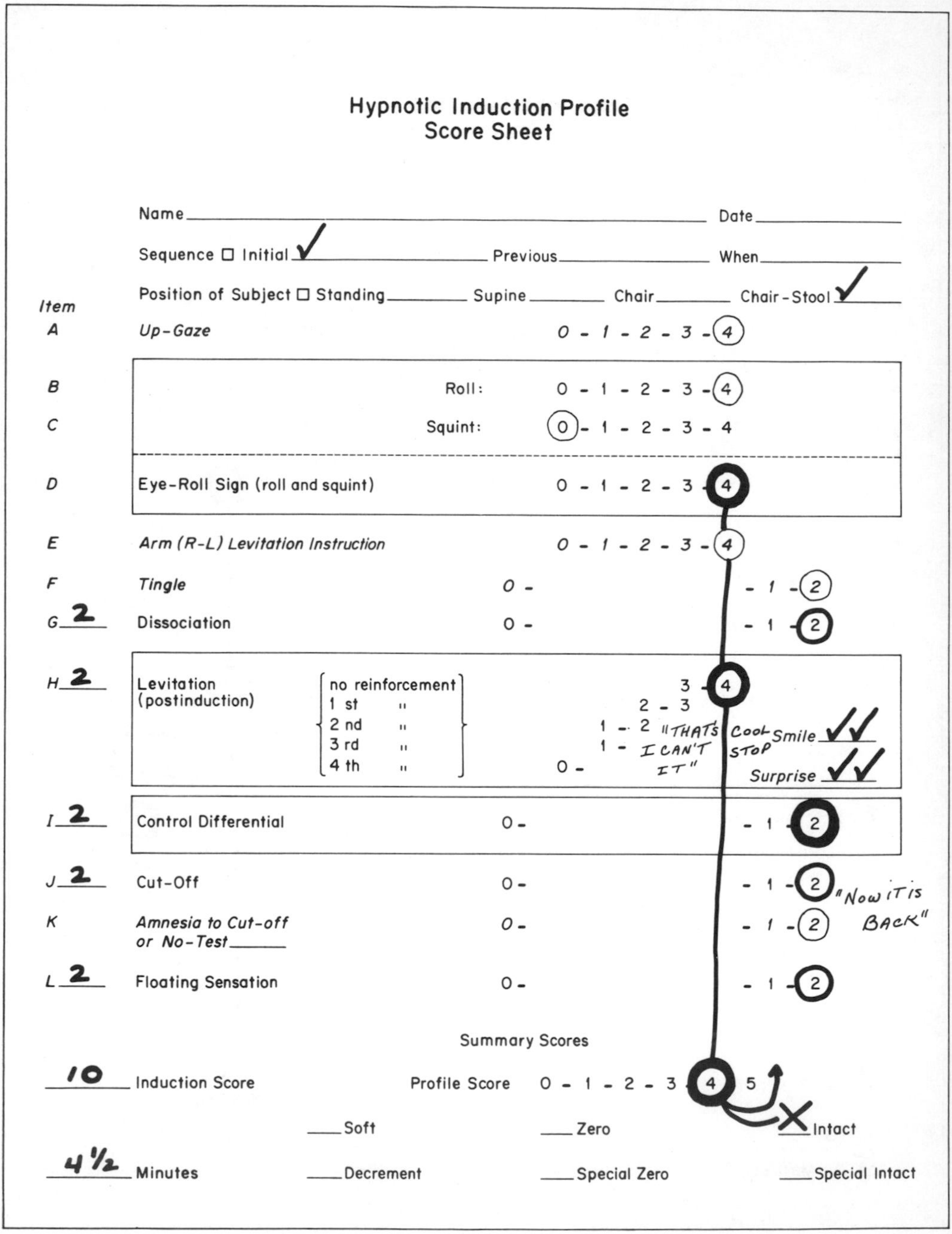

Hypnotic Induction Profile
Score Sheet

Name _____ Date _____

Sequence ☐ Initial ✓ _____ Previous _____ When _____

Position of Subject ☐ Standing _____ Supine _____ Chair _____ Chair-Stool ✓

Item			
A	Up-Gaze		0 - 1 - 2 - 3 - ④
B	Roll:		0 - 1 - 2 - 3 - ④
C	Squint:		⓪ - 1 - 2 - 3 - 4
D	Eye-Roll Sign (roll and squint)		0 - 1 - 2 - 3 - ④
E	Arm (R-L) Levitation Instruction		0 - 1 - 2 - 3 - ④
F	Tingle	0 -	- 1 - ②
G **2**	Dissociation	0 -	- 1 - ②

H **2** — Levitation (postinduction)

no reinforcement		3 - ④
1 st "		2 - 3
2 nd "		1 - 2 "THATS Cool Smile ✓✓
3 rd "		1 - I CAN'T STOP
4 th "	0 -	IT" Surprise ✓✓

I **2**	Control Differential	0 -	- 1 - ②
J **2**	Cut-Off	0 -	- 1 - ② "Now it is BACK"
K	Amnesia to Cut-off or No-Test _____	0 -	- 1 - ②
L **2**	Floating Sensation	0 -	- 1 - ②

Summary Scores

10 _____ Induction Score   Profile Score   0 - 1 - 2 - 3 - ④ 5

_____ Soft   _____ Zero   ✗ Intact

4 ½ _____ Minutes   _____ Decrement   _____ Special Zero   _____ Special Intact

Figure 4-15:   4-Intact Profile Configuration, Possible Grade 5

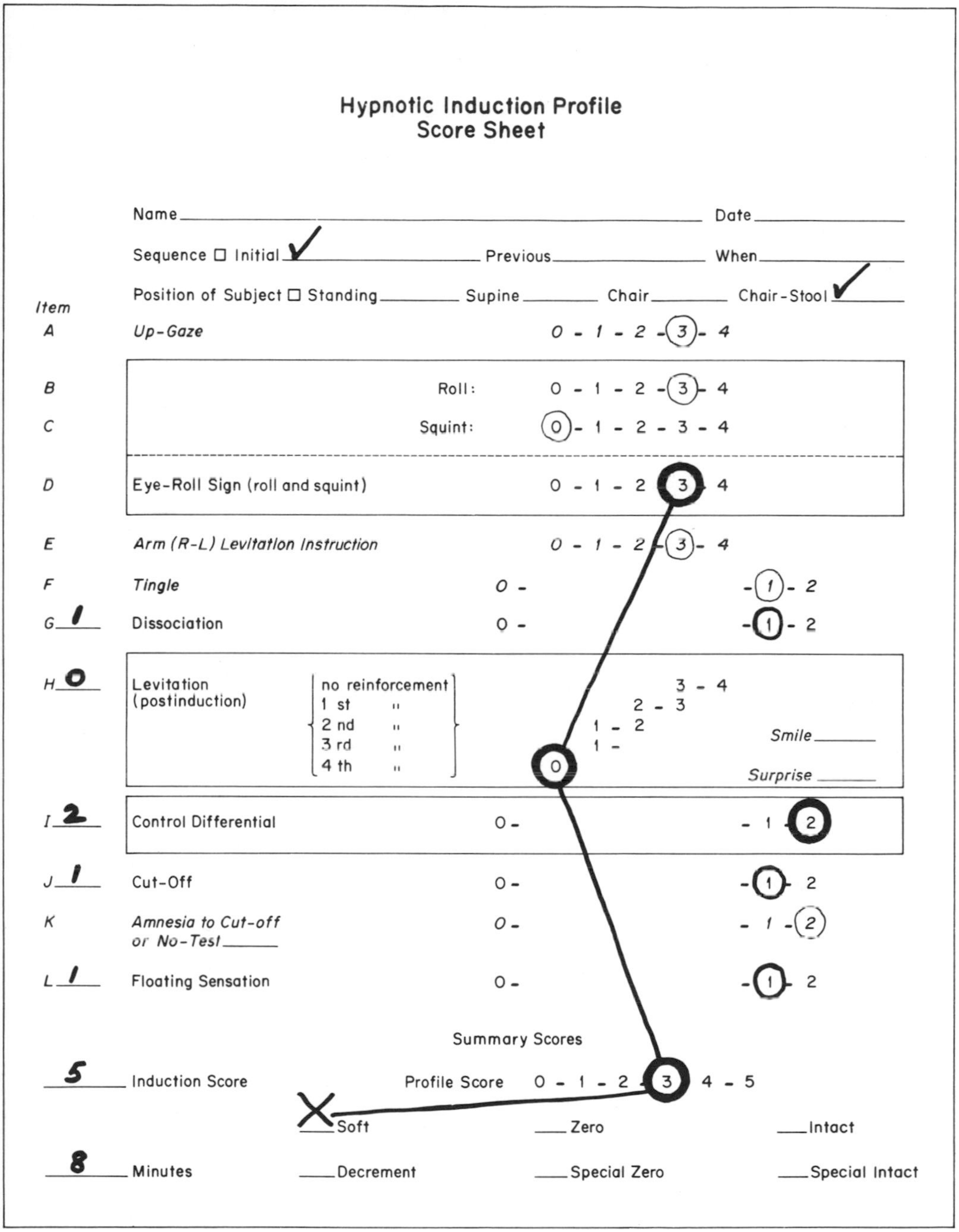

Hypnotic Induction Profile
Score Sheet

Name_____ Date_____

Sequence ☐ Initial ✓_____ Previous_____ When_____

Position of Subject ☐ Standing_____ Supine_____ Chair_____ Chair-Stool ✓

Item		
A	Up-Gaze	0 - 1 - 2 -(3)- 4
B	Roll:	0 - 1 - 2 -(3)- 4
C	Squint:	(0)- 1 - 2 - 3 - 4
D	Eye-Roll Sign (roll and squint)	0 - 1 - 2 -**(3)**- 4
E	Arm (R-L) Levitation Instruction	0 - 1 - 2 -(3)- 4
F	Tingle	0 - ... -(1)- 2
G **1**	Dissociation	0 - ... -**(1)**- 2
H **0**	Levitation (postinduction)	no reinforcement / 1st " / 2nd " / 3rd " / 4th " — 3 - 4 / 2 - 3 / 1 - 2 / 1 - **(0)** — Smile_____ Surprise_____
I **2**	Control Differential	0 - ... - 1 -**(2)**
J **1**	Cut-Off	0 - ... -(1)- 2
K	Amnesia to Cut-off or No-Test_____	0 - ... - 1 -(2)
L **1**	Floating Sensation	0 - ... -(1)- 2

Summary Scores

5 _____ Induction Score   Profile Score   0 - 1 - 2 -**(3)**- 4 - 5

X _____Soft   _____Zero   _____Intact

8 _____ Minutes   _____Decrement   _____Special Zero   _____Special Intact

Figure 4–16:   Soft Profile Configuration

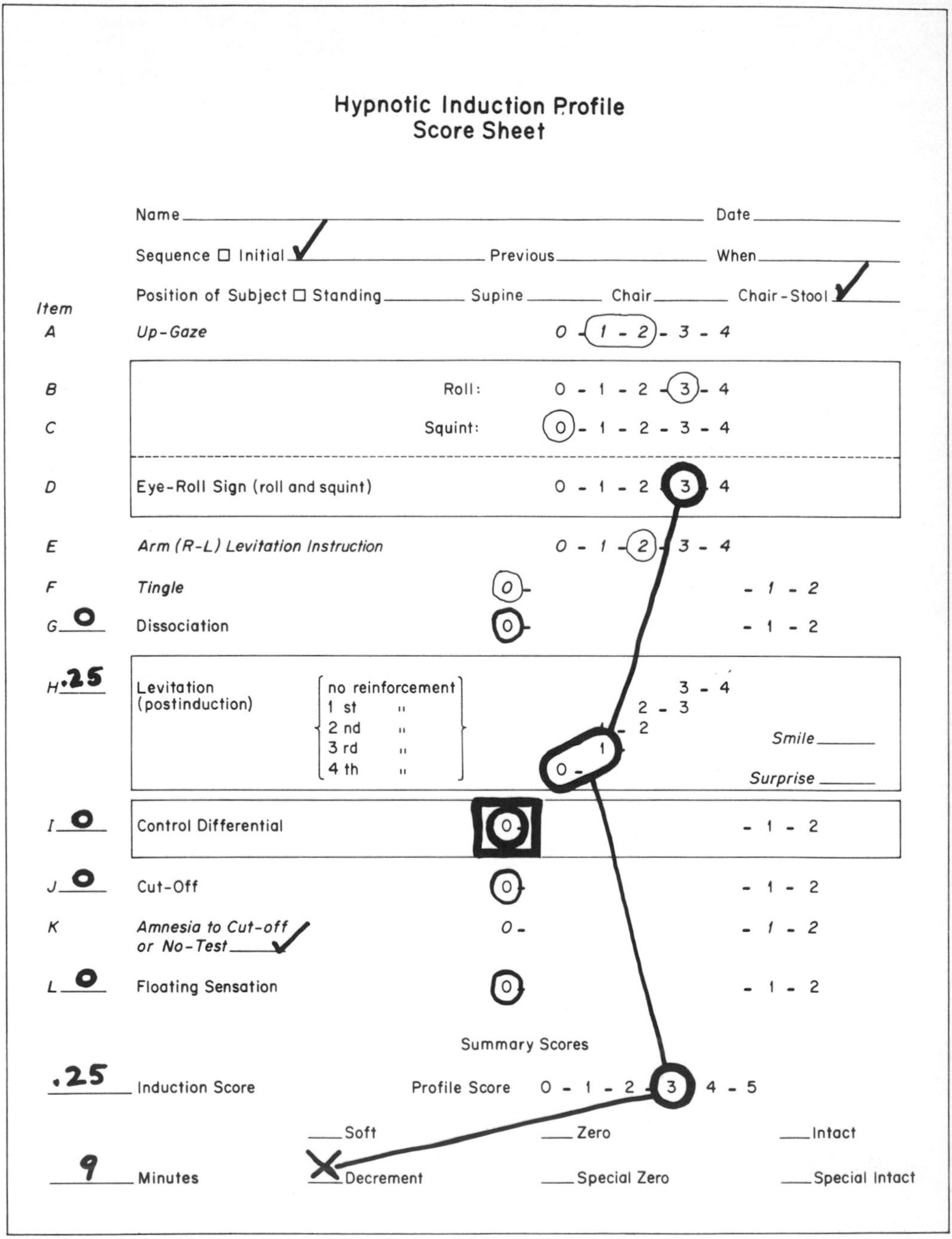

Hypnotic Induction Profile
Score Sheet

Name _____ Date _____

Sequence □ Initial ✓_____ Previous _____ When _____

Position of Subject □ Standing _____ Supine _____ Chair _____ Chair-Stool ✓

Item		
A	Up-Gaze	O -(1 - 2)- 3 - 4

		Roll:	O - 1 - 2 -(3)- 4
B			
C		Squint:	(O)- 1 - 2 - 3 - 4

D	Eye-Roll Sign (roll and squint)	O - 1 - 2 -**(3)**- 4

E	*Arm (R-L) Levitation Instruction*	O - 1 -(2)- 3 - 4

F	*Tingle*	(O)-	- 1 - 2
G **O**	Dissociation	(O)-	- 1 - 2

H **.25**	Levitation (postinduction)	no reinforcement 1 st " 2 nd " 3 rd " 4 th "	3 - 4 2 - 3 2 1 O -	*Smile* _____ *Surprise* _____

I **O**	Control Differential	[O]	- 1 - 2

J **O**	Cut-Off	(O)-	- 1 - 2
K	*Amnesia to Cut-off* *or No-Test* ✓	O -	- 1 - 2
L **O**	Floating Sensation	(O)-	- 1 - 2

Summary Scores

.25 _____ Induction Score   Profile Score   O - 1 - 2 -**(3)**- 4 - 5

_____ Soft   _____ Zero   _____ Intact

9 _____ Minutes   ✗ Decrement   _____ Special Zero   _____ Special Intact

Figure 4-17:   Decrement Profile Configuration

shows positive potential for trance, but inability to experience it. This decrement represents the inability to express hypnotic potential, a variety of nonhypnotizability which the HIP distinguishes from nonhypnotizability due to lack of potential, as in the straight zero profile. A decrement profile can also be described as a trance capacity that begins in the zone of intact hypnotizability (as indicated by positive ER)—but concentration is not sustained and the score collapses out of this zone (zero CD score). The label for the decrement pattern incorporates the ER score and the term "decrement." Example: ER = 2.5, Lev = 1.5, CD = 0; the profile score is called a "2.5-decrement." In practice, most decrement profiles show a zero Lev score. For an example, see Figure 4–17.

The profile category is often further described and identified by the ER score. For instance, 3 decrement refers to a decrement profile pattern in which ER score was 3. Similarly: 1.5 intact (regular); 2 special intact; 3.5 soft, etc. (The terms "grade 4" or "grade 3" are occasionally used and refer only to regular intacts.)

THE INDUCTION SCORE

The induction score for each profile is completed by adding the scores of the following five items:

Item G	Dissociation (Di)
Item H	Posthypnotic Arm Levitation (Lev)
Item I	Control Differential (CD)
Item J	Cut-Off (CO)
Item L	Float (Fl)

The induction score = Di + ½ Lev + CD + CO + Fl. The range of the induction score is from zero through ten. For example, a subject who scores 1 for Di, 3 for Lev, 2 for CD, 2 for CO, and 1 for Fl would obtain an induction score of 7.5.

Note that Lev, scored on a continuum of zero through four, is divided by two in calculating the induction score, although the four-part range is used in the profile score. Lev is halved in order not to give this item a differential weight in the induction score.

	0	0.5	1.0	1.5	2.0
Lev value as part of the induction score	0	0.5	1.0	1.5	2.0
Lev as represented on score sheet				3	4
			2	3	
		1	2		
		1			
	0				

For example, a recorded score of 2.5 (that is, a 2 and a 3 are circled) would be rescaled (½ Lev) and added to the induction score as 1.25.

Relationship Between the Two Summary Scores. Certain relationships between the induction score and the profile score are necessary simply as a result of the way the HIP is constructed. Because the decrement profile is defined as a score on CD (and thus, as zero on CO), the induction score can be no higher than 6.0. Similarly, because the Lev score on the soft profile is usually zero, the induction score in practice falls at 8.0 or below.

Clinical Uses of the HIP

A METHOD OF SELF-HYPNOSIS

After you have completed the profile, you are in a position to teach the subject how he or she can utilize this capacity to shift into a state of attentive concentration in a disciplined way.

This is how it is done. I am going to count to three. Follow this sequence again. One, look up toward your eyebrows, all the way up; two, close your eyelids, take a deep breath; three, exhale, let your eyes relax, and let your body float.

As you feel yourself floating, you concentrate on the sensation of floating and at the same time you permit one hand or the other to feel like a buoyant balloon and allow it to float upward. As it does, your elbow bends and your forearm floats into an upright position. Sometimes you may get a feeling of magnetic pull on the back of your hand as it goes up. When your hand reaches this upright position, it becomes a signal for you to enter a state of meditation. As you concentrate, you may make it more vivid by imagining you are an astronaut in space or a ballet dancer.

In this atmosphere of floating, you focus on this:

Here you insert whatever strategy is relevant for the patient's goal, in a manner consistent with the trance level the patient is able to experience. It is best to formulate the approach in a self-renewing manner which the subject is able to weave into his everyday life style. The patient must sense that he can achieve mastery over the problem he is struggling with by "reprogramming himself"—often identified as an "exercise"—by means of a self-affirming, uncomplicated reformulation of the problem.

For example, the patient who is attempting to gain control over a habit such as smoking can learn to induce self-hypnosis, and at this point repeat a summary of his treatment strategy: "Smoking is a poison for my body. I need my body to live. I owe my body this respect and protection." The patient can practice this strategy every one or two hours, just as he would any exercise.

Now, I propose that in the beginning you do these exercises as often as ten different times a day, preferably every one to two hours. At first the exercise takes about a minute; but as you become more expert at it, you can do it in much less time. You sit or lie down and, to yourself, you count to three. At one, you do one thing; at two, you do two things; at three, you do three things At one, look up toward your eyebrows; at two, close your eyelids and take a deep breath; and at three, exhale, let your eyes relax, and let your body float. As you feel yourself floating, you permit one hand or the other to feel like a buoyant balloon and let it float upward as your hand is now. When it reaches this upright position, it becomes your signal to enter a state of meditation in which you concentrate on these critical points.

Here you restate in an abbreviated but even more direct way, and in as simple a formula as possible, what the patient is to review for himself each time he does the exercise.

Reflect upon the implications of this and what it means to you in a private sense. Then bring yourself out of this state of concentration called self-hypnosis by counting backwards this way.

Three, get ready. Two, with your eyelids closed, roll up your eyes (and do it now). And, one, let your eyelids open slowly. Then, when your eyes are back in focus, slowly make a fist with the hand that is up and, as you open your fist slowly, your usual sensation and control returns. Let your hand float downward. That is the end of the exercise. But you will retain a general feeling of floating.

If necessary, demonstrate by doing it yourself. Then repeat the sequence of entering the trance state so that the patient can watch it. Then, while you supervise with direction, the patient repeats it again.

By doing the exercise every one to two hours, you can float into this state of buoyant repose. You have given yourself this island of time, twenty seconds every one to two hours, in which you use this extra-receptivity to re-imprint these critical points. Reflect upon them, then float back to your state of awareness, and get on with what you ordinarily do.

CAMOUFLAGE FOR SELF-HYPNOSIS

People do not always have the privacy to do the exercise. What follows is a modification of the exercise so that it can be done in public every one to two hours.

Now, suppose one or two hours pass and you want to do the exercise. You do not have privacy and do not want to make a spectacle of yourself. Here is the way you do it. There are two changes. First, you close your eyes and then roll your eyes up so that the eye roll is private. People seeing the uncamouflaged eye roll may get frightened. Second, instead of your hand coming up like this . . .

Demonstrate arm levitation as it was done in the hypnosis session.

Let it come up and touch your forehead. To an outsider the exercise looks like you are thinking about something . . .

Demonstrate a camouflaged arm levitation.

In twenty seconds you can shift gears, establish this extra-receptivity, re-imprint the critical points to yourself, and shift back out again.

You may be sitting at a desk or a table, or you may be in a conference, in which case you lean over on your elbow like this, with your hand already on your forehead, you close your eyes, roll them up, and shift into a trance state.

Demonstrate.

Let us try it again . . .

Repeat the camouflage technique. This time instead of demonstrating, have the patient try it.

By doing the basic or camouflage exercise every one to two hours during the day, you establish a private signal system between you and your body so that you are ever alert to this commitment to your body.

Elaborate on this instruction with reference to the treatment strategy you have used.

FURTHER TESTING TO IDENTIFY GRADE 5

The highest score on the regular HIP is a grade 4. All 4s are potentially 5s (Spiegel, H. 1974b). The criteria used to test further trance capacity follow:

1. Ability to sustain posthypnotic sensory and motor alterations. For testing, the subject is placed back into trance by utilizing the same three-step induction outlined in the first part of the HIP procedure. The subject is then administered one of the following instructions when in trance. The instruction is given so that the subject understands he is to comply with the sensory or motor alteration after leaving the formal trance state. A cut-off signal is included to terminate each instruction. Examples which satisfy this criterion are: positive or negative visual or auditory hallucinations, or limb paralysis, flaccid or rigid, in response to a posthypnotic signal.
   a) *Positive* hallucinations: "see a bird when the door closes," or "hear music when you move your legs."
   b) *Negative* hallucinations: "not hear voices of anybody but mine" (the hypnotist).
   c) *Motor paralysis*:   "when out of trance your left arm will be limp. When I touch your left shoulder your arm strength will return," or "clasped fingers are stuck together and you are unable to open hands until I stroke your wrists."

In all these tests, the sensorimotor distortions terminate with the cut-off signal.

2. Total spontaneous amnesia to the entire hypnotic experience, i.e., without being signalled to have amnesia.
3. Ability to regress to earlier age levels and experience age in *the present tense* with appropriate verbal, motor, and affective behavior for that chronological age. For example: "this is no longer the present time; you are going back into the years; you are getting younger; twenty-four years old, seventeen years old, eleven years old, six years old; today you are four years old, this is your fourth birthday. When I touch the side of your eyes you'll be able to open your eyes and talk with me. Later, when I touch your forehead, your eyes will again close. Ready!"
   "Hello, what's your name."
   "Anything special today," etc.
   If responses are appropriate for that age and in the present tense, this is the grade 5 level. If responses are somewhat appropriate and somewhat regressive with some historical perspective apparent, this scores at the 4 or 5 level. If there is no regression response at all, the score remains at the 4 level.

If all three tests reveal positive response, this identifies a grade 5 (about 5 percent of the population). If the subject responds positively on some but not all the above criteria, he is given a score of 4 to 5. If the subject does not score positively on any of these tests, the score remains 4. Grades, 4, 4 to 5, and 5 are treated with essentially the same clinical strategies.

PART II

The HIP as a Diagnostic Probe

5

Apollonians, Odysseans, and Dionysians: A Hypothesis

I felt a cleavage in my mind,
As if my brain had split;
I tried to match it, seam by seam,
But could not make them fit.
Emily Dickinson
"I Felt a Cleavage in My Mind"

The cluster hypothesis is a generalization derived from our observations of the clinical pattern of patients who had been given the Hypnotic Induction Profile and who had intact scores, i.e., excluding softs and decrements. These clinical observations were compared with other measures, including independent diagnoses and psychological testing. Three major types seemed to emerge from the data, Dionysian, Apollonian, and Odyssean. First we will describe these types briefly and then discuss them in more detail. Supporting research data follows in Chapter 10.

Dionysians

The chariot of Dionysos is bedecked with flowers and garlands, panthers and tigers stride beneath his yoke. If one were to convert Beethoven's 'Paean to Joy' into a painting, and refuse to curb the imagination when that multitude prostrates itself reverently in the dust, one might form some apprehension of Dionysiac ritual. Now the slaver emerges as a free man: all the rigid, hostile walls which either necessity or despotism has erected between men are shattered. (Nietzsche [Golffing F., trans.] 1956)

Our initial observations about the Dionysian personality style grew out of some intriguing psychological problems encountered by patients in the 4 to 5 range on the HIP. (Spiegel, H. 1974). These individuals had a high eye roll and high response on the behavioral aspects of the test. Our observations of these grade 5 patients resulted in the impression that they had certain clusters of characteristics which were more or less consistent with their high hypnotizability and with the fact that they spontaneously slipped into trance states. They adopted a naive posture of trust in relation to many if not all people in their environment; were prone to suspend critical judgment; had a tendency to affiliate easily with new events (one patient would become nauseated every time her friend's sick dog was nauseated); and demonstrated a telescoping of their sense of time so that their focus was almost exclusively on the present rather than in the past or the future. They further demonstrated a tendency to employ extreme trance logic (Orne 1959) in that they were relatively comfortable with logical incongruity, and had excellent memories and an unusually good capacity for intense and focused concentration.

In addition, patients with high hypnotizability and considerable psychological dysfunction showed a fixed personality core of beliefs which was relatively nonnegotiable even though these individuals were in other ways very compliant. Especially troubling was their role confusion and fixed sense of inferiority: these two characteristics often served as a rationalization for a naive posture of trust and uncritical acceptance of environmental cues. These patients tended to say to themselves: "Who am I to know anything about this, compared to the person who is directing me?" As one might expect, they were very prone to spontaneous trance experience and uncritical acceptance of casual comments as posthypnotic signals.

Apollonians

It then occurred to us to look for what we will call Apollonian characteristics in the low and nonhypnotizable patients within the intact range of the HIP. We expected to find these people more cognitive, organized, critical, and aware of the periphery in their style of concentration. We have found clinical and research data to support this hypothesis.

The stage for contrasts was set. As an alternative to Dionysos, Nietzsche describes Apollo:

> Apollo is at once the god of plastic powers and the soothsaying god. He who is etymologically the 'lucent' one, the god of light, reigns also over the fair illusion of our inner world of fantasy. The perfection of these conditions in contrast to our imperfectly understood waking reality, as well as our profound awareness of nature's healing powers during the interval of sleep and dream furnishes a symbolic analogue to the soothsaying faculties and quite generally to the arts, which make life possible and worth living. But the image of Apollo must incorporate that thin line which the dream image may not cross under penalty of becoming pathological, of imposing itself on us as crass reality; a discrete limitation, a freedom from all extravagant urges, the sapient tranquility of the plastic god. (Nietzsche [Golffing F., trans.] 1956)

The ongoing theme of Apollonian individuals is control and reason over passion. As we scrutinized those with low grades on the HIP (that is, less than 2) we found that they put tremendous emphasis on reason and understanding and were very much prone to planning for the future and to employing their critical faculties to the utmost. One patient who proved to be an intact-1 spent most of the first session debating the issue of free will—whether in fact all hypnosis was self-hypnosis or whether the hypnotist would be implanting something in her mind by hypnotizing her. It was only at a second session that we simply could set aside these arguments, having heard them, and proceed with the profile.

Certain clusters of characteristics were generally present among low-intact patients. They were steady, unemotional, organized individuals. They were not devoid of passion, but were far more prone to value reason than passion.

Odysseans

For Nietzsche, the ground between Apollonian reason and Dionysian ecstasy was filled by the Greek tragedians. We will describe those people with mid-range scores on the HIP with reference to their extreme characteristics. We have named them after Homer's tragic hero, Odysseus, a man whose name literally means "trouble," or "to give pain and receive pain."*

Walking beneath high Ionic peristyles, looking toward a horizon defined by pure and noble lines, seeing on either hand the glorified reflection of his shape in gleaming marble and all about him men moving solemnly or delicately,

* We are indebted to Professor Jacob Stern of the Department of Classics at City College, City University of New York, for reviewing our data and suggesting the term "Odyssean."

with harmonious sounds and rhythmic gestures: would he not then, over-whelmed by this steady stream of beauty, be forced to raise his hands to Apollo and call out: 'Blessed Greeks! how great must be your Dionysos, if the Delic god thinks such enchantments necessary to cure you of your dithyrambic madness!' To one so moved, an ancient Athenian with the august countenance of Aechylus might reply: 'But you should add, extraordinary stranger, what suffering must this race have endured in order to achieve such beauty! Now come with me to the tragedy and let us sacrifice in the temple of both gods.' (Nietzsche [Golffing F., trans.] 1956)

This quotation reminds us that many Greek temples had altars both to Apollo and to Dionysos; that the greatness of Greek tragedy was its embodiment of the never-ending tension between the desire and capacity to experience extremes of joy and sorrow, and the hope that reason would provide a clarity and order in human experience to transcend mere sensation. To Nietzsche, tragedy represented a high artistic expression of the fact that the tension between reason and passion is never elim-inated in human experience; it is rather to be savored and suffered. Hence the Greek tragic vision that man can never fully succeed in the satisfaction of his desires and yet he is never far from the will to achieve what is beyond himself.

This third group is the vast mid-range (grades in the 2 to 3 range on the HIP) composed of mixtures of these opposing qualities. We call the group Odysseans, named for a wanderer of fluctuating moods, capable of heroic bravery and profound despair—not a mythical deity, like Apollo and Dionysos, but a mythical man. For these individuals the tension between reason and feeling is in some ways more trouble-some than for Apollonians and Dionysians. Odysseans are less settled and are more compelled to find a formula for integrating their con-flicting pressures, a formula that Nietzsche described as the stuff of which tragedies are made. And yet these individuals are often produc-tive, normal people who have the kinds of life crises that we have learned to identify as part of normal growth and development.

In the structuralist sense, all phenomena are best understood not merely as things in themselves but rather in the context of alternative possibilities. Thus, even those people who comprise the majority of the normal population are best understood in terms of the possible, extreme personality characteristics of which they represent a kind of integration. We have broadly characterized Odyssean style in terms of action/despair. Such individuals fluctuate between periods of absorption and involve-ment in life, and periods of a more critical and at times despairing review of—or response to—this activity. Their clusters of characteristics will be explained in the remainder of the chapter with illustrations from our own clinical experience and from literary sources.

Other Sources of the Apollonian–Dionysian Model

The application of Western mythology to clinical psychiatry may seem somewhat strange, but the use of such myths is not unknown to the behavioral sciences. Ruth Benedict, in her classic book *Patterns of Culture* (1934), applied the Apollonian–Dionysian model to her analysis of the culture contrasts between the Pueblo and Plains Indians. She found that the Zuni tribes, with their carefully constructed and highly organized pueblos, represented a kind of Apollonian model of native American culture in which reason and ceremony were highly valued. The Navahos, who lived on the Plains, had a much less structured society with more emphasis on feeling and activity, and were better characterized as Dionysians. This marked cultural contrast is conveyed by the Pueblo Zuni jewelry with its careful inlay and geometric shapes, in contrast to the more dramatic and heavy Navaho jewelry with its flowing lines of silver and respect for the natural outlines of the stones. Thus, encouraged by the explanatory fertility of Benedict's model, we have attempted to expand and apply it to clinical psychiatry.

A serious, yet amusing, use of these mythological types is found in a letter to the editor of *Science* by the Nobel Prize winner Szent-Gyorgyi (1972). He wrote:

Wilhelm Ostwald* divided scientists into the classical and the romantic. One could call them also systematic and intuitive. John R. Platt† calls them Apollonian and Dionysian. These classifications reflect extremes of two different attitudes of the mind that can be found equally in art, painting, sculpture, music, or dance. One could probably discover them in other alleys of life. In science the Apollonian tends to develop established lines to perfection, while the Dionysian rather relies on intuition and is more likely to open new, unexpected alleys for research. Nobody knows what "intuition" really is. My guess is that it is a sort of subconscious reasoning, only the end result of which becomes conscious.

These are not merely academic problems. They have most important corollaries and consequences. The future of mankind depends on the progress of science, and the progress of science depends on the support it can find. Support mostly takes the form of grants, and the present methods of distributing grants unduly favor the Apollonian. Applying for a grant begins with writing a project. The Apollonian clearly sees the future lines of his research and has no difficulty writing a clear project. Not so the Dionysian, who knows only the direction in which he wants to go out into the unknown; he has no idea what he is going to find there and how he is going to find it. Defining the unknown or writing down the subconscious is a contradiction *in absurdum*. In his work, the Dionysian relies, to a great extent, on accidental observation. His observations are not completely "accidental" because they involve not merely seeing things but also grasping their possible meaning. A great deal of conscious or subconscious thinking must precede a Dionysian's observations. There is an old saying that a discovery is an accident finding a prepared mind. The Dionysian is often not only unable to tell what he is going to find, he may even be at a loss to tell how he made his discovery.

Being myself Dionysian, writing projects was always an agony for me, as

---

° W. Ostwald, *Grosse Männer*, Akademische Verlagsgesellschaft GMBH, Leipzig, 1909.
† R. J. Platt, personal communication.

I described not long ago in *Perspectives of Biology and Medicine.** I always tried to live up to Leo Szilard's commandment, "don't lie if you don't have to."† I had to. I filled up pages with words and plans I knew I would not follow. When I go home from my laboratory in the late afternoon, I often do not know what I am going to do the next day. I expect to think that up during the night. How could I tell then, what I would do a year hence? It is only lately that I can see somewhat ahead (which may be a sign of senescense) and write a realistic proposal, but the queer fact is that, while earlier all my fake projects were always accepted, since I can write down honestly what I think I will do my applications have been invariably rejected. This seems quite logical to me; sitting in an easy chair I can cook up any time a project which must seem quite attractive, clear, and logical. But if I go out into nature, into the unknown, to the fringes of knowledge, everything seems mixed up and contradictory, illogical, and incoherent. This is what research does; it smooths out contradiction and makes things simple, logical, and coherent. So when I bring reality into my projects, they become hazy and are rejected. The reviewer, feeling responsible for "the taxpayer's money," justly hesitates to give money for research, the lines of which are not clear to the applicant himself.

A discovery must be, by definition, at variance with existing knowledge. During my lifetime, I made two. Both were rejected offhand by the popes of the field. Had I predicted these discoveries in my application, and had these authorities been my judges, it is evident what their decisions would have been.

These difficulties could perhaps be solved to some extent, by taking into account the applicant's earlier work. Or, if the applicant is young and has had no chance to prove himself, the vouching of an elder researcher acquainted with the applicant's ability may be considered. The problem is a most important one, especially now, as science grapples with one of nature's mysteries, cancer which may demand entirely new approaches.‡

Albert Szent-Gyorgyi
Institute for Muscle Research
Marine Biological Laboratory
Woods Hole, Massachusetts

This letter emphasizes a theme that is central to our approach: in many people the distinctions we are describing are differences in style and are not indicative of psychopathology. The Dionysian has an intuitive sense, as Szent-Gorgyi describes it, which can be very useful but which lacks the structure and planning that characterizes the Apollonian.

Psychiatrists and many laymen tend to use short-cut descriptions of a person's style of living or thinking by resorting to pathological-like labels, without necessarily intending to imply a predominance of psychopathology—e.g., "hysterical type," "obsessive type," "schizoid-like," "depressive type," "manic-like," "obsessive-repulsive," "psychopathic." Usually it is necessary to smile or joke or make quick disclaimers along with the term so as not to be misunderstood. We agree that there are clear personality traits which are more or less distinct, but these traits can be clearly alluded to by descriptive terms which do not imply pathology or behavior deviance. People differ in many ways that are healthy. And so we employ neutral, nonclinical, but perhaps somewhat dramatically exaggerated labels to describe the main character types.

° Szent-Gyorgyi. *Perspect. Biol. Med.* 15:1, 1971.
† Szilard, personal communication.
‡ Reproduced with author's permission. From *Science* 176 (1972):196.

As has been done before, we go back to the Greeks and adopt three clear but overlapping labels: Apollonian, Dionysian, and Odyssean. With these categories, personality and character differences can be discussed without implying value judgments about health or illness.

The Compulsive Triad

We will now discuss the differences among these three groups—Dionysians, Apollonians, and Odysseans—in more detail. We have devised a system to visually represent the significance of these different hypnotic capacities. The system is designed so that it focuses not on hypnotizability per se, but on utilizing a cluster of behavioral transformations which we have named the "compulsive triad" (see Fig. 5–1.) The triad is composed of three consistent features: amnesia to the context of a signal; compulsive compliance with the signal, and rationalization of the compliance. Variations in these features characterize the differences among the three groups. For example, a type of compulsive triad observed in a hypnotic subject follows:

During the administration of the HIP, a patient who proved to be moderately hypnotizable was asked to explain the sudden change in sensation in his left arm after the cut-off signal (touching his elbow) had been given. He looked at his arm, noted that it was indeed no

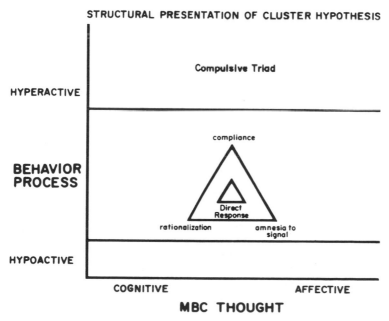

STRUCTURAL PRESENTATION OF CLUSTER HYPOTHESIS

Figure 5–1

longer upright, and then commented that: "It feels different now because the circulation is better—you get more blood circulating when your hand is down." He denied any memory of having his elbow touched, although he conceded that it might have happened when his arm was stroked. He also denied remembering any instructions regarding a change in sensation in his arm.

In this case the patient demonstrated clearly all three aspects of the compulsive triad: he developed an amnesia for the cut-off signal; felt a compulsion to comply with the signal and did so by letting his arm float back down to the chair; and invented a rationalization for his behavior which did not include any memory of the original signal. A more highly hypnotizable subject emphasizes compliance with the signal without an explanation. He is amnesic for the signal and singularly uncurious about how the event occurred. On the other hand, a subject with low hypnotizability is more likely to say: "I think I remember your saying that when you touched my elbow something would happen— did you touch it?" He complies reluctantly with the signal, and then is sure to provide some rationalization, such as: "I prefer to have my hand down now anyway."

This triad, which appears so clearly and in such a short period of time in a hypnotizable individual, can be seen as one type of a far more general phenomenon. We often find ourselves compelled to act for reasons which in varying degrees we have forgotten. When pressed for an explanation, we invent what amounts to rationalizations for our behavior. This is not to say that we are never aware of the reasons for our conduct; but generally the determining factors are so complex that our "reasons" are almost certainly to some degree rationalizations.

A general example of the compulsive triad operating in a person not hypnotized may be in the obsessional rituals of an obsessive-compulsive neurotic. He feels a compulsion to act in compliance with his obsessional ideas. He has at least some degree of amnesia for the conflicts which gave rise to his obsessions and rituals, and he frequently has a complex structure of rationalizations for his behavior. One purpose of intensive psychotherapy can be to overcome some of the amnesia so that rationalization comes closer to the original signals, which are perhaps largely internally generated, with the hope that the patient's compulsive need to comply with the rituals will also diminish.

The sizes of the compulsive triad triangles in Figure 5–1 and in succeeding figures in this chapter represent variations in the rigidity and nature of the compulsve triad phenomena. The smaller triangle, labeled "direct response," indicates the relatively less compulsive nature of a behavioral response to a direct request than the response to a posthypnotic suggestion, or in a neurotic ritual. The input signal is mostly remembered rather than forgotten, the rationalization for the behavior is therefore quite close to the actual signal given, and compliance is relatively noncompulsive. It is closer to being a rational choice; the individual hears the request, remembers it, and makes a more or less conscious decision about whether or not to comply. Hence there is little distance between the signal, the reason, and the compliance, and the triangle is small. A larger triangle suggests that the input signal is less remembered, the rationalization is further from the original impetus for the behavior, and compliance is relatively compulsive in nature.

The point is that a common pattern of behavior can be discerned in widely different situations, types of people, and levels of hypnotizability among people. The persistence of this pattern in diverse situations suggests that it may be the key to a more general transformation in which we are constantly engaged between thought and behavior, or in our specialized language from the myth–belief constellation to the process of interaction with the world (Spiegel, H. and Shainess 1963). We are constantly confronted with the problem of trying to understand our behavior and with the fact that the reasons we provide ourselves can never fully take into account all of the social, interpersonal, and unconscious forces that influence our behavior. We do not defend the deterministic thesis that all behavior is merely the result of external and internal forces, like a vector diagram in physics; nevertheless, we do exist in a complex field of forces which influences our behavior.

We constantly face the problem of assessing our behavior in an effort to see whether or not it lives up to our cognitive concepts of ourselves. Every action is an expression of our conscious and unconscious belief system as it is integrated with interpersonal and social forces. Our behavior can be viewed as a statement that translates a complex of beliefs. It is never a simple statement and we contend that it is usually ambiguous because there is likely to be some rationalization and amnesia about the forces which motivated the behavior. At the same time, the behavior is likely to be seen by the person as representative of himself and his beliefs—an expression of himself.

Dionysian Versus Apollonian

The cluster hypothesis is a series of generalizations regarding characterological styles and traits which seem to be related to trance capacity as measured by the Hypnotic Induction Profile. These traits are an amalgam of clinical experience, reviews of psychological testing, answers to questionnaires, the literature on traits associated with hypnotizability, the neurophysiological literature, and studies of hypnotizability and psychopathology, much of which will be reviewed later. Our generalizations are operational rather than absolute. We consider them correct insofar as they can be empirically validated but, more important, they prove clinically useful in constructing an appropriate approach to the patient and the patient's problem. They are not so much categories as guidelines, ways of quickly tuning in to the interactional style of the patient so that brief and effective intervention is facilitated and decision

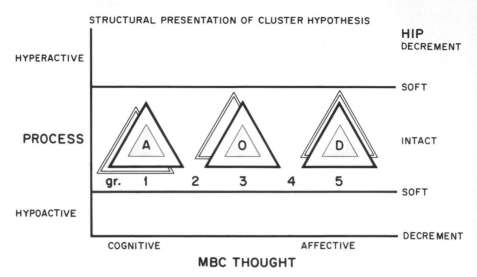

Figure 5–2

making in regard to the appropriate long-term intervention, if necessary, is made more rational and effective.

It is apparent that people differ in somewhat predictable and classifiable ways in their systems of beliefs and premises and in their styles of behavior. As a beginning we will compare and contrast the styles of people in the Dionysian and Apollonian groups, that is, those who are extremely hypnotizable and those who are barely hypnotizable (Fig. 5–2), utilizing the compulsive triad model of compulsive compliance, rationalization, and amnesia.

For Dionysians, rationalization is in the service of compliance; for Apollonians, compliance is in the service of rationalization. As a crude generalization, more highly hypnotizable people value feeling and action over reason and are relatively unconcerned about the explanation of motives: a Dionysian may present an explanation in a disinterested way and be prone to accept paradoxes and conflicts in describing his reasons which would stymie an Apollonian (Orne 1959). The capacity of Dionysians to tolerate logical incongruities has been previously described in the clinical setting (Spiegel, H. 1974). It was noted that tolerance for such logical incongruities is not solely a characteristic of the trance state, but is a more general aspect of human existence.

COGNITIVE AND AFFECTIVE DISSONANCE

Cognitive dissonance has been discussed in some detail by Festinger in his classic work on the subject (1957). Festinger noted that the degree of logical conflict between two beliefs or between a personal belief and an observation in the world leads to behavior which is designed to reduce the dissonance. Often this behavior does not challenge an aberrant belief; rather, it seeks to distort perception of the reality. This behavior occurs by gathering together a group of supporters who share a view of the world which denies some obvious reality. Festinger's important work seems to focus largely on cognitive dissonances, that is, logical contradictions involving conflicting beliefs, or beliefs and conflicting perceptions. The behavior observed was often of an organizational nature. That is, those individuals who were disappointed in their belief that a flying saucer would rescue them from a disintegrating earth set about organizing others to confirm the validity of a modified prophesy of doom.

Although we know of no studies relating hypnotizability to cognitive dissonance phenomena, we speculate that the type of cognitive dissonance described by Festinger is especially characteristic of the Apollonians, for whom logical paradoxes are of critical importance. The problem for the Dionysian is what we call "affective dissonance"; the Dionysian is troubled more by conflicting emotional ties or commands and less by logical or cognitive paradoxes. For a Dionysian, conflicting loyalties or instructions from valued people in his life create a crisis which is resolved by seeking support from someone who can transcend the conflict, or by shifting allegiances back and forth.

Cognitive dissonance is less problematic for the Dionysian, as has been demonstrated in experiments with highly hypnotizable individuals who can, for example, hallucinate the absence of an individual who is seated in the room. These perceptual distortions make it relatively easy to eliminate cognitive paradoxes, although the Dionysian is prone to suffer with affective dissonances. Conflicting loyalties rather than conflicting ideas create the most pressure for change in a Dionysian. Our clinical experience indicates that the obverse is true for the Apollonian. Manipulating loyalties, in the sense which Festinger describes it, is important to the Apollonian only in the service of reducing cognitive dissonance. For the Dionysian, cognitions and perceptions are altered in the service of reducing affective dissonance which often involves conflicting loyalties.

An historical example follows of affective dissonance and its consequences in a person whom we presume to have been a Dionysian. At first glance, one may think that all Dionysians are so compliant that they inevitably become followers rather than leaders. This is not necessarily so; much depends upon the social matrix and support systems available and used by the person.

Mary Baker Eddy, the founder of Christian Science, was a woman whose influence endures in our culture. Without undertaking a psychohistory project, we refer only to a few relevant reported events in Wilbur's (1907) biography of Mrs. Eddy, who personally approved the manuscript.

She was "delicate in health from birth." Later her condition was called "spinal weakness." It was necessary for her to be carried from room to room by her father during her childhood and adolescence. When she eventually married and gave birth to a son, "she was far too ill to nurse her child," who was raised by a wet-nurse.

Ultimately she heard of a hypnotist, a student of Mesmer's, one Phineas P. Quimby to whom she went for help. Under trance ". . . the relief was no doubt tremendous. Her gratitude was unbounded. She felt free from the excruciating pain of years. Quimby himself was amazed at her sudden healing." He was also amazed at her interpretation that the transformation occurred because Quimby mediated this effect between herself and God.

This dramatic description of her sudden hypnotic responsiveness, sudden cure, and the complete fulfillment of her expectations seems so authentic and typical of the Dionysian seeking of relief from stress that we infer she was a grade 5. In retrospect it appears that during her earlier years she unconsciously used pain and weakness as a means of eliciting attention and concern from her family. The "spinal weakness" was a somatic metaphor rather than a physical disability. She then employed her "cure" to elicit even more attention, now directed toward her strength and mastery rather than toward her weakness. Thus in a few years she emerged as a recognized healer and leader, gathering converts from the ranks of the healed, their relatives, and friends.

Interestingly, her conflict was one of loyalties rather than ideas. The miraculous fact of her cure was less troubling than the conflict over to whom she owed loyalty for the result. She initially felt quite fond of Quimby, but then quickly decided that her healing was due to God, and shifted her allegiance. In Mrs. Eddy's words: "It has always been my misfortune to think people better and bigger than they really are. My mistake is, to endow another person with my ideal, and then make him think it is his own . . ." (p. 94). Her growing recognition helped her to confirm her new loyalty. She could deal with adversity and criticism by offering to her critics the opportunity for a new relationship with God. To this day, attendance at a Christian Science service is an intense and emotionally involving experience.

In summary, the highly hypnotizable person tends to readily comply with a signal, forget it, and rationalize casually about the meaning of his behavior. He conveys his relative disinterest in the predominance of reason and a willingness to affiliate with new modes of action. By contrast, the person who is hypnotizable at a low level complies with a signal in a more rigid and methodical way and is more interested in providing a consistent rational explanation for his behavior. He demonstrates his belief in reason via his behavior and the explanation for it, although he may be more or less amnesic for the hypnotically induced causes of his action.

Major Groupings of the Cluster Traits

We have organized the clusters of traits which characterize the Dionysians, Apollonians, and Odysseans into four major groupings (Fig. 5–2): spatial awareness, time perception, myth–belief constellation (content), and processing.* These traits are related to the trance experience itself, but the trance state need not be formally induced for them to be manifested. They are indicative more of a presence or absence in an individual which makes itself felt in the style of concentrating, feeling time, interacting with other people, and working with ideas. We will start out by discussing the contrast between the Dionysians, the highs, and the Apollonians and later we will discuss the more ambiguous and balanced picture presented by the Odysseans.

SPATIAL AWARENESS

The first structure involves an individual's awareness of himself in space, or his capacity for focal absorption along the lines of the work of Tellegen and Atkinson (1974). The dialectic of focal and peripheral awareness, so critical in the trance state itself, is a factor in all our experiences of concentration. We tend to describe ourselves as concentrating better when we lose touch with surrounding stimuli and focus intently on one or two points. Our concentration is always, to some degree, divided between focal and peripheral awareness. At different times we surrender more or less of one to the enhancement of the other: the trance state is characterized by a relative increase in focal as opposed to peripheral awareness. This capacity to focus intensely can be tapped without a formal trance induction and characterizes the Dionysian style. These people tend to concentrate so intensely for example, when watching a play or movie, that they lose their bearings in space and often report a sense of surprise and a need for reorientation at the end of the performance.

By contrast, the Apollonian's attention tends to be more widely scattered, scanning for conflict and comparison. He sacrifices some degree of focal intensity, but is less likely to be misled by one particular path in a train of concentration—for example, he is more likely to keep his bearings when doing a test. Thus the Apollonian style of concentration is characterized by a predominance of peripheral awareness in relation to focal awareness. These individuals never seem to lose track of where they are or of alternative issues in the way that Dionysians do, although Apollonians are, of course, also capable of intense concentration.

---

* The data which we have to support these hypotheses will be presented in chapter 10, as will a review of the pertinent literature in chapters 6 and 7.

TIME PERCEPTION

Dionysians tend to telescope time, putting greater emphasis on the present (See Figure 5–4). With their intense absorption in the now, they tend to lose sight of past and future. An objection may be raised that one of the characteristics of the highly hypnotizable individual is his capacity to relive the past with dramatic intensity and surprisingly good recall of detail. This is indeed true, but the distinguishing feature is that the past is relived as though it were the present, and in the reliving, past and future are likewise ignored. Their view of the past can be compared to freezing a frame on a motion picture reel. They are the kind of people who live for the moment and who are not overly given to worrying about past precedents or future consequences.

By contrast, Apollonians seriously view the past and the future, being very aware of the importance of the past and the pressure exerted by the future. They are inclined to carefully think through the consequences of what they do, and to weigh alternatives. Apollonians tend to see

STRUCTURAL THEMES AND HYPNOTIZABILITY

GRADE: Hypnotic Induction Profile	0	1	2	3	4	5
CHARACTER TYPES	APOLLONIAN		ODYSSEAN		DIONYSIAN	
A) Space Awareness (Absorption)	Focal ⁄PERIPHERAL		FOCAL-PERIPHERAL		FOCAL⟍ Peripheral	
B) Time Perception	PAST-FUTURE		PAST-PRESENT-FUTURE		PRESENT	
C) Myth–Belief Constellation (Premises)	Affective ⁄COGNITIVE		AFFECTIVE-COGNITIVE		AFFECTIVE⟍ Cognitive	
1) Locus of Interpersonal Control	INTERNAL		INTERNAL-EXTERNAL		EXTERNAL	
2) Trust Proneness	LOW		VARIED		HIGH	
3) Critical Appraisal	IMMEDIATE		VARIED		SUSPENDED	
4) Learning Style	ASSIMILATION		ACCOMMODATION		AFFILIATION	
5) Responsibility	HIGH		VARIED		LOW	
6) Preferred Contact Mode	VISUAL		VISUAL-TACTILE		TACTILE	
D) Processing	Premise ⁄IMPLEMENT		MIXED		PREMISE⟍ Implement	
1) Writing Value	HIGH		VARIED		LOW	

(left margin label: STRUCTURES)

Figure 5–3

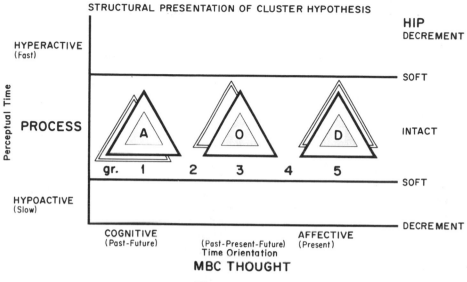

Figure 5–4

things in parallel that Dionysians view in series, to borrow a metaphor from electronics. They have a tendency to avoid the gratifications of the moment as somewhat illusory and misleading, in favor of the satisfactions of careful planning.

MYTH–BELIEF CONSTELLATION

Reference to Fig. 5–3 will indicate that the myth–belief constellation, the mixture of intrapsychic familial and cultural beliefs which creates an individual's perspective on himself and the world, has been divided into six substructures. Numerous related distinctions exist among the groups and this discussion is more descriptive than exhaustive.

This concept of a myth belief constellation or "metaphor mix"' is consistent with Ortega's description (from *On Love: Aspects of a Single Theme*) of our perception of reality:

Strictly speaking, no one see things in their naked reality. The day this happens will be the last day of the world, the day of the great revelation. In the meantime, let us consider our perception of reality which, in the midst of a fantastic fog, allows us at least to capture the skeleton of the world, its great tectonic lines, as adequate. Many, in fact the majority, do not even achieve this: they live from words and suggestions; they lead a somnambulent existence, scurrying along in their delirium (1957, pp. 38–39).

The difference in the myth–belief constellation—the mixture of private assumptions about the world related to intrapsychic development, family beliefs, and cultural myths—is characterized by the affective–

cognitive dialectic. Dionysians as a rule tend to operate more on their gut feelings about what is right. They view reason as helpful but not definitive, and they tend to trust in their gut judgments about people and making decisions. By contrast, Apollonians value reason more than feeling. They tend to be distrustful of feeling, in the belief that following one's feelings can lead to trouble, and that having a reason for doing something should be the ultimate arbiter of human conduct. This broad distinction implies differences, which will be presented, in the way Dionysians and Apollonians relate to others and acquire new information. In summary, Apollonians tend to be head-oriented, Dionysians heart-oriented.

LOCUS OF INTERPERSONAL CONTROL

The interpersonal styles of the two groups can be compared. Dionysians are characterized as operating somewhat on a radar that picks up affective signals. They are quite sensitive to the feelings of people around them and are prone to absorb and identify with such feelings. They are less interested in the ideas of others than in their actions and feelings. Apollonians seek confirmation in the thoughts of others which they compare carefully with their own thinking. They help to rationalize what they do by seeking confirmation of their own ideas in other people. Nonetheless, they use their own ideas as a primary reference and as such they can be described as moving more on their own gyroscope than on radar. They utilize social support as a way of confirming their own mental processing.

Dionysians are rather prone to allow other people to control their relationships, at least overtly. The kind of individual who says "I would rather let him decide" is often a Dionysian. On the other hand, when many Apollonians are asked "When you are in a close relationship do you like to let the other person make the decisions or do you like to be in control of things yourself?" they will frequently respond with a knowing look, "There's no doubt about it, I like to be in control."

TRUST PRONENESS AND CRITICAL APPRAISAL

Our clinical experience indicates that Dionysians in general are prone to trust others in a relatively naive and uncritical fashion. Those with high trance capacity who come to psychiatric attention often report major problems in their lives resulting from naive and uncritical acceptance of other peoples' ideas. But this is a personality tendency even when it does not lead to serious difficulties.

A noted researcher, extremely competent and critical within his field of expertise, found himself repeatedly the victim of high-pressure salesmen. He once walked into a large department store, came out slightly dazed, and went home to report to his wife that he had acquired a brand new refrigerator. His wife looked him and said, "Why there's nothing wrong with the refrigerator we have now, why did you get it?"

He responded, "Well the salesman was so nice and it seemed like such a good idea at the time."

This example indicates a related attribute of the highly hypnotizable individual, a relative proneness to suspend critical judgment. This researcher, who was highly critical and somewhat distrusting in his work, found that in other areas of his life he was far too prone to trust people and to suspend his own critical judgment. The normal scanning awareness that he was hardly in need of a refrigerator was suspended in the face of his willingness to trust a stranger. By comparison, Apollonians tend to be extremely critical of external input and very prone to compare and contrast alternatives. They often describe themselves as skeptics by nature and may even be too reticent to get involved in new activities or enterprises without researching them carefully. This hypothesis receives some support in the work of Roberts and Tellegen (1973), indicating an incidence of greater proneness to trust among highly hypnotizable individuals.

LEARNING STYLE

The learning style of the two groups can also be contrasted. Dionysians tend to learn by affiliation; they are characterized by an ability to throw themselves into new disciplines with relative ease; they tend to soak up new concepts. The Apollonians tend to learn rather more methodically. For example, they are unlikely to affiliate with a new school of thought without examining it tenet by tenet, piece by piece, before making a decision. Thus their learning style is characterized more as assimilation than affiliation.

We have some clinical experience indicating that individuals with what is called a photographic memory or with truly prodigious recall for certain details tend to be Dionysians. The capacity for seemingly total recall of detail has many characteristics of hypnotic age regression. One dental student reported feeling that he cheated on his final examinations because he was able to picture the pages and diagrams of his textbooks in his mind while answering the questions. Interestingly, though, when it came to applying this book learning to his clinical work, he found himself in serious trouble. He was able to recall the textbook material, but he had not integrated it into his physical behavior so that it would be useful to him in the coordination of his hands during clinical practice.

Normal learning involves a combination of affiliation and assimilation and these extremes are presented to illustrate the point, not to imply that Dionysians never assimilate or that Apollonians never affiliate.

RESPONSIBILITY

Although the sense of responsibility has many developmental and cultural determinants, Dionysians as a group do not particularly pride themselves on being responsible, although they may fulfill structured social and vocational roles in a highly responsible manner. They tend to look to others for the guidelines of appropriate conduct; to live with a series of intense involvements rather than with involvement on a continuum; and knowing this, they tend to neglect certain of their responsibilities at any one time. Apollanians often pride themselves on being extremely responsible. Their sense of organization of past and future make them hesitant to commit themselves, as illustrated by their high critical appraisal and assimilating style of learning; but once they make a commitment they usually stick with it. They are often seen as the Rock of Gibraltar by their families, and their steadiness is a major asset. For example, it is our clinical impression that although it is somewhat more difficult initially for an Apollonian to make the commitment not to smoke, once he has made it he is much more likely to stick with it than a Dionysian.

PREFERRED CONTACT MODE

Interestingly, Dionysians prefer tactile sensory input as compared with Apollonians who prefer more distant visual stimuli. When our patients are asked whether they would prefer to see or to touch a new object, the Dionysians are much more inclined to say they would prefer to touch it and the Apollonians to say that they would rather see it. Our clinical experience is that those forms of therapy which involve some sort of physical sensory input, such as body-space sculpting and massage, seem to find ready acceptance among the highly hypnotizable and to heighten resistance among the lows.

PROCESSING

Finally, the style of behavioral processing or implementing of ideas seems to differ between Dionysians and Apollonians. As a rule, Dionysians are content to toy with ideas in their mind; to think and rethink things in an intense but somehow casual way. They are also more likely to achieve satisfaction from dreaming up new ways of doing things than from the actual process of implementing. Apollonians prefer the satisfaction of seeing that an idea is executed correctly. They often prefer to write out ideas as part of their process of thinking them out. They tend to be the kind of people who don't believe something unless they see it in print, in contrast with Dionysians who are more likely to retain information transmitted orally.

Case Examples: Apollonian and Dionysian. These traits, among others, characterize differences among the people on the ends of the spectrum of intact but high or low hypnotizability. These differences include spatial and temporal orientation, interpersonal behavior, and processing of ideas. The differences convey the importance of action, the value of feelings as opposed to thought, and many other assumptions about the world and oneself.

The following two cases illusrate the distinctions between a typical Dionysian and a typical Apollonian. N.M. was a 25-year-old married woman who came for evaluation of a motor weakness which had not been responsive to medical treatment for two years. She was a warm, engaging person who scored 4 on the HIP and also scored positively on the extra tests for grade 5. On questioning, she acknowledged having most of the attributes of the Dionysian. In addition, she reported having a good eidetic memory and having a special problem in saying "no." She had encountered difficulties in establishing her household because of standards imposed on her by her husband's parents. They expected her to be the manager of servants and lady of leisure, and she secretly preferred to be more active and independent in running her home. However, she found it impossible to assert herself in this matter, doubting her own right to have such feelings. Her physical disability became her way of overtly complying with the family pressure and at the same time making a metaphorical statement that the situation was damaging to her.

Psychological testing revealed her to be an intelligent and basically intact woman with some hysterical features, depression, and guilt. She evidenced a sense of being at the mercy of her environment, easily threatened by external forces, and yet frightened by solitude. The tester noted that she retreated from her own hostile impulses because of a need to be a "good girl," especially to authority figures. She was described as frightened, insecure, and dependent. She was seen as somewhat preoccupied with her physical problems and in considerable emotional pain. There was evidence of some immaturity, but none of psychosis or organicity. The diagnosis was conversion hysteria.

She responded rapidly to treatment with self-hypnosis (see Chapter 18 on conversion symptoms for further discussion of this aspect of the case) once pain and physical dysfunction were resolved. With certain cognitive guidelines provided by the therapist, she also made important changes in her way of relating to her in-laws.

Her high hypnotizability was consistent with her other Dionysian attributes—her good memory and capacity to concentrate, her sense of immersion in a situation, her proneness to trust and take direction from others, and the ease with which she employed somatic metaphors for expressing problems.

H.D., a 54-year-old married scientist and father of two children, scored 1–2 on the HIP. He reported exclusively Apollonian features when questioned, such as orientation to the past and future rather than to the present, a tendency toward critical examination of new information, a tendency to be controlling in relationships, and a general head rather than heart orientation. He was quite successful in his career. He had come for help to stop smoking and succeeded. In addition, he had some interpersonal difficulties, including a reputation for being hard and controlling and a preoccupation with guilt—he had married out of a sense of guilt over pregnancy and viewed his marriage as an experience of duty rather than passion.

He was engaging yet judgmental with the therapist, noting several times during the first session his "satisfaction" with the rapport established. Some months after the first session, the therapist (H.S.) received in the mail a copy of an important lecture delivered by the patient with the following handwritten notation: "This lecture was written (and will be delivered) without smoking, thanks to H.S." This tone of self-confidence bordering on grandiosity permeated subsequent contacts with him.

Psychological testing revealed him to be an extremely intelligent, ambitious, and achievement-oriented man. The tester noted: "It is thus small wonder that, lacking a compassionate, empathic, emotionally giving personality, he has hurt others or failed to understand their personal errors or problems in the compulsive pursuit of his own goals." He was described as assertive and dominant with obsessional defenses and an introspective style. The tester noted the following: "His personal strivings and needs supersede any awareness of the needs of others; he is responsive to the pushes and pulls and strains within himself, to his fantasies, plans, needs, and goals, but not to any expression of similar needs on the part of others." He was found to be clearly nonpsychotic but willful, brooding, and somewhat obsessional.

The picture that emerged was of a man puzzled by the fact that people seemed to respect but not like him. He had solved problems all his life, but emotional bonds seemed somewhat defiant of the organized solutions which had marked his career. He was clearly dominant and structured, capable of perceiving alternatives and yet out of tune with his own emotions and those of the people around him.

Although both of these patients had psychological problems, on the broad spectrum of mental illness they were well within the healthy realm. They had productive careers and families despite their difficulties. Their personality styles were in many ways polar opposites. N.M. was insecure about herself, dependent, emotional, and vulnerable to external manipulation. She responded to extreme external pressure with depression and a somatic metaphor of dysfunction. H.D., on the other hand, was self-confident, ruminative, organized, and estranged from his emotions. He viewed life in terms of problems rather than feelings, and elicited respect rather than affection from others.

About twenty-five high-powered industry executives recently met for a seminar. They were introduced to the cluster hypothesis and to the relationship between eye roll and personality traits. Of the entire group, only one executive had an eye roll above 2. His was 3–4, and he identified himself with most of the Dionysian features. His Apollonian colleagues asked him how he managed to be so successful in controlling an important power position. He said that when he was a college student his rich, successful uncle had warned him, "If you want to make it in this world, you'd better learn to be an S.O.B. like me." Using his uncle as a model, he affiliated with his market-place manners and learned them well.

Bemused by this new look at himself, he said "Today when I leave my office, I suppose I'll leave that Apollonian cloak on the desk, because I am a different person at home with my wife and children."

The group voted to call him a "closet Dionysian." The Dionysian's capacity to affiliate with models makes this understandable. The reverse is not as easy; for an Apollonian to adapt to a Dionysian style requires so much analysis and questioning that it usually is not feasible.

The Odysseans

The previous characterizations have been presented as dialectical oppositions. We recognize that no pure oppositions exist and for each trait some aspect of its opposite exists in each person. Focal and peripheral awareness provide perhaps the best illustration of this dialectical reality. Even a profoundly regressed hypnotized person retains some scanning awareness and can respond to commands and outside stimulation. The most obsessional critical person has somewhat of a capacity to suspend scanning awareness and to focus intently.

But we see more of an integration of these oppositions in the Odyssean group, those within the middle range of hypnotizability. They are difficult to characterize because they tend to have a more balanced synthesis of the opposites presented in the preceding pages. In a sense, they show the most integrated mastery of their dialectical position. They tend to balance focal and peripheral awareness. Thus, they are capable of considerable absorption but they tend not to become so involved in their focal task that they lose their spatial orientation as the Dionysians do. Their time sense is more balanced, incorporating aspects of the past, the present, and the future with no overall emphasis on one over the others.

Their approach toward affective versus cognitive standards of truth is also more balanced. Their premise system, which we identify as the myth–belief constellation, tends to emphasize both affective and cognitive components. Odysseans seem to be less prone to imbalance; that is, to overemphasize either affect or cognition as being solely important. They respond to questions about interpersonal control by saying that it depends on the situation; in some situations they like to maintain control and in others they like to let the other person make the decisions. They tend to be only moderately trusting of other people and to make limited use of critical appraisal. Often their approach is not an exact amalgam of these oppositions; rather, it varies depending on the situation. In some situations Odysseans note that they tend to be more critical and skeptical, whereas in others they are more trusting and accepting.

Their style of learning can be characterized as accommodation—a compromise between affiliation and assimilation. Odysseans recognize that they must change in the process of learning, but they also tend to actively transform new information into a usable form. In this sense, the term accommodation is similar to Piaget's use of it in developmental psychology to suggest that the process of learning involves both active interaction with the environment and the necessity of change in the learner (1954). Odysseans view themselves as moderately responsible and have no extreme preference for sensory mode, either visual or tactile. Likewise, they take pleasure in both developing and implementing new ideas and do not clearly show preference for either oral or written language.

In relation to the Dionysians, who can be characterized as changing themselves to absorb directions and new ideas from their environment, and the Apollonians, who have rather firm rational standards to which they bend their environment, the Odysseans may best be seen as a group of individuals for whom the problem of changing in response to the world around them is especially important. These individuals recognize some necessity to modify themselves in response to pressures from the outside, but such change is not automatic and the necessity to change carries problems with it. Any change requires a capacity to give up and mourn old ways of believing and being. Odysseans may have periods of sadness or despair in their normal development which involves giving up old parts of themselves as they change. More serious stress may elicit pathological states of depression or withdrawal, but in general a certain amount of sadness is a normal part of their lives.

This kind of changing can be characterized as the action/despair syndrome. Odysseans tend to alternate on the compulsive triad model between compliance and a kind of affective rationalization. They will act, but later reflect and wonder why. Their rationalizations will not be far from the original input. They can immerse themselves in the here-and-now but then retreat to the broader perspective of past and future. Their approach to life is the most dialectical in an obvious and un-conscious way: they weigh alternatives, tend to comply and rationalize their choices, but do not give excessive weight to either aspect. They seem in many ways to be a synthesis of the extremes outlined earlier for Dionysians and Apollonians, but they have special characteristics of their own.

The outstanding characteristic of people in this mid-range group is a periodic fluctuation throughout their lives between intense activity and contemplative withdrawal from this activity, marked by despair and diminished productivity. The actress described below sought psychiatric help during such a period of despair in her career. She scored 2–3 on the HIP.

B.L. was a 40-year-old marrried actress and college graduate. She sought help on the advice of her coach because of anxiety about perform-ing a new production. She described herself as meticulous, demanding, and a perfectionist about her own performance. She was terribly con-cerned about this new anticipated play, having a feeling that she would not meet her usual standard. Since she had no previous psychiatric his-tory and revealed an intact profile, and the performance was due within a week, the entire session was focused upon training her to use self-hypnosis to bring about a state of relaxation. She was taught to experience a sense of floating relaxation, which she practiced experiencing in the trance state throughout the day as a means of mastering her performance anxiety.

One month later she returned, feeling exhilarated. The play was a success, the critics had acclaimed her performance, and she herself felt that she performed better than she had in the recent past. Her coach also confirmed her success. She now expressed a curiosity as to why she had gotten into such a jam. Responding to her curiosity, we undertook a more detailed exploration of her career and personality structure, and obtained psychodiagnostic testing.

Her first husband was a possessive and controlling man who used her as an extension of his own theatrical career, although he did give her early training and opportunities to perform. For many years she did not challenge his direction, but came to realize as she matured that he was stifling her development. She finally made the decision to divorce him and to pursue her career on her own. In retrospect, she and her teachers realized that her early experience had been too scattered and she had received too much undiscriminating praise, hindering her personal and artistic growth. Several years later she remarried, this time choosing a more secure and independent man, who was supportive of her career but not overly invested or dependent on it.

In spite of her happiness in this much better marriage, and her continued prominence, critics pointed up something which she was more and more willing to admit to herself, that she was not fully expressing her talents. As she became more frightened of performing, she recognized that she was conveying this uncertainty to her audience. The critical reviews of one performance in particular, several years earlier, were so negative that she decided to reexamine her career in order to learn from the experience. She sought further coaching after having considered and rejected the idea of an early retirement. She began to rebuild her confidence, in terms of both the technical aspects of her craft and her personal life.

Psychological testing revealed that she was an intelligent but somewhat emotionally constricted woman entering an important transition period in her life. Her desire for approval had made her cautious, vigilant, and overly dedicated to achievement. The testing indicated that she was opening up and getting in touch with underlying feelings of depression, guilt, extreme sensitivity, and vigilance towards other people; however, the psychologist noted that these feelings were related to assertive rather than aggressive strivings within her. She seemed unused to self-searching or personal preoccupation, but had newly developed concerns about her own anxiety. In sum, she was seen as a constricted, moderately depressed person with conflicts revolving around dependence, independence, guilt, and anxiety. There were obsessional features, especially her perfectionism on the Bender Gestalt, along with affective components of depression and guilt.

The picture emerged of a woman who was a synthesis of extremes. She showed some preoccupation with perfectionism, achievement, and a tendency toward emotional constriction. At the same time, she was capable of experiencing depression and anxiety, and had been sufficiently insecure and compliant to allow herself to be exploited by the more domineering people in her life. She experienced herself as caught between her desires for achievement, and her emotional doubts about her motives and the quality of her performance. Her first marriage had served to confirm her doubts about her worth as a person, although her second marriage helped her develop a greater sense of self-assertiveness, value, and feeling worthy of being loved. Her career had undergone a similar fluctuating course. Early in her career she had emphasized intense activity, and had been in some senses an overachiever. She then entered a period of despair and withdrawal, during which she doubted the entire value of her talent and work. It was only by going through a life crisis that she utilized her doubt to improve her actual performance.

She thus typifies the action/despair syndrome of the Odyssean group, and the Odyssean compromise between the extremes of Apollonian perfectionism and Dionysian emotionality and compliance. It is interesting that her curiosity was stimulated for the difficult exploration necessary to gain this perspective on her life only after she underwent a mastery experience in relation to therapeutic intervention, and further, that this insight with regard to her life came in her fifth decade.

As a middle group on the hypnotizability spectrum, and by far the largest group, Odysseans are closest to what may be called a normal or healthy population. They seem able to integrate the advantages of hypnotizability without becoming victimized by a kind of exaggerated proneness to using the trance state. We do not mean to imply that there are no healthy people in the other groups or that Odysseans are all healthy. Rather, we are describing a tendency toward the integration of different capacities. An article of faith with us is that the healthier people are, the more difficult it is to describe them with any degree of accuracy. Their very freedom to choose makes them less predictable.

The Concept of Personality Style

We have thus far outlined characterological differences among the three clusters as distinguished by the Hypnotic Induction Profile. A word about the distinction between character style and neurosis is now in order. This discussion pertains to the Apollonian, Odyssean, and Dionysian groups containing people in what is commonly described as the normal–neurotic spectrum, and excluding those with serious character, thought, affective, or organic disorders. The latter will be discussed later.

We have described people with certain styles of thinking, feeling, relating to others, and concentrating, among other styles. As such, they comprise the range of normal human differences. Even those on the extremes—for example, a grade-1 Apollonian who is highly cognitive or a grade-5 Dionysian who is quite affect-oriented and compliant—may lead normal lives. We predict, however, that should such people undergo psychological stress, either internally or externally generated, they would be likely to decompensate in ways predictable for their character style.

The Apollonian probably will bind whatever uncomfortable affect he is feeling with obsessional rationalizing and compulsive rituals. The Dionysian will exaggerate the tendency for compliance and find new people to comply with in order to avoid thinking about old problems, and develop dramatic new affects to isolate and replace uncomfortable ones. Our point is that each group will have characteristic modes of neurotic decompensation, or they may never get into neurotic difficulty. The Apollonians tend to decompensate in the obsessive–compulsive direction, the Odysseans in the direction of alternating between periods of action and despair or depression, and the Dionysians in the direction of hysteria. These characteristic types of decompensation are represented in Figure 5–2 by the light, displaced triangles. In terms of the three aspects of the compulsive triad, the Apollonians tend to degenerate into rationalization, the Dionysians into compulsive compliance, and the Odysseans to fluctuate between compliance and depressive reflection.

CENTERING

This brings us to the concept of "centering" (see Figure 5–5). In subsequent chapters we will go through the uses of this perspective on personality differences in psychotherapeutic exploration. It is worth noting now, however, that as a rule we consider it a realistic goal for psychotherapy to help a person get back to the center of his characterological tendencies from a decompensated position. Looking at the structural diagram, Dionysians are encouraged to think more and do less in good psychotherapy. Some mixture of consolation and confrontation is recommended to help Odysseans deal with swings between action and despair which may have gotten out of hand.

The main point is that we try to help a person understand and accept his own personal style but to keep it within manageable limits. We never expect to make a hand-washing rationalist out of a Dionysian nor a seductive, dissociated complier out of an Apollonian. We hope to help people center on their own capacities and limitations.

The distinction between a characterological style and a neurosis has been explored increasingly with the growth of ego psychology in the psychoanalytic movement. Shapiro (1965) discusses some of these possibilities in his book, *Neurotic Styles*. Although he emphasizes the pathological rather than the adaptive aspects of the neurotically related styles, both aspects are conceptualized:

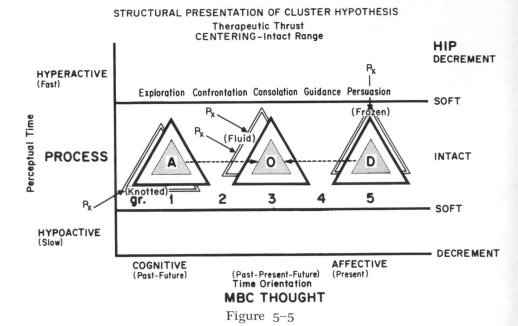

Figure 5-5

I do not mean to say that any single mode or style can describe all areas of an individual's functioning, but only that styles or modes may be found that are capable of describing general aspects of function (such as cognition, emotional experience and the like), modes that themselves will then be related and organized. Such consistencies of individual functioning as those between symptom and adaptive trait may be conceived as reflecting such general modes giving shape alike to symptom and nonsymptom, to defense against impulse and adaptive expression of impulse. They are presumably slow to change and therefore guarantee not only an individual's consistence but also his relative stability over long periods of time. (p. 4)

He goes on to describe four types of neurotic style: obsessive–compulsive, paranoid, hysterical, and impulsive. We see the obsessive–compulsive as he describes it as a decompensated Apollonian subgroup, and likewise the hysterics as decompensated Dionysians. Certain aspects of his descriptions are congenial with ours; others are not. For instance, in discussing the realm of affect for hysterics and obsessionals, he says:

In the hysterical style, for instance, affective experience virtually dominates the individual's existence. In the obsessive compulsive style on the other hand, affective experience as a whole shrinks . . . (p. 30)

We agree. Nonetheless, he contrasts obsessional and hysterical attention in a way which is not consistent with our experience. He describes the obsessional's attention as having "intense, sharp focus" (p. 27). He divorces from his discussion of the actual concentration, the constant effort required by an obsessional in the process of concentrating. We have observed that the attention of obsessionals is constantly labored.

He does discuss their attention to detail and their problem with distraction:

They concentrate and particularly do they concentrate on detail. (p. 27) Elements on the periphery of attention, the new or the surprising, that which can only be apprehended impressionistically—all these are only potentially distracting and disruptive to the obsessive compulsive, and they are avoided exactly by the intensity and the fixed narrowness of his preoccupation with his own idea or aim. (p. 30)

We observe that the obsessional is indeed always caught up in a pre-occupation with the periphery, in the struggle to keep it out of his focal attention. His very struggle with such "distractions" makes them an important aspect of his concentration. In describing the rigidity of the obsessional's thought process, Shapiro refers to the similar "stimulus bound" quality of patients with unspecified organic impairments:

What I am describing here is, of course, what we call "flexibility." I am suggesting that cognitive flexibility may be described as a mobility of atten-tion of this sort, a volitional mobility of attention. Now, we concluded before that obsessive-compulsive intellectual rigidity also was characterized by some special limitation of attention. Can we say that, notwithstanding the obvious disparity between the obsessive compulsive's and the brain-damaged person's rigidity, they have this feature in common: that both are characterized by some general loss or impairment of volitional mobility of attention? (pp. 26–27)

Again, we agree. Further, this aspect seems related to Shakow's (1971) Segmental Set Hypothesis regarding schizophrenia, which is one illness which may befall a deteriorating obsessional. Shakow argues that the fundamental lesion in schizophrenia involves an inability to maintain a major set:

By "major set" I mean, the difficulty in maintaining any state of readiness for response to a coming stimulus, the state which facilitates the optimal response called for by a given situation. . . . It would appear that the schizo-phrenic difficulty lies in not being able to keep to the major set and being drawn to adopting minor ones. (p. 309)

We cite this research on schizophrenia to support our thesis that the admittedly stimulus-bound and detail-conscious nature of obsessional attention represents not so much intensity of concentration as difficulty with it. It is labored concentration, always threatened by details which cannot be ignored easily.

The hysterics do not have such struggles. Shapiro aptly describes them:

They seem to feel as if they were virtually weightless and floating, attracted here, repelled there, captivated first by this and then by that. (p. 121)

They easily dissociate peripheral events without apparent effort. We attribute this to a capacity for intense focal and hypnotic-like concen-tration as distinct from the obsessional style. Here we disagree with Shapiro's statement that: "Hysterical cognition seems relatively lack-ing in sharp focus of attention." (p. 112) An hysteric's capacity to throw himself into new affects and behavior requires a kind of intense, receptive concentration, although it is not detailed or strenuous. We certainly agree with his description of hysterics as impressionable (p. 114). However, we question both his statement that hysterics are deficient in knowledge (p. 115), and his tired assertion that hysterics can safely be referred to by the pronoun "she." Our studies indicate no correlation between hypnotizability and gender, nor between type of neurotic decompensation and gender.

As a whole, then, it is clear that aspects of *Neurotic Styles* are quite consistent with the aims of our studies, including Shapiro's emphasis on the description of traits which are consistent with but not included in a specific neurotic pattern. Our major effort is to develop such an approach to the point where character style and neurotic style are separate but related areas.

SUMMARY

In terms of the compulsive triad model presented at the beginning of this chapter, certain predictable differences in an overall sense characterize Apollonians, Odysseans, and Dionysians. Apollonians emphasize rationalization and are relatively noncompliant—they value reason above all. Dionysians compulsively comply with external signals, whether presented in a formal hypnotic setting or not, and are frequently amnesic to the signals. They have little interest in rationalizing their behavior, however. Odysseans fluctuate between periods of intense activity and times of withdrawal and despair, alternating between compliance and rationalization. Then tend to value both reason and action, with the balance shifting back and forth during the course of their lifetimes.

We have presented our approach to systematizing and summarizing clinical data about personal attributes related to hypnotizability, as measured on the intact range on the HIP. The three clusters of attributes, Apollonian, Odyssean, and Dionysian, seem related to low, mid-range, and high performance on the Profile. In chapter 10 we will present the clinical data we have in support of this hypothesis. First we will review the pertinent literature relating hypnotizability to both personality characteristics and neurophysiology.

6

Review of the Literature: Hypnotizability and Personality

Any attempt to relate the hypnotizability to clusters of personality style and psychopathology must take into account the intense and frequently disappointing efforts in the last fifty years to relate hypnotizability to performance on a variety of psychological tests and clinical measures. A large and divided literature on the relationship between hypnotizability and personality characteristics does exist. Each tentative correlation seems more than matched by a failure to consistently relate an aspect of personality to trance capacity. This is surprising in view of the relative simplicity and stability of existing measures of hypnotizability. As David Rosenhan has said, ". . . it is nevertheless an odd situation that a trait as stable as hypnotizability should yield no stable correlates with other measurable dispositions." (Rosenhan 1969)

We have reviewed the literature on personality correlates of hypnotizability in order to identify areas which are consistent and inconsistent with our cluster hypothesis. Major contributions in this area have been made in recent decades as the concept of hypnotizability as a trait became firmly established. In this chapter we will review the literature relating this trait to various pencil-and-paper psychological tests in a normal population.

New evidence has recently been presented which supports the widely accepted hypothesis that the trait of hypnotizability varies among individuals but is relatively stable in a given individual over time. Morgan,

Johnson, and Hilgard obtained a test–retest correlation of .60 with a ten-year interval between administrations of the Stanford Hypnotic Susceptibility Scale, Form A—despite major changes in life circumstances of the subjects (Morgan et al. 1954). Such a relatively stable trait with such clear individual variance should surely be related to some other traits.

In broad strokes, the literature at first cites disappointing efforts to relate standard psychological tests to standard measures of hypnotizability. A more empirical, grounded, theory approach gradually yielded more results; several groups found that measures of hypnotic-like experience in normal life were positively correlated with hypnotizability. The research literature now demonstrates that good hypnotic subjects knowingly or unknowingly make frequent use of their trance capacity. This fact influences elements of their behavior and their style of experiencing events around them. The trend in research on hypnotizability and personality suggests that fruitful correlations most likely will emerge from personality measures which are grounded in aspects of the hypnotic experience.

Early Studies

In 1947 Brenman and Gill reviewed the literature on personality and hypnotizability and came to the following conclusion:

> It must be apparent even from this brief survey of the meager literature that there is neither clinical nor experimental data sufficient to draw any conclusions regarding either the personality characteristics of the good hypnotic subject or the psychiatric syndromes that are most susceptible to hypnosis. There exist reports of successful hypnosis in almost every nosological category, and there also are reports of utter failure in all. (Brenman and Gill 1947)

Two major reviews of the literature written twelve years apart later indicated a trend toward cautious optimism about correlations between personality traits and hypnotizability. Deckert and West (1963) noted a general correlation between hypnotizability and intelligence. Hilgard (1975) noted the development of four promising areas: "imagery, imaginative involvements (absorption), creativity, and cerebral function (especially hemispheric laterality)." We will review the neurophysiological data in chapter 7.

A wide variety of pencil-and-paper personality tests have been employed. Davis and Husband in 1931 compared a scale of hypnotic susceptibility which they had developed to a series of tests measuring intelligence, maladjustment, introversion, prejudice, and affectivity. Their findings were generally negative, with the exception of a .34 positive correlation between hypnotizability and intelligence, and a tendency for "introverted" females to be more hypnotizable. They used this data to deny Janet's assertion that hypnotizability is related to neurosis (Davis and Husband 1931).

Hypnotizability and Sociability

In the mid-1950s, Weitzenhoffer and Weitzenhoffer and also Barber utilized the Guilford-Zimmerman Temperament Survey and came up with conflicting findings. The Weitzenhoffers tested Charcot's assertion of a link between neuroticism and suggestibility, with negative results. They found no significant correlation between hypnotizability and the Guilford-Zimmerman scale in a population of two hundred college students (1958).

Barber did a similar study in a population of only eighteen college students. He found significant correlations between hypnotizability and such traits as ascendance, sociability, emotional stability, and objectivity, and a negative correlation with a trait he labeled "restrained." These findings led him to assert the "good guy" theory of hypnotizability, linking hypnotizability to desirable character traits (1956). However, serious questions must be raised about Barber's results, due to his small sample size and the Weitzenhoffers' contrasting results in a larger sample.

Barber later did a much larger study with college students who were given the Marlowe-Crowne Scale of Social Desirability, the Edwards Personal Preference Schedule, measuring personal needs such as autonomy and dominance, and the Jourard Self-Disclosure Scale. His findings were generally negative and he attributed the few significant correlations to chance in a large sample. He then turned to emphasizing the greater importance of interactional variables and the demand characteristics of the situation.

Levitt et al., in the early 1960s correlated results on the same scales—using the Guilford-Zimmerman Temperament Survey and the Edwards Personal Preference Inventory, among others—with the Stanford Hypnotic Susceptibility Scale. In a small sample they found that low-anxiety, high-dependency individuals were highly hypnotizable. However, the high-anxiety and low-dependency complementary group was not refractory. Thus they found that certain combinations of attributes had predictive value, although the converse combinations did not (Levitt and Brady 1963). Their suggestion that a pattern approach be taken—that is, looking for patterns or combinations of traits in correlation with hypnotizability—became an increasingly common theme in later literature.

In a second study Levitt et al. measured personality correlates of nonhypnotizability in a larger group. They noted the following:

The refractory students are less friendly, outgoing, credulous and tolerant of others, and more aggressive, dominant, independent, critical and suspicious. They are also more anxious and tend toward greater emotional instability. (Levitt et al. 1965)

These results nicely complemented the earlier study of Barber (1963) at the time he was espousing the "good guy" hypothesis of hypnotizability. Our data suggest that in the results of the Levitt study two groups were combined: those who were indeed emotionally unstable, and those with Apollonian characteristics, who were notably less credulous, tolerant of others, more dominant, independent, critical, and suspicious.

Several studies pursued the relationship between hypnotizability and interpersonal orientation. Bentler found consistent positive correlations between hypnotizability and subjects who described themselves as "docile, dependent"; "cooperative, overconventional"; and "responsible, hypernormal" (Bentler 1963). Roberts and Tellegen studied self- and group ratings in interpersonal trust in relation to the Harvard Group Scale of Hypnotic Susceptibility (Shor and Orne 1962). They tested a population of undergraduates who knew one another fairly well. The students who rated themselves as highly trusting proved to be very hypnotizable. However, being rated by others as very trusting did not indicate enhanced hypnotizability (Roberts and Tellegen 1973). There was some evidence that high hypnotizability was associated with perceiving oneself as trusting, dependent, cooperative, responsible, and nonanxious. Low hypnotizability was related to being aggressive, independent, critical, and anxious, as well as emotionally unstable.

The Maudsley Personality Inventory

A number of studies were done with the Maudsley Personality Inventory. Furneaux and Gibson (1961), associates of Eysenck, studied a population composed of fifty-five college students and forty-four adults, readers of a radical journal. To complicate their methodology, they dropped twenty-two subjects as "liars" on the basis of a lie scale which they administered. They found that the "liar" group was on the whole less hypnotizable. Among those labeled "honest" there was no simple correlation either with the well-known extroversion–introversion dimension, or with stability–neuroticism. However, they found stable extroverts and neurotic introverts relatively more hypnotizable than neurotic extroverts. These data added to the growing chorus of opinion that a single measure would not suffice; combinations of factors seem more productive in relating personality to hypnotizability.

The peculiar assortment of subjects in the Furneaux and Gibson study led other investigators to question their positive results (Hilgard and Lauer 1962). Evans (1963) also criticized the study: he reworked the data and questioned the separation of the group labeled "liars." He noted that other studies had not shown significant differences in the hypnotizability of those labeled "liars." Recalculating the results with the "liars" group added no significant findings, although there was a trend relating suggestibility to stablity and introversion—a result which conflicts with the original study.

A later study by Vingoe (1966) utilizing the Eysenck Personality Inventory was negative, although Vingoe noted that extroverts were more willing to participate in the experiment and were better predictors of their own hypnotizability. Along similar personality dimensions, Duke (1968) reported no correlation between hypnotizability and a scale of inner–other directedness based on David Reisman's work.

Likewise, Silver (1973) found no relationship between hypnotizability and the use of repression as a defense, although he did find that a relatively "bright" mood was related. Silver speculated that relative happiness might be a significant predictor, especially just before the assessment of hypnotizability, but also as a trait. His study supports the idea that hypnotizability is consistent with general mental health. This reflects our own finding that those who are significantly depressed are not hypnotizable.

The Minnesota Multiphasic Personality Inventory (MMPI)

It was inevitable that hypnotizability studies would be done with the widely used MMPI. As with previous efforts, the results were mixed, at best. In 1950 Sarbin published a long paper in which he discussed his concept of hypnosis as a role-taking behavior. In it he briefly mentioned a study with seventy undergraduates in which he utilized the MMPI and unstated criteria of hypnotizability. He discarded approximately half the subjects as nonhypnotizable and reported that the Hysteria scale of the MMPI significantly differentiated somnambulists from those capable of a light trance.

Although the technique of dropping half the subjects may be considered questionable, Sarbin may have happened upon his interesting finding by doing so; dropping those subjects we classify as decrements, and leaving the subjects with intact moderate and high hypnotizability. The role-theory portion of the paper does not seem to take into account the fact that a trance may occur easily without formal induction. And calling hypnosis a role does not account for the significance of individual variance in hypnotizability.

An earlier study by Eysenck contradicts this finding. He tested sixty subjects equally divided as to sex and a clinical diagnosis of hysteria or nonhysteria (either normal or depressive). He found no distinction in hypnotizability among the groups, noting only that highly hypnotizable people tended to be more intelligent. Utilizing various behavioral measures of suggestibility, he also isolated factors designated as primary and secondary suggestibility. Primary suggestibility consisted of ideomotor measures, and was described as more reliable (Eysenck 1943). The usual ambiguities attending diagnosis and the role of experimenter expectation seem especially applicable to this study.

Wilcox and Faw (1959), utilizing the MMPI and personal diaries, found that highly hypnotizable subjects were on the whole better adjusted. They found a group among the less well adjusted but hypnotizable portion which scored high on the Hy scale of the MMPI. The less hypnotizable group showed signs of depression, insecurity, and distraction by bizarre thoughts and feelings. In spite of these findings, no relationship was found between hypnotizability and diagnosis of neurosis, or behavior or thought disorder (Faw and Wilcox 1958). We expect this last finding; their study merges subjects having intact but low hypnotizability with those more seriously impaired individuals who would probably have decrement profiles on the HIP. The results of the Wilcox and Faw study do imply a general relationship between hypnotizability and mental health.

Subsequent studies with the MMPI were not so encouraging. Schulman and London (1963) found no impressive correlations between the MMPI and the Stanford Hypnotic Susceptibility Scale, but they noted a tendency for more susceptible people to score as less aggressive and more compliant. They concluded with the refreshing suggestion: "It is time to stop doing studies like this one and to seek a fresh approach."

Not heeding this advice, Zuckerman et al. (1967) found no significant correlations between the MMPI and the Harvard Group Scale. They found, as did Silver, that emotional state was relevant. In this case highly hypnotizable subjects were as a whole less hostile. They argued from this study that affect states are more important than affect traits in measuring hypnotizability. Their conclusion seems somewhat hasty in view of the ambiguous distinction between an affect state and a trait —certainly many affective states are characteristic of people even if not picked up as such on the MMPI. Thus, although several earlier studies with the MMPI seemed promising, more recent work with it and other standard personality measures indicates the difficulty of establishing reliable correlations with these instruments.

Hilgard and Lauer employed a different personality scale, the California Personality Inventory (CPI) in a population of more than 200 undergraduates and compared the results with the SHSS. They found no reliable correlation and pointed to promising work with questionnaires to measure hypnotic-like experiences, as more useful than evaluation with standard paper-and-pencil measures (Hilgard and Lauer 1962).

Hypnotizability and Hypnotic-Like Experiences

Some interesting results have come from this direction, notably the work of Shor et al., Ås et al., and Tellegen and Atkinson. In various ways they constructed scales of experiences in ordinary life which are reminiscent of the trance state and related such experiences to formal measures of hypnotizability.

In an early study Shor (1960) found that undergraduates quite commonly reported hypnotic-like experiences. He and others then administered a questionnaire including inquiries about the intensity of the "hypnotic-like" experiences. They found no convincing correlations between hypnotizability and the frequency of occurrence of hypnotic-like experiences, but they did find impressive positive correlations with the intensity of such experiences. They then made observational measures of hypnotizability and found that the intensity of hypnotic-like experiences correlated especially well with those subjects who proved to be highly hypnotizable. They went on to assert: "It follows further that multiple correlation composed of both ability and nonability factors would predict hypnotizability along the entire continuum of hypnotizability" (Shor et al. 1962). (This is the kind of approach we are attempting to employ in studying hypnotizability in relationship to nonhypnotizability.) Then, utilizing their concept of "plateau" hypnotizability—that is, that some training is needed in order to reach reliably a given subject's optimal state—Shor ran a complex series of correlation studies on a population of people skewed in the direction of much experience with hypnosis and high hypnotizability. Citing Rosenthal's studies of the effects of expectancy on outcome, Shor noted that it is not unlikely that the investigator's particular interest might lead to false correlations through sampling errors or through variations in the interactions between the experimenter and subject.

They expected no correlation between personality characteristics measured by the MMPI, other tests, and hypnotizability. They discovered, in fact, no significant correlations with any of the measured personality traits. By their own description the population studied was relatively highly hypnotizable, which may have obscured differences; one would see only the variance between the moderates and highs rather than between the lows and highs. Surprisingly, they found a negative correlation between hypnotizability and intelligence, as measured by the Wechsler-Bellevue Intelligence Scale Form II, and a positive correlation between hypnotizability and female gender. They did, however, confirm their earlier observation of a clear correlation between personal hypnotic-like experiences and hypnotizability (Shor et al. 1966).

A study of cognitive control by Goldberger and Wachtel (1973) provided independent confirmation of one aspect of Shor's studies. They found a high tolerance for unrealistic experience and a high resistance to interference in the more hypnotizable individuals. Orne, however, sought to limit the concept of the applicability of hypnotizability to the general life experience of the good subject. He denied the existence of a general tendency toward compliance among good hypnotic subjects and cited as an example a study in which he asked individuals who had previously been hypnotized to mail postcards back to him on a daily basis. He found no relationship between hypnotizability and the number of postcards returned. He also found good subjects somewhat less punctual for appointments than poor ones.

Orne proposed that the crucial leverage in hypnosis is the capacity to create distortions of perception and memory which then can lead to changes in behavior rather than a tendency to comply (Orne 1966). His findings are interesting but one wonders about the demand character-istics of the experimental situation. Our experience is that highly hyp-notizable individuals are quite sensitive to subtle cues: is it possible that Orne's individuals somehow sensed that excessive compliance was not encouraged? Time is another consideration in reviewing these experiments. In our experience, highly hypnotizable individuals tend to throw themselves into a succession of activities with intensity. Orne's subjects may have begun complying with signals from other people. What he observed may have been a shift in compliance rather than the lack of it.

Ås took a similar approach in studying the relationship between scores on the SHSS and the personal experiences questionnaire admin-istered to fifty male undergraduates. He found significant correlations which indicated that the more hypnotizable students had a greater number of experiences in four areas: 1) "Peak experiences," 2) "ex-periences of unusual states," 3) "wish to indulge in emotions and sen-sations with the feeling of just letting go," and 4) "the feeling that by and large, other people are to be trusted." Ås noted that composite scores of experience items correlated more significantly than any individual experience (Ås 1962). A factor analysis of a similar study on a larger population of female undergraduates yielded two factors, one dealing with the sustaining of the suggested effect over a short period of time, and the second involving a capacity for psychological change and social "influenceability" (Lauer 1962).

The studies of Ås, Lauer, and Shor yielded promising indications that a measure of subjective experience of trance-like states is related to formally measured hypnotizability. As the dependent variables be-came more flexible and closely related to the phenomena measured by the independent variable, hypnotizability, the results improved. But this was not true uniformly. Derman and London attempted to replicate some of the findings by administering a questionaire drawn from the work of Shor and Ås, along with the Harvard Group Scale, to some 400 undergraduates. In spite of finding no impressive correlations, they considered the personal experience study promising. They concluded with an idea so simple that it is often overlooked: "If one wishes to assess and understand hypnotic susceptibility, the more powerful approach may be to examine hypnotic susceptibility directly" (Derman and London 1965).

Hypnotizability and Imaginative Involvement

A major recent work in this direction is Josephine Hilgard's *Personality and Hypnosis: A Study of Imaginative Involvement* (1970). She was interested in discovering early-life developmental experiences which correlated with later hypnotizability. She employed intensive interviews which were later correlated with the results of the Stanford Hypnotic Susceptibility Scale. She found the capacity for deep imaginative involvement particularly important:

> We found that the hypnotizable person was capable of a deep involvement and almost total immersion in an activity, in one or more imaginative feeling areas of experience—reading a novel, listening to music, having an ecstatic experience of nature, or engaging in absorbing adventures of body or mind. (Hilgard 1970)

Utilizing a retrospective approach, Hilgard went on to speculate that certain patterns of family involvement may allow for the development of hypnotizability. She found such patterns in her more highly hypnotizable subjects. She discussed three major developmental factors; the first was an early deep involvement of a noncompetitive nature, such as reading, or other experiences which challenge the imagination. The second factor was a history of punishment given in a firm but helpful manner by the parent. Some willingness on the part of the subject to submit to impartial authority was also involved in this factor. The third factor was a strong history of identification with the opposite-sex parent.

There are always problems with retrospective analyses; it is never clear which came first. Did the inherent trance capacity influence family development, or vice versa? Such studies as Hilgard's cannot resolve this issue, which is further complicated by the fact that older children are in general more hypnotizable as a group than adults. Only after adolescence do relatively stable trance patterns emerge (Morgan 1973). Nonetheless, Hilgard's findings regarding imaginative involvement do suggest that certain styles of interacting with other people and with the sensory world are associated with high hypnotizability.

Finally, an interesting study by Tellegen and Atkinson, utilizing a personal experiences questionnaire approach, lends support to Hilgard's description of the importance of imaginative involvement. They reported that "absorption," defined as a "capacity for absorbed and self-altering attention" (Tellegen and Atkinson 1974), was highly correlated with hypnotic susceptibility. The questionnaire which they developed covered such areas as absorption, dissociation, trust, impulsiveness, and relaxation, and they administered it to 500 female undergraduates. They compared scores on this questionnaire with the modified version of the Harvard Group Scale of Hypnotic Susceptibility and did a complex factor analysis which indicated that absorption was the most highly correlated factor with hypnotizability. The absorption factor was statistically distinct from the introversion–extroversion and neuroticism dimensions. They described the trait as an ability to absorb oneself in perception, a kind of heightened reality in what is observed:

We suggest, in a similar vein, that the attention described in absorption items is a "total" attention, involving a *full commitment of available perceptual, motoric, imaginative, and ideational resources to a unified representation of the attentional object.* (p. 276)

This trait sounds consistent with our description of the predominant mode of attention (focal) and method of learning (affiliation) for Dionysians. This ability to throw oneself into something, to involve oneself intensely in an experience, is part of what we call the trance state. It is a capacity often utilized, though unrecognized as such, by those individuals with high trance capacity.

SUMMARY

It can hardly be said that the results of this psychological literature attempting to relate personality traits to hypnotizability are unambiguous. Nevertheless, certain trends do seem confirmed. High hypnotizability has been related to a generally "bright" mood, and a somewhat naive and trusting approach to people, as well as to emotional stability. Low hypnotizability has been associated with being less outgoing, and rather more critical and suspicious. Hypnotizability has been associated with hysteria, and also found unassociated with hysteria. Combinations of attributes such as stability and extroversion, along with lessened anxiety, have been related to hypnotizability. The occurrence of hypnotic-like experiences in ordinary life, a capacity for imaginative involvement, and an ability to experience absorption have all been related to high hypnotizability.

The research that we have cited has focused mainly on personality attributes of highs rather than lows, but it does point to some useful distinctions as the dependent variables have come to approximate aspects of the trance experience itself. It seems clear from this literature that highly hypnotizable individuals experience other aspects of their life using the trance mode and that this experience in turn effects their personality structures. While our cluster hypothesis regarding the attributes of the highs, mid-range, and lows goes considerably farther than the data cited may allow, in general this body of research is not inconsistent with our hypothesis.

We will now review the clinical literature relating hypnotizability and psychopathology.

7

Review of the Literature: Neurophysiological Aspects of Hypnosis

Lateral Eye Movement and Hypnotizability

There is a growing and promising literature relating various aspects of neurophysiological functioning and hypnotizability. In 1969 Bakan reported a positive correlation between hypnotizability and a measure called laterality of eye movement which had been discovered by Day (1967). In this measure, the subject was placed opposite the examiner who had a neutral background behind him. The subject was asked a series of questions and the examiner noted the initial lateral deviation of gaze as the subject began to respond to the question. In general, two-thirds of the subjects characteristically looked to either the left or the right more than 70 percent of the time. They were thus characterized as "right lookers" or "left lookers." This measure theoretically was related to the hemisphere which is used more frequently or given priority by the subject. Predictably, right hemispheric priority, associated with "left looking" was correlated with higher hypnotizability in Bakan's study.

Gur and Reyher (1973) tested the hypothesis that since left lookers seemed more prone to a "right hemispheric" style of interaction, involving emotions and subjective feelings, they might do better with an induction procedure tailored to this manner of thinking. Conversely, right lookers might score higher on a hypnosis scale constructed to emphasize a more intellectual, cognitive style. This study did not replicate Bakan's earlier findings in that, when they used the standard Harvard Group Scale of Hypnotic Susceptibility (HGSHS) (Shor and Orne 1962), they did not find a significant difference in the hypnotizability of left and right lookers. They found that the specially tailored scales did not increase hypnotizability beyond what was measured by the HGSHS. The scale tailored for left lookers, although mildly enhancing the performance of left lookers, reduced the performance of right lookers. The scale tailored for right lookers was similar in having little affect on the group for which it was designed, and in reducing the response of the opposite group.

In a later study, Gur and Gur (1974) studied the effects of handedness, sex, eyedness, and also lateral gaze in relation to hypnotizability. Their studies supported Bakan's findings that left lookers were more hypnotizable than those who looked to the right. In studying handedness, they failed to support an earlier finding of Bakan's (1970) that left-handed subjects fall into the extremes of hypnotizability, either high or low. They noted that left-handed individuals who were also left-eyed; that is, who using their left eye as the preferential visual focus for lining up objects, tended to be more hypnotizable than those subjects who were left-handed but right-eyed. They also found that the significance of the relationship between left-looking and higher hypnotizability was supported in right-randed males and left-handed females. It should be noted that the results for left-handed females were a "mirror image" of those for right-handed males; that is, higher hypnotizability for right-handed males was correlated with eye movements to the right.

Thus, Gur's findings support the lateralization of brain function hypothesis in relation to hypnotizability and contribute to the idea of dividing data in terms of sex and handedness. Their work also implies that the completeness of lateralization may be an important factor in hypnotizability. That is, individuals with some incomplete division of brain function may prove to be less hypnotizable.

The "state/trait" controversy has entered the field of eye laterality research as it has for hypnotizability (Sarbin 1972). Kinsbourne (1972) reported that deviation of gaze seemed related to the nature of the question under consideration. Among right-handed subjects, a task which called for verbal cognition elicited eye movements to the right, whereas those tasks involving spatial integration produced a prevalence of eye movements to the left. This content distinction did not hold up among left-handed subjects, suggesting to the investigator that verbal and spatial intellectual capacities are more evenly distributed among right and left hemispheres in left-handed individuals.

In a well-designed study Gur (1975) and Gur et al. (1975) reported a model for reconciling the argument between researchers such as Bakan and Day, who view lateral deviation of gaze as a trait representing hemispheric preference in an individual, and Kinsbourne, who views laterality of gaze as reflecting the nature of the question. They found that the experimenter's position in relation to the subject was the crucial issue. With the experimenter facing the subject, as in Bakan's experiment (1969), the subject demonstrated a characteristic deviation of gaze regardless of the question. However, when the experimenter was seated behind the subject and eye movement was recorded by hidden camera, deviation of gaze was in general more closely related to the spatial or verbal nature of the question—reflecting Kinsbourne's work. They postulated that the experimenter seated in front of the subject was a situation of confrontation arousing high anxiety which forced the subject to fall back upon his characteristic or most comfortable cognitive style. The situation described by Kinsbourne (1972), in which the experimenter sat behind the subject, may have allowed for maximum task attentiveness and therefore elicited a deviation of gaze reflecting maximum activation of the involved hemisphere. This clarification of the situation was accepted by Kinsbourne (1974).

Thus lateral deviation of gaze indicates hemispheric preference in an individual as a trait, and may also reflect a state in which a subject reflects in the deviation of his gaze the preferential involvement of the contralateral hemisphere. The failure of Gur and Reyher (1973) to demonstrate major changes in hypnotizability based on the modifications they made in the induction procedures adds weight to the argument that hypnotizability is a trait rather than a state. The connection between laterality of eye movement and hypnotizability may well be a reliable finding which is confounded by state variables such as position of the experimenter.

However, Erlichman et al. (1974) failed to replicate Day's, Bakan's, and Kinsbourne's findings of a relationship between initial lateral direction of gaze and type of question (verbal versus spatial) in a study that did not involve hypnosis. On this basis Erlichman et al. questioned the hypothesis that lateral eye movements reflect cerebral-hemispheric task differentiation. They did note that verbal questions elicited significantly more downward gaze movements than spatial questions. Presuming that the trance experience has more to do with somatosensory and spatial awareness than verbal integration, this finding implies a relationship between downward eye movement and nonhypnotic experiences. It would not be inconsistent with our observation that the capacity to look up while closing one's eyes (the eye roll) seems significantly associated with trance capacity in a normal, psychologically healthy population (Spiegel 1972), although the eye roll is a measure of capacity rather than frequency of upward eye movement.

In review of clinical data on the lateralization of conversion symptoms, Stern (1977) confirmed an old observation of a higher incidence of left-sided over right-sided sensory and motor alterations. He noted that this occurred regardless of handedness, thereby arguing against the "convenience" theory that the difference could be accounted for by subjects choosing to impair the functioning of the functionally less important nondominant side. This work lent support to the notion of differential cerebral lateralization of function in relation to affect. In addition, much of the early work on hypnosis grew out of interest in hypnotic treatment of hysterical conversion symptoms (Ellenberger 1970).

The Measurement of Alpha Activity

These behavioral observations lead one to expect promising results utilizing measures such as electroencephalograph alpha activity. There have been several reports of a positive correlation between EEG alpha activity and the hypnotic state. Nowlis and Rhead (1968) reported a positive correlation between the presence of EEG alpha rhythm and hypnotic capacity. It should be noted that their subjects were in the resting state and had not been given instructions for a trance induction at the time of the EEG measurements. This study suggested that the crucial variable in relation to alpha was the capacity to experience hypnosis, rather than the formal induction of a trance state.

The study was consistent with the report of London, Hart, and Leibovitz (1969) who correlated the presence of EEG alpha with hypnotic capacity regardless of whether the subject was given any instructions. Bakan and Svorad (1969) reported a negative correlation between resting EEG alpha and right eye movements. They also found a significant negative correlation between hypnotic capacity and right eye movements. Travis et al. (1973) found that a matched control group given hypnotic instructions showed no greater signs of enhancement of alpha activity than a group given similar enhancement training without a trance induction.

These results, although negative, gave support to the trait idea of hypnotizability. Subjects were selected on the basis of "abundance of alpha emitted during the first reinforcement practice session." To the extent that the capacity to produce alpha is related to hypnotizability we can presume that the experimenters chose subjects of equal hypnotic capacity and demonstrated that a formal induction was not necessary to evoke whatever trance capacity the subject had.

Morgan, MacDonald, and Hilgard (1971) developed an alpha laterality score determined by comparing alpha from the right and left hemispheres. They found higher alpha activity in highly hypnotizable subjects but attributed some of the variance in alpha activity in different hemispheres to the nature of the task. That is, they found that analytic tasks stimulated proportionately less alpha activity in the left hemisphere and spatial imagery and music tasks stimulated relatively less alpha in the right hemisphere. They pointed out, however, that differences in the difficulty of the tasks might be responsible for some of the variance. Their work raised the question of whether various measures of lateralization of function might be related to the task before the subject rather than to a characteristic emphasis on the function of one or the other hemisphere.

In a later study (Morgan et al. 1974), the same group replicated earlier findings and added a more difficult music task, presumably a right hemispheric function. Nonetheless a preponderance of right over left alpha was indicated, implying more left hemispheric involvement. They attributed this finding to the high difficulty of the task. In view of the previously discussed connection between spatial imagination and hypnosis, they also found that the overall proportion of right hemispheric alpha elicited during hypnosis was comparable to that found during nonhypnotic spatial tasks.

Sensory-Evoked Responses

Galbraith et al. (1972) studied sensory-evoked response in relation to hypnotizability. They found a consistent relationship between hypnotizability and the capacity to produce a visually evoked response to an appropriate rather than irrelevant stimulus. They found similar results for auditory-evoked responses. They used these results to discuss the selective attention processes involved in hypnotizability.

The present results also have important implications concerning the mechanism of hypnotic susceptibility. Assuming that larger evoked response amplitudes imply increased attention as the majority of studies seem to implicate, it would appear that subjects high in hypnotic susceptibility selectively attend to relevant information. That is, they appear to comply with an externally imposed task (flashes, etc.). The subjects low in hypnotic susceptibility on the other hand appear to do just the opposite. Their larger evoked response amplitudes to an irrelevant evoking stimulus suggest that they tend to pay attention to the distractors. (p. 512)

This description is consonant with our discussion of hypnosis in terms of focal and peripheral awareness. It provides some experimental support for our hypothesis that Dionysians are expert at mobilizing their focal attention and minimizing their peripheral awareness and that Apollonians always tend to maintain their scanning awareness, even while concentrating. This data is also consistent with the research data we have cited by Tellegen and Atkinson (1974) regarding the relationship between absorption and high hypnotizability.

Cerebral Lateralization

The work of Galin and his group, although not specifically related to hypnotizability, is clearly relevant to this field, since they explored neurophysiological bases for differences in cognitive style and psychological functioning. They involved themselves in the eye movement research by studying the eye movement responses of individuals with different vocations (Day 1967). They compared ceramicists and lawyers in an effort to contrast individuals who use predominantly spatial versus verbal cognitive functions. They found no significant differences in lateral eye movement between the two groups, but they did find that the ceramicists made more upward movements and fewer downward movements than lawyers. Furthermore they found that both groups responded to verbal questions with significantly more downward eye movements than to spatial questions (Galin and Ornstein 1974). Erlichman et al. repeated this finding (1974).

This study also lends support to our hypothesis that the eye-roll measurement—that is, the capacity to look up while closing one's eyes —is significantly related to hypnotizability in an intact population. The trance state seems to tap the kinesthetic and sensory modes represented by nonverbal responses. Upward eye movements were found more prevalent in responses given by individuals who work with three-dimensional spatial configurations than with words. It must be noted that looking up is different from the eye roll itself. The tendency to look up rather than down may have some connection with the eye-roll process.

Galin's group studied various EEG measures as well. They found some relationship between the ratio of right to left hemispheric activity. The ration was higher by a significant margin in verbal and arithmetic tasks as opposed to spatial tasks; since the hemisphere primarily engaged in the specialized cognitive activity demonstrated proportionately lower EEG activity (Doyle et al. 1974; Galin and Ornstein 1972). This group also studied evoked potentials in relation to lateral brain asymmetry and found a similar lateral brain asymmetry in right/left ratio of evoked potential, reflecting verbal versus spatial tasks. However, they found that the lateralization hypothesis was better supported by alpha asymmetry in EEG (Galin and Ellis 1975).

In a conceptual article Galin (1974) reviews the literature on cerebral lateralization and speculates on a relationship between these findings and psychological functioning. Utilizing data from commissurotomy studies he draws this distinction:

It is important to emphasize that what most characterizes the hemispheres is not that they are specialized to work with different types of material (the left with words and the right with spatial forms); rather, each hemisphere is specialized for a different cognitive style; the left for an analytical logical mode for which words are an excellent tool and the right for a holistic Gestalt mode which happens to be particularly suitable for spatial relations as well as music. (p. 573)

He emphasizes the coexistence of these two different modes or functioning hemispheres and cites our varying recognition of two coincident cognitive processes as a model for understanding in neurophysiological terms what has been referred to as unconscious process and repression:

But we have good reason to believe that the experience of mental unity is to some extent an illusion, resulting in fact from exactly the conventions of language and law that Sherrington cites "The strength of this conviction (of unity) is no assurance of its truth." One of the most striking features of the commissurotomy syndrome is that the patients (at least the hemisphere that can be interviewed) do not experience their obvious duality; they do not notice anything missing after the operation. (p. 576)

There is a striking parallel between these commissurotomy patients with their obvious and unsynthesized duality, and hysterical patients we have seen with what is called the multiple personality syndrome. Such patients experience themselves as being either one or the other of two or more personalities and do not consider it strange that one or the other seems to occupy their body at any given time. They may have no memory on a conscious level of what occurred when the other personality was "out." One personality may be harsh, hostile and unabashedly, sexually provocative and the other may be meek, dependent, and reticent. All the patients that we have seen with multiple personality syndrome have been highly hypnotizable and this dissociative capacity is clearly related to their multiple personality syndrome. Without exception they have been able to switch from one personality to another utilizing the hypnotic state.

Thus it makes sense to us to extrapolate from Galin's speculations to the idea that trance capacity is involved in this mediation between right and left hemispheric functions. *La belle indifference*, associated with hysteria, may be related to the anosognosia of stroke patients with right parietal lobe lesions. Furthermore, lateralization of brain function seems relevant to the occurrence of hysterical symptoms. Galin cites Ferenczi's observation that there is a prevalence of left-sided hysterical symptoms. This clinical impression has been documented by Stern (1977).

Galin formulates that we are an amalgam of our relatively independent right and left hemispheric functioning; that some fairly precise ideas about cognitive style can be gleaned in relationship to the relative priority given the functioning of one or the other hemisphere. There is an obvious parallel to the personality styles we have described as Apollonian, Odyssean, and Dionysian. We conceive that Apollonians clearly and primarily function in the left hemispheric mode emphasizing verbal, mathematical, and analytic processes. On the other extreme, Dionysians favor their right hemispheric functioning, emphasizing what Galin would call holistic and Gestalt modes. We picture the Odysseans as being a mid-range between the two extremes and utilizing a more balanced input from both right and left hemisphere.

Schwartz et al. (1975) have added to the research in lateral eye movements by adding the emotional/nonemotional dimension to spatial and verbal distinctions. They found that emotionally laden questions elicited left eye movements significantly more often, indicating right hemispheric activation and that spatial emotional questions elicited the most left eye movement; while verbal nonemotional questions elicited the most right eye movement. Their work adds to the picture implicating the right hemisphere in emotional as well as spatial tasks. There have been a number of clinical reports which emphasize this cognitive–affective distinction. Flor-Henry (1976) reported lateralized EEG spikes in patients with serious thought and affective disorders. Predictably he found subtle EEG foci in the left hemispheres of patients with thought disorders, and right hemispheric foci in patients with affective disorders.

In a detailed review of 160 patients with right- or left-sided hemispheric lesions, Gainotti (1972) found that patients with left-sided lesions tended to demonstrate signs of the "catastrophic reaction" involving depression and anxiety, especially those with serious aphasia. Those with right-sided lesions demonstrated the "indifference reaction" involving relative disinterest in or denial of their symptoms, and neglect of the contralateral half of the body and of space.

Metzig et al. (1976) utilized an intriguing measure of lateral asymmetry, involving the degree of rotation of the right versus the left thumb when placed in opposition with the fifth digit, to distinguish between bipolar and unipolar manic depressives. Statistically, right-handed subjects who demonstrated greater rotation capacity of the right thumb than the left when placed in opposition to the fifth digit proved more likely to have bipolar manic depressive illness. Those who showed greater rotation of the left thumb were far more likely to have unipolar depressive illness. Normal controls had equal left and right thumb opposition. Thus the differential distribution of thumb rotation in the two groups as compared with normals suggests some neurophysiological overemphasis on right hemispheric functioning in the unipolar patients.

These experiments are difficult to evaluate; studies of dysfunction or ablation of parts of the brain really demonstrate not what the affected area does, but what the rest of the brain does in the absence of appropriate input from the affected area. Nonetheless, these studies do provide some evidence suggesting that emotion, particularly elation, may be more a function of the intact right hemisphere and that depressive preoccupation with dysfunction is enhanced by left hemispheric impairment. While hardly clearcut, these data lend some support to our speculation that among individuals with right hemispheric dysfunction, decompensation involves an important affective component, although that component may be expressed as denial or indifference. Individuals with left hemispheric dysfunction may show decompensation involving difficulties such as ververbalization, rumination, and thought disorder.

"Hand Clasp" and Hemispheric Preference

We have found an interesting correlation between hypnotizability as measured by the HIP and a possible measure of hemispheric preference which we describe as the "hand clasp" (Spiegel, H. et al. 1978). Subjects were asked to clasp their hands together, interlocking fingers while holding their hands in front of their chest. The examiner noted which thumb and corresponding fingers were on top in this position. Every patient had a characteristic choice in the hand clasp, noting that clasping hands in the opposite manner felt "awkward." Handedness was then determined by asking each subject which hand he preferentially used for motor activities and whether he had ever been switched as a child.

Of the 946 patients studied, approximately half clasped their hands in such a manner as to favor the dominant hand. A statistical association was found between lower hypnotizability and right-handed subjects who placed their right hand on top in the hand clasp. Highly hypnotizable subjects were statistically likely to have a nondominant hand clasp. There was also a weak but statistically significant, positive association between eye-roll score and type of hand clasp in the direction of more nondominant hand clasps among those with higher eye rolls. We hypothesized that the hand clasp measurement indicates a preference for the functioning of the hemisphere contralateral to the hand on top. Thus, the association of this hand clasp phenomenon with hypnotizability is consistent with the related hypothesis that the capacity for hypnosis is a sign of preference for right hemispheric functioning, a concept which has considerable support in the literature cited.

Pribram's Studies: Sensory Input Redundancy

The hemispheric lateralization hypotheses have been best studied in relation to hypnotizability, but there is other intriguing work relating brain function and individual differences. Pribram (1961, 1969a, 1969b) explored the possibility that input whch alters the redundancy of sensory input systems may account for differences among individuals along dimensions such as "effective–affective" and "esthetic–ethical." His data indicated that decreasing circuit redundancy provides the organism with a relative insulation from new input data and enhances its capacity to make choices, or to organize the data on its own terms. This mode of integration provides an increased number of alternatives in processing the new data, a style which Pribram likened to Piaget's concept of assimilation (Piaget 1954). In contrast, a mechanism which increases circuit redundancy also increases vulnerability to new input and decreases critical decision-making opportunities, a process more like Piaget's accommodation. Pribram's data indicated that posterior-temporal cortical input tended to decrease sensory redundancy, and frontal-limbic input to increase it.

It is conceivable that differences in cognitive style may reflect or be related to a predominance of a) redundancy inhibition with an emphasis on perceiving alternatives (Apollonians), or b) redundancy enhancement with a higher vulnerability to the influence of input (Dionysians).

In a later paper, Pribram and McGuinness (1975) related these findings to the difference between "activation" and "arousal." They described arousal as the availability of channel capacity for processing information, influenced by the amygdala. Activation, on the other hand, represented a more specific somatomotor attention mediated by the basal ganglia. The hippocampus seems to mediate between the two systems, with a tension existing between "chunking"—that is, increasing redundancy and lumping together new information—and "parsing," or categorizing. This concept may also allow for integration of recent work on neurotransmitters. Pribram and McGuinness suggested that the arousal of redundancy inhibiting system was predominantly serotonergic, and that the activation system with its connections in the basal ganglia logically would be dopaminergic.

There seems to be some parallels between the "arousal" concept and normal scanning awareness as well as between "activation" and hypnotic attention. The close affinity between somatosensory experiences and the induction of trance is compatible with the relation between activation and the somatomotor system as described by Pribram.

In summary, we speculate that the highly hypnotizable individual is more prone to input from the frontal-limbic system and the basal ganglia, employing enhancement of redundancy in processing sensory input. Lows may be more prone to employ posterior-temporal connections and the amygdala, thereby diminishing redundancy and vulnerability to new input, and increasing critical review of alternative choices. We have absolutely no data to support these speculations of a relationship between hypnotizability and the alteration of redundancy systems; nonetheless, there seems to be sufficient convergence of concepts from related fields that the relationship deserves comment.

MacLean's "Triune Brain" Concept

MacLean (1977) postulated the "triune brain" with "three quite different mentalities," two of which lack the power of speech. In hierarchical terms he identified reptilian complex, paleomammalian (limbic system), and neomammalian patterns. He further postulated corresponding forms of mentation: protomentation, i.e., drives and impulses; emotomentation, i.e., "cerebral processes underlying what are popularly recognized as emotions"; and ratiomentation. He speculated that three corresponding patterns of time and space awareness exist. In a metaphorical sense "the reptilian brain provides the basic plots and actions; —the limbic brain influences emotionally the developments of the plots; while the neomammalian brain has the capacity to expound the plots and emotions in as many ways as there are authors." Since words are not adequate to intercommunicate among these levels, we continuously grapple with the head–heart dilemma.

This representation of brain function in some ways may be an oversimplification; it nevertheless provides a plausible neural basis for our clinical observation of a Dionysian–Odyssean–Apollonian spectrum which roughly parallels the reptilian, limbic, and neomammalian patterns of integration.

Greenberg: Reticular Flexibility and Eye Roll

Greenberg (1977) postulated a "biological basis of trance capacity." The eye roll, up-gaze, and arm levitation involve skeletal muscles. The eye roll sign is especially interesting to him:

The motor nuclei for control of the extra-ocular muscles are located in the brain stem, as is the motor nucleus which is involved in control of the levator palpebrae. Although certain integrative motor neurons for eye movement are located in the motor cortex, there is a great deal of sub-cortical integration of eye movement. In particular, the medial longitudinal fasciculus (MLF), which receives contributions from the vestibular subsystem and from the Reticular Activating System (RAS) plays an important role. In addition, the superior colliculi appear to integrate eye-movements sub-cortically and receive significant reticular afferents. Clearly, as well as the up-gaze and eye-roll movements can be conceptualized by third-order neurons in the cortex, the functional capacity cannot exceed that permitted by reticular integration in the brain stem. In other words, *it is herein postulated that the complex movements of up-gaze and eye-roll have a final common integrative component within the mid-brain reticulum acting on the oculo-motor nuclei. It is this integrative factor which may reflect a general capacity of the reticular system for flexibility and which also may account for a biological basis for limbic-thalamic integration.* By reticular flexibility is meant the capacity of the RAS to shift focal attention sharply on one or two areas, and to do so rapidly. It also may reflect the capacity for rapid integration of externally suggested movements by means of flexible reticular function. Once the concept of levitation has gained entry into the midtemporal, and perhaps parietal, cortex, its rapid transfer to the effector neuron complex may very well hinge on reticular activation which fosters such transfers. This would imply that Up-Gaze, Eye Roll, and Initial Arm Levitation, all motor functions, depend to varying degrees on a rapidly adaptable reticular system. This is a plausible, internally consistent, but unproven hypothesis.

The preceding hypothesis moreover, also yields two theorems, namely (a) that a lesser degree of reticular flexibility and adaptability leads to *greater* difficulty in trance induction, and (b) that a greater degree of reticular flexibility leads to greater ease of trance induction.

Further development of the hypothesis of reticular flexibility with respect to trance capability leads to the concept that trance is induced when recticular activation is localized focally and *not* diffused generally. It is consistent with the point of view that the trance state is a special state of attention and arousal and *not* a sleep state. Thus, ideation, emotion, and sensation, led through appropriate cortical, limbic, and thalamic pathways may be facilitated or inhibited by virtue of focusing the reticular system on particular functions. The RAS then can permit integration of ideation, emotion, and sensation so that a new ideational complex is immediately available to the posterior temporal and parietal areas as well as to the conceptual motor areas. The process of hippocampal to mid-temporal transfer is essentially bypassed, or hastened, although there may be hippocampal memory storage. This mechanism may also be involved in amnesia, when it occurs, and in post-hypnotic suggestion. It is also important to stress that the availability of *limbic* input to the reticular system and the cortex may be correlated with reticular flexibility.

Thus, the biological basis of trance capability may depend on an integrating function of the RAS, whereby thalamic and limbic impulses are integrated with left and right sided cortical components. Although the right brain is important in body image ideation, the left brain is equally important in ideation concerning value system and attitudes. Trance capability probably depends on right–left *integration* rather than the ascendancy of one side or the other. The apparent emotion readily available to people who can experience trance clearly is most probably a product of the availability of limbic impulses to the cortex via direct connections and as well as by means of a very well-functioning RAS . . . . To summarize, it is herein *postulated* that trance capability is related to reticular flexibility as indicated by the Up-Gaze and Eye-Roll. This reticular flexibility allows for emotional factors to reign more freely and for limbic-thalamic integration to occur in conjunction with bilateral cortical integration. These phenomena, in turn, lead to a capability to focus attention on events of interest to the organism in a trance state.

Greenberg's emphasis is not so much on right–left hemispheres as it is on the vertical hierarchical relationship between the RAS and cortex, and the RAS and limbic system. Greenberg's postulation regarding the role of the limbic system in focal attention is roughly consistent with Pribram's description of limbic involvement in redundancy enhancement. If further research continues to reveal co-variance between clinical behavior patterns and neurophysiological circuitry, as indicated by this ER hypothesis, we can view the eye roll as a useful indicator at the psychoneurophysiological interface.

We will shift now from neurophysiological research and theory to clinical neurological data. A study of emotionally disturbed and brain-damaged children by Jacobs and Jacobs (1966) indicated that, in comparison with normal children, disturbed children were less able to be hypnotized and had less clearly established hemispheric preferences. Keeping in mind that children are generally more hypnotizable than adults, they went on to note, "When a child is unable to achieve a trance state, one must be aware of the possibility of brain damage" (p. 273).

Certain authors have taken a categorically opposed position to the idea of hypnotizability as a trait and they consequently argue against the validity of any physiological correlates of hypnosis. Sarbin and Slagle (1972) critically reviewed the physiological literature, justifiably questioning some of the more vague physiological correlates such as changes in heart rate, respiratory rate, steroid levels, and so on. They were critical of the London et al. study cited earlier, relating EEG alpha activity to hypnotizability in a rather circular fashion. They noted that relaxation as well as hypnotizability is related to the presence of EEG activity and, therefore, they attributed the differences to levels of relaxation as opposed to degrees of hypnotizability. Their argument fails to take into account the consistency of individual variance—a major weakness of the "role demand" critique of hypnotizability as a trait. Call it relaxation rather than hypnosis if you will, but how is it that some people consistently do it better than others?

SUMMARY

The literature reviewed here involves various behavioral, electro-encephalographic, and clinical measures of left and right hemispheric functioning and priority. There is growing evidence that the left and right hemispheres do different things, perhaps simultaneously, and that individuals differ in their characteristic utilization of these two hemispheres. Measurements such as laterality of eye movement, alpha activity, evoked response, vertical eye movement, the eye roll, and the hand clasp indicate that individuals have a characteristic, preferred style for the functioning of one hemisphere over the other, independent of handedness. This preference may be related to certain kinds of sensory experiences and cognitive styles. There is also clearly a task-related component to these measures; verbal and mathematical tasks elicit left hemispheric functioning by a number of measures, and spatial and emotional tasks elicit right hemispheric functioning.

Nonetheless, experimental conditions have been created which maximize the characteristic expression of preference and minimize the effect of task-related preferences. This approach is consistent with the systematic assessment of hypnotizability, in which social and task pressures are important but individual variance in capacity is primary. There is also evidence that patterns of integration of the neuraxis, such as frontal-limbic versus posterior-temporal, and basal ganglia versus amygdala, may relate to differing styles of paying attention.

Enough data is accumulating in regard to differences in cognitive style as related to neurophysiological functioning that our hypothesis— that in a clinically useful way one can distinguish among styles as Apollonian, Odyssean, or Dionysian—is, if hardly proven, at least plausible. In remaining sections of this book we hope to make this distinction clinically useful: with additional knowledge about the preferred cognitive style of the patient as elicited by the systematic assessment of hypnotizability, the astute clinician will be in a position to "speak the patient's language" and choose the most appropriate treatment strategy for his patient's particular cognitive style.

8

The Hypnotic Induction Profile and Psychopathology

The fourth group consists of individuals who have in common a disordered trance state with little functional trance capacity. They are distinguished from those in the other three groups by their performance on the Hypnotic Induction Profile and by the fall-off of their behavioral response from the physiological predictor, the eye roll. This group comprises two types of profile: soft and decrement. The *soft profile* is intermediate between intacts and decrements. The levitation response is at the zero level although the eye roll and the control differential are positive. In the *decrement profile* the control differential is always negative and the eye roll is positive regardless of the levitation response. Our data clearly indicate a correlation between relatively severe psychopathology and decrement profiles and suggest that a soft profile is consistent with less florid but still serious pathology of a characterologic or depressive type. This data will be presented later.

As Figure 8–1 illustrates, we have divided the serious psychological disorders roughly into categories of thought and affect following Bleuler's time-honored distinction. It is our impression, as yet unestablished statistically, that severe decompensations in Apollonians tend to lead to thought disorders, and that decompensations in Dionysians tend to lead to affective disorders. The Odyssean style seems most related to reactive

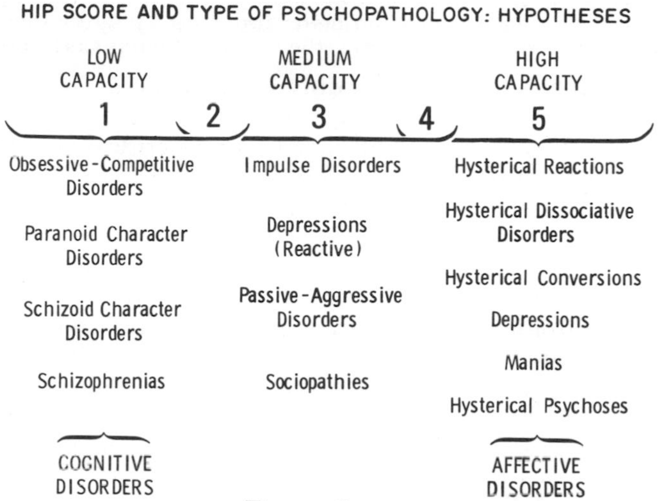

HIP SCORE AND TYPE OF PSYCHOPATHOLOGY: HYPOTHESES

LOW CAPACITY	MEDIUM CAPACITY	HIGH CAPACITY
1 2	3 4	5
Obsessive-Competitive Disorders	Impulse Disorders	Hysterical Reactions
Paranoid Character Disorders	Depressions (Reactive)	Hysterical Dissociative Disorders
Schizoid Character Disorders	Passive-Aggressive Disorders	Hysterical Conversions
		Depressions
Schizophrenias	Sociopathies	Manias
		Hysterical Psychoses
COGNITIVE DISORDERS		AFFECTIVE DISORDERS

Figure 8–1

depression and withdrawal and to sociopathy; disorders primarily of behavior, with mixed affective and thought components. Such a working dichotomy between disorders of affect and thought is well established in classical psychopathology. In his work *Lived Time* Eugene Minkowski reviews Bleuler's contribution in clarifying this distinction:

Bleuler expresses the difference existing from this point of view between the schizophrenic and the manic depressive by a formula which has since become famous. He said that we have no affective contact with the first while this contact is maintained in the second.   (Minkowski, 1970, p. 72)

Minkowski then reviews the utility of connecting descriptions of people who are quite disturbed to those within the normal range of human behavior:

In genealogical research it is given an even more solid basis for this attempt to establish an inner bond between the overall behavior of the alienated on the one hand and normal individuals on the other. It is always the presence or absence of affective contact in the environment that serves as the guide for this comparison. (p. 73)

Thus he is arguing that a description of all people based on the degree of affective connection is useful. The extremes of manic-depressive illness on the one hand and schizophrenia and schizoid states on the other serve as guideposts for the classification of "normal" behavior. He goes on to provide a distinction among more normal people which is highly relevant to a discussion of trance capacity:

In taking up Kretschmer's research Bleuler is led to the notions of schizoidism and syntony. In going beyond the domains of characterology he sees in them the expression of two fundamental principles of life. Syntony alludes to the principle that allows us to vibrate in unison with the environment, while schizoidism on the contrary designates the faculty of detaching ourselves from that environment. Moreover these two principles, in spite of their apparently contradictory character, do not exclude each other. The one is as indispensable as the other . . . . that is, far from being two contrary forces they have to do with two different sides of our being, the one as essential as the other. (p. 73)

The concept of "vibrating in unison" with the environment sounds very much like what we would describe as intact trance capacity and the corresponding "detachment" as the more critical nontrance state. Different people are capable of different degrees of "vibration" and "detachment," and a given person will be in different states at different times. Yet this sensitivity to the environment is a relevant and useful variable and seems also connected to the relative importance of affect in an individual's life; hence, the connection between severe affective and thought disorders and the range of more normal human differences. We are indebted to Fromm-Reichman (1950) and Sullivan (1953) for the perspective of mental health and mental illness as a continuum with underlying dynamisms which differ in degree but not in kind. The serious disorders are distinguished along the spectrum of thought/affect, and also in terms of relative hyper- or hypoactivity, as illustrated in Figure 8–2. We will first describe the disorders which primarily involve thought.

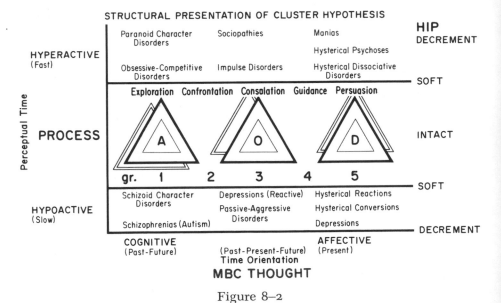

Figure 8–2

Cognitive Disorders

Paranoid Character Disorders. These individuals are quite actively suspicious and often harbor isolated delusional systems although functioning in some ways reasonably well. They tend to ward off a feeling

of overwhelming anxiety with rigid suspicions. Unlike overt schizophrenics, however, they tend to be provocative and aggressive rather
than withdrawn. They are likely to have decrement profiles.

Obsessive-Competitive Disorders. In severe forms of these disorders,
the person is quite rigid and unresponsive to his environment but complies in a fixed manner to inner compulsions with a relatively unchanging system of rationalization which is quite important to him.
Such people exalt their reasons for doing things although their reasoning
can actually be quite bizarre. They are absorbed in their processing of
events and are expressing their desire to suppress feeling in their obsessional activity. They tend to be so rigid that their rationalizations,
characteristically isolating and displacing hostile feelings, are quite far
from the real sources of their behavior. When these people decompensate
further they tend to develop thought disorders. They frequently have
soft or decrement profiles. For a lucid presentation of this syndrome,
see Nemiah's book, *Foundations of Psychopathology* (1961).

We choose the unconventional label "obsessive-competitive disorders"
rather than the standard "obsessive-compulsive" for this group because
compulsive behavior is at least equally or more evident in the Dionysian
who compulsively complies to external signals. Compulsive behavior
exists throughout the psychopathological spectrum. Apollonians with
obsessional features are more uniquely characterized by the competitive
nature of their compulsive behavior. They are likely to place cues from
others in a competitive context and their compulsive behavior is likely
to be a response to an internal system of beliefs. Interpersonal com-
petitiveness especially characterizes this group.

Schizoid Character Disorders. On the low-processing side and below
the Apollonian group are individuals whose lives are characterized by
serious withdrawal from contact with others. They tend to be somewhat
depressed but differ from those who are primarily depressed in having
an apathetic and withdrawn quality rather than being dysphoric. They
have some tendency toward thought disorder but are often neither autistic nor psychotic. They face what writers in the English object-relations
school have referred to as the "schizoid dilemma," (Fairbairn 1954), a
sense of desperate dependence tied with a foreboding that involvement
spells destruction. Thus they constantly fight people off while desperately
wanting them. They rigidly avoid compliance with outside signals and
adhere to their own inner compulsions in order to avoid entangling
involvements.

Schizophrenia. These people tend to be quite fixed and rigid, refractory to outside signals, bound by primary-process impulses. Their reasoning is so bizarre and far from its original sources, utilizing the compulsive triad model, that it is called autistic. Paradoxcally, these individuals
are unusually committed to understanding exactly what is happening
to them: their rationalizing becomes quite distorted and fixed; they are
willing to distort their behavior in the direction of conforming to "rational" if autistic explanations; and they may also distort perception in
that direction. Thus their rigid compulsive triad conveys a good deal

about their extreme commitment to autistic reason and to their rejection of feeling, although they occasionally suffer breakthroughs of intense and uncontrolled affect.

This state of mind is elegantly described by Claude Levi-Strauss in the following account of the opposition between normal and pathological thinking, contained in a discussion of shamanism:

From any nonscientific perspective (and here we can exclude no society), pathological and normal thought processes are complementary rather than opposed. In a universe which it strives to understand but whose dynamics it cannot fully control, normal thought continually seeks the meaning of things which refuse to reveal their significance. So-called pathological thought, on the other hand, overflows with emotional interpretations and overtones in order to supplement an otherwise deficient reality. For normal thinking there exists something which cannot be empirically verified and is therefore "claimable." For pathological thinking there exists experience without object or something "available." We might borrow from linguistics and say that so-called normal thought always suffers from a deficit of meaning whereas so-called pathological thought (in at least some of its manifestations) disposes of a plethora of meaning."

(Levi-Strauss, 1963, p. 181)

It would be misleading to interpret these patterns as simply a choice of symptoms, as a neurotic might substitute anger for anxiety. Rather, these people seem to be making the best of their limited capacity to concentrate and integrate thought and feeling. There is a kind of desperation in their attempts to make the irrational rational, and a fear of dominance by strong feelings, which one schizophrenic patient referred to as "eruptions." With a relatively rigid triad of rationalization, compulsive compliance, and a kind of amnesia, they attempt to make the best of a bad situation. Faced with what Laing has described as "ontological insecurity," a sense of nothingness underlying everything, they cling to something fixed desperately (Laing 1963).

Bleuler's classic description of schizophrenia included a discussion of the deterioration of attention which is consistent with our observations of decrement performance on the HIP:

As a partial phenomenon of affectivity attention is affected with it by deterioration. Insofar as interests are extant—in milder cases this means for the majority of events, in severe cases at least for the emotionally charged activity (such as the working out of plans for escape)—attention appears to be normal at least according to our present methods of observation. However, where affect is lacking, there will also be lacking the drive to pursue the external and internal processes, to direct the path of senses and the thought; i.e. active attention will be lacking.

Passive attention is altered in an entirely different manner. On the one hand it is evident that the uninterested or autistically encapsulated patients pay very little attention to the outer world. On the other hand, however, it is remarkable how many of the events which the patients seem to ignore are registered nevertheless. The selectivity which normal attention ordinarily exercises among the sensory impressions can be reduced to zero so that almost everything is recorded that reaches the senses. Thus, the facilitating as well as the inhibiting properties of attention are equally disturbed. (Bleuler, E. 1950, Trans. Zinkin, J., p. 68).

What Bleuler observed among schizophrenics was a breakdown in processing capacity, both an inability to adequately direct active attention, or what we would call focal concentration, and a difficulty in filtering out aspects of passive attention, or what we would call peripheral awareness. This disordered state of attention is characterized on the HIP by an inability to attend to the ribbon of concentration necessary to respond to the hypnotic signals, in spite of a positive eye roll.

The previously quoted work of Shakow and his segmental set theory may throw more light on this problem and its relation to the phenomenon of hypnosis. In developing his segmental set theory, Shakow has come to believe that the fundamental lesion of schizophrenia is an inability to sustain concentration over time. He has developed precise measurements of this capacity that show marked differences between schizophrenic and normal populations (Shakow 1974). Such an observation is consistent with the common clinical finding of distractability among schizophrenics and it may also be related to thought processes which we describe as autistic. We distinguish schizophrenic autism from a manic flight of ideas in that we can follow the flight, but get lost trying to understand autistic thoughts. These irreconcilable gaps in autistic thought may be related to a sudden discontinuity in concentration. This is precisely the kind of cognition measured by the Hypnotic Induction Profile, and it is closely related to the broken ribbon of concentration seen in the decrement profiles.

Affective Disorders

Mania. On the other extreme of the spectrum are severe psychopathological disorders with a major affective component, illustrated on the right side of Figure 8–2. Manics are dominated by affect and tend to be overwhelmed by their activity. They act constantly and their capacity to comply with an external signal is disordered at best. Their clinical state is usually dominated by cyclical periods of mania and depression, with depression often present below the surface even during the elated periods (Kotin 1972). They exhibit compulsive hyperactivity and a relative insensitivity to outside signals. These individuals frequently have soft or decrement profiles, but we believe the pattern of performance on the profile to be somewhat different from that of schizophrenics. Research is being done now to determine whether in fact these individuals have high eye rolls and decrement performances in contrast to schizophrenics, who we predict would have a 1 or 2 eye-roll score and a decrement behavioral performance on the HIP.

Hysterical Psychosis. Clinically, these people appear quite floridly psychotic but often the drama of their condition, especially its affective dimension, separates it clearly from schizophrenia and sometimes from mania. These patients respond to severe environmental stress with rapid psychotic decompensation from a previously good level of functioning. They may be delusional and have ideas of reference, loose associations, and affect which ranges from bland indifference, approaching flatness, to intense agitation. They frequently mobilize tremendous attention and anxiety from their social network. These patients often recompensate rapidly, especially when appropriate intervention is made in their environment.

Michael was a 15-year-old male who was first presented to the hospital emergency room in an agitated and combative state and was placed in four-point restraints. He told the admitting physician that he was "possessed by demons of Satan." His family noted that he had begun speaking "in a bizarre awful voice, uttering obscenities, grunting, growling, and sniffing like a wild animal." On admission his affect was noted as "flattened and mildly depressed"; he was suicidal and delusional; and his proverb interpretation was concrete, religiously oriented, and personalized. He was initially diagnosed as psychotically depressed, and a few days later as schizophrenic.

Michael and his twin sister were the youngest of five siblings in a middle-class, religious, Lutheran family with no prior psychiatric history. Three months prior to admission, Michael had been displaced from the bedroom he shared with his brother and had been moved to the bedroom of his 22-year-old, sexually active sister who was away at nursing school during the week but who returned on weekends, sometimes with her fiancé. Ten weeks prior to admission he had become involved with his first girlfriend but she left him six weeks later. At that time he made a suicide gesture and a minister told him that it was "Satan's work."

One week after admission, the patient was administered the Hypnotic Induction Profile. His initial score was a 4 to 5 and he was able to regress to his past as though it were the present. Using this regression technique he was able to relive the "possessed" states which had become periodic during his hospitalization. He was taught to bring on the attacks and thereby control them and he was placed on low-dose antipsychotic medications. Family therapy began, emphasizing that the family remain calm during his "attacks" and also that he get a bedroom of his own. He had a second brief hospitalization, was taken off medication, and at one year follow-up had had no recurrences and was doing well. The final diagnosis was hysterical psychosis (Spiegel, D., and Fink 1978).

This case illustrates the dramatic quality of hysterical psychosis, and also its susceptibility to external control. The patient was rewarded for learning to bring on and then control his psychotic states. He had a high-intact profile and his high hypnotizability was useful in differentiating the diagnosis from schizophrenia. Some of these patients may have decrement or soft profiles as well, but this case serves to illustrate that a hysterical patient may be quite psychotic and still be highly hypnotizable.

The differential diagnosis between hysterical psychosis and manic-depressive illness may also be difficult. We have seen several patients who were diagnosed as manic-depressive but were poorly controlled on lithium: they had high-intact profiles and responded well to a therapeutic strategy employing self-hypnosis for anxiety reduction and behavioral control.

H.L. was a 52-year-old married mother of two who had suffered with manic-depressive illness for ten years. At age 46 she was placed on lithium. Two years of careful adjustment of the medication resulted in some improvement, but her mood swings were not adequately controlled. She was referred for adjunctive treatment with self-hypnosis and scored 3 to 4 soft on the profile. Her responses to the cluster survey were in the Odyssean–Dionysian range. She was taught how to use self-hypnosis with emphasis on creating a sense of floating as a means of defusing her inner sense of pressure and anxiety. She was maintained on the same level of lithium, but with the aid of this exercise she was able to contain her mood swings and has done well with it since then. As she improved, her repeat profile score changed to a 3 to 4 intact.

We realize that there are many areas of overlap and disagreement within psychiatric nosology. We have not even included the complex entity of schizo-affective disorders in our schema. Distinguishing among manic-depressive psychosis, hysterical psychosis, hyperactive schizophrenia, and the anxiety-ridden obsessive disorders can be quite difficult. We are currently engaged in studying the relationship between patterns of performance on the Hypnotic Induction Profile and these different but related diagnostic entities.

Hysterical Dissociative Disorders. This group includes fugue states and other hysterical conditions often associated with hypnotic phenomena. Repression is the primary defense; the patient avoids a painful conflict by focusing intently on a single aspect of his life or perhaps even by surrendering his customary identity. These patients generally have soft or intact high profiles. They frequently respond well to structured therapy and abreaction is often helpful. Regression techniques can be useful to demonstrate to the patient in a dramatic and immediate way his capacity for dissociation. This approach is a first step toward teaching mastery and control over the dissociation. (See chapters 20 and 22.)

Hysterical Reactions. These include the more withdrawn hysterical conditions in which the individual avoids a problem area in his life by retreat and by assuming an affect of *la belle indifférence.* These withdrawal responses are often a reaction to some severe environmental stress. The patients may have high-intact or soft profiles.

Hysterical Conversions. These include the severe and immobilizing conversion symptoms such as paralysis and stocking-glove anesthesia of limbs. Patients with such symptoms in acute form tend to have high-intact profiles. Those with conversion symptoms in chronic form who have accumulated massive secondary gain and have become trapped by their own disability are more likely to have soft or decrement profiles. They may be chronically depressed as well.

When dealt with acutely, these symptoms are often rapidly reversible.

Case Example: A medic was returned from the battlefield unable to use either of his legs, although no organic basis for his disability was discovered. He and his unit had come under heavy fire. Just as the sergeant ordered the unit to retreat, the patient heard a friend cry for help and saw the foot of a soldier who might have been his friend lying behind a rock. However, he obeyed the order and retreated and his friend never returned. He had presumed that his friend was still alive and that the foot he had seen belonged to his friend. He was overwhelmed with remorse at not having tried to rescue him, although he had indeed obeyed orders.

This man was highly hypnotizable (he was seen before the HIP was developed) and was able to regress to the past as though it were the present. The intervention involved having the medic picture the situation he had fled on the battlefield with one modification, that the foot he had seen was facing downward, the implication being that the man was already dead. The soldier came out of the trance state with a sense of "discovery"; his friend was already dead and there would have been no point in trying to rescue him. Within a few days he regained the ability to walk and was returned to active duty.

His high trance capacity (most likely in the 4 to 5 range) was utilized to help this soldier cope with his overwhelming sense of guilt and entertain the probability that his friend was already dead. With that he was able to disengage the somatic message that he should not have moved from the spot where his friend was wounded and he regained the ability to walk. (Spiegel, H. 1965) For further discussion of hysterical conversion symptoms see chapter 20.

Depression. This group, characterized by withdrawal and dysphoric affect, shows little willingness to comply with any external signals. Reason becomes morbid rumination, with guilt and self-criticism the predominant theme. The feeling of sadness overwhelms all of their functioning and this affective state overshadows the actual reasons which exist in the world as a cause of sadness. The massive interference that a serious depression causes in an individual's intrapsychic and interpersonal functioning likewise seems to show itself in performance on the Hypnotic Induction Profile. Depressed individuals often have soft or decrement profiles. A decrement performance in a mid-range or high patient who otherwise seems fairly intact has been helpful to us in picking up a masked depression which has otherwise been overlooked.

A man in his 40s sought help with hypnosis for recurrent muscular aches and muscle fatigue which had become so severe that they often hampered his work as an auto body repairman. He was a tall, strong, vigorous, single man who reported mild sleep disturbance and some decrease in appetite but no dysphoric mood. He related well and seemed to have minimal secondary gain from his pain and fatigue. He had an extensive medical work-up which included checking for an intracranial lesion and myasthenia gravis. All the medical and laboratory findings were negative. He scored a 3 decrement on the Hypnotic Induction

Profile. On the basis of this score, along with some somatic signs of depression, he was started on a tricyclic antidepressant. Three weeks later his pain and muscle fatigue began to improve and two months after that visit his pain syndrome had resolved on an adequate dose of tricyclic medication. This man had somatized his depression and when the depression was treated his somatic symptoms improved. In this case the profile was helpful in making the correct diagnosis and in finding more effective treatment than hypnosis for this individual.

It has been our clinical experience that when Dionysians decompensate they tend in the direction of depression, at times of psychotic proportions. Even if depression is not the primary diagnosis, it is frequently associated with the more severe decompensations of highly hypnotizable patients. This type of depression is distinct from the ruminative and less affective-laden despair of some decompensated Apollonians.

Disorders of the Mid-Range Group

We will now discuss the decompensated states which we have seen in association with mid-range soft and decrement profiles. This consists of those individuals with eye rolls in the 2 to 3 range and either zero levitation and a positive control differential, a soft pattern, or zero control differential, a decrement pattern.

Sociopathies. These people are highly active. Their emphasis is on manipulation and action rather than on feeling, and their affect is commonly described as shallow, rather than overwhelming as with manics or flat as with schizophrenics. They tend to be suspicious of others and are well known for resistance to compliance with external signals. They are more inclined to busily engage in getting other people to comply with their purposes than to be at all receptive toward accepting input from others about their behavior. Their compulsive rationalizing of their feelings and behavior often serves to justify the behavior after the fact, frequently in a somewhat paranoid fashion. Many sociopaths have clear paranoid features; underneath their manipulative hyperactivity is a delusional, paranoid core. Action is what counts for these individuals, and they often respond best to a highly structured and disciplined therapeutic approach.

Characteristic of their position which is near the Odyssean group, they are often described as being "pseudonormal." Havens* has described the sociopath as someone who gives an interviewer the feeling that he, the patient, is more normal than the interviewer. Sociopaths create an impression of normalcy which is useful to them, yet they are compelled to act in such a way as to avoid any real feelings. It is in this area that we believe many of the patients described as borderline by

---

* Havens, L. L., personal communication, 1970.

Grinker et al. (1968), Kernberg (1975), and others belong. We expect in borderline patients with decrement profiles such characteristics as micropsychotic episodes; the tendency to project and manipulate, to split objects in their world into good and bad ones; shallow affect; and a strong tendency to act rather than feel. However, they may be hard to distinguish from those patients diagnosed either as sociopaths or as having paranoid character disorders. We thus see them as being decompensated Apollonians or Odysseans with paranoid and sociopathic features.

K.U. was a 23-year-old, separated father of three. He was seen for psychiatric evaluation after his arrest on charges of rape and murder. The crime was a particularly brutal one, and the defense argued that he suffered from a "dual personality" and was therefore psychotic during the crime. His parents were divorced when he was an infant, and his mother's remarriage was marked by repeated separations. He completed high school, had no prior criminal record, and had worked as a laborer prior to his arrest.

The HIP was administered and he scored a 2 to 3 soft pattern with an induction score of 5. The survey of cluster characteristics yielded mixed features. Formal psychological testing revealed the following information:

K.U.'s test results indicate poor identity formation, characterized by marked feelings of inadequacy, inferiority, schizoid tendencies, depression, and depersonalization. Feelings of loneliness and emptiness pervade the test responses, suggesting a borderline personality disorder. If stressed too far where tolerance for ego deflation has reached an impasse, a sharp lack of impulse control may definitely reflect his (lack of) ability to cope adequately with the stress-inducing situation. His borderline structure is primarily a developmental defect, in which a fundamental deformity or inadequacy of ego-functioning prevails.

In short, he was found by the court to be characterologically impaired, but neither hysterical, psychotic, nor legally insane. The psychological test results and the initial impression generated by the profile score were consistent with the diagnosis of a borderline sociopath. Without a high-intact profile score, hysterical dissociation or so-called "dual personality," was unlikely. On the other hand, one would expect to see a 1 or 2 decrement profile if the subject was schizophrenic. The 2 to 3 soft pattern was a statement of his marginal psychological functioning with poor impulse control. He was not so impaired that the ribbon of concentration was entirely disrupted, but his trance capacity was hardly so profound that it could be invoked to explain the postulated dissociative episodes. He was, in fact, found to be sane and guilty by the court.

It is our experience that the profile has been useful in making the difficult distinction between borderline schizophrenia and primitive hysteria, the latter having high-intact profiles, and the former often having soft or decrement profiles. This difference in the pattern of performance when hypnotizability is tested may be a reflection of a critical clinical distinction. Hysterics may have serious loss of function, exhibit psychotic symptoms, and be quite manipulative; but the underlying conflicts are usually of a positive libidinal nature. One establishes rapport easily with them, and they tend to be, if anything, too trusting and dependent in therapy. Thus their willingness to "go along" with the hypnotic protocol is not surprising. Genuine borderlines, on the other hand, tend to be somewhat hostile and paranoid. Coping with hostility and negative transference is the major work in psychotherapy with them (Kernberg 1975). Thus it is hardly surprising that as a group they tend not to allow themselves to experience sensorimotor changes characteristic of the trance state. Their underlying hostility and suspicion interferes. The implications of this distinction for psychotherapy will be further discussed in the section on appropriate psychotherapy (chapter 21).

Impulse Disorders. This group includes individuals who have a similar tendency to act rather than feel, but the trait is less rigid and bound in hostility than in those characterized as sociopaths. This group includes individuals with a specific impulse problem in one but not all areas of their life, such as some addictions or compulsive gambling. They may be more prone to soft rather than decrement profiles, are often more functional in other areas of their life, and are less paranoid and suspicious. It is not hard to see how a patient's paranoid stance with regard to the world would interfere with allowing himself to experience many somatic sensory alterations at the request of another person.

Reactive Depressions. This is a large group consisting of many fundamentally intact individuals who suffer a relatively severe depression in response to a life stress. For a period of time they may become immobilized with decreased energy, interest, and involvement with others. At such times their profile may become soft. We have some clinical data to suggest that after recovery from the depressive episode the intact mid-range trance capacity is re-established. As noted earlier, members of the Odyssean group are prone to periods of depression between periods of activity. This group of reactive depressives constitutes a fraction of the normal neurotic group whose depression becomes serious and immobilizing.

Passive-Aggressive Disorders. In this group we include individuals with characterological passive-aggressive traits, not merely those with such patterns in isolated neurotic form. Their relationships tend to be permeated with a quiet hostility and they use their inaction in a calculated and manipulative fashion. At the same time they often feel quite empty, lonely, and mistreated. They generally have soft or decrement profiles.

As a rule these members of the soft and decrement group have a relatively fixed and inflexible pattern of responding, exemplified by a rigid and distorted compulsive triad. They tend to distrust and fail to respond to new input, either ignoring or transforming it so thoroughly that it becomes virtually unrecognizable. They compulsively comply to an internally generated theme much more than to any external input and they are not open to outside direction and change. Furthermore, they are often densely unaware of the determinants of their compulsive activity; their reason serves not to illuminate but to justify their compulsive patterns of behavior. They have in common a poor hypnotic performance and are unresponsive to hypnotic signals, relative to their rather rigid adherence to their internally generated preoccupations.

CONCLUSION

These reflections are an attempt to assimilate a vast body of psychiatric data. The primary point is that the style of hypnotizability seems to be correlated with a large number of other personal traits and problems: what is tapped in the trance state may broadly transform the individual's world view of himself, and his capacity and willingness to learn and act, into a brief and measurable behavioral performance.

The association between patterns of performance on the Hypnotic Induction Profile and various clusters of character style and psychiatric disorders is presented with some supporting evidence but is hardly an absolute or final picture. Rather, it is hoped that organizing the spectrum of personality styles and psychiatric disorders in this way will prove clinically useful in thinking through differential diagnosis with the help of a brief assessment of hypnotizability. We have enough data to assert that the presence of intact-high hypnotizability should arouse the clinician's index of suspicion that his patient is reasonably functional and has an intact, usable capacity to concentrate. In contrast, we have data to suggest that the presence of a soft or decrement performance on the HIP is consistent with more serious psychopathology. However, no such statistical association is absolute in an individual case. Such associations are best used to sharpen and refine a clinician's diagnostic impression based on standard intervention techniques, including history and mental status examination. It is hoped that the Hypnotic Induction Profile will prove useful enough to be incorporated as part of the mental status examination of the patient.

9

Review of the Literature: Hypnotizability and Severe Psychopathology

Conflicting literature exists concerning the hypnotizability of seriously disturbed patients. Researchers have variously asserted that schizophrenics are not at all hypnotizable and that they have the same trance capacity as normal individuals. We have chosen several of the most systematic papers with differing points of view to analyze critically. There is a much larger anecdotal clinical literature which seems to us less helpful and hence will not be reported. We focus here on the relationship between hypnotizability and psychotic symptomatology since the work on neurotic symptoms has been reviewed in the chapter on hypnotizabiilty and personality.

In 1964 Abrams published a review of the literature to date on the use of hypnosis with psychotic patients. He referred to three studies (Wilson et al. 1949; Gale and Herman 1956; Heath et al. 1961) of hypnotizability among psychotics and compared some of their results to Hull's distribution of hypnotizability in a normal population. His overall conclusion was that, although some psychotic patients seemed hypnotizable, as a group they were markedly less hypnotizable than the general population. He went on to note:

Certain factors have been suggested as causing the psychotic to be less hypnotizable. They would appear to be related to poor contact with reality, chronicity, deterioration, and uncooperativeness.

(Abrams, 1964)

Abrams was interested in the treatment of psychotics with hypnosis, and took pains to note that some patients diagnosed as schizophrenic seemed hypnotizable, although on the whole they were not. This review, however, utilized the hypnotic "depth" concept which has largely been abandoned in the research literature in favor of hypnotic susceptibility or preferably hypnotizability. The issue is the trance capacity of the of the individual rather than the so-called "depth" of any given trance experience.

At about the same time, Barber et al. (1964) did a careful study of hypnotizability as rated by the Barber Suggestibility Scale among a population of 253 chronic schizophrenic patients. He noted that 59 patients were "untestable"; that is, they were uncooperative. He found the remaining group somewhat susceptible, but on the low side as compared with normals (1.3 to 1.8 as compared with 2.2 to 3.5 on an 8-point scale). He concluded that it was difficult to hypnotize chronic schizophrenics. His results implied lessened hypnotizability of this group. In addition, the elimination of a quarter of the sample as untestable further indicated the inability of schizophrenics to be hypnotized. This problem plagues most studies of hypnotizability among psychotic patients; that is, many patients are so disturbed that they cannot cooperate. Yet in a study comparing the tendencies of populations, it seems reasonable to include those incapable of cooperating as nonhypnotizable.

In several studies on the hypnotizability of psychotic patients, Kramer noted equal or enhanced susceptibility as compared to normals. In the first study he administered the Stanford Hypnotic Susceptibility Scale (SHSS) to 25 psychotic inpatients (6 others refused) and found higher than normal scores (Kramer and Brennan 1964). In a later study, he administered the Harvard Group Scale of Hypnotic Susceptibility (HGSHS) to 25 of 28 patients chosen (3 would not cooperate) and found the normal and psychotic groups equally hypnotizable. Three of the 25 were later diagnosed as psychoneurotic. Among psychotic patients the correlation of self and observer rating of hypnotizability was much lower than in normals: .43 versus .83 to .91 (Kramer 1956). In a third study, Vingoe and Kramer (1966) questioned their own results when only 15 of 46 patients completed the project. The uncooperative patients had similar diagnoses to those who complied with the protocol, and thus the two groups seemed not to differ.

The results of the retesting of 9 of the original 15 subjects in the Hypnotized group, and the fact that the general level of contact in such a chronic group is extremely variable, suggests that the hypnotizability of the chronic psychotic hospitalized patient may be of a fairly unreliable nature. (p. 53)

Although Kramer and his associates were inclined to think of psychotics as quite hypnotizable, the problems involving even minimal cooperation in a hypnotic testing situation could not be overlooked.

Gordon (1973), utilizing the Stanford Hypnotic Susceptibility Scale, Form A, reported significantly higher hypnotizability in a group of 32 schizophrenic subjects as compared with a group matched for age and drawn from a general medical and surgical inpatient service. It should be noted that the administration of the scale was modified to delete any reference to the term hypnosis. Lavoie et al. (1973) obtained conflicting results when he utilized the same assessment procedure with a group of 56 chronic psychotic patients, primarily schizophrenics, compared to a normal group score as defined by Hilgard (1965). Lavoie emphasized the distractability commonly associated with schizophrenia as a factor which impaired concentration and therefore hypnotizability in their sample. Of particular interest is the fact that they found no psychotic patient scoring in the highest range of 10 to 12 on the SHSS.

Utilizing a modified version of the Davis-Husband Scale (1931) and the outmoded hypnotic depth concept, Polak et al. (1964) reported that 16 of 28 chronic psychotic patients were at least somewhat hypnotizable. In a more sophisticated study, Green (1969) utilized a modified version of the SHSS and obtained scores among psychotic patients similar to those reported as a norm for college students. Webb and Nesmith (1964) employed a simple postural sway measure on a much larger group of patients and normals (N = 490). They found significantly more responsiveness among the normal population.

There have been numerous clinical reports of hypnosis used to treat psychotic illnesses with varying degrees of success (Scagnelli 1974, 1976; Zeig 1974). They will not be discussed in detail because this chapter focuses on diagnostic implications of hypnotizability rather than the therapeutic uses of hypnosis with psychosis. It is worth noting, however, that in general this literature describes some psychotic patients who respond quite well to hypnotic technique, and others who are quite unresponsive. These results are interesting from a diagnostic perspective and are consistent with the idea that at least some highly hypnotizable psychotic patients suffer from an hysterical psychosis rather than schizophrenia. These may well be the kind of patients who have responded to hypnotic techniques.

A clinical article written by Copeland and Kitching (1937) deserves comment in this regard. They presented 20 cases in which hypnosis was artfully employed in both the diagnosis and the treatment of inpatients. Of particular interest is their discussion of several patients who were seemingly psychotic, but were easily hypnotized and subsequently recovered quite quickly. Those cases which were not hypnotizable had worse outcomes, more consistent with the course of severe affective or thought disorder. The authors concluded:

Here we would point out what we find to be one of the values of hypnosis. Without exception, cases which presented as true psychosis could not be hypnotized. If susceptibility to hypnosis developed, we were compelled to revise the diagnosis. (p. 328)

The absence of any highly hypnotizable patients, according to the SHSS in Lavoie's previously cited study with carefully selected psychotic patients, is consistent with our hypothesis. Combined with the clinical observations of Copeland and Kitching, these clinical and research data indicate that there may be something unusual about psychotic patients who prove to be highly hypnotizable in formal testing. Some of them may be unusual schizophrenics, although there is evidence that many schizophrenics have an impaired capacity to concentrate and tend not to be hypnotizable to a significant degree. It is our impression that some of these highly hypnotizable, psychotic patients are suffering from what can best be termed hysterical psychosis, but which is probably mis-diagnosed as schizophrenia.

We are especially intrigued by the work of Flor-Henry (1976) who, using neuropsychological tests and power spectral analysis of the EEG, indicated that the schizophrenic syndrome and psychopathy are mani-festations of neuronal disorganization in the dominant orbital-frontal-temporal regions, and the manic-depressive syndromes reflect disor-ganization of the nondominant anterior limbic structures. Later, Flor-Henry et al. (1977) reported that the obsessional syndrome is related to a loss of normal inhibitory processes in the dominant frontal area. These findings are strikingly consistent with our hypothesis.

Hoppe (1977) reminds us that in 1895 Freud pointed toward a unification of psychiatry and neurophysiology. He studied split-brain patients and reported: "The similarity and operational thinking between patients suffering from psychosomatic illnesses and split-brain people has led me to the hypothesis of a 'functional commissurotomy' in cases of severe psychosomatic disturbances."

Although some researchers and clinicians report normal or high hyp-notizability among seriously disturbed populations, the previously cited results support the hypothesis that there is, at the least, something unusual about the hypnotic performance of psychiatrically disordered individuals. They tend to cooperate erratically and to demonstrate dis-ordered concentration. As we have noted, Shakow's work with schizo-phrenics (1971, 1974) provides a possible explanatory system for this observation in a schizophrenic group of patients. Thus this data is in general consistent with our own findings that patients with thought, character, or affective disorders show little functional hypnotizability, and frequently have soft and decrement profiles.

Our clinical impression is that such patients demonstrate an inter-ference in their physiological capacity for hypnosis. This fall-off is represented on the HIP by the gap between the eye-roll measurement and measurements of levitation and control differential. Their behavioral and subjective performances are below the biological baseline. For schizophrenics, this may be due to the fragmentation of attention and concentration—their distractibility and loose associations. For those with paranoid or obsessional character disorders, the trance experience may arouse too much anxiety, suspicion, and fears about the operator con-trolling the patient. Sociopaths may fear that the hypnotic situation makes them too vulnerable to manipulation, a projection of their own style of dealing with others. Those with serious depressions may be so narcissistically withdrawn and devoid of energy that they cannot at-

tend to the input signals. Manics, on the other hand, may be so ener-
gized and grandiose that they disdain following the instructions which
are part of the trance induction.

Regardless of the phenomenology of the subject's experience, our
observations on the HIP indicate a fall-off of hypnotic performance
from the biological baseline in association with serious psychiatric dysfunction, and this position seems to have some support in the research
and clinical literature.

Research Findings

The Cluster Hypothesis

Our hypothesis that three distinct clusters of personality traits exist which characterize individuals in the high, mid-range, and low-intact spectra of hypnotizability grew initially out of clinical experience. In particular, observations were made among highly hypnotizable patients that indicated such trance-related features as a naive posture of trust, a tendency to readily affiliate with new ideas, and a tendency toward intense involvement with other people with a dependent quality. We then looked clinically for complementary characteristics among individuals with intact-low profile scores and we defined certain characteristics of Apollonians in contrast to the Dionysians. Finally a mid-range group, the Odysseans, was described and characterized primarily by the "action-despair syndrome," a tendency to fluctuate between periods of intense activity and involvement in the world and periods of withdrawal and despair over the "meaning of it all."

In view of the well-documented difficulties experienced by many researchers in relating trance capacity to personality traits (see chapter 6) we have made efforts to support our clinical impressions with more systematic clinical research that builds on work which has been done in the field. The literature previously cited gives support to the notion that there are distinct characteristics among the highly hypnotizable; including a capacity for imaginative involvement, a tendency to intense absorption, a proneness to having hypnotic-like experiences in everyday life, and some tendencies toward a bright mood and an easygoing, affiliative manner. Low-hypnotizables on the other hand have been shown to be somewhat more withdrawn, reserved, and less cheerful.

Some preliminary, clinical research results follow which are somewhat supportive of our cluster hypothesis but are hardly definitive. We are still in an early stage of this research, engaged in expanding and refining our hypotheses and in seeking suitable methods of testing them. Nonetheless, because the cluster hypothesis is broad and goes beyond existing reports in the literature, we feel it is important to include the data we have which supplements our clinical impressions.

In one study a group of raters utilized detailed psychological testing reports as a basis for classifying the patient's personality style as Apollonian, Odyssean, or Dionysian and consequently predicting the patient's hypnotizability. The records of 40 psychiatric outpatients were used for this study. The patients had come primarily for psychiatric treatment of a symptom-oriented nature. Neither the patient nor the clinician were aware at the time that the hypnotic or psychological evaluation would be utilized for research purposes. Thus the motivation was solely for treatment. The patients were given the Hypnotic Induction Profile and were referred for clinical psychological testing which included the Weschler Adult Intelligence Scale, Figure Drawings, the Sentence Completion Test, the Bender Gestalt, the Thematic Apperception Test, and the Rorschach. The cases were selected randomly, with the exception that all soft and decrement profiles were excluded. The names were removed so that raters could not identify the individuals involved.

The raters, two psychiatrists and a research assistant,* familiarized themselves with the test reports. One of the psychiatrists (H.S.) had seen the patients in the study and had administered the Hypnotic Induction Profile; however, the patients had been seen some years previously, they were not identified by name, and two cases were dropped when there was individual recognition. The predictions were made on a seven-point scale from pure Apollonian through Odyssean to Dionysian. The three raters independently read and evaluated each case. Then the psychological report was read aloud and a group decision was made, which became the final prediction. Confidence ratings were introduced as a means of resolving disagreements on scoring in certain cases.

Results. Correlational analysis demonstrated that the group prediction of hypnotizability based on reading the psychological reports was significant: $r = .32$, $p < .05$. The individual predictions were positively correlated but not significant for two of the three raters, and the interrater reliability was between .44 and .50, which is generally considered acceptable for clinical measurements. All of the raters' individual meas-

* Herbert Spiegel, David Spiegel, and Marc Aronson.

TABLE 10-1A

Questions and Scoring for Apollonian—Odyssean—Dionysian Personality Inventory.

A.   Space Awareness. As you concentrate on watching a movie or a play, do you get so absorbed in what is going on that you lose awareness of where you are? If "no," circle "A." If "yes" (clarify further by asking) "do you ever get so absorbed that when the curtain comes down you are surprised to realize you are sitting in a theatre?"

If "yes" circle D.
If "no" circle O.
If "not that much" circle O.

B.   Time Perception. In general, as you perceive time do you focus more of your attention upon the past, present, or future—or all three equally?

If the spontaneous answer is "past-present" or "present-future" circle OD.
If past and/or future, circle A.
If all three circle O.
If present, circle D.

C.   Myth-Belief Constellation (Head-Heart). The French philosopher Pascal once said, "The heart has a mind which the brain does not understand." He said that there are two kinds of mind, the heart-mind and the brain-mind. As you know yourself, which of these two minds do you give priority to?

If brain or mind, circle A.
If both or variable, circle O.
If heart, circle D.

C-1.   Interpersonal Control. As you relate to another person, do you prefer to control the interaction or do you prefer to let the other person take over if they wish?

If the spontaneous answer is "control interaction," circle A.
If both or "it depends" circle O.
If control is given to other person, circle D.

C-2.   Trust Proneness. In you proneness or tendency to trust other people, where would you place yourself on a scale of average—above or below?

If low or below average circle A.
If average or moderate circle O.
If high or above average circle D.

C-3,4.   Critical Appraisal and Learning Style. As you are learning something new, do you tend to critically judge it at the time you are learning it, or do you accept it and perhaps critically judge it at a later time?

If judgment is immediate, circle A.
If both or varied circle O.
If judgment is suspended or accepted, circle D.

C-5.   Responsibility. As you sense your responsibility for what you do, where do you place yourself on a scale of average, above or below?

If highly responsible or above average, circle A.
If average or moderate, circle O.
If low or below average, circle D.

C-6.   Preferred Mode of Contact. If you are learning something new and you know in advance that it is of such a nature that you can learn it clearly, safely, and equally well by either seeing it or touching it, which would you prefer—to see it or to touch it?

If the response is to see or visualize, circle A.
If both modes are used or valued equally, circle O.
If the response is "touch," circle D.

D.   Processing. When you come up with a new idea, there are two parts to it; one is to dream it up, and the other is to figure out how to do it. Of these two parts which gives you a greater sense of fulfillment?

If the response is to dream or think up an idea, circle D.
If both are satisfying or if it varies, circle O.
If the response is implementing or carrying out an idea, circle A.

D-1.   Writing Value. As you come up with or work out a new idea, is it necessary to write notes or do you feel your way through without writing?

If response is "must rely upon writing notes," circle A.
If response indicates minimal or small amount of writing, circle O.
If response is "without taking notes," circle D.

TABLE 10-1B

Scoring Sheet

Name _____

Date _____

Structural Cluster Survey
Apollonian - Odyssean - Dionysian

			A	O	D
A)	Space Awareness (SPACE)	Low	A		
		Medium		O	
		High			D
B)	Time Perception (TIME)	Past - Future	A		
		Past - Present - Future		O	
		Present			D
C)	MBC: Head - Heart (CONTENT)	Head	A		
		Both		O	
		Heart			D
	1) Interpersonal Control	Self	A		
		Varied		O	
		Other			D
	2) Trust Proneness	Below Average	A		
		Average		O	
		Above Average			D
	3) Critical Appraisal	Immediate	A		
	4) and Learning Style	Varied		O	
		Suspend			D
	5) Responsibility	Above Average	A		
		Average		O	
		Below Average			D
	6) Preferred Mode	Visual	A		
	of Contact	Both		O	
		Tactile			D
D)	Processing (PROCESS)	Implement	A		
		Varied		O	
		Imagine			D
	1) Writing	High	A		
		Varied		O	
		Low			D

urements correlated at the .7 level with the overall group score. We believe that the group rating was more reliable than any individual prediction because of the complexity and wealth of information in the psychological report. The group was better able than any one individual to consider and balance conflicting information.

These data suggest that predictions of hypnotic capacity may be made with significance based on an evaluation of psychological structure. The correlation of .32 accounts for approximately only 10 percent of the variance between the two measures, but it is high enough to suggest a significant relationship between the measures. This examination also was made difficult because the psychological tester was not involved in the rating; the raters were forced to make conclusions based on someone else's testing, which tends to obscure the data. Furthermore, the psychodiagnostic reports were designed to establish the degree of psychopathology rather than character style, and so provided only indirect information for our purposes. We conclude that this study seems promising if not definitive.

We are now in the process of developing a questionnaire to be administered in an interview format, regarding the various characteristics of the personality clusters we have described. This questionnaire has not yet been tested for reliability and validity. Although the questions seem to have some face validity, our preliminary testing indicates that a number of factors may distort the answers we receive. The questions we have designed are reproduced in Tables 10–1 A and 10–1 B.

In particular, our early results indicate that cultural, social, economic, and gender factors strongly influence the responses that individuals give to these questions. It seems almost impossible for a poorly educated working-class man to admit that he thinks with his heart rather than with his head, for example. It is hardly chic these days for a liberated upper-middle-class professional woman to admit that she prefers to let the other person in her relationship make the decisions. Few working-class or middle-class individuals are likely to admit that they consider themselves less responsible than average.

The other problem in administering these questions is that their contextual meaning for the subject is quite variable. A very trusting individual who was raised in a family of extremely trusting people may have been labeled by his family as the skeptic: he may view himself as a skeptic, although in relation to the broader variety of mankind he is actually extremely trusting. We are working to resolve these problems. Our preliminary data indicates some possible relationships between items such as spatial awareness, time perception, the heart–head axis, and preferred mode of contact with hypnotizability, as measured by the HIP.

Clinical Research: Psychopathology and the Hypnotic Induction Profile

We have accumulated a body of research data relating soft and decrement patterns of performance on the Hypnotic Induction Profile to serious psychopathology. The three studies which follow present evidence for the hypothesis that hypnotizability as measured by the HIP is a function of relative mental health characterized by integrated concentration; and that an impairment or collapse in hypnotizability as represented by soft or decrement profiles indicates a high probability of the presence of serious psychopathology.

We initially made this clinical observation among psychiatric outpatients. Patients with diagnoses as diverse as sociopathic personality, severe character disorder, schizophrenia, severe depression, mental retardation, neurological deficit such as early Parkinsonism—or those heavily sedated or tranquilized—all tended to obtain decrement profiles on the HIP. The unifying feature in these diagnostic groups seemed to be an impairment of the ability to maintain a state of focal concentration in which a given input is integrated under a wider "umbrella" set. It was postulated that a severe psychopathological condition, because of associated impairment of focal concentration, would reduce hypnotic capacity and result in lower hypnotic performance than the biological potential represented by the eye roll would indicate—hence a decrement profile. The following studies have also been reported elsewhere (Spiegel, H. et al. 1975; Spiegel, H. et al. 1977).

STUDY I

As an initial, rough test of the hypothesis, 100 patients in the psychiatric division of Bellevue Hospital in New York City were selected by hospital staff who were unaware of the hypothesis for testing with the Hypnotic Induction Profile. The tester* in turn was unaware of each patient's specific diagnosis; he knew only of their inpatient status and thus that the psychiatric diagnosis was probably serious. Of the 100 patients tested, 95 proved to have decrement profiles. Each of the 95 subjects had a diagnosis of serious psychiatric disturbance; two-thirds were schizophrenic and the remainder carried diagnoses of psychopathic personality and psychotic affective disorders. Such a clear relationship between the decrement profile and severe psychiatric disturbance was encouraging but not wholly convincing, since the tester was familiar with the hypothesis and knew that the subjects were psychiatric inpatients.

Despite its limitations, this study indicated that the decrement profile was associated with severe psychological disturbance and that the nondecrement profile was associated with an absence of active psychotic symptoms. These results led to a more carefully designed and controlled study of the original hypothesis.

STUDY II†

The relationship between HIP scores and psychological status was evaluated with a group of psychiatric outpatients.

Patient Sample Information on 105 patients who had been referred to the office of the senior author for evaluation and psychotherapy was incorporated into this study. The information was gathered as part of routine psychotherapeutic treatment. Originally, information was collected on 110 patients seen sequentially. Data on five of these patients were incomplete or unscorable and they were dropped from the study. Group assignments in the study were made on the basis of the presence or absence of severe psychopathology. Demographic characteristics of patients in the two groups are comparable, as shown in Table 10–2.

Method. As part of the therapeutic evaluation, the Hypnotic Induction Profile was routinely administered during the first session. All HIPs were scored by both the induction and the profile method. Shortly there-

---

* John T. Janics M.D.
† This report was prepared by drawing on work reported by Spiegel, H. et al. (1975) and Spiegel, H. et al. (1977), which contains more detailed findings and data analysis. These same data are examined from the point of view of the validity of the HIP as a psychodiagnostic instrument in the Appendix.

TABLE 10-2

Demographic Characteristics According to
Severity of Psychopathology.

	Mild to Moderate Psychopathology (N = 56)	Severe Psychopathology (N = 49)
Sex (percent)		
Male	63	61
Female	37	39
Education (percent)		
with high school		
or less	25	9
with some college	14	24
with college degree	61	67
Age		
Mean	37.4	35.6
S.D.	10.7	10.5

after, these patients were referred to a clinical psychologist for psychological testing. The referrals were made as part of the therapeutic program and neither the patient, the physician, nor the psychologist was aware at the time that the information would be used in a research project.

The psychologist's reports were based on the Wechsler Adult Intelligence Scale (Wechsler 1955), the Machover Draw-a-Person Test (Machover 1949), the Sentence Completion Test (Irvin 1972), the Visual–Motor Gestalt (Bender 1946), the Rorschach (1954), and the Thematic Apperception Test (Murray 1943). The reports then were submitted to an independent psychiatrist who was unfamiliar with the patients, unaware of their HIP grades, and uninformed about the hypothesis. He in turn distributed the reports on a five-point mental "Health–Illness" continuum. The five categories were: A) healthy; B) moderate neurosis; C) severe neurosis; D) probable psychosis, severe character disorder,

TABLE 10-3

Means and Standard Deviations of Induction
Scores for the Five Health-Illness Groups.

Severity of Psychopathology	N	Induction Score Mean	S.D.
No neurosis (A)	10	8.7	1.1
Moderate neurosis (B)	46	7.7	2.6
Severe neurosis (C)	20	5.5	3.2
Probable psychosis (D)	28	5.8	3.0
Obvious psychosis (E)	1	3.0	0.0
Total	105		

severe depression, or schizophrenia (latent); and E) obvious psychosis. The patient distribution is represented in Table 10–3. (Categories A through E were also labeled 1 through 5 for the purpose of statistical analysis.) The relationship was examined between the patient's psychological status, as determined by the psychiatrist, and the patient's HIP grade, as determined by both induction and profile scores.

Induction Score Results. Although it was found that the induction score means of the Health–Illness groups descended in nearly stepwise order according to rated severity of psychopathology (Table 10–3), only two groups were used for the purpose of statistical analysis. This procedure insured adequate group sizes and also at least partially vitiated the problem of the reliability and validity of the H–I ratings. Because the psychologist's reports (rather than firsthand observation) were the basis of H–I ratings, use of two H–I raters would not have helped in the establishment of reliability in this case. We reasoned that most clinicians would feel capable of reliably assigning patients to one of two groups (moderate to no neurosis, versus severe neurosis to probable or obvious psychosis) on the basis of detailed psychological testing performed and reported by a seasoned psychologist. However, without seeing the patient, the requirement that each patient be assigned to one of five groups would probably lead to reasonable skepticism regarding the meaningfulness and replicability of group assignment. Therefore, H–I groups A and B were collapsed, forming a group ($N = 56$) which was characterized by the absence of severe psychopathology. Health–Illness groups C, D, and E were collapsed and characterized by relatively severe psychopathology.

Table 10–4 shows the induction score distributions of the two H–I groups.* If scores of 6 and below are considered low, as they usually are in clinical work with the HIP, the predicted difference between the two groups is apparent; 73 percent (24) of the scores in this range belong

TABLE 10-4

Frequency and Percentage Distributions of the Induction Score According to Severity of Psychopathology.

Induction Score	Mild to Moderate Psychopathology		Relatively Severe Psychopathology	
	No. of Cases	% of Total	No. of Cases	% of Total
Low (0 to 6.0)	9	(16%)	24	(49%)
Medium (6.25 to 9)	31	(55%)	24	(49%)
High (9.25 to 10)	16	(29%)	1	(2%)
Total	56	(100%)	49	(100%)

* The distribution of induction scores in this sample is virtually identical to the distribution observed in the normative clinical sample of 1,339 consecutive, private psychiatric patients, including the patients selected for the present study (Spiegel, H. et al. 1976). Although both samples showed a large proportion of high scores, the mode of the sample given here was one point higher (9 instead of 8).

to the group with severe psychopathology.* The mid-range scores (6.25 to 9) are a poor predictor. Unexpectedly, though, Table 10–4 also shows that the induction score provides maximal separation of the two groups at the top of the range; 94 percent (16) of the scores 9.25 to 10 were earned by patients in the group with mild psychopathology ($p < .0003$).

On the basis of the induction score (o to 6 predicts severe psychopathology and 6.25 to 10 predicts mild psychopathology), the probability of correctly assigning a patient to the relatively healthy group was .84, compared to a sample base rate of .53. However, the probability of correctly assigning patients to the relatively less healthy group was only .49, no improvement over the base rate of .47. For the whole sample, the hit rate on the basis of the two categories of the induction score (o to 6 and 6.25 to 10) was .68, a small improvement over the .53 base rate.

Profile Score Results. Table 10–5 presents the relationship between severity of psychopathology and the intact versus nonintact profile patterns. The two types of nonintact profile pattern, soft and decrement, showed equally high concentrations in the group with H–I ratings of C, D, and E. For this reason, definitions of these subtypes are not presented here. However, it should be noted that clinical use of the HIP suggests that the decrement profile pattern is a less ambiguous predictor of severe psychopathology than the soft pattern.

Support for the hypothesis of an association between the nonintact pattern and severe psychopathology was clear: 80.5 percent (29) of the nonintact profiles were obtained by patients with H–I ratings of C, D, or E. Again, this proportion is highly unlikely on the basis of chance alone ($p < .001$). Correspondingly, 73 percent (49) of the intact profiles were obtained by patients in the larger, relatively healthy group.

On the basis of the intact profile pattern, the probability of correctly assigning the patient to the relatively healthy group was .875, approximately the same as the accuracy rate using the induction score. The accuracy rate was .59 among the less healthy group, slightly better than the hit rate using the induction score. The hit rate for the sample as

TABLE 10-5

Relationship between Severity of Psychopathology
and Type of HIP Profile Pattern.

	Patients with Intact Profile Pattern	Patients with Nonintact Profile Pattern
Mild to moderate psychopathology	49	7
Severe psychopathology	20	29

° The binomial probability of observing this distribution by chance alone is very small: $z = 3.00$, $p < .002$, unidirectional.

a whole (.74) was also slightly higher than the hit rate using the induction score.

Comparison of Profile Pattern and Induction Score. The induction score (0 to 6 and 6.25 to 10) and the profile pattern (intact or non-intact) led to prediction of the same degree of psychopathology (mild to moderate versus relatively severe) in 93 of the 105 cases. Of the remaining 12 cases, the psychiatric rating and the profile pattern agreed in nine and the psychiatric rating and the induction scores agreed in three. Thus, the two scores bear approximately the same relationship to severity of psychopathology; and when the predictions of the scores disagree, the profile score is slightly more accurate.

STUDY III*

Study III evaluated the prediction that patients with decrement pro-files show more severe psychopathology than patients with straight zero profiles. The definition of both grades includes failure of the con-trol differential item and demonstration of little or no hypnotizability. Theoretically, a zero eye roll indicates a lack of the innate physio-logical capacity to engage in this style of concentration, and therefore indicates a consistent lack of any hypnotic engagement. A decrement profile indicates an inability to use the given physiological attribute to maintain a focused concentration set. Because severe psychopathology impairs the capacity for focal concentration, the discrepancy between potential and usable hypnotic capacity should predict the presence of serious dysfunction.

In this study, therefore, we hypothesized that the zero profile would show a lesser degree of association with severe psychopathology than the decrement profile, and that zeros and intacts would show no differ-ence in severity of psychopathology.

Patient Sample. A group of eight patients with HIP grades of zero had independent psychological evaluations performed on them. The sample size was determined by case availability. There were no other patients with zero HIPs on whom we had independent psychological evaluations. This is consistent with the finding that only 5 to 6 percent of 4,300 HIPs had zero grades. (Spiegel, H. et al. 1976)

Method. Using the same Health–Illness rating system employed in the previous study, an independent psychiatrist identified two of these eight patients as having moderate neurosis, four as having moderate to severe neurosis, one as having severe neurosis, and one as being obviously psychotic. The patients were then grouped on a two-point Health–Illness scale.

Of the patients with zero profiles, 25 percent (two) were assigned by the rater to the group characterized by relatively severe psychopath-ology (C, D, and E ratings), compared to 80.5 percent of the nonintacts. This difference is highly significant (Fisher exact probability = .005);

* We wish to acknowledge Martin T. Orne's suggestion that we study the incidence of psycho-pathology among patients with zero profiles.

it confirms the impression that a zero score on control differential and/or arm levitation predicts severe psychopathology *only in the presence of a positive eye roll*. This finding suggests that the ER (eye roll) and the profile score have particular value in the identification of patients with severe psychopathology.

Correlation of ER and Induction Score. We have reported that in an unselected sample of 1,023 private psychiatric patients, the correlation of ER and induction scores was .22 ($p < .01$) (Spiegel, H. et al. 1976). In the same article it was reported that the ER/induction score correlation was much higher (.52, $p < .001$) in a selected sample of nonpsychotic patients. This nonpsychotic group was made up of the same patients whose Health–Illness ratings in study II placed them in the mild to moderate psychopathology group. The same correlation was calculated for the group that scored in the severe psychopathology category. In this group the correlation between ER and induction score was low and nonsignificant* and the difference between the two groups was significant.†

Although the sample size was small, this study demonstrates that the relationship between eye-roll score and hypnotic performance on the HIP has predictive value in regard to psychopathology. Individuals who had comparable performances on the levitation and control differential measures but who also had zero eye rolls were less likely to have severe psychopathology than those with positive eye-roll scores. The implication is that individuals with a positive ER and a soft or decrement profile pattern experienced a fall-off from their biological hypnotic potential.

COMPARISON OF THE STUDIES

In Study II the profile distribution beween the Health–Illness groups was so clear-cut that the association of the decrement profile with severe mental illness became predictive. The Study II results were supported by the findings for induction scoring. However, the distribution of induction scores between the Health–Illness groups, especially in the low range, was not as distinct as the parallel profile-scoring distribution. These findings (Study II) indicated that severe psychopathology is associated with nonhypnotizability as represented by nonintact profile grades (soft and decrement) and low induction scores. Conversely, general mental health is associated with hypnotizability as depicted by zero and intact profile grades, as well as by high induction scores on the HIP.

The zero and decrement profiles depict nonhypnotizability in different ways. Study III indicated that the zero profile reflects the nonhypnotizable extreme of the intact hypnotizability continuum; that is, hypnotizability to the zero degree.

The individual with a decrement profile in contrast has "fallen off"

---

* $r = .15$; $p > .05$, $n = 49$
† $z = 2.3$, $p < .05$

the hypnotizability continuum; such a person has the capacity for, but is refractory to, the hypnotic experience. The variance caused by unidentified decrements in the general population may account for the wide-ranging and contradictory results to date in research which relates hypnosis and personality or hypnosis and psychopathology (cited earlier). Study III supported the uniqueness of the relationship between decrements and severe psychopathology. Decrement and zero profiles are both characterized by zero control differential scores. Study III in effect showed no connection between the control differential score alone, and psychopathology. An eye-roll score greater than zero differentiates both decrement and intact profiles from the zero profile. Other studies (Spiegel, H. et al. 1976) have shown no connection between eye-roll scores alone, and psychopathology. Consequently, the diagnostic clinical uses of the HIP are dependent upon the entire profile configuration.

The statistically significant increase in the percent of decrements with increasing psychopathology implies that seriously disturbed patients are unable to use their physiological capacity for disciplined concentration. This is consistent with Shakow's (1974) finding that the schizophrenic has difficulty maintaining the "major set" for total integrated control while negotiating new input signals. In other words, the psychotic patient struggling with distracting internal and external stimuli is unable to set aside these stimuli enough to focus his attention, shift into, and maintain an altered state of receptive concentration or hypnosis.

Thus our clinical research indicates a connection between serious psychopathology and extremely low scores using the induction scoring method or decrement and soft profile scores. More specific work remains to be done, especially in relating the size of the gap between eye-roll score and hypnotic performance to the type of psychopathology involved. As the cluster diagrams indicate, we postulate that 1 or 2 decrement profiles are more consistent with schizophrenia; and that individuals with 3 and 4 eye rolls but with decrement performances are more likely to have serious affective disorders. These more complex studies of specific differential diagnosis and patterns of performance on the HIP are currently being undertaken.

PART III

Using Hypnosis in Treatment

11

Formulating the Problem

Should I, after tea and cakes and
ices,
Have the strength to force the
moment to the crisis?

T. S. Eliot
"The Love Song of
J. Alfred Prufrock"

Introduction

Hypnosis and therapy, like man and woman, are different but related
in interesting ways. In understanding the relative role of hypnosis in
therapy, it is useful to establish a spectrum of all the therapies as a
background (See Figure 11–1). The intact zones from 1 to 5 on the
HIP are the target areas in which hypnosis has its most direct applicability. As indicated in the diagram, there are a variety of therapeutic
modalities already in use that can be usefully employed with the Apollonians, Odysseans, and Dionysians. The major role of hypnosis in these
established treatment modalities is to facilitate the primary treatment
strategy. In essence, hypnosis can contribute an extra leverage effect
which adds to the impact of a given therapy and often leads to shortening
that procedure. Although many therapists choose the treatment modality by intuitive judgment, logistical preference, or ideological bias, our
approach suggests that there is a systematic way to determine which of
these various modalities is most appropriate for a person with a given
problem.

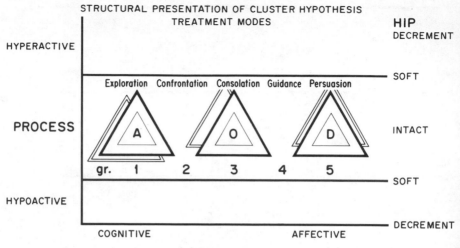

STRUCTURAL PRESENTATION OF CLUSTER HYPOTHESIS

Figure 11–1

We will present one approach to brief, symptom-oriented treatment, called "restructuring," which employs hypnosis and is designed to be maximally adaptable for all individuals within the intact range of hypnotizability. By virtue of being brief, it is designed for teaching a patient in one session and involves a mixture of cognitive and emotional components. Restructuring serves as a first step in the treatment process, as a kind of therapeutic trial. If it works and the symptom is alleviated, the patient may go on to symptom mastery in other areas or may simply be satisfied with the result. If it fails or if the patient's curiosity is aroused regarding further explanation of his symptom, we seek to employ the information gathered from the HIP and the rest of the clinical data in systematically selecting an appropriate intensive treatment strategy.

The structure of the remainder of the book reflects this treatment approach. After presenting our approach to the use of hypnosis in symptom-oriented treatment, we discuss the uses of hypnosis in selecting an appropriate intensive psychotherapy, and in treating the highly hypnotizable patient. In the next section we present in some detail our theoretical approach to the use of hypnosis in brief psychotherapy. We arrive at the selection of a treatment strategy after reviewing hypnotizability assessment and its implications for a given patient's personality structure and relative state of mental health. This parallels the clinical encounter in which a history is taken, the patient's hypnotizability is assessed and discussed with him, and the therapist is then prepared to recommend a treatment approach and teach the patient how to use it.

What follows is a distillate of our approach to incorporating hypnosis into psychotherapy. We have endeavored to present the approach in some detail, both from a theoretical perspective and through enumerating treatment strategies. Follow-up data on the effectiveness of two of the interventions are reported in the Appendix. It is hoped that the reader will be able to evaluate and use this material in the context of his own interests. We present it not as the only approach available, but as one which we have found to be theoretically and clinically appropriate, efficient, and effective. This section is not intended to be a comprehensive review of the variety of reported uses of hypnosis in psychotherapy. This task has been done well in other texts to which the reader is referred (Erickson 1967; Erickson et al. 1976; Frankel 1976; Meares 1960; Weitzenhoffer 1957; Wolberg 1948; Crasilneck and Hall 1975).

Time for Psychotherapy

When the major emphasis in therapy is on rapid and brief treatment, often in one session, an approach is needed which necessarily demands rapid and accurate problem assessment and commitment to change on the part of the therapist and the patient. It demands an atmosphere not of leisurely exploration but of urgency, a commitment to getting on with living, and a focus on clear assessment of results. For such an approach to be successful, the patient must view his time with the therapist as an opportunity for growth and change: he must value his time and that of the therapist. Although this effort toward rapid intervention is desirable but not mandatory in most instances, it is critical for effective therapeutic momentum to prevent or treat the early phases of traumatic neurosis (Kardiner and Spiegel 1947 [also see pp. 297–302 on abreaction]).

Before going on to discuss brief treatment strategies, it seems worthwhile to discuss the importance of time in relation to psychotherapy. We have already noted that individuals have quite different views of time. Apollonians tend to concern themselves with past and future; Dionysians tend to live for the moment; Odysseans tend to shift between present and past or future considerations; and schizophrenics tend to live in a timeless world of primary process. Likewise, different psychotherapies have within them different, implicit views of the passage of time, and they convey varying messages to patients about the value of time.

It is an intriguing hypothesis that one can productively look at the kinds of human behavior which normally enter the view of psychiatrists in terms of one factor: time. It can be argued that many neurotic and even psychotic processes are ways of dealing with the passage of time—that they are in fact ways of creating the illusion that time does not move on—that it is not moving at all, it is circular, or it can be stopped at will.

Numerous philosophers have concerned themselves with the phenomenon of time. At least as far back as Aristotle, there has been a trend of describing time in spatial terms of arguing that time can be adequately measured by the movement of an object at a fixed rate of speed along equal distances. Aristotle essentially tried to lay a strip of time on the ground and measure it by spatial standards (Hope 1961). This idea was crucial for the development of scientific thought. After all, the very notion that experiments can be reproduced requires a capacity to hold certain circumstances constant. It is necessary to be able to assume that one five-minute period is essentially the same as any other, in order to quantify and replicate results. The clock is the perfect symbol of the translation of time into spatial terms. Temporal motion is translated into uniform circular motion. This model provides a uniform and reproducible representation of time.

Yet this model has certain limitations. It cannot capture what is truly unique about time in relation to space—its irreversibility. Clocks do not generally run backwards, but they can; and in any event, by running forward they wind up in the same place. Movement in time, as distinct from movement in space, is unidirectional and irreversible. No spatial metaphor can capture this, since any object can theoretically move in any direction in space. The directional nature of time seems to take on relatively little significance in the physical universe: molecules can join and separate, atoms split and fuse, tides come in and go out. These events occur in time, but in any reasonable sense are quite reversible. It is possible that in astronomical thinking there is a place for time, in terms of speculating about the formation of the universe and the stars, novae, and solar systems. These events may indeed be irreversible. But in our palpable physical universe, events seem reversible.

This is no longer the case where living matter is involved. We begin to utilize historical terminology, such as "evolution." Primitive, single-celled organisms seem to divide and reproduce endlessly, although there is research indicating that cells cannot reproduce indefinitely (Hayflick 1965; Martin, et al. 1970). As the complexity of life grows, so does its fragility, along with the concept of irreversible change and development.

This is particularly clear for homo sapiens, who in varying ways is aware of the relentless passage of time. Each life, once extinguished, is *gone*. No human has endless time, and each passing moment of "now" enters history. We change ceaselessly as we grow, becoming what we have been and evaluating what we would like to be. Folk wisdom is full of such phrases as "you can't go back" to make it clear to us that time is irreversible.

Phenomenological and existential thinkers of the nineteenth and twentieth centuries have paid special attention to this phenomenon, focusing on individual perception of life and its time. Merleau-Ponty, the French phenomenologist, prefers to reverse the Aristotelian error and alter space to fit a temporal metaphor. He discusses traveling from home to work, suggesting that when a new obstacle arises or the traffic is worse, the trip takes longer and the goal is actually farther away. Thus he measures space by the intended activity of the person wishing to traverse it, and his experience of the time it takes him (Merleau-Ponty 1962).

Bergson pursued these speculations farther. He focused on the irreversible nature of time as opposed to space, and linked these to the primacy of human experience (Bergson 1960).

The passage of time in human life is both exciting and anxiety-provoking. Each moment is new; it provides an opportunity for change and growth. Each moment, however, also provides an opportunity for disaster and death. Each day that we survive brings us closer to the inevitable end of our lives. Thus we face the passage of time with ambivalence at best. The psychoanalytic tradition is rich with descriptions of "timelessness" in the time sense of young children; the unconscious, especially as exemplified in dreams; and psychoses:

The processes of the system *Ucs.* are *timeless;* i.e., they are not ordered temporally, are not altered by the passage of time; they have no reference to time at all. Reference to time is bound up, once again, with the work of the system *Cs.*

(Freud, Vol. XIV, 1963, p. 187)

Young children have no real understanding of the inexorable, unidirectional flow of time. In dreams one moves effortlessly forward and backward in time and space. Given the psychoanalytic principle that the behavior of children and psychotic patients are expressions of primary process, and that dreams are expressions of otherwise repressed unconscious material, we can draw evidence to assert that a sense of timelessness permeates the unconscious. To the extent that neurotic and psychotic processes can be viewed as eruptions of unconscious conflicts and as failures of repression, we expect the unconscious sense of timelessness to show itself in neurotic and psychotic symptoms. In fact, there may be an essential interplay between the unconscious presumption that time does not move on and the perpetuation of the neurotic or psychotic symptom. The very preservation of the symptom carries with it a sense of indifference about the passage of time. The rigidity of a neurotic pattern of keeping other people at a distance, for example, presupposes that these other people will always be available to be fended off. The transference neurosis can blossom only if the transference object is available for projection.

The hysteric can throw himself into a series of intense but unfulfilling relationships, as though past and future never existed. The obsessional destroys any sense of spontaneity by forcing interactions into a constricted pattern of obsessions and rituals. The schizophrenic copes with his overwhelming anxiety by forcing events into a rigid and autistic pattern of thinking. In various ways, all these psychopathological patterns presume that somehow time can be stopped. An illusion is created that the same pattern of behavior can go on indefinitely, that in this way time repeats itself. The fantasy of being able to control and manipulate time is consistent with the eruption of primary process, with the grandiose unconscious notion that one is above the limits of time. It understandably reduces anxiety to convince oneself that time can be transcended because it makes the problem of mortality more academic than real.*

Thus, there seems to be a close relationship between an individual's implicit sense of the passage of time and his psychopathological state. Denying the passage of time can be viewed as a defense against the anxiety aroused by the forward rush of time. Many neurotic and even psychotic defenses—isolation, displacement, avoidance, denial, and projection, for example—can be seen as an attempt to avoid and yet master the movement of time; to act as though time were really like a clock and one could start over, be young again, avoid the significance of the moment. These defenses deprive a situation of its newness, making a situation seem familiar even when it is not entirely familiar. Growth comes to an individual as he learns to seize each moment for what he can, rather than expend psychological energy in denying its importance and its fleeting quality.

IMPLICATIONS FOR PSYCHOTHERAPY

These speculations lead us to ponder the temporal structure of psychotherapy and how it is related to the temporal anxiety of patients. Levi-Strauss, in discussing myth and music, referred to them as "instruments for the obliteration of time" (1969). He might just as well have been alluding to certain aspects of psychotherapy. Two types of time in therapy will be explored; the length of sessions and the length of treament.

Psychiatrists, especially the psychoanalytically oriented ones, are famous among physicians for their firm adherence to a fixed schedule of fifty-minute hours. Psychiatrists have, in fact, less clearly structured work to perform with patients than internists and surgeons, who must do physical examinations, take blood tests, and so on. As a rule, surgeons are paid for their treatment; psychiatrists for their time. Outcome is usually far more apparent and measurable for surgical than for psychotherapeutic procedures; the section of inflamed and bleeding bowel is removed successfully or it is not. If it were only this easy to assess the mastery of anxiety or depression!

Surgeons emphasize accurate diagnosis and rapid action to prevent worsening of the condition; psychiatrists generally emphasize careful assessment and deliberate action. Surgeons often foster dependency and reliance on their ability to cure the patient—to do something to and for him. Psychiatrists have less of a concrete nature to "do to and for" a patient and focus more on process, making a point of discouraging dependent transference expectations and emphasizing the fact that the patient must effect any cure largely by himself. The content

---

* The authors are indebted to Professor Irvin Yalom for raising this issue.

of interaction in psychotherapy is far more vague and this also applies to the issues of life and death which often sharpen the focus on temporality. Surgeons often and directly confront life and death issues; psychiatrists less often, as with a threat of suicide, and usually indirectly. Psychotherapists seem to respond to this lack of clearly defined content with a rather rigid temporal structure. Surgeons see a patient not for a fixed period of time, but only long enough to get the task accomplished. Certain psychotherapists have become critical of this fixed temporal structure and are leaving their time more open-ended or turning to marathons to increase the intensity of the encounter.

Nonetheless, psychotherapists in general choose to make a fixed period of time the common denominator of their relationships with patients. The realities of scheduling dictate this fixedness. The fact that a therapist is in effect selling a fixed portion of his time also gives him a kind on anchor which enables him to keep other aspects of his interaction more independent. For example, if a patient seeks his opinion about a given situation, he can make it clear if necessary that what is paid for is his time, and that by paying the fee the patient is not purchasing his agreement on any particular issue. What results is a kind of uniform division of time pervading the psychotherapist's practice. Instead of converting time into space, we employ the old adage "time is money." Such a division of time into identical blocks may be as good a compromise as is possible for the psychotherapist.

It is also interesting to consider the implications of the psychiatrist's use of his time with his patient. The therapist can be seen as responding to the patient's anxiety about time passing him by with what amounts to an obsessional defense: by implication, the psychiatrist suggests that his way of dealing with the passage of time is to make all units of time as much the same as possible so that time seems to repeat itself. Patients often complain early in treatment that the doctor must have many patients, and that they all must seem the same to him. The structure of the psychiatrist's schedule reinforces this anxiety.

Psychiatrists occasionally do extend the fifty-minute hour to a longer but still rigidly fixed period, such as an hour for family work or an hour-and-a-half to two hours for groups. The overt need is for more time in the presence of more people, to sort out the complex patterns of interaction which occur among them. But it is interesting to wonder as well about the fact that more time is spent with units which have a life longer than any given individual. Therapists often refer to their groups as "having a life of their own" once they get going, and the groups will even meet without them when they are on vacation. In any event, the time generally remains tightly structured, although more is given where the metaphorical life of the patients as a group transcends that of any one individual.

The time taken for psychotherapy is another interesting measure. There is a suggestion that therapists may be inadvertently fitting into their patients' "time neurosis" in the way they structure the overall length of therapy. When Freud first developed psychoanalysis, the average course of treatment was approximately six months. One stopped what one was doing and journeyed to Vienna to be analyzed by the master. In view of the time involved, it was not terribly unreasonable for Freud to ask the patient not to make any major life decisions, to avoid the acting out of transference material. Analysts currently view such analyses as incomplete, and the treatment has expanded to a course of three to five years. Kleinian analyses can go on for eight years or more. Patients are often asked not to make major life decisions, such as job changes or marriage, for at least the first year of analysis, if not the whole treatment. As this happens, the therapist may be playing into the unspoken wish for time to be endless. It reinforces the fantasy that one can retreat from life and enter a period of suspended animation, and that everything will be the same when one again emerges; opportunities will not have been lost and one will not have grown older. Many patients are indeed relieved at the suggestion that they not make any major decisions, and are glad to comply with other requirements of the therapy for the sanction of not having to get on with their lives. Thus the very decision to reflect in therapy, especially over a long period of time, can have the effect of reinforcing a patient's attempted withdrawal from the flow of life.

One may speculate that, as measured by the hard stick of temporality, a good therapeutic intervention involves making it clear that the time spent in therapy is precious; to the extent that it is wasted with avoidance, denial, and even transference development, an opportunity for real contact and exchange is being lost. Such defenses presume that the other object will always be around to be warded off, and a reminder that such is not the case may give the patient the impetus to explore and master the parts of himself which prevent his utilizing the therapy experience as something new and important in his life.

There is a large and growing literature in the field of brief psychotherapy. Notable examples are the work of Mann (1973) and Sifneos (1972). These are carefully structured attempts to adapt psychoanalytic techniques to a time frame of approximately three months. The focus is limited to a core conflict or problem, but the emphasis is on change through insight. This development in the psychoanalytic approach amounts to a recognition of the need to acknowledge the importance of time, but the technique is still insight- rather than symptom-oriented. Furthermore, it amounts to lengthy brief treatment; if symptom mastery can be achieved in one session, why have twelve?

Numerous other symptom-oriented approaches exist, including behavior modification, biofeedback, and psychopharmacology. Their differences from the approach presented here will be taken up in a later chapter. It suffices to say that the assessment of hypnotizability for maximum utilization of existing trance capacity is crucial, and may indicate that another brief or even intensive treatment is in order. It should indicate as well those patients who are capable of very rapid change.

Two questions should be investigated when a patient brings a symptom to a psychotherapist: Why did the symptom arise? and Why does the symptom continue? Insight-oriented therapists tend to focus on the former question; yet the latter question is in many ways far more important; and the two questions are not the same. A symptom exacts a toll on the patient, his friends and family, and his colleagues, every hour and day that it continues. The secondary loss generated by a symptom, in terms of anxiety and humiliation, may well serve to cement its existence in the life of the patient. For example, mild performance anxiety may initially lead to a series of personal and vocational humiliations which destroy future opportunities and reinforce the anxiety. Thus a therapeutic technique which emphasizes symptom removal as quickly as possible and in a realistic fashion is respectful of this toll and of the relentless passage of time. Some patients may not respond to this brief intervention, which should be clearly determined, and they may want to go on to alternative brief or more intensive treatment. But this approach emphasizes making a disciplined effort at rapid symptom mastery, first by assessing those who are presumably capable of it with the HIP, and then by teaching them how to better mobilize their own resources. Time is not on our side; we must try to master it or it will master us.

The Clinical Challenge

Bearing in mind the importance of providing an optimal therapeutic strategy in a minimal amount of time, the therapist is confronted with no small challenge. Patients present a variety of symptoms which are at times clearly described, and other times vague. A given complaint may be only the "tip of the iceberg," an evasion; or it may in fact represent a well considered and thorough presentation of the problem. The therapist elicits a welter of information regarding the patient's psychological state, his biological capacities, and his social setting. The crucial issue is to sift among this material and select the most relevant problem or problems to be dealt with at that time.

Good clinical work requires an attitude that can be described as a "soft focus," a synthesis of disciplined investigation and a kind of intuitive sense. We make no pretense that there is an ultimate truth that the therapist and patient will stumble upon and use. Rather, the hope is that they will quickly collaborate on finding a relevant and plausible problem in the wealth of data provided by the patient.

The Hypnotic Induction Profile can provide a systematic starting point in the organization of this data. It provides some information regarding the patient's relative state of mental health, and about his personality style. The relationship between patterns of performance on the HIP and these factors is discussed in detail earlier in this book. The data provided by the HIP constitutes a starting point, a baseline for organizing further clinical data in a disciplined fashion.

In formulating the problem, it is also necessary to gather data about a patient's psychological motivation and capacity, his biological abilities, and his social environment. This information can be organized in such a way that it helps to define both the problem and the patient's resources for meeting that problem. Some of the information may serve to modify or invalidate the initial hypotheses yielded by the profile measurement. It is hoped that the profile information will be used as a disciplined but not rigid means of focusing the inquiry.

THE WELDON MODEL

How do we go about formulating a problem? There are many approaches, but we have been impressed by a model developed by Weldon, who postulated three major kinds of dilemmas: a difficulty, a puzzle, and a problem (Weldon 1945).

A difficulty is a simple inconvenience which does not require too much discernment or diagnostic appraisal to identify. The aim in approaching it is self-evident—to remove the difficulty as an obstacle. For example, if one wants to go from point A to point B and a chair is in the way, it is self-evident that in order to avoid hitting the chair one walks around it or moves it. The dilemma posed by that chair is a "difficulty."

A puzzle is a game with a set of rules which are all known. It is clear to the person challenged by the puzzle that it is possible, with appropriate ingenuity, to solve the challenge by following the set of rules. He may fail, but nevertheless it is possible to find a solution.

A problem is an ambiguous dilemma upon which we impose a puzzle form to give ourselves a sense of clarity. In the complexity of the human condition, it is literally impossible to identify all the problems that relate to a person's existence. But in this complex maze it is often clinically possible to select a sampling and apply to that aspect of the maze a puzzle form. By identifying appropriate rules of conduct to solve this puzzle, one hopefully can influence other aspects of the person's condition. In other words, the mastery of the puzzle that is imposed upon the problem can lead to a ripple effect into other phases of the person's life—you solve a problem by imposing a puzzle form upon it.

For example, one of the most frustrating and challenging areas in medicine is dealing with terminal illness. Some years ago Dr. Jesseph* was serving as a research surgeon at the Brookhaven Laboratories Hospital on Long Island, New York. He was developing new radiation therapy techniques for cancer. His ward contained twenty-five women, all dying of metastatic breast cancer. They knew they were terminally

---

* Dr. John E. Jesseph is currently Professor and Chairman, Department of Surgery, Indiana University School of Medicine, Indianapolis.

ill, which was one of the conditions for being accepted on this research ward. The patients were told that no matter what happened, there was always something the staff could do.

One morning the doctor noticed that he was drinking his fifth cup of coffee while reading the *New York Times*. He startled himself by asking, "Why am I drinking so much coffee? I don't even like coffee." He then experienced a "moment of truth" in which he frankly acknowledged to himself how difficult it was to leave the dining room, go into the ward, and face those twenty-five dying women. At the time the research program was not doing well, the results were not promising, and he was discouraged by the progress of the study. He happened to remember reading about the possibility that hypnosis could be used effectively in pain control and he found an announcement of a course in hypnosis that was being offered at Columbia University. He signed up for the course and managed to travel a hundred miles back and forth for seven Saturdays to learn about hypnosis. After the fifth session he had learned enough about pain control with hypnosis to be able to induce trances in all his patients on the ward, and he taught them how to alter their perception of pain. By the end of the course two weeks later, he reported that: 1) with the daily use of hypnosis for pain control, the patients were able to reduce their analgesic drugs to one-third the previous level; 2) reports of nightmares were reduced by 90 percent after the introduction of self-hypnosis; and 3) not the least important, the doctor himself returned to having only one cup of coffee at breakfast. He observed that, despite the difficulties they were having with their radiation research, he did have the sense of re-establishing himself as a physician who at least brought comfort to his patients by offering them an opportunity to develop a sense of mastery during this stressful period.

Several months later we were invited to the hospital to visit the ward, which had a strangely serene atmosphere. We observed four women sitting at a table playing bridge and at the same time using self-hypnosis to contain their pain. Sitting in the corner in a rocking chair and knitting was a mother superior, also a patient, who said: "When the doctor introduced this use of hypnosis to all of us on the ward, it made such an impressive change in our feelings about ourselves that I have put myself in a dilemma I never expected. Sometimes in my prayers I am tempted to thank Dr. Jesseph before I thank God."

Another way of stating the Weldon postulate is that, by applying the puzzle form to a problem, we are recasting the problem into a workable form. This brings to mind the Rheinhold Niebuhr prayer which asks God to "Give me the strength to change that which can be changed, the courage to accept that which cannot be changed, and the wisdom to tell one from the other." The Weldon formula offers us an art form in which we learn to ask the appropriate question which enables us to discover effective models for dealing with that particular question. Above all, it enables us to approach a problem without the temptation of becoming dogmatic. Ortega y Gasset wrote: "Whoever aspires to understand man, must throw overboard all immobile concepts and learn to think in ever-shifting terms" (1957). However, the choice of puzzle is not arbitrary. One must be sure that it relates to the problem.

The choice of the puzzle may be irrelevant. For example, during World War II I (H.S.) met a battalion surgeon standing alongside a jeep that was rigged up with ingenious equipment enabling him to carry three litter cases and simultaneously administer plasma. I was so impressed by the unusual design that I immediately made notes of the equipment and asked the surgeon where I could manage to appropriate the material for it. As we were talking I noticed that he seemed to be alone with his driver and I interrupted to ask where his battalion was. The function of a battalion surgeon is to be physically with the men to offer immediate medical care and evacuation, if necessary. He pointed due east and said, "I estimate they are about a mile up there." This immediately dampened my enthusiasm for the ingenious jeep. It brought into focus the distinction between technology and appropriate treatment. This surgeon had become so involved in developing his technology that in the process he removed himself from the scene, and in effect deprived his men of appropriate emergency treatment where they most needed it. He had applied an inappropriate puzzle to the problem at hand.

The clinical task is to apply the Weldon principle to therapy, which involves systematically scanning the external and internal problems and resources; combining this information with the results of the HIP; and then estimating which aspect of this array of problems invites the application of a useful puzzle form.

History and Examination

The history includes the usual information about age, sex, marital status, place of birth, referral source, formal education, work history and current employment, previous illnesses and psychiatric therapy, hospitalizations, current medication, and previous experiences with hypnosis.

The history of the condition bringing the patient for help is an important opportunity for defining the current issue. If the presenting complaint is a circumscribed statement in itself, further history is in general not helpful. However, if the complaint is diffuse, vague, ambiguous, or covers many facets of the person's life, then further investigation is necessary to look for one definable and hopefully representative aspect of the total complaint that can be approached for psychotherapeutic intervention. The long-term expectation is that if a circumscribed problem is approached and the person can learn to master this one area, a ripple effect will extend to the other difficult areas in the person's life.

As part of the general psychiatric evaluation, it is assumed that issues such as constitutional endowment, physical condition, age, sex, economic condition, treatment time available for the patient and the doctor, situational setting of the treatment atmosphere, and the therapist's willingness and ability to provide the appropriate therapy for the patient are all taken into consideration. Our focus here will be on dealing with specific judgments in relation to the Hypnotic Induction Profile.

As the patient's history is taken, a mental status examination is concurrently conducted by the clinician. The presenting symptom is often not the main reason for the patient to be at the therapist's office. Developing a sense of perspective is part of learning to do the clinical evaluation. Even if the therapist perceives the complaint simply as a camouflage, it is possible that dealing with it as a symbolic or meta-phorical statement can have a therapeutic effect. At other times it may be necessary to break through the camouflage and have an open con-frontation about the critical issue in the therapeutic encounter. Some-times someone in a decompensating depression who presents himself for treatment is in some way looking for another failure experience. This cue may be a good indication to delay further treatment until the depression is dealt with directly.

Even if it seems that a much longer history is relevant, or that a long-term, introspective investigation over many sessions is obviously necessary to clarify issues, it is useful to suspend this further history and investigation and to examine the patient with the Hypnotic Induc-tion Profile. At this point the cluster questions are presented, which usually takes three to five minutes (see chapter 10). After that the formal HIP is performed, taking another five to ten minutes. The com-bination of the brief history, the presenting symptom, the hand clasp, the cluster data, and the HIP now establishes the setting in which further exploration can be done or treatment procedures begun.

External Considerations

ENVIRONMENTAL FACTORS

It is important to assay relevant social factors which may have been important precipitatants in creating a symptom, or in creating sufficient pressure on the patient that he now seeks help for the symp-tom. For example, the death of a relative with lung cancer may result in a sufficient crisis in a smoker that he turns for help in stopping the habit. A patient may find that a previously manageable phobia is creating a serious obstacle to the development of his career. For ex-ample, a plane phobia may prevent a young executive from doing necessary traveling; one man found himself under acute stress after receiving a promotion which necessitated his traveling by plane.

It is helpful to take account of the patient's educational, vocational, social, and family status, since this information can help to define the problem more precisely or give information about the patient's momentum for change. At other times the social and family data can provide a means for effecting change.* The therapist may be able to alleviate stress in the patient's environment. In closed social systems, such as in the army or other institutions, the authority vested in a physician can be used to bring about relief. However, in an open democratic society this particular leverage is not easily available. Inviting family involvement can be an important part of the treatment atmosphere. For example, in the case presented previously as an example of hysterical psychosis, one of the major therapeutic interventions simply involved negotiating with the family for the patient to have his own bedroom and be removed physically from a situation which would inspire overwhelming anxiety in almost anyone—that of sharing a bedroom with a sexually active sister.

As another example, a young medical student who proved to be a grade 5 presented himself as having anxiety, insomnia, difficulty concentrating, and disrupted social relations. In a compliant way characteristic of grade 5s, he had adopted his father's premise that the only way to be a man was to financially support himself, even through medical school, where he was a good senior student. His father was financially comfortable and had never had any reason to suspect his son of exploiting his financial resources. The patient held several outside jobs in addition to pursuing his studies, and had become increasingly isolated because of the pressure of studies and work. The primary intervention in this case was a phone call to the father, asking him to rethink his position about his son needing to be financially independent while still in medical school, rather than a few years later, when he would be earning his own income as a house officer. His father provided him with more money; the anxiety, insomnia, and difficulty in concentrating disappeared; and the boy began to lead a more normal life.

It is unusual that one can make such a simple and effective intervention in the patient's social support system. Nonetheless, family and friends often provide additional leverage in defining the problem and effecting change.

SECONDARY GAIN AND SECONDARY LOSS

The treatment atmosphere is an excellent occasion to allow the patient to reorder his understanding of the power or impact of his symptoms in terms of secondary gain and secondary loss. The secondary gain is especially apparent in demoralized life situations. It is an un-

---

* For a discussion of the significance of the external environment in considerations of social intervention, see: Leichter and Mitchell 1967; 1977.

conscious attempt on the part of the subject to use the perpetuation of the disabling symptoms as a means of extracting more and more benefit from the disability. An insidious concomitant is the emergence of secondary loss, which is at first so subtle that no one is aware of it. It involves a potential loss in self-respect and the transition from being an active person, no matter how imperfect, to being an invalid. Unless this subtle emergence of the loss of self-respect is identified early, it can become institutionalized in the treatment atmosphere. Months or even years may go by before the person recognizes the severity of this secondary handicap.

Case example: J.H. was a thirty-nine-year-old woman, married for eleven years, living comfortably in a midwestern town. Ever since child-hood she had been suffering with the symptoms of dog phobia. As a child, adolescent, and young woman, she accrued many benefits from this symptom because it attracted attention and supportive care. During her courtship with her husband, he regarded this symptom as a sign of feminine cuteness and welcomed the opportunity to protect her when necessary. But as his successful business interests developed and as she got older, it became more and more of a nuisance to him and his friends. At times he mentioned this, but it in no way affected the symptom.

On one special evening, he was entertaining some important business clients at an elegant restaurant and someone walked into the restaurant holding a white poodle. At the sight of the dog, the patient suddenly jumped up from her seat, turned over the table, and spilled wine and food on the gowns and evening dress of her husband's guests. At this point her husband became enraged. He grabbed her by the arm, took her to a telephone booth at the restaurant, phoned a doctor in New York, and in her presence said to him, "Doctor, I've had it. I'm putting my wife on a plane first thing tomorrow morning and I want you to either fix her up or keep her there." The shock of hearing this clear-cut message from her husband clarified something to the patient that had been ambiguous for some time. Clearly, the secondary gain accruing from her phobia was at an end and instead there was the warning of mounting secondary loss. She complied, and flew to New York.

Initial examination revealed, in addition to other relevant history, that she profiled at an intact 2 to 3 level. It was also quite clear that she was highly motivated and quite prepared to tackle the problem seriously. She was given instructions on how to restructure her perspective toward dogs. In the course of the next few weeks and with the help of a cooperative friend who owned a dog, she instituted a gradual desensitization and reorientation toward dogs to the point where she held the dog in her hand, and permitted him to lick the palm of her hand. At this point she knew she had recovered, phoned her husband, and asked him if, when she returned home, he would buy her a dog as a pet.

In this case, the rather precipitous shift from secondary gain to secondary loss was a major factor in the treatment momentum. The fact that her husband no longer considered her symptom cute, but viewed it as a serious threat to their marriage, shifted the equilibrium she had established so that she was open to therapeutic intervention.

Secondary loss can be neutralized early, if in the treatment atmosphere a state of flux is developed by the physician to enable the person to re-evaluate his resources, both positive and negative, and establish new perspectives that put emphasis on his strength. Compensation policies developed and fostered by the Veterans' Administration and many insurance companies unfortunately either do not take the secondary gain factor into account or, despite its importance, ignore it and tend to encourage its perpetuation by paying people to remain sick. This becomes further emphasized when, from the patient's point of view, he is punished for getting well; compensation is reduced or removed completely. Recovering sometime before he is able to resume his previous level of functioning creates a serious moral dilemma in the patient's private life; to give up a disabling symptom when he is able to, may undermine financial security. A system that puts pressure on a recovering person to maintain disability in order to receive compensation complicates the rehabilitative atmosphere. This is one of the cogent arguments for insurance companies to develop policies of lump sum settlement rather than teasing the patient into unnecessary chronic invalidism.

Unknown numbers of veterans have played the game of being professional invalids until the peak years of their lives passed them by, only to realize in retrospect that to give it up would no longer allow them to get involved in the mainstream of living as a productive or creative person. This problem is compounded by the fact that such patients often form the kind of support systems around the network of the helping institution that ordinary people do in their work and social environment. Some of these patients really have no good alternative and face too great a loss of social connectedness in relinquishing their patient status.

This problem of economic or other compensation for psychiatric dysfunction points up the fact that secondary gain insidiously becomes secondary loss. Crisis intervention theorists have described a crisis as a time when old equilibria are shaken up, and new methods of coping are established (Caplan 1964). There is a certain critical period, usually of one to five weeks, during which the individual is relatively open to new or alternative coping strategies.* After that time he tends to become fixed in his new adaptation and the same amount of input has less effect. This is another way of saying that timing is critical and that a small intervention, occurring before secondary gain and loss have become cemented into the life style of the patient, can be far more effective than even major intervention at a later point.

---

* The Chinese ideogram for "crisis" consists of two characters, one denoting "danger," the other "opportunity."

One of the major lessons learned in World War I from a psychiatric point of view was that once a combat soldier was evacuated beyond the sound of the guns for disability reasons, it was extremely difficult to get him back into a combat situation and to fight effectively, even though he may technically have recovered from his physical trauma. This was overlooked in the early days of World War II, but later there were some occasions when it was possible to take advantage of this knowledge.

For example, during World War II a battalion was trapped in a valley, unable to move forward or backward. It was exposed to a constant dive-bombing and artillery attack without any opportunity to fight back. There were many simultaneous casualties and the situation was clearly frightening.

As this was occurring one of the medical aid men roamed about the field, even though we were ordered to stay in our foxholes, and in his dazed wandering he unconsciously veered toward the rear. His sergeant ran after him and tackled him, throwing him to the ground to avoid flying shell fragments. The soldier in his confused state cried out, "I can't stand it anymore! I can't stand it anymore! I must get out—I must get out!" The battalion surgeon, pressed to hold onto all personnel that he had, grabbed the soldier by his collar and directly said to him, firmly and clearly, that under no circumstances would he be evacuated, except when physically wounded or dead. The only way out would be on a litter. Once that message was clearly understood, the soldier was ordered to dig himself a hole and stay there until ordered out. He did, in fact, dig the hole deep enough to give him ample protection. That evening the battalion surgeon visited him, and, although he was still trembling and shaken, he agreed with the surgeon that he felt he could take hold of himself. The following morning, before the fighting resumed, the aid man went over to the surgeon and thanked him for helping him gain control of his fear. For the rest of that campaign, the soldier served competently and courageously as a combat aid man. In the ensuing month the surgeon was wounded and evacuated to the States.

Two years later the surgeon received a letter from this aid man at Christmas, with the information that he (the soldier) had served successfully, been wounded, and recovered. He took occasion to wish the surgeon a merry Christmas and a happy New Year. For several years after, the surgeon received a Christmas card, renewing contact and conveying a sense of both warmth and appreciation for the help that the man had received in maintaining his sense of dignity and self-respect.

There is no doubt that if the surgeon had evacuated this man as a psychiatric casualty labeled "combat fatigue," this soldier would have joined myriads of others in the assembly line of accepting compensation for disability. The annual Christmas cards seemed to be statements of reaffirmation that he preferred the option of being a man with his self-respect intact.

In this situation secondary gain and loss were prevented before they started. It is rare that a therapist finds himself in a situation which permits such preventive work. However, it is often possible to intervene along with the patient and his environment in such a way as to minimize secondary gain and secondary loss. The following case examples illustrate this point.

H.T. was a thirty-seven-year-old single woman who was a buyer in a department store in a large city outside New York. One rainy night as she was waiting in her car for a red light, a truck hit her car in the rear, causing a condition that was diagnosed as a "whiplash." In the inevitable litigation, it was very clear that she was in no way responsible for the accident, and that the truck was. Her response to physiotherapy was poor; there were no physical or laboratory signs to support the discernible pathology, although she had been diagnosed as a whiplash casualty. Because of her poor response to traction and physiotherapy, she was advised by her internist to travel to New York to get help with hypnosis for pain.

She arrived at the doctor's office in a chauffered limousine, and indicated that she was registered at a Park Avenue hotel, one of the most luxurious in the city, and was prepared to stay in the city as long as the doctor found it necessary to cure her. Her profile was 1 to 2, intact. The therapist immediately confronted her with the importance of litigation aspects of the case and taught her some self-hypnosis exercises to reduce muscle tension in her back and neck muscles, and to develop a psychological numbness in the painful area. But, following these instructions, she was given this clear-cut advice:

1. It was clear that she had a good case in court and it was also clear that the insurance company knew that.

2. In order to get the best benefit from the exercises with self-hypnosis, she would do herself a great favor by returning home as soon as possible, engaging a competent lawyer, and demanding the best lump sum settlement possible. After reaching her settlement, if by that time the pain was still present, she should then return for further instructions and extensions of this therapy using self-hypnosis.

She was surprised that the therapist limited the treatment to only one session; she had traveled all this distance and had been looking forward to a long stay in New York. That night she called her lawyer, and with his agreement and encouragement, did in fact return home and within two months managed to arrange a satisfactory lump sum settlement with the insurance company. At the same time, she was in weekly phone contact with the psychiatrist in New York and continued with the self-hypnosis relaxation exercises. By the time the settlement was completed, her whiplash syndrome had disappeared.

She regarded her trip to New York as a "miracle experience" and told her referring doctor so. She said she could not understand how the power of hypnosis could so quickly contain and eliminate the pain, when the previous therapies had failed.

What is intriguing is that the effective operational therapeutic factor was this woman's unconscious acceptance of getting the money issue settled as quickly as possible, and her willingness to realize that she was too young and had too many interesting things to do in life to get blocked into a lifelong battle for bits of money from the insurance company. She tended to underplay the secondary gain and loss factor and to attribute the success of this encounter to hypnosis.

Internal Considerations

SELF-ESTEEM

It is helpful to bear in mind that virtually any symptom which brings a patient to a doctor for help constitutes an assault on that person's self-esteem. He may have suffered some public humiliation, for example with a phobia, or he may feel privately constricted. In any event, the restoration of the patient's previous level of self-esteem is an important consideration. It is even possible that, as a consequence of therapy, the patient's self-esteem is enhanced beyond the pre-illness level. However, the first goal in the treatment encounter is to cope with the deficit in self-esteem associated with the illness.

This process of restoration can begin even during the data-gathering phases of the treatment session. If the therapist establishes an atmosphere of collaboration with the patient, in which the patient actively participates in defining the problems along with the therapist, his intelligence and capacity to achieve perspective on his own life in this way are acknowledged rather than belittled. It is important from the very beginning to convey to the patient that he is seen as a person with a problem, rather than as a sick object. This means acknowledging his strivings to overcome the symptom, as well as the dimensions of the symptom itself and establishing an atmosphere of cooperation in the service of mastery—rather than coercing or manipulating the patient for a given objective result.

The following case example helps make this point. I (H.S.) am not proud of my role in this event, but it happened at a time when I was a young psychiatrist in the army, in World War II, and I had just learned how to use hypnosis. I was working in the psychiatric section in the station hospital at Fort Mead, and a young black infantryman was brought in with a paralyzed left arm. After examination we diagnosed it as hysterical paralysis, and with my fresh knowledge I induced hypnosis and immediately removed the symptom. Then, with a posthypnotic signal, his left arm paralysis would return each time I touched the back of his neck. The returned symptom could be removed by another preestablished signal. The drama of this procedure attracted a great deal of attention in the hospital, and as a result it was repeated many times over a period of a week. Even the commanding officer of the hospital came to watch it happen. To my embarrassment, I must admit that there was an almost circus-like atmosphere around the case. Finally we decided that the show was over and with a sense of reluctance I sent the man back to duty because it was hard to give up such a "good" patient.

Within three days he was readmitted to the hospital with both arms and legs paralyzed. That taught us a great lesson. By going into a greater state of paralysis he answered our lack of sensitivity and our awareness of the humiliation that he had been going through by being used as a vaudeville performer. He was again rehypnotized, and again all the paralysis of both upper and lower limbs was removed. This time we related to him as a person, instead of as an amusing object. I learned that he was having difficulty in a company that had combined both black and white soldiers with a sergeant who was not terribly competent in dealing with racial problems. In discussing the matter with him, I learned that this situation was the factor that provoked the symptom; his "paralyzed" arm prevented him from punching the sergeant in the mouth. Respecting his complaint, and apologizing for our conduct, it was then possible to establish a liaison with the reassignment officer and have him assigned to a more appropriate unit, which he accepted. A six-month follow-up revealed that he was still working effectively as a soldier in the new unit.

This was clearly an instance in which the dignity and self-respect of the patient were totally ignored. His evident therapeutic potential was not mobilized until attention was paid to his dignity and self-esteem, and the therapeutic effect was then sustained. This case could have been misunderstood as an example of the inevitability of symptom substitution or the danger of hypnosis. In fact, the critical issue was the initial disregard for the patient's self-respect.

MOTIVATION AND INCENTIVE

There are some patients who believe that their only contribution to the treatment situation is to bring their bodies into the doctor's office. Harry Stack Sullivan had an approach that effectively dealt with this issue. Without saying it directly, he inferred by his conduct with the patient during the first interview this question: "Why should I be interested in you or your problem?" In that atmosphere, the patient sensed his obligation to get involved in the interaction with the therapist. In this manner, Sullivan subtly evoked a mobilization of incentive and motivation to get the therapy moving.

Unless there is adequate incentive on the patient's part, the potential for using a capacity for change can be lost or paralyzed. Sometimes simply focusing upon its importance is enough to make this factor operational. Even with other favorable treatment factors, the therapy can ultimately result in failure without this motivation. At times, it can be important enough to delay further treatment until the patient develops adequate motivation. This is especially true for individuals who have low-intact profiles, the Apollonians. Since they have a low leverage effect from their hypnotizability, motivation compensates for the reduced leverage. For example, it is quite common for the Apollonian to successfully use self-induced hypnotic numbness for pain control when he is highly motivated; but when he becomes indifferent, his perception of pain returns. In contrast, the Dionysian, because of his high leverage effect with self-hypnosis, can maintain the compensatory numbness from the self-hypnosis exercise even when motivation is less than optimal.

Another interesting reflection on motivation is that in our early studies with cigarette-smoking control, we discovered that the person with the least likelihood to succeed with the procedure to stop smoking was the widowed or the divorced person in his fifth decade or older, who had no children or close family ties. This was apparently a situation in which the absence of external family supports has a profound influence on the patient's internal sense of motivation to make a change which could well prolong his life.

DISTANCING

Another consideration in assaying the capacity for change involves providing an opportunity to perceive alternatives; that is, to develop a sense of distancing. Once the problem is identified and related to the personality tendencies of the patient, spelling out alternatives to deal with the problem becomes an exercise in preparing the person for making a choice. One of the major difficulties which emerges in therapy is a sense of entrapment. When the therapist enables the patient to see the problem in such a perspective that alternative choices become apparent, he challenges the patient to make a choice and to consolidate his commitment to the decision. It helps to make the patient aware that a symptom is usually a double statement, one of stress as well as the capacity to respond to that stress. For example, fever is a statement that the body may be invaded with bacteria, and at the same time that the body is defending itself against the invasion by raising the temperature, which enhances the body's capacity to combat the bacteria.

It also helps to reformulate the symbolism of the symptom into a less extreme form. Many symptoms unnecessarily dramatize a problem and are overreactions to a given stress. A therapeutic approach which attenuates but does not eliminate the symptom may immediately acknowledge the communicative effort that the symptom represents, and at the same time establish the momentum necessary for entirely phasing out the symptom under new conditions of security. Throughout this process, insight as such may be minimal.

Case Example. A 40-year-old lawyer was unable to swallow food or drink unless his wife held her hand on his throat, or unless she sat at his left side so that he could touch her as he ate with his right hand. He was anxious, tense, and depressed, and could not sleep without sedation. This condition had existed in various degrees of severity since he was forced to leave his native country one year before. At that time a revolution had instituted a dictatorship that would have imperiled his life if he had not drastically revised his allegiance to friends and clients within the country. Instead, he chose to flee to the United States to carry on his work.

He had been in treatment with various physicians for several months, but the crisis that led to his referral to me (H.S.) was a series of social and business meetings with important persons in regard to his legal work in the near future. Among other anxieties, the anticipation of humiliation by not being able to swallow food or drink at these impending functions led him to near panic. We had time for three sessions, one hour a day for three days, in which to work.

He was able to go into a grade 3 to 4 trance state. Among other data, these associations were elicited: his vengeful anger at his partner for betraying him, his transient hope that his exile would be brief, his need to build a new life here, his concern about his mother back home and in need of an eye operation, his fear of never seeing her again, and his statement, "I have to swallow all this."

During the second session as the patient was in a trance, I introduced the notion that he was mixing metaphors; that is, it seemed clear that there was something he could not swallow and still maintain his dignity as a person, but was this something food, or was it perhaps guilt about his mother, or was it the dictatorship that he could not accept for himself? That night he slept without sedation for the first time in over a year. When he returned the next day, he said the phrase "mixing metaphors" had turned in his mind ever since he had left the day before. In the trance he almost ecstatically declared that he now saw more clearly than before that to be a man he must not swallow (i.e., accept) the course of his partners, but he must swallow food and drink to survive as a person.

He was brought out of the trance. He jumped up and paced back and forth, declaring, "Now I am sure I can do it." I presented him with a glass of water, then a cracker. He swallowed with ease. His eyes popped with excitement. At his request, I called in his wife and brother who were in the waiting room. He demonstrated his regained capacity to swallow to them. His wife clapped her hands and wept with joy.

Having spelled out the alternatives, the freedom to use these alternatives becomes a focal issue. Circumstance, economic issues, and a variety of other milieu factors are all important; but once they are dealt with, the therapist must focus on the exercise of freedom. Typically, the highs may want to attenuate this exercise of freedom by taking into account the sensitivities of others, whereas the lows may immobilize themselves through the exercise of their own internal judgment.

CAPACITY FOR CHANGE

It is our hypothesis that the HIP can be used as a source of information regarding the given patient's capacity for change. The clearest distinction in this regard is between patients who score in the intact range versus those who are softs and decrements. Because of the association between a soft and decrement profile and severe psychopathology (see chapters 8 and 10), these patients as a group show relatively little capacity for internalized commitment and change. Intervention techniques involve medication and external support, rather than the eliciting of collaboration and commitment.

We will now turn our attention to patients in the intact range on the HIP, who are presumed to have a high capacity for change. We take an intact performance on the HIP as a message that the patient's capacity to concentrate is likewise intact and capable of being mobilized. He should be able to attend to a task, such as making a change in his behavior. In other words, the intact profile is a statement of intact capacity to change. In particular, we look for an ability to mobilize internalized commitment and to sustain this commitment until closure is achieved on the problem. These individuals are as a group capable of understanding and making use of environmental support, and at the same time filtering out interference in the environment and minimizing secondary gain and loss. Consistent with the generally good pattern of mental health among the intact group, we expect that their self-esteem is not terribly damaged, that they have considerable motivation and incentive to make an improvement in their lives, and that they have sufficient ego functioning to distance themselves from their symptom and consider alternatives. Clearly, this is a very broad group of people and they show wide variation.

By this point in the interview, it is hoped that the therapist has elicited special strengths among these factors and pinpointed special problem areas. We find it useful to invoke the Apollonian–Odyssean–Dionysian distinction in organizing this information and in deciding how to approach the patient.

In general, Apollonians are somewhat less flexible than the other groups, and more critical regarding the necessary conditions for change. They are prone to ask numerous questions about a proposed treatment strategy and are often quite hesitant about getting involved in it. However, if they accept a treatment approach, they are likely to internalize it and maintain the change with closure. They are also relatively independent of interfering environmental forces.

Dionysians, on the other hand, do not usually exercise the same critical judgment before affiliating with the new treatment strategy. As a consequence, they can accept the strategy; but whether it is well internalized, sustained, and becomes an accepted change with closure, is more dependent upon the support system around them, both positive and negative. Therefore, it is especially important to bear in mind social and environmental factors when making a problem assessment with the Dionysian. These factors may be especially important in producing a complaint, and they are certainly important in sustaining any change.

The mid-range group, the Odysseans, tend to be less critical than the Apollonians in the initial acceptance of the new treatment approach or in the choice of alternatives. At the same time, they do not show the same easy affiliation with new ideas as Dionysians. As a consequence, they represent a mid-range both in their flexibility to change and in their ability to need or respond to support systems in order to sustain a change.

SUMMARY

The therapist's task is to collaborate with the patient in reviewing and simplifying the data he has assembled, to work out an effective strategy for action. We employ the Weldon Model to make clear the point that the therapeutic approach is not *the* answer to *the* problem; rather, *an* answer to *a* problem. It is one of several possible puzzle forms that can be applied to a given problem.

Often the most difficult task for the therapist is identifying the relevant problem in the first place. We have attempted to make somewhat more systematic the intuitive art of problem assessment. This is hardly a formula, but rather a road map. Taking into account such factors as support systems, secondary gain and loss, self-esteem, motivation, distancing, and the capacity for change, the therapist should have a fairly reliable estimation regarding the most important problems and the patient's own resources in coping with them.

12

Restructuring

This chapter is written with the presumption that we are working with a patient who is compartively well integrated, who scores in the intact range of the HIP, and who has a clearly defined and reasonable sypmtomatic complaint for which brief treatment is appropriate. The therapist and the patient have either tacitly or overtly reached a decision that the symptom can be approached with a brief treatment strategy, and that long-term intensive psychotherapy is either not indicated or might be appropriately considered after a trial of brief treatment.

Having taken a history and administered the cluster questionnaire and the HIP, we have a clear idea of the problem to be addressed and the capacity and motivation of the patient for dealing with the problem. Our task now is to develop a treatment strategy employing self-hypnosis which mobilizes as many of the patient's personal resources as possible in the service of effecting a change. This is particularly important regarding long-term outcome of treatment. It is not difficult to think of ways of "ordering" a patient to relinquish a symptom with or without hypnosis. The problem is that if such a strategy should work, the interpersonal message is that the responsibility and credit rest with the therapist rather than with the patient. Thus the patient feels no enhancement of self-esteem; he has merely chosen a brilliant therapist. If the strategy should fail, the patient feels justified in being angry and disappointed in the therapy rather than in himself.

The same kind of problem occurs when so-called aversive behavioral techniques are employed. These techniques tend to be unpleasant, and although the concept was derived from the field of operant-conditioning psychology, it is well known that a rat learns far better from positive than negative reinforcement (Bandura 1969, pp. 347–348). For example, to tell a patient in the trance state that from now on cigarettes will smell and taste like excrement is to create more problems than one solves. The therapist is relying on the drama and strength of the trance experience alone rather than on instilling the real conviction that smoking is harmful to one's body. Furthermore, it is the strength of an illusion: the patient knows that he has enjoyed the taste of cigarettes, and an artificial distortion of this fact does not address the fundamental problem of a conflict between one kind of enjoyment and the associated damage to one's body.

Occasionally more amusing consequences of this type of intervention occur. One psychiatrist who was experimenting with such an aversive technique for smoking received a frantic phonecall from a patient several hours after his treatment session. "My house smells awful" the patient complained. The doctor inquired "Why, are you still smoking?" "No," the patient replied, "but my wife is." The psychiatrist was then obliged to modify the posthypnotic suggestion to include only the smell of cigarettes which the patient smoked.

What follows is an attempt to describe the construction of a treatment strategy for making use of naturally occurring self-protective mechanisms and dissociative states. The types of problems appropriate to this approach include smoking, weight control, pain control, phobias, insomnia, stuttering, asthma, and other less common behavioral and psychosomatic disorders. As an example, we will present the model used for smoking control and then discuss in some detail the reasons for this particular strategy and the thinking behind it. This may help the therapist become familiar enough with the approach that he can use the model and its theoretical background for adapting the approach to the particular problems with which he is confronted. Later in this chapter we will present some of the philosophical reasoning behind our treatment strategy in more detail.

We will examine the elements required for constructing a self-activating treatment strategy using self-hypnosis. In this section we provide a working model with which a therapist and patient can formulate any one of a number of psychiatric problems or symptoms (including many not discussed specifically in this text) into a brief and workable exercise for self-hypnosis. This formulation is useful for dealing with a large variety of problems that call for enhancement of control. The fundamental conception is the goal of helping the patient to develop a new frame of reference which includes his old and problematic behavior, but in a different perspective.

To start out, let us examine several generalizations about the manner in which patients relate to a troublesome symptom such as smoking.

Time Concept

We have found it helpful to express these generalizations in terms of the patient's view of the passage of time. As a rule, people with a symptom which they have not mastered seem to occupy one of two extreme positions with regard to time, although they may alternate between the two. For example, those who panic in a phobic situation or feel victimized and overwhelmed by an urge to smoke or overeat tend to see time as an unceasing rush from which they are helpless to extricate themselves. The image is that of a person in a canoe, caught in a furiously rushing stream, unable to control the course of the boat. Such a smoker becomes anxiously preoccupied, lighting cigarette after cigarette, as if to confirm his knowledge that he is trapped by the habit and that it will lead to his downfall.

However, the very extremity of this view forces some individuals to take refuge in avoidance, a kind of *la belle indifference*. Such a person may carry on smoking or phobically avoid certain situations as though there were no consequences to his actions. In this situation friends and family members may be distraught, all the more so because of the patient's apparent denial or avoidance. He in turn may reinforce his manner of unconcern as a defense against the anguish around him. It is not uncommon to find smokers who seem convinced that lung cancer and emphysema can happen to other people but not to themselves. Or they will say things like, "By the time I get to be old enough to have cancer, I won't want to live anymore anyway." This manner of denial corresponds to a static or frozen representation of time, in which time is presumed to repeat itself. For such a person, the present seems unconnected to past and future consequences: yet by a simple transformation, this position really implies its opposite—panic and submission.

The avoidance of real consequences implies that there is something overwhelming which is being avoided. The more massive the denial, the easier it is to slip into panic when faced with the consequences of something like smoking or a long-feared phobic situation. Thus one position really implies the other, and a given individual may flip back and forth between avoidance and panic with no change in his basic orientation. On the other hand, some individuals characteristically employ one defense or another. It is our impression that Apollonians tend to employ anxious obsessional preoccupation, and that Dionysians are prone to avoidance and denial.

A particularly good clinical example of this paradigm of temporal distortion is the case of the stutterer. The treatment for stuttering with self-hypnosis will be discussed later (in chapter 19), but it is interesting to note here that many stutterers are actually "rushing" into speech, although they sound as if they are speaking haltingly and slowly (Brady 1971). They are thrown off their normal temporal rhythm while speaking, and alternate between periods of prolonged delay in producing sounds and attempts to run too many sounds together at once. Thus they literally alternate between a rushing and a freezing of speech. The therapeutic approach described later, building on the work of Brady, requires that the patient establish for himself a leisurely but regular rhythm around which he can orient his speech. This requires that he neither rush nor freeze the flow of his speech.

The temporal model applies to the resolution of other symptomatic problems. Effective utilization of time requires an integration of the two extreme, opposing views of it. We can learn to see time as neither vanishingly brief or as infinite. Problem resolution requires a recognition that a real problem exists and that it is not overwhelming.

The Paradox of Fighting Against One's Self

Many people manage to make changes in their lives only with the feeling of "forcing themselves" to fight the symptom. The pressure of time is taken seriously, the toll of time is weighed, but a tremendous amount of emotional energy is expended in maintaining the change. For example, someone on the brink of death may give up smoking, or a person may fight a phobia because not to do so would mean economic ruin. In this type of forced change, the smoker feels that he is depriving himself of a pleasure, rather than that he is doing himself and his body

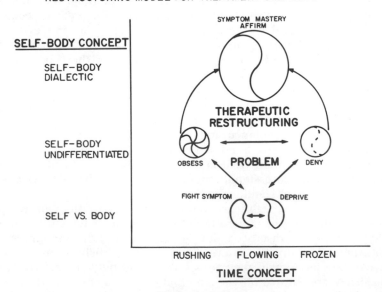

RESTRUCTURING MODEL FOR TREATMENT STRATEGY

Figure 12–1

a favor. Often he becomes so unpleasant to people around him that friends and family members beg him to resume smoking and to reassume his old manner toward them.

Such a change is often made as a deprivation rather than as a positive assertion of self; and as such, it is unstable. A person in this situation often has the feeling that he cannot manage two problems at once, and as soon as some other pressure develops in his life, he reverts to the old pattern of avoidance and denial. This pattern of problem involvement is illustrated on Figure 12–1. The labeled figures represent alternative approaches to a problem. An individual may alternate between obsession about and denying a problem. If he attempts to solve it by fighting the symptom, he experiences a sense of deprivation and emotional strain. The corresponding temporal attitudes we have described are illustrated on the abscissa of the diagram.

Self-Body Concept

On the ordinate of the diagram is another dimension which clarifies the distinction between immersion in a problem and gaining mastery over it. This dimension is the type of relationship between one's self and one's body as implied by the position one takes regarding a given problem. A position of obsession with the problem or denial of it implies that the person makes no clear distinction between himself and his body. He does not distinguish between desire and need, impulse and action. In the case of smoking, if he experiences a psychological desire to smoke, he assumes that his physical behavior must follow suit. Or if he is coping with his anxiety about smoking by denying its consequences to his body, the implicit assumption is, "If I do not think tobacco will harm my body, in fact it will not harm my body." Psychological construct and physical experience are not distinguished.

However, if the pressure of the passage of time becomes sufficiently strong, the person may cope by fighting the problem—fighting smoking, for example—in essence, fighting his own body. His position then becomes, "It is me versus my body: I want and need to smoke, but my body will not let me." The more he asserts that he is against smoking, the more powerful the idea of smoking becomes. In this context, fighting a symptom is a testimony to the symptom's strength. When God said to Adam and Eve, "Don't eat the apple," the end of Paradise was at hand. The individual has a sense that he is opposed to his body, defining himself in his desire in terms of what his body is not. Signals from his body are thus to be avoided, for they suggest that the body is winning the battle. The individual is forced to deprive himself of real contact with a part of himself, and he comes to feel that he is "denying himself." This is true in two senses; the individual may feel that he is literally denying himself some gratification such as smoking, and he may also feel that he is denying any positive relatedness to his body because he is in the paradoxical position of fighting his body.

Aversive techniques fall into this category of problem resolution. They put the patient in the position of fighting his symptom. Such an approach may appeal to the masochistically oriented individual, to whom the concept of self-punishment is familiar. He may succeed in stopping smoking by fighting his body, but the masochistic dynamism goes unchallenged or is even gratified and reinforced. Also, the individual treated with aversive techniques is in the uncomfortable position of being vulnerable to what has been called "symptom substitution" (see chapter 1)—for example, the substitution of overeating or interpersonal nastiness for smoking. In this position the individual is uncomfortable and out of tune with himself, but his new problems are more relevant to the way he is attempting to change the habit than to change itself.

Restructuring: The Dialectical Resolution

The therapeutic restructuring section of the diagram suggests a means for constructing a new perspective in which to view an old problem. The patient is invited to view the relationship between himself and his body as dialectical. That is, neither is he his body nor is he entirely separate from it. He cannot ignore his body, but he is not the same as his body. Thought and act are related, but are not the same. Impulse cannot be denied, but it also need not be followed by activity. Sensations are real, but not absolute. An individual can influence his body, but within limits. He is different from his body but cannot live without it. The individual is invited to restructure the relationship between himself and his body, hence the term "restructuring strategy." In overcoming a symptom, he affirms what he is rather than fighting or denying it.

In the case of smoking, the affirmation of relatedness is achieved by focusing on the patient's relationship to his body during the trance state in this manner: 1) for my body, smoking is poison; 2) I need my body to live; 3) to the extent I want to live, I owe my body this respect and protection. Here the focus is on affirmation of self and body through protecting the body. The emphasis is placed on establishing a relationship of respect between one's self and one's body. It logically follows that in the course of establishing this relationship, one will naturally give up smoking. The habit becomes less important rather than more important, as it would through obsession or avoidance in regard to the impulse, or through fighting it. One is not fighting it, rather one is seeing that it can become less important when the focus is instead on the relationship to one's body. The habit itself is placed in perspective and the individual is invited to rearrange his view of himself and of his body in the process.

This technique is separate from but closely related to the trance state. The dissociated state experienced during the Hypnotic Induction Profile is used as a model for suggesting therapeutic possibilities. The emphasis is on maintaining a dual focus. The patient learns to perceive his body in new ways. In this process he explores his capacity for relatedness to his body. He learns that it can provide him with new sensations and also that he has more control than he thought over the sensations that he experiences. The crucial measure in the profile, the control differential, also suggests to a person that he can alter his control over his body; that is, he feels that he has more control over one hand than the other. Thus the trance experience can teach an individual that he and his body are not the same, and that he can alter his relationship to his body in interesting ways.

Since the trance state is characterized by intense focal concentration with diminished peripheral awareness, it can be used to maximize an individual's restructuring or reorientation to himself and his body. He can use the receptive attentiveness of the trance experience to intensify his focus on protecting and respecting his body. Consequently, he can diminish his potential for being distracted by the desire to smoke, or becoming caught up in old ways of viewing the problem.

This intense central focus with diminished peripheral awareness becomes a model which can be employed in various ways depending on the symptom. For example, one can use the concentration to focus on respecting one's body, or one can use the diminution of peripheral awareness to filter out unwelcome physical signals such as pain. In the treatment strategy for pain, the input signals are reprocessed in a new way: the patient is taught to alter his relationship to his body by setting up a filter between the painful physical signal and himself, a filter which takes the hurt out of the pain. This technique will be discussed in detail later (chapter 17). But again, it involves helping the patient reorient his relationship to his body.

Conversely, such a technique can be used to help an anxious person avoid getting his body caught up in emotional tension. For example, he can be taught to picture interpersonal difficulties on an imagined movie screen while maintaining a sense of floating, relaxed buoyancy in his body. This visualization technique is a method of developing a sense of relatedness between self and body, but in this case the filter is established using the metaphor of the screen to prevent painful psychological signals from influencing the body unduly.

The restructuring approach is represented in Figure 12–1 by a variation on the old yin–yang model, the classic symbol for a dialectic. As an individual develops this paradoxical sense of distance from his body and inseparability from it, of both being his body and being different from it, he can learn a sense of mastery over a symptom by putting it in a new perspective. This is what is meant by therapeutic restructuring;

the patient restructures an old problem in a new way. This new approach takes account of the relentless passage of time, but it does it in such a way that the patient feels he is affirming rather than denying himself. In this sense the therapeutic strategy is designed to take advantage of an individual's natural nurturing and protective urges, and it becomes self-reinforcing because he feels affirmed by what he is doing. He is reinforcing his own sense of himself and therefore he is minimally in need of external reinforcement or commands in order to maintain the change. This is the general model for depicting a problem or symptom and for restructuring it in such a way that change becomes a mastery experience and an affirmation of self. Further examples will follow.

THE NINE-POINT MODEL

This notion of altering premises in order to extricate oneself from a reciprocating cycle of paradoxical demands has been discussed in *Change* by Watzlawick, Weakland, and Fisch (1974). We have been influenced by their explication of the self-perpetuating nature of paradoxical interactions which we have placed in the context of transformation, although we disagree with their notion that therapeutic interactions necessarily require manipulation as opposed to clarification. If one is encouraging a patient to enlarge his perspective of himself, one is inviting his collaboration, not manipulating.

Their use of a geometric puzzle as a way of getting across their idea of second-order change is instructive (see Figure 12–2). The problem posed is to connect a series of nine dots arranged in three parallel rows, using four connected straight lines, and without lifting the pencil from the paper. The problem is insoluble as long as an individual accepts the unwritten visual premise that the lines must stay within the confines of an imaginary box. When he expands his perspective and allows the lines to wander into the surrounding space, he can solve the problem. This is an example of the Weldon model described earlier, of applying a puzzle form to a problem. It simplifies a situation which gets the message across to a patient that he can take a new approach to an old problem. We often use this puzzle with Apollonian patients who are intrigued by its intellectual challenge; it becomes a metaphor for re-

The Nine-Point Puzzle

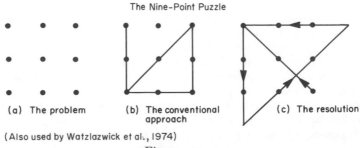

(a) The problem   (b) The conventional   (c) The resolution
                             approach

(Also used by Watzlazwick et al., 1974)

Figure 12–2

structuring an approach to an old problem. Change becomes a natural consequence of the new perspective rather than a forced issue, leaving the patient with a sense of mastery rather than deprivation.

SUMMARY

If the patient does not differentiate between himself and his body, he is vulnerable to obsession or denial. With either dynamism he may succeed in controlling the symptom, but he is prone to find himself in a context of fighting his body. He feels diminished as a person, the victim of forces beyond his control, which results in a chronic sense of deprivation. If such a patient accepts the premise "I am a smoker" and unwittingly assumes thereby that he is the equivalent of his smoking behavior, then to stop smoking means giving up his identity as a person.

On the other hand, if a patient learns to relate to his body in a dialectical sense, he views the symptom or habit as only one of his many attributes as a person. Then if he chooses to respect his body and not smoke, the choice does not challenge his status as a person, and it in fact enhances his sense of mastery toward his body and himself.

Philosophical Background

In this section we present the philosophical background and structure of the restructuring strategy. Restructuring is employed in conjunction with self-hypnosis in the treatment of a variety of problems, including habits, pain, phobias, and insomnia. The details of utilizing this approach will be further discussed in subsequent chapters. In its most general sense, the strategy involves an effort by the therapist to crystallize the patient's problem into a few succinct ideas. These ideas help the patient incorporate the idea of change through self-affirmation in a fundamental sense, which includes an acceptance of the unending dialectical struggle between life and death. The ideas are developed in an attempt to help the patient focus on his relatedness to himself and his body, and to concentrate on what he is for, in this context, rather than what he is against. The aim is that it will become clear to the patient that he has within himself the ability to confront his own dialectical struggle and to make the choice between life and death.

It has been said that one has not "lived" until one has been close to death. The phrasing might better be: one cannot appreciate life without being aware of death. We make thousands of choices every day, most of which involve taking a position concerning our physiological or psychological death. We constantly affirm our desire either to live and be free, or to choose death and bondage.

In seeking to explain any mode of therapy, one employs a vast range of theoretical explanations, from the feeling that in personal experience "it has worked" to careful statistical studies documenting efficacy. How-ever, whether articulated or not, every therapeutic approach has at its base some assumptions about the nature of man. The key philosoph-ical elements of our restructuring approach may be understood in light of the personality theories of three of the men who laid the founda-tion for existential philosophy: Hegel, Kierkegaard, and Heidegger.

The group of people who count themselves as existentialists is a vast and heterogeneous array. Some who exclude themselves from any such membership deserve it more than many who loudly proclaim affinity with the title. As an operational rule, we defined as "existential" those philosophies in which "existence" is considered inseparable from or prior to "essence," the ultimate reality of what can be known. Tradi-tionally, essence was considered ontologically prior to mere existence, which was seen as an imperfect example of essence. A brief review of the history of Western philosophy may clarify this distinction.

IDEAL VERSUS REAL

Plato and Socrates created the framework within which the major controversies in philosophy developed. The tension between the "ideal" and the "real" was explored in their dialogues. They raised the question of whether truth lay in the realm of ideas or objects. It does not do justice to the complexity of their writings to label them idealists, al-though this has often been done. They certainly did present a com-pelling argument for the primary importance of ideas and logical constructs. Others, like Aristotle and much later the British empiricists, put the major emphasis on the primary importance of perception of objects.

This philosophical tension between the ideal and the real has taken many forms—subjectivity versus science, among others. The contro-versy was alive in the medieval period in the tension between the in-creasingly rigid scholastic idealism and various objectified and at times pagan rules and rituals. St. Thomas, however, dealt with this tension by conceiving of a kind of spirit–body dualism. Descartes built on this with his well-known mind–body dualism, but he relegated primary importance to the realm of ideas.

MIND AND PERCEPTION

Kant brilliantly attempted a synthesis of the structure of the mind and the reality of perception. His fundamental contribution to Western philosophy was his establishment of the necessity of the relationship between the structure of the mind and perception. What can be known is fundamentally related to our mental capacity to know. His notion that perhaps the resolution of the tension between knowledge and per-ception lay in paying attention to the integration of mind and body in man, provided the background for Hegel's fundamental contribution.

This philosophical dialogue corresponds in a loose sense to the first two metaphors of Ortega which were referred to in the Introduction: the stamp on sealing wax relates to the empiricist position, and the box and its contents relates to the idealist position, defended in its most sophisticated form by Kant in his *Critique of Pure Reason* (trans. Smith 1965).

HEGEL'S DIALECTICAL FRAMEWORK

These alternative schools of thought, empiricism and idealism,* formed the essential background for Hegel's dialectical revolution, which in turn laid the fundamental groundwork for existential thinking. In simplified terms, Hegel viewed the empiricist versus idealist debate as resolvable only within a dialectical framework: man is both ideal and real, not one or the other; man is both existence and essence, and neither. Thus Hegel made existence and essence coincidental and inseparable. Existentialists later purported to go even farther and place existence prior to essence in importance, and yet the dialectical approach permeates the writing of many of the most prominent existential thinkers.

The theory behind the restructuring approach assumes that man is neither existence nor essence, but in a dialectical sense is both. The human dialectical experience will be examined, first within the more abstract paradoxes of Hegel, and then with the more concrete approach provided by the restructuring strategy.

In his major work, *The Phenomenology of Mind* (Baillie, trans. 1961), Hegel developed a world view focused on his dialectical understanding of the human spirit. He saw the self as constantly reconciling its opposites: uniqueness with the abstract universality of thought; freedom with the inevitable limitations that freedom imposes. The self is free to relate to these paradoxes in many ways. Hegel wrote primarily in an historical context, as though Western society as a whole were gradually coming to self-awareness, but the process can be seen as a metaphor for the development of individual self-awareness as well. Originally, an individual may be totally ignorant of the conflicts within himself. As he confronts these oppositions and his self-consciousness emerges, he is often at first overwhelmed by them; he becomes the "Unhappy Consciousness, the Alienated Soul which is the consciousness of self as a divided nature, a doubled and merely contradictory being." (1961, p. 251)

By working through the dialectic of these various conflicts, the Alienated Soul develops a new unity, but it also becomes something different, or altered, in the process:

° For the sake of simplicity we are placing in one group avowed empiricists such as David Hume, and philosophers of an inductive bent such as Aristotie. Both might better be called "realists." They have in common an overriding respect for the primacy of sense perception, although many realists consider the sense experience an opportunity to have more general laws revealed, and in that sense they are indirectly idealists.

This dialectic process which consciousness executes on itself—on its knowledge as well as on its object—in the sense that out of it the new and true object arises, is precisely what is termed Experience. (1961, p. 142)

An individual feels himself to be entirely unique, yet he thinks in abstract universal ways which deny his uniqueness. The dialectic takes each part of that paradox to its extreme and shows how it collapses into its opposite; in the process the self becomes these two previously "irreconcilable" opposites. That is, the individual considers himself absolutely unique, yet the very term "unique" is an abstract word suggesting a trait common to all individuals, rendering the unique universal.

This is not merely linguistic trickery. When we think about our uniqueness, we do it in words, which then become the means of communicating ideas, i.e., of transcending our own uniqueness. Our uniqueness is a strong bond with other human beings, a property common to all humans. However, our uniqueness has no meaning unless it can be contrasted with our universality. We are all human and we are all unique: we are not merely "unique"; our uniqueness is universal.

To repeat the paradox: universality is an abstract idea which has no meaning if it does not apply to any individual case. In fact, any single abstract idea is a unique one, differing from all other universal or abstract ideas. Thus the analytic process by itself is shown wanting, and the individual transcends the paradoxes which result from it through a dialectical synthesis. The dialectical process thus becomes one in which the individual is able to absorb the paradoxes of his existence and create a new kind of unity within the self which recognizes these conflicts and internalizes them.

Similarly, the self must deal with the paradox of freedom and necessity. The self's very freedom is a necessary contingency of life: one is forced to choose all the time, even in denying that there is any choice. Yet the notion of being bound means nothing without the concept of the alternative of not being bound. We cannot speak of necessity without invoking freedom. The individual must absorb both his freedom and his boundaries to transcend the alienation produced by these self-conflicts.

The understanding of this dialectical process takes time, and on any given issue an individual can be at various stages in realizing the paradoxes which comprise his personality. The elements of the dialectic are inherent in any situation; we can hardly fault anyone for failing to make a dialectical step if the step is never even a possibility.

The conflicts between such elements as freedom and necessity or individuality and universality, along with many others, are inherent in any situation, and an individual may have many degrees of success in reconciling them. This process of reconciling opposites is constant, never complete, never entirely undone; the process itself is dialectical. To fully grasp the meaning of the dialectic, it is necessary to approach it with a new frame of mind which is not strictly analytical. It is tempting to see dialectic as merely a new form of idealism, just a new and more complex model to which imperfect reality approximates itself. The dialectic is not an object, but rather a living process in which knowledge is created. It utilizes logic and perception, but is misunderstood if viewed as an object in itself. In fact, the critical dialectical step is to see how form and content merge, rather than separate. It is in this sense that we understand Ortega's third and most important metaphor of light, referred to in the Prologue. The process of knowing is inseparable from what is known. The dialectic is part of a process of becoming, through which we struggle to overcome our self-alienation, an alienation which results from such arbitrary dysjunctions as between uniqueness and universality, freedom and necessity, knowing and what is known.

KIERKEGAARD AND THE IDEA OF "RELATING"

Hegel's illumination of man's dialectical nature was expanded upon by Kierkegaard, who is usually referred to as the father of existential philosophy. While disagreeing with Hegel on many issues, Kierkegaard was profoundly influenced by his study of the dialectic. A kind of dialectical irony permeates his writing style, and his discussion of man existing in paradoxical relation to himself is, in fact, a dialectical formulation. His approach is more literary and personal than Hegel's, and helps fill out the dialectical theory of personality:

The self is a relation which relates itself to its own self, or it is that in the relation (which accounts for it) that the relation relates itself to its own self; the self is not the relation but (consists in the fact) that the relation relates itself to its own self. Man is a synthesis of the infinite and the finite, of the temporal and the eternal, of freedom and necessity, in short it is a synthesis. (Kierkegaard [Lowrie, trans.] 1954, p. 146)

In these few sentences of rigid prose at the beginning of *The Sickness Unto Death*, Kierkegaard comes as close as he ever did to briefly stating what a person is. In good dialectical fashion, he hastens to warn us what a person is not as well. It is dangerous to talk only about what a person is, for this is to reduce him to a "what," a thing devoid of the subjectivity which is the basis of our humanness. What he points out is, we exist in that we relate to all things: to ourselves, to our fields of experience, to our environment, to other people. Lest any be tempted to fasten on this "relationship" as though it, too, were an object (people often picture the steel rod connecting the two ends of a dumbbell), Kierkegaard reminds us that the self can relate to any given relationship we care to name; the self exists through the fact that it does relate. Hence, it is always beyond our grasp.

The two key words in understanding Kierkegaard's theory of personality are "paradoxical" and "relationship." The self is a paradox in that it consists of the dialectical opposites of freedom and necessity, universality and individuality. It is a set of relations, but more than that, it is always able to relate beyond any given set of relations. Where Hegel used the term "self-alienation," Kierkegaard uses the term "despair." The first chapter of *The Sickness Unto Death* is entitled "That Despair is the Sickness unto Death." This sickness is a result of the self willing itself to be dead, lifeless, devoid of the power to relate. This despair (and hence, sickness) occurs when the self treats itself as an object; for example, when a person considers himself nothing more than a given social role, set of ambitions, or collection of habits. A person moves beyond despair when he gives up these "dead" images of himself by acting as more than an object. In *Fear and Trembling*, for instance, Kierkegaard praises Abraham as one who became himself by giving up his image as leader of a great race of people and by being willing to sacrifice Isaac (1954).

This dialectic may be considered a life and death struggle. In one sense, sterile constructs compound a "dead," reified understanding of man in which the living, dialectical relatedness that is man's nature is reduced to simple, unchanging statements or ideas. Anyone who chooses to view himself in either purely universal or purely unique terms is denying his fundamental ability to relate. He treats himself as though he were an object, and death is the literal reduction of a living being to the status of an object.

THE CONFRONTATION WITH DEATH

Martin Heidegger expanded upon this theme. He viewed the confrontation with death as a critical step in the individual freeing himself to recognize his possibilities of relating. Death, for Heidegger, is the ultimate possibility; it is ultimately certain, but its timing is absolutely uncertain. The confrontation with death reminds us that we are not all the things we might think we are, or even could become, because that confrontation makes it manifestly clear that we might not exist:

. . . (death is) the possibility of the impossibility of any existence at all. . . . It is the possibility of the impossibility of every way of existing. . . . Being-towards-death, as anticipation of possibility, is what first makes this possibility possible, and sets it free as possibility. (Heidegger 1972)

Death is best understood in a dialectical sense: it is both a distortion of human freedom to relate, and a reminder of our limitless possibilities in relating. An individual can either be cowed by death, and circumscribe his life with fears and limitations, or he can face it and expand his ability to make choices.

Philosophy and Psychotherapy

This philosophical background provides a context for understanding the implications of the restructuring approach, which we will explore after a brief parallel discussion of the history of psychotherapeutic strategies. The overall aim of the dialectical revolution in philosophy is integration—synthesis—rather than analysis. Analysis is hardly discredited or abandoned, since in a dialectical sense synthesis has no meaning without analysis. But the thrust of this approach is to view understanding as a tool rather than a goal. Knowledge and experience are to be united rather than dissected.

PSYCHOANALYSIS

Parallels are evident in the psychiatric setting. A major current of thought to be reckoned with in any discussion of therapeutic strategy is clearly psychoanalysis, which has been a major influence on our thinking. Yet as the name itself demonstrates, the aim of the treatment is analytic, towards separation and understanding of subjective processes. This is done with the conviction that such an understanding will make the unconscious conscious, the irrational rational, and thus will lead to growth. The connection between this thinking and biological reality is one of the weakest parts of the Freudian system. The instinct theory underlying drives and the economic system of energy replacement are not widely accepted by many modern psychoanalysts, and are ignored by most experimental psychologists. But the bulk of Freud's analysis of subjectivity has survived, leaving us with an irony; that as he explored subjectivity, he wound up with an object. Psychoanalysis led to objective descriptions of human behavior which were productive, but which at the same time led to the blurring of distinctions among individuals and to a presupposition that the analyst knows more about a person than the person himself knows. The analyst may well know different things than the analysand knows about himself, but the contradiction inherent in such a position suggests that something has gone astray.

Jean-Paul Sartre discussed this paradox in some detail in an article in *Ramparts*, in which he described disruption of an analysis when the patient brought in a tape recorder in an effort to gather "objective" information about the analyst. The latter became quite angry and defensive. Sartre's suggestion was that if turnabout is not fair play, then the analysis is doing something more than it claims. The desire to analyze is converted into a power operation in which the person becomes objectified. The power to know someone becomes the power to limit rather than free him (Sartre 1969).

A further irony appears in Freud's own methods of exploration, which contained many dialectical as well as analytic elements. He developed not one but three typographies of the human psyche: first, unconscious—preconscious—conscious; next, ego—superego—id; and finally, eros and thanatos. The course of his work seems like a dialectical reworking of the same yet different phenomena. He was attempting to integrate opposites as suggested in each of the three groupings, and yet felt that no one description sufficed. The relations among the three typographies are complex at best. The final distinction of eros and thanatos has a particularly existential flavor, and is the least used in standard analytic treatment. An excellent review of Freud's work and a discussion of his thinking in relation to Hegelian dialectic is contained in Ricoeur's book, *Freud and Philosophy* (1970).

Thus the psychoanalytic method hints at integration of mind and body, but its tendency is heavily in the direction of separation and the objectification of subjectivity. The technique is most closely allied to the idealist schools in philosophy, which most highly value rational ideas about affect. The Ortega metaphor of the box and its contents is apt for the analytic method, which seeks to explore and explain the contents of the unconscious.

BEHAVIOR THERAPY

By contrast, newer methods of behavior therapy primarily developed in the United States make a point of ignoring subjectivity and focusing on objective behavioral change. B.F. Skinner (1938, 1957), a founder of the operant-conditioning approach to the study of animal behavior, chooses to view the mind as a "black box" and behavior as nothing more than the product of input. This position is most closely allied to the empiricist schools in philosophy, especially Hume and other British empiricists. Ortega's first metaphor of the stamp and the sealing wax is clearly appropriate to the behavioral approach. The "black box" view of the mind does create some philosophical problems, for the predictibility of a response in relation to a given stimulus suggests some nonrandom organization of the mind.

This operational simplification of the brain seems to represent what Bateson refers to as "dormitive hypothesis," one which "put(s) to sleep the critical faculty within the scientist himself" (Bateson 1972).* By this he means a pseudoexplanation that represents an agreement by scientists to spend no further time examining a phenomenon. In fact, he likens an explanatory principle to the black box concept: "a conventional agreement between scientists to stop trying to explain things at a certain point" (Bateson 1972, pp. 39–40). It should at least be recognized that such a simplification may make life easier for the investigator but it is certainly no closer to the truth. To reduce the brain to the sum of inputs and outputs is to belittle it, even if it seems to become more "understandable" in the process. At best the black box assumption may be useful for the purposes of simplifying complex data, but Skinner's attempt to elevate this technique to the status of philosophical reality is misleading.

The therapists who have based their work on operant-conditioning models follow in more or less ignoring subjective responses and in their having a uniform interest in behavior. They concern themselves with objective reality, and yet it is a peculiar kind of objective reality influenced by many factors—social, interactional, physical, economic,

---

* This idea is related to the concept of "contextual rigor" developed by Hope Jensen Leichter (1974).

and so on. Furthermore, the whole is more than the sum of its parts, and this technique overlooks the importance of the subjective decision to enter treatment and stay in it. Some change may come, but to ignore the intellect is to insult it, and this insult is bound to be part of the outcome. The subject struggles with the program or the therapist instead of with himself.

In spite of or perhaps even because of this objectifying orientation, proponents of behavioral modification techniques report success in changing behavior. Many people prefer to treat themselves as objects, and they are relieved by an opportunity to deliver themselves into the hands of an authoritarian figure who will make the decisions for them, once they have made the decision that they want to be changed. Such techniques do indirectly elicit the cooperation of the patient when they are applied in a noncoercive atmosphere. The crucial difference between this model and the restructuring strategy has to do with the dependence of the patient on the treatment strategy iself. For example, behavioral modification programs require considerable effort in constructing a hierarchy and applying it to a graded series of experiences, or they involve a pattern of negative reinforcements directed toward extinction of a given piece of behavior. They are thus often unnecessarily elaborate and cumbersome.

Psychoanalysis and behavior modification occupy opposite positions on the spectrum of the psychotherapies. The former focuses on the realm of ideas and the latter focuses on behavior. The analytic position suggests that it is the person who counts and not his symptom; those who practice behavior modification deliberately focus on the symptom and not the person. There are situations where either approach may be the most appropriate because of its focus on person or symptom. As discussed previously, the unstructured exploration of psychoanalysis may be most appealing to an Apollonian person, and the structure of behavior modification may work well with a Dionysian or with an Apollonian who gets involved in the structure of the technique.

RESTRUCTURING

It is in this context that the restructuring model is employed. It is meant to occupy a middle ground between the idealist and empiricist positions, to consider both the person and his symptom. Ortega's third metaphor of "clarity inside life, light shed on things" (Marias 1970, p. 280) is appropriate. The contact with the therapist is viewed as an opportunity for the patient to change his life if he so chooses. It is a chance to "seize the moment" in the Kierkegaardian sense.

The goal is to help the patient avoid subjective escapism from the realities of his life on the one hand, and to avoid the trap of objective determinism on the other. The "sick" individual in a psychiatric sense, or the "unhappy consciousness" in the Hegelian sense, may be seen as one who despairs of transcending the paradoxes which confuse his selfhood. He decides that he is at one or another of the extremes, although he is usually unaware of consciously having made any such decision. The common denial, "Well, I really had no choice," is an instance of our tendency to escape from our real freedom to choose.

At one extreme, some people insist that there are forces manipulating their minds. In this way they feel they have no choice at all. They see themselves as absolutely bound and predetermined. The opposite extreme turns out to be similar. Some people operate on the premise that they are entirely free of all restraints, failing to recognize the element of necessity within their own spirit. They act as though subjective wish were equivalent to real action. They often manipulate the people and world around themselves in an effort to change a subjective state of mind. Thus they feel determined by their environment, yet they feel they have unending power to change the environment. They feel free to do anything which seems to improve their feelings, but also feel trapped by the necessity of creating a comforting environment. Such people, often described as sociopaths, are bound by their compulsions to act "freely" of all constraints.

In our formulation, a relatively healthy person is one who has successfully integrated such conflicts, and who can therefore act on the basis of the inevitable conflicting elements which make up the human self. He seeks to merge subjective desires with real limitations. He "seizes the moment" because he realizes that he is free to act, but will not be so forever. Recognition of the value of life is inseparable from recognition of the absoluteness of death. Freedom has no meaning without the limitations of necessity, nor subjectivity without the anchor of objectivity. This is the "essence" of the dialectic. To the extent that people recognize and integrate these opposites, they master their lives.

The restructuring strategy seeks to incorporate this dialectical approach into psychotherapy. The concept is to crystallize a treatment approach which takes into account both a person's limitations and his abilities, and then formulates them in a simple and useful way. The idea is neither to focus only on the reasons for doing something, nor only on consequences; but to focus on potential methods of integrating motivation with consequence. The focus is on affirmation of the person as an integrated whole, rather than on aversion or denial. We do not say "don't." The negative injunction is rather an inferred consequence of the primary strategy. The term "restructuring" emphasizes the idea that this therapy helps an individual place an old problem in a new perspective.

This approach requires formulating a problem in dialectical terms as a conflict of oppositions which can then be integrated in a variety of ways, giving the person a choice. For example, if the problem is the habit of smoking, the focus of the treatment, as discussed in the previous section, would be around three critical points which the patient would be asked to repeat and remember: 1) For my body, smoking is a poison; 2) I need my body to live; 3) To the extent that I want to live, I owe my body this respect and protection. This technique reminds the subject that he has a relationship to his body, several, in fact. His body allows him life; he decides what goes into it and what does not. It is then suggested that he make the choice of either treating his body with new respect, or of conceding that he is willing to give up the life it provides him.

For this point of view, the first statement is particularly important: "For my body, smoking is a poison." It is a formulation which allows the patient to get some "distance" from his body, to relate to it in a new way. He can now accept that he has a desire to smoke, but having the desire does not prove that he must smoke. He is merely reminded of the importance of protecting his body, reinforced in the third statement.

Several relationships are thus suggested: you can potentially harm your body; you owe your existence to your body; you can be a protector of your body if you choose. To the extent that you choose to smoke, you are killing yourself—both in the literal sense and in the sense that you are treating yourself as an object, not a self-willing relationship, as long as you consider yourself slave to an image. The dialectical nature of the restructuring strategy is particularly seen in its approach to the mind–body problem. The patient comes to understand that he is not the same as his body but neither is he entirely separate from it. He is not absolutely bound by physical urges, but he cannot escape the fate of his body. He can relate freely to his body, but he must relate to it.

Thus the formula is an attempt to reconcile opposition, while recognizing the conflict. To use the smoking-habit analogy, the first statement, "For my body, smoking is a poison," is a universal. The second, "I need my body to live," suggests to the patient his individuality. The third statement, "To the extent that I want to live, I owe my body this respect and protection," is a dialectical synthesis of the universal rule and the patient's individuality.

The patient is not merely the universal rule; he can choose to poison his body. But his uniqueness is not unlimited; his life is subject to some rules. The dialectic of freedom and necessity is highly relevant to this series of statements. The patient is free to choose whether he is to live or die. He cannot escape this freedom, and hence the dialectical paradox that he is "bound" to choose.

It is this very paradox to which the restructuring strategy addresses itself: recognize that you are free to choose, and then make your choice. You are not so free that you can avoid choosing, and you are not powerless in the face of your desire to smoke. The therapist brings the individual to self-consciousness about this particular objectification of himself—"I can't live without a cigarette," the determinist position, or "I won't have any problems with smoking," the subjective escape—in the Hegelian sense that he is an "unhappy consciousness, a divided and merely contradictory being." At the same time, the therapist offers the patient a dialectical step beyond his dilemma: to make a choice and thus reconcile his freedom and his necessity, his subjectivity and his objectivity, his individuality and his universality.

This formulation is the core of the treatment program. If the patient is hypnotizable, and after his trance capacity is determined, he is taught a self-hypnosis exercise which incorporates a review of the dialectical formulation every one to two hours. Further discussion with the patient centers around the theme of choice among real alternatives. It also contains an exploration of the self-defeating nature of telling oneself not to do something. This pure negation merely affirms the importance of the habit. The technique is rather to affirm oneself and therefore naturally change the habit.

Thus the patient affirms that he is in the process of changing a habit, overcoming a phobia, or mastering pain. This perspective may help to explain the "ripple effect" that has been noted after successful habit control in one area (Spiegel and Linn 1969). Many people who begin to affirm themselves by stopping smoking discover that they also lose weight, work better, or overcome old hysterical phobias without necessarily intending to. The message goes far beyond any given problem: you are free to relate to yourself in any way you choose, so why not choose to affirm your freedom of will? When a person stops treating himself as an object in one area, he is likely to affirm his fundamental relatedness in other areas as well. He is not depriving himself of gratification, and may even be exhilarated to discover that he is finally treating himself as a person.

These gains may also have interpersonal consequences. A crucial aspect of Kierkegaard's thinking which relates to this therapy is that to treat oneself as a person, one must treat others as persons as well. To treat others as objects is to attempt to reduce them to the status of objects, which is despair. A good word for this objectification is manipulation, a term often applicable to human interaction on any level. To the extent that a person treats himself less like an object, he is less likely to treat others as objects.

CONCLUSION

This technique formulates in simple terms the essence of a dialectical conflict, and then offers the patient a choice. He comes to see himself as neither absolutely bound nor absolutely free, but rather as having an opportunity to affirm his freedom to choose. This opportunity in therapy is an occasion to move toward resolution of the blind alleys of pure objectivity and pure subjectivity. It is an attempt to integrate the significance of behavioral change with an understanding of the subjective meaning of the act. Pure analysis does not suffice, and pure behavioral pressure also is not satisfactory. Understanding is utilized to the degree that it helps clarify the relationship of mind and body. The hypnotic mode is utilized to intensify focal concentration upon this potential for revising one's relationship to oneself. The hypnotic mode also suggests a more comfortable integration of mind and body; the mind is active and intent as the body is floating and relaxed. Mind and body do not struggle against anxious preoccupation or physical tension. Rather, the trance state implies a capacity to synthesize which then can be utilized in the integration of thought and behavior.

The restructuring strategy seems particularly well suited to use with hypnosis. For people capable of a meaningful trance state (operationally, the intact groups), the message of relating to oneself in new ways corresponds naturally with the sense of floating and relating to one's body in a new way by means of hypnosis. The capacity for intense concentration is tapped in the trance experience, and it can work to reinforce the dialectical message.

TREATMENT STRATEGIES: SHORT TERM

13

Smoking Control

The cigarette smoking habit and its sequelae constitute one of the major health problems in the Western world today. Since the Surgeon General's report in 1964, unknown numbers of people have stopped smoking. Some simply stop without professional help. Many fail and seek further help. These people are the habituated hard-core smokers who are motivated to come for a fresh approach to the problem. To simply tell them that smoking is bad and that they should stop is absurd. They know that. To delve into the reasons they started to smoke is irrelevant, because at the time most adults of today started smoking it was not known to be harmful. No matter what reasons are uncovered, the critical information is not there. Smoking was not known with any certainty to be malignant until 1964. The reasons for stopping the habit were then based on information not available when the smoking started. This specific habit became a fair starting point to study habit change without taking the time to explore the reasons behind the habit.

This is the closest model we have in the West to Zen therapy. The inferred premise in Zen therapy is that the patient is a student who has much to learn and further, that the therapist (priest) is a teacher. The priest knows and lives the Zen way and that is why he is a teacher. The patient is obviously not living the Zen way, hence the symptoms.

Since the patient is present to learn and the Zen therapist knows what to teach, why spend the time listening to the patient? It is better to let the patient be quiet and listen to the therapist. In fact, in the first phase of Morita therapy the patient is isolated in his room and is instructed to be quiet and prepare to learn.

Using this model, the time spent for clinical history is brief—less than five minutes. It includes the number of years of smoking, the average amount of cigarettes, and the high and low range on a daily basis. Did the patient stop for any long period of time in the past? Also, who in the household smokes besides the patient? What physical symptoms are apparent now, and what events precipitated the decision to look for help at this time? We would like to understand what convergence of events, realizations, or external pressures made the patient decide to try to stop smoking at this time. It usually involves some kind of family pressure or, even more often, some experience of physical deterioration, for example, shortness of breath, leg pain with mild exercise, chronic coughing, chest pains; or a warning from a physician about heart disease, emphysema, or lung cancer. During this period informal scanning is done to rule out the rare patient who is about to decompensate into psychosis or depression.

Then the cluster survey and HIP are done. Based on these results, the instruction phase begins. If the patient is an Apollonian, the tone of the discussion is that of solving a puzzle, using the nine-point puzzle. If Dionysian, the focus is toward the emotional appeal of the body's innocence. The approach to Odysseans varies. The nonintacts get the same instruction, but geared to their attentiveness and motivation without the use of the formal trance state.

The Self-Hypnosis Exercise

After the trance experience of the profile measurement, the patient is told:

> You see, you were not asleep. Hypnosis is a method of concentration. It is better identified as a feeling of floating. It is like having a double focus or parallel awareness, like being here and alongside yourself at the same time. This enables you to be optimally receptive to your own thoughts. The strategy that you use in this receptive atmosphere is what we take up next.
>
> I am going to count to three. Follow this sequence again. One, look up toward your eyebrows, all the way up; two, while looking up, close your eyelids, take a deep breath; three, exhale, let your eyes relax, and let your body float.
>
> And as you feel yourself floating, you permit one hand or the other to feel like a buoyant balloon and allow it to float upward. As it does, your elbow bends and your forearm floats into an upright position. Sometimes you may get a feeling of a magnetic pull on the back of your hand as it

goes up. When your hand reaches this upright position, it becomes for you a signal to enter a state of meditation.

(One option is to have this section on tape. It gives the therapist a four-minute rest, and offers the message in another form.)

In this state of meditation, you concentrate on the feeling of floating, and at the same time, concentrate on these three critical points:

The first point is: For your body, smoking is a poison. You are composed of a number of components, the most important of which is your body. Smoking is not so much a poison for you as it is for your body specifically.

The second point is: You cannot live without your body. Your body is a precious physical plant through which you experience life.

The third point is: To the extent that you want to live, you owe your body respect and protection. This is your way of acknowledging the fragile, precious nature of your body, and at the same time, your way of seeing yourself as your body's keeper. You are, in truth, your body's keeper. When you make this commitment to respect your body, you have within you the power to have smoked your last cigarette.

Notice how this strategy puts the emphasis on what you are for, rather than what you are against. It is true that smoking is a poison and you are against it, but the emphasis is upon the commitment to respect your body. As a consequence of your commitment, it becomes natural for you to protect your body against the poison of further smoking.

Observe that when you make this commitment to respect your body, you incorporate with it a view toward eating and drinking which reflects your respect for your body. As a result, each eating and drinking experience in itself becomes an exercise in disciplined concern for your body. You can, if you wish, use this same exercise to maintain your ideal weight while protecting your body against the poison of further smoking.

Now I propose that in the beginning you do these exercises as often as ten different times a day, preferably every one to two hours. At first the exercise takes about a minute, but as you become more expert, you can do it in much less time.

The exercise is as follows: You sit or lie down, and to yourself, you count to three. At one, you do one thing; at two, you do two things; and at three, you do three things. At one, look up toward your eyebrows; at two, close your eyelids and take a deep breath; and at three, exhale, let your eyes relax, and let your body float.

As you feel yourself floating, you permit one hand or the other to feel like a buoyant balloon and let it float upward as your hand is now. When it reaches this upright position, it becomes the signal for you to enter a state of meditation.

In this state of meditation you concentrate on these three critical points:

1. For your body, not for you, for your body smoking is a poison.

2. You need your body to live.

3. You owe your body this respect and protection.

Reflect on what this means to you in a private sense, then bring yourself out of this state of concentration called self-hypnosis by counting backwards in this manner.

Now, three, get ready. Two, with your eyelids closed, roll up your eyes (and do it now). And one, let your eyelids open slowly. Then, when your eyes are back in focus, slowly make a fist with the hand that is up and as you open your fist slowly, your usual sensation and control returns. Let your hand float downward. That is the end of the exercise, but you retain a general feeling of floating. (end of tape)

(The patient is now out of the formal trance state and his eyes are open.)

This floating sensation signals your mind to turn inward and pay attention to your own thoughts—like private meditation. Ballet dancers and athletes float all the time. That is why they concentrate and coordinate their movements so well. When they do not float they are up-tight, and they do not do as well.

Now I am going to review the basic principles of the strategy, and then we will go back to the exercise so you will know it before you leave. You do this exercise every one to two hours. Each time it takes about twenty seconds. Your body is entitled to twenty seconds every one to two hours, and during this twenty-second period you let the world take care of itself and you pay attention to this issue between you and your body. Making use of this extra receptivity, you now re-imprint the three points. Notice that this is not a scare technique, but rather a reminder of two important facts: for your body smoking is a poison and you need your body to live. The third point is the commitment: to the extent that you want to live, you owe your body this respect and protection. Shift back to your usual awareness and go about doing what you do. This is like reinforcing a program in a computer. To date the best computer made is the one you have in your head.

If I had my way, I would ask you to spend the next week living in a tobacco shop to emphasize the point that the issue is not the presence of tobacco, but rather your private commitment to your body even in the presence of tobacco. Anybody can stop smoking if you lock them in a room and don't give them tobacco, but that in no way internalizes the change. You know that you are internalizing the change when in the presence of tobacco you decide to give priority to your body.

The biggest mistake that you can make in this is to tell yourself that you must not smoke. That is precisely wrong That is like telling yourself "Don't have an itch on your nose." What happens if you concentrate on not having an itch?

PATIENT: You have got an itch on your nose.

DOCTOR: Try this one, "Don't think about purple elephants." Or, "Don't think about swallowing." Free people don't like to be told "don't." Why not use that knowledge if you want a strategy that can work? You can use it this way. Turn it around and you come up with a corollary which is equally true. It is more effective to change behavior when you do it on the basis of something you are for. Approach it this way: yes, you will respect and protect your body. In the course of protecting your body from smoking you have radically changed your behavior but you feel it as "yes" rather than "don't smoke." Do you see the difference?

At this point, with Apollonians, present the nine-point puzzle as shown in Figure 12–2 (see chapter 12). After the patient tries to solve the puzzle and either succeeds or is shown the answer, he is told the following:

Staying within the system is like saying: "Run, don't run; go, don't go; smoke, don't smoke." This does not solve the problem. But if you approach it from the outside and see yourself as your body's keeper, by offering your body this respect and protection, you indirectly control the habit.

For Dionsyians and most Odysseans:

Now, you can sharpen your focus on this if you look at yourself in this double sense. There is you and your body. You are your body's keeper, and your body is your physical plant. There is something precious and helpless about your body. It is just like with a baby. When you put poison into your body it can do nothing but accept it and make the best of it. But when you realize that you *are the one putting the poison there, you have some questions to ask yourself. Which side are you on? Are you for your body or are you not? Are you for living or are you not? If you are not for living, keep on smoking. But if the idea of living is still enticing, then you have a built-in obligation to give your body the respect that it deserves.*

(For all types)

What you are learning here is in essence an art form. It is the art of learning how to control an urge. And in that connection, there is a basic principle: if you mean to control an urge, don't fight it. If you fight it you only make it worse than it already is. But what you can do is to ignore it. And you can ignore it this way. When the urge to smoke occurs, admit it. But at the same time acknowledge that you have this commitment to respect your body. You now have two urges at the same time, the urge to smoke and the urge to respect your body. Lock them together. If you emphasize one, you have to ignore the other. If you choose to emphasize this commitment to your body, then you are simultaneously ignoring the urge to smoke. There is an axiom of human behavior that goes like this: any facility or any urge—biological or psychological—will eventually wither away if you repeatedly do not satisfy it and ignore it. This is true even for something as basic as muscles. Do you know what happens to muscles if you don't use them?

PATIENT: Yes.

DOCTOR: *Atrophy. The same thing is true with urges, even urges that are biologically rooted. For example, many people are privately skeptical of the celibacy of the Catholic clergy. But the impressive truth is that those nuns and priests who take their vows seriously are celibate. Once they get through a transition period, they no longer have sexual urges; it phases out. The same thing is true for another urge that is biologically rooted, and that is hunger. When Ghandi went on his forty-day fast, by the fifth day he observed that although he was weak, he was no longer hungry. Dick Gregory described that. Caesar Chavez described that. Thousands of soldiers all over the world have described that in combat. When they are cut off from supplies and are found several days later, the last thing they are interested in is food; they are so absorbed in such important things, like not getting killed or captured, that often they have to be reminded to eat.*

Now, there is a lesson. If you take urges that are biologically rooted and if they wither away by being ignored because your emphasis is elsewhere, certainly an acquired habit like smoking will also wither away if you learn to ignore it by emphasizing this commitment to respect your body. However, if you antagonize yourself by saying, "don't smoke," or if you tease yourself by cutting down, then you are in trouble. Because to cut down means that although you are smoking less at the time, the tease is working. Whereas if you channel your energy so that you keep reaffirming this commitment to respect your body, such is your new perspective toward your body that if an urge to smoke comes along, it gets so locked into this momentum of respecting your body that you are able to ignore it rather than fight it. That is the principle of the exercise.

Now, I'm going to do it. I'm going to ask you to watch me. Then I will ask you to do it again. After that I will show you a camouflaged way of doing it so that even in the presence of others you can do it without attracting attention. But this basic way assumes that you have privacy. In privacy it goes like this. You sit or lie down. To yourself you count to three. One, look up; two, close your eyes, take a deep breath, and exhale; three, eyes relaxed, body floating, let one hand float up like a balloon. In this position imagine yourself floating and to yourself repeat the three points: For my body smoking is a poison. I need my body to live. I owe my body this respect and protection. Reflect upon this. Then, three, get ready; two, with your eyelids closed, roll up your eyes; one, open slowly, fist open, down, and that is the end of the exercise. Got it. You do it now and I will give you your directions. One—no you don't have to take your glasses off. You ordinarily wear them, don't you?

PATIENT: Yes.

DOCTOR: All right. One, look up; while looking up, two, close your eyelids and take a deep breath; three exhale, eyes relaxed, body floating, and let one hand float up just like a balloon. In this position imagine yourself floating and at the same time you repeat to yourself the three points. Although ordinarily you say this to yourself, on this occasion we will do it aloud. After each point you repeat it after me. For my body smoking is a poison.

PATIENT: For my body smoking is a poison.

DOCTOR: I need my body to live.

PATIENT: I need my body to live.

DOCTOR: I owe my body this respect and protection.

PATIENT: I owe my body this respect and protection.

DOCTOR: Reflect on what this means to you in a private sense. Then, bring yourself out of this state of concentration this way. Three, get ready; two, with your eyelids closed, roll up your eyes, and do it now; and one, let your eyelids open slowly. Now, when your eyes are in focus, slowly make a fist with the hand that is up, open your fist slowly, let it float, and that is the end of the exercise. I will give you those three points in print later, as a reminder.

All right. Now, suppose you want to do the exercise and you don't have privacy. You camouflage it this way. Two changes. First, close your eyelids, then roll your eyes up so that the eye roll is private. Second, instead of your hand coming up like this [forearm floating upward], let it come up like this [hand to forehead]. So to an outsider it looks like this. Watch me. For my body smoking is a poison. I need my body to live. I owe my body this respect and protection. Who would know that you're doing the exercise? In twenty seconds you shift gears, establish this extra-receptivity, re-imprint the three points to yourself—and shift back out.

By doing the basic or camouflaged exercise every one to two hours, you establish a private signal system between you and your body so that you are ever alert to this commitment to respect your body. When your hand reaches out for a cigarettes or you find yourself wanting to smoke, admit it. But at the same time do this [stroke eyebrow]. This gesture activates the last time you did the exercise. It activates that third point: I owe my body this respect and protection. By doing this you are again locking in the urge to smoke with the urge to respect your body. By reaffirming respect for your body, you are ignoring the urge to smoke rather than fighting it.

Now, the temptation to fight the habit is there. But, there's something deceptive about that, because there are two sides to it. On the surface you have the illusion of feeling virtuous. Aha! I'm fighting it. But because you're fighting it, you're making it worse. In fact there is an ancient Japanese Zen parable that deals with this precise phenomenon. It's a story of a jackass tied by a long rope, one end around its mouth and the other end to a pole. As long as it thinks like a jackass, it pulls and pulls. All it gets out of that is a sore mouth and a tighter knot. When it *stops thinking like a jackass, it discovers it doesn't have to pull on the rope, and if it doesn't pull, the rope slackens. With the rope slack, it can walk around, lie down, go here, go there and when the rope is slack long enough, even the knot gets loose. Do you see the point? That is the point here. Do you have a pet dog?*

PATIENT: Not at the moment, but I hope to very soon.

DOCTOR: *All right. Suppose you have one. Now, you're going to feed the dog some food. You open up a package and you read on the label a statement that says, "The Surgeon General has determined that this food is danger-ous to your dog's health." Would you feed the dog that food? Why not give your body the same consideration you would give to a dog? Isn't that startling?*

This brings into focus that sometimes things are so obvious we ignore them. One thing which is obvious is that your body is innocent. Your body doesn't know that smoking is poison. You know it, but your body doesn't. When you realize that your body has this trusting innocence and depends upon your judgment, it sharpens your sense of responsibility. For example, when you cross a street, you take certain precautions. Have you noticed when you are supervising a child crossing the street, how much more careful you are? Do you see how natural it is to respond to the trusting innocence of a child? If you look at your body as this trusting innocent part of you, do you see how natural it can be to take a position of respect and protection toward your body? That is just the point here.

Now, in essence, what you're learning here is this: instead of doing the pedestrian thing of fighting cigarettes, take an outside point of view and use a natural resource you have anyhow, namely the compassion that you would show toward any trusting, innocent living creature. If you look at your body as this trusting, innocent living creature that depends upon your judgment, of course you will show it the respect that it deserves. Do you see how different that is from saying, "Don't smoke"?

PATIENT: Yes.

DOCTOR: *That is just the point here. So you are ending up radically changing your point of view toward your body and radically changing your smok-ing behavior. But you are doing it in an atmosphere of an affirmation experience instead of in a fight. That's it. I'm going to give you a copy of those three points and a card, and ask that you send the card back in about a week so that I can learn how you are doing.*

The patient is then given an opportunity to ask questions, and then the session is ended. The entire procedure usually requires one forty-five minute session.

Follow-Up Data[*]

In a six-month follow-up study of 615 cases treated with one session of self-hypnosis, we obtained a 44 percent response rate to the question-naires; 121 of these patients reported that they were still not smoking

[*] Some of this data has been presented elsewhere in more detail (Spiegel, H. 1970a; 1970b).

after six months. If we make the assumption that all of those who did not return the questionnaire had resumed smoking, this would mean that 20 percent of the sample were not smoking six months after one session. This method of data analysis undoubtedly makes for a certain percentage of false negative reports. Kanzler et al. (1976) found that 75 percent of their subjects responding to a mailed questionnaire were not smoking. Telephone follow-up to the nonresponders revealed that 27 percent of this group were not smoking. One can extrapolate from these results to estimate that perhaps one-quarter of the nonresponders are still not smoking. However, in view of the amount of speculation necessary, a more conservative evaluation of the results seems to be in order.

A study on a much larger sample of patients is currently under way in an effort to clarify the ambiguities of the first study. The data are presented in the Appendix.

Although we do not have data on a control group, and it can be presumed that a certain percentage of these patients might have stopped without the intervention, it is worth noting that in general this was a population which was referred only after other efforts to stop smoking had failed. We have thus labelled them as "hard core" smokers who had experienced repeated frustration in the past in attempting to quit smoking.

This single-session treatment approach is the briefest intervention reported, using hypnosis. It has been reviewed in the literature. Nuland (1970) suggested that further treatment sessions in selected cases might improve the treatment outcome. Wright (1970) commented on the importance of placing the responsibility for the treatment result on the shoulders of the patient. Perry and Mullen (1975) employed the three-point self-hypnosis strategy described here and obtained comparable results, 13 percent abstinence at three-month follow-up. They found no correlation between hypnotizability (not measured by the HIP) and abstinence, but when they divided the patients into high and low hypnotizables and included those who did cut down on smoking, they found a relationship between hypnotizability and positive outcome. It may be that in this low hypnotizable group they included those who would score as softs and decrements on the HIP, who would likely have a poorer outcome. They noted that given the low percentage of subjects reporting abstinence, further investigation of the problem of motivation is in order.

There are numerous techniques reported which employ hypnosis in the treatment of smoking behavior. Crasilneck and Hall (1970) and Hall and Crasilneck (1968) reported a four-session approach utilizing a series of hypnotic inductions, with suggestions that craving cigarettes would be reduced and that the smoking habit was damaging to the body. When they studied a sample of 75 patients they found that 82 percent of those who responded, or 73 percent of the total sample, were not smoking at an average of two years after the treatment.

Kline (1970) reported on a twelve-hour therapy treatment for smoking which employed hypnosis for the purposes of intensifying smoking deprivation, with a subsequent reduction of tension. He reported that one year later 88 percent of the treatment group were not smoking.

Nuland and Field (1970) reported on a modification of their approach to the use of hypnosis in the treatment of smoking, in which they de-emphasized hypnotic depth and concentrated on self-hypnosis. They employed a flexible and unstated number of treatment sessions, and reported 60 percent abstinence on follow-up at six months. They emphasized developing a relationship with the therapist and explorations of motivation if the patient failed to stop after the first session.

Pederson et al. (1975) performed a controlled study in which they compared six weekly group-treatment sessions with and without hypnosis, and with a control condition. They reported that 56 percent of the hypnosis-with-counseling group were not smoking after three months, a much better result than that for the counseling group alone (12 percent), or the control group (0 percent). This brief but well-done study is one of the few with a control group. Critical reviewers often dismiss reports of 20 to 30 percent rates to a treatment approach as comparable to a spontaneous cure rate. It is therefore worth noting that in this study none of the members of the control group stopped smoking. Any positive response was likely due to the treatment intervention.

Watkins (1976) reported on a five-session approach emphasizing suggestions of relaxation and coping with anger. Fifty percent of the initial subjects were not smoking after six months. Johnston and Donoghue (1971) reviewed a variety of other techniques using hypnosis.

In a thorough review of the behavior-modification literature on smoking control, Keutzer et al. (1968) reported on a variety of techniques, including systematic de-sensitization, reciprocal inhibition, and aversion. They noted that aversive techniques in general were ineffective, and that various group clinic techniques and approaches using hypnosis seemed quite effective. However, they cautioned that the factor of rapport with the therapist in the hypnotic situation made it difficult to compare results in what were otherwise controlled studies.

CONCLUSION

There is a problem in comparing studies, due to possible differences in patient samples. The effectiveness of various therapeutic strategies will not be firmly established without systematic study of a larger number of patients over a longer period of time. Clearly, short-term results can be misleading. However, taken as a group, these studies suggest that hypnosis can be quite effective in facilitating the cessation of smoking. It is entirely possible that a more intensive or extensive therapeutic input would result in a higher percentage of responders. It is also possible that offering a more prolonged or involved treatment tends to select for those patients who are more committed to stopping smoking. The ultimate goal is the maximum therapeutic response to a minimum of necessary time and effort expended. It may well be that for a certain subsample of patients, subsequent sessions would be helpful at intervals following the initial restructuring. It is at least clear that a patient who has had difficulty in the past in stopping smoking can be helped in one session, utilizing self-hypnosis. Given the prevalence of the smoking problem and the serious medical consequences which attend it, a public health perspective dictates using the simplest technique which can be employed most widely to help the greatest number of patients. For some patients, the opportunity to place their problem in a new perspective suffices. Others may benefit from more involved treatment, and still others may be unresponsive to any approach. Even if only one in five patients consolidates his decision to stop smoking, this is a major opportunity for clinicians to practice preventive medicine.

14

Eating Disorders

Obesity

Our use of hypnosis with obesity will be presented as an edited transcript of a session with an overweight patient. We present the approach in this manner in order to convey the clinical flavor of the interaction, and not as a prescription to be followed exactly. Good psychotherapy requires an integration of therapeutic principles with the personal style of the therapist, as well as with the psychological style of the patient. This technique is also modified somewhat to fit the personality characteristics of the patient, as will be described.

The treatment generally occurs in one or two sessions if the patient exceeds his normal weight by less than 15 percent. More seriously overweight patients require periodic reinforcement sessions. A brief medical and psychological history is taken, along with data on marital and family status, education, and employment. The HIP is performed and explained to the patient, and then the patient is taught an exercise in self-hypnosis which emphasizes the concept of eating with respect for his body. A typical session then proceeds as follows:

There are basic principles concerning eating and dieting which I would like to discuss with you. Then I will show you how to do the self-hypnotic exercise for weight control, and finally I will discuss some other guidelines. But first, the basic principles.

1. Choose a Varied Diet. It is useful each day, once you are acquainted with all the different diet programs, to decide for yourself what you are in the mood for that day. Sometimes you may be in the mood for a vegetable day, sometimes a high protein day, sometimes a liquid day. Most of these diet programs are equally good, so it is all right to shift from one to the other from day to day if it gives you a chance to decide each day which one you are in the mood for, so that it becomes your commitment, it takes on more meaning than blindly following what somebody tells you to do. The major issue is the total number of calories that you take in relation to your physical activity. Whether you get the calories from one kind of food or another doesn't make too much difference, as long as basic nutritional needs are met.

2. *Change Your Relationship to Your Body.* As important as calories are, fighting calories is too narrow a focus. It is so narrow that you cannot possibly pay attention to it around the clock. In order to adopt a new point of view toward your eating behavior, regard today as the day in which you are radically changing your whole philosophy of life. In that context you are changing your point of view toward your body, and as a consequence you are changing your eating behavior. By giving it this broad base, you can keep this concept with you around the clock. You are changing your philosophy of living in relation to your body and, as a result, your eating behavior.

3. *Accept Responsibility for Your Eating Behavior.* It is very tempting to blame your eating behavior on your parents, your wife, the mayor, Watergate, the moon, the tides. As soon as you see the absurdity of that you will realize that of all the things you do in life, there is nothing in which you are more clearly 100 percent responsible for than your eating behavior. Reflect on the fact that most of the things you do in life have to take into account other considerations or other people, but in your eating behavior you are in business for yourself.

4. *Prepare for Normal Weight.* While you are losing weight, it is mandatory that you learn to reacquaint yourself with your body, so that you prepare yourself to meet your body at your normal weight. It will be like meeting a long-lost friend and, having prepared yourself for the meeting, you will be in a position to hold on to that friendship indefinitely. If you do not prepare yourself to meet your body at your normal weight, then even if you get your weight down you will have an eerie feeling of being like a stranger in your own body and you will go right back up. The preparation for this is mandatory if you want to make a long term success of it.

THE SELF-HYPNOSIS EXERCISE

Now with that in mind I am going to show you this exercise. You will do this exercise every one to two hours, each time taking only twenty seconds. First I will show you how you do it if you have privacy, and then later I will remind you of the camouflaged way of doing it. If you have privacy, it goes like this: you put one arm there and one arm there and one, look up to the top of your head; and while looking up, two, close your eyes and take a deep breath; and three, exhale, let your eyes relax, let your body float, and as you feel yourself floating you permit one hand or the other to feel like a buoyant balloon and let it float upward. As it does, your elbow bends and your forearm floats into an upright position. When it reaches an upright position, this becomes your signal to enter a state of meditation in which you concentrate on this imaginary floating and at the same time on three critical points:

1. For your body overeating is in effect poison. This is just like the situation with water; you need water to live but too much water will drown you. Similarly, you need food to live but too much of this very same food in effect becomes poison.

2. You cannot live without your body. Your body is the precious physical plant through which you experience life.

3. To the extent that you want to live your life to its fullest, you owe your body this commitment to respect it and protect it. This is your way of

acknowledging the fragile precious nature of your body and at the same time it is your way of seeing yourself as your body's keeper. You are in truth your body's keeper.

When you make this commitment to respect your body, you have within you the power to so radically change your eating and drinking behavior that each eating experience becomes for you an exercise in disciplined respect for your body integrity. Lock this concept in mind so it becomes a posthypnotic signal that you give to yourself. Then bring yourself out of the state of meditation this way: three, get ready; two, with your eyelids closed, roll up your eyes; and one, let your eyes open slowly. Then when your eyes are back in focus slowly make a fist with the hand that is up, open your fist slowly, and let it float down and that is the end of the exercise.

We are going to go back to that exercise later but before I do, I want to point out four major ways in which "thin eating" differs from "fat eating." Then I will offer you two guidelines for establishing your own middle range between these extremes.

Now, to the differences.

1.   A thin person looks at food as fuel, like filling up a gas tank and driving off. A fat person fills up the gas tank but then he sees additional fuel in the pump and he reasons like this: "Well, since it is there I might as well take more." But since the tank is full, he sprays gas on the back seat and the front seat. Perhaps he feels a little silly and rationalizes by saying, "This is a good way to keep the upholstery clean." That's not only silly but it is mischievous.

2.   No matter how delicious the food is, once his appetite is satisfied, a thin person regards that extra food on the plate as belonging either in the icebox or in the garbage can. The fat person, without admitting it to himself, reasons like this: "It's a shame to put it into that garbage can: I might as well put it into this garbage can." At that point the fat person is abandoning respect for his body integrity without admitting it to himself.

3.   There are two major kinds of ceremonies regarding eating: temporal and social. If mealtime comes around, a thin person eats if he is hungry. If not, he will skip it. If a fat person is not hungry when mealtime comes, he or she reasons like this: "Well, I guess I don't feel hungry, but I may get hungry, therefore I had better eat." This involves denying the signal from the body that it doesn't need food.

On social occasions a thin person eats if he is hungry; if not, he will take a token bite to socialize. A fat person reasons like this: "I don't want to make my guests uncomfortable," or "I don't want to embarrass the hostess," or "I don't want to appear like a square peg in a round hole so I'll just eat like everybody else." Again he denies the message from the body that it doesn't need food.

4.   The fourth difference is a more subtle one, and that is the way we use our symbols or metaphors, especially our body metaphors. We all live our lives using metaphors at various times. For example, if I say to you, "He gives me a pain in the neck," you know exactly what I mean. But if somebody is bothering me and I wait until my neck muscles get so tensed up that they produce pain before I get the message, that is taking a good metaphor too far. Similarly, we may want something of a psychological or social nature; we may want it so much that we formulate it privately in terms of having a hunger or thirst for it. But the desire can get so vivid that we feel if we eat food we are actually going to satisfy our desire, and that is where the deception takes place. As Laing puts it, this is the error of confusing the menu with the meal.

Now how does all this come into focus? It is not necessary to constantly psychoanalyze all these factors or we wouldn't have much time for anything

*else, but there are two guidelines that can help keep a sense of balance
between these extremes.*

*The first guideline is this: always, always eat with respect, with respect
for your body. Because if you respect your body you are never likely to
regard it as a garbage can. The more important part of that perspective is
that you avoid the biggest trap of all, which is to tell yourself "Don't eat
that." Once you get caught in that trap you are losing. It is like telling
yourself, "Don't have at itch on your nose." Do you feel it? Or, "Try to think
about not swallowing." Free people don't like to be told "don't." When God
said to Adam and Eve, "Don't eat the apple," that was the end of Paradise.
This is a basic observation about the human condition. Why not use this
knowledge if you want to devise a strategy that can work? You can use it
this way: turn it around and you have a corollary, which is that a far more
effective way to change behavior is to do it on the basis of something you
are for. So if you approach it this way, you will respect and protect your
body. In the course of protecting your body from overeating you can radically change your behavior, but you feel it as "Yes, I respect my body"
instead of "Don't eat that."*

*The second of these two guidelines is going to surprise you. Learn to eat
like a gourmet. Why a gourmet? Because a gourmet pays full attention to
every swallow. Every swallow is a total encounter with food. He is aware of
the touch, the taste, the smell, the temperature, the texture of the food, and
with such total involvement that it is incredible how much fulfillment and
enjoyment he gets out of each swallow. In fact, this whole process not only
helps you to radically change your eating behavior, but it brings joy back to
eating again. The gourmet does not make the mistake of saying, "Oh I
swallowed that food, but I don't remember what it tastes like, I had better
take another bite." The reason a gourmet does not make that mistake is
because each swallow is such a total involvement that the memory of it
stays with him. He doesn't have to keep getting reinforcements of new
food because he knows fully what the experience was. The stereotype that
gourmets are overweight is just not true. Most of the great gourmets of the
world are either of normal weight or are underweight.*

*Now let's pull all of this together: you have the recurrent urge to eat and
drink, and the urge to respect your body, which you reinforce by doing this
exercise every one to two hours. Lock these two urges together until you
form a psychological filter and then ask yourself the question, "Does this
intended food reflect respect for my body?" If it conforms to the program
that you have committed yourself to for that day and the answer is yes,
eat it and enjoy every swallow. But if the answer is "No, it does not con-
form to my program for the day," then, instead of fighting food, by emphasizing this respect for your body you are ignoring the urge to eat rather than
fighting it. Do you see that difference?*

*Now with that in mind let's go back to the exercise. One arm there and
one arm there: one, look up, while looking up; two, close your eyes and
take a deep breath; and three, exhale, eyes relaxed, body floating, and let
one hand float up just like a balloon. When it reaches the upright position,
this becomes your signal to enter a state of meditation in which you concentrate on this imaginary floating and at the same time on the three
critical points. Although ordinarily you say them to yourself, on this occasion we will do it aloud. Repeat each point after me.*

DOCTOR: *For my body overeating is a poison.*

PATIENT: For my body overeating is a poison.

DOCTOR: *I need my body to live.*

PATIENT: I need my body to live.

DOCTOR: *I owe my body this respect and protection.*

PATIENT: I owe my body this respect and protection.

DOCTOR: *Take a few seconds to reflect on what this means to you in a private sense. Then bring yourself out of this state of meditation this way: three, get ready; two, with your eyelids closed, roll up your eyes; and one, let your eyes open slowly. Then when your eyes are in focus slowly make a fist with the hand that is up, open your fist slowly, and let it float down and that is the end of the exercise. I will give you those three points in print as a reminder and you will notice that the concept is similar to the smoking exercise but it has an intermediate step, which involves asking yourself the question, "Does this intended food reflect respect for my body?" which means, does it correspond to your program for the day. That is, you make a decision regarding whether it is for your health or for your death. The guideline has to be your choice of diet for the day.*

Now suppose you don't have privacy. You camouflage the exercise with two changes. (The therapist demonstrates.) First you close your eyes, then roll your eyes up so that the eye roll is private; second, instead of your hand coming straight up, let it come up and touch your forehead. To an outsider it looks as though you may have a headache. Then repeat to yourself: "For my body overeating is a poison, I need my body to live, I owe my body this respect and protection." In twenty seconds you shift gears, establish your sense of receptivity, reimprint the three points to yourself, and shift back out again. By doing the basic or camouflaged exercise every one to two hours, you establish a private signal system between yourself and your body so that you are ever alert to this commitment to respect your body. If your hand reaches out for food or drink or if you find yourself wanting to eat, admit it. At the same time do this, stroke your forehead. This gesture activates the last time you did the exercise, especially that third point: "I owe my body this respect and protection." By doing that you are again psychologically locking in the urge to eat with the urge to respect your body. By forming the psychological filter you ask yourself the question, "Does this food reflect respect for my body." If it conforms to your program for the day, the answer is yes. Then eat it and enjoy it. If the answer is no, then instead of fighting the food by emphasizing respect for your body, you ignore the food.

The temptation to fight food is there, but it is deceiving. On the surface you have the illusion of feeling virtuous, "I'm fighting it." But beneath the surface you are making it worse because you are fighting it. There is an old Japanese Zen parable about a jackass tied by a long rope, one end around its mouth and another end tied to a pole. As long as it thinks like a jackass, it pulls and pulls, and all it gets out of that is a sore mouth and a tighter knot. When it stops thinking like a jackass, it discovers that it doesn't have to pull on the rope and that if it doesn't pull, the rope slackens. With the rope slack it can walk around, lie down, go here, go there—and when the rope is slack for a while, even the knot gets loose.

Do you have a pet dog?

(Patient says yes.)

DOCTOR: *Suppose your veterinarian says to you: "The dog is too fat, and if you want it to grow up and be a good pet you have to control its food." Would you do it?*

(Patient nods yes.)

DOCTOR: *Why not show your body the same consideration you show your dog? There is something startling about that because it brings into focus some things that are so obvious we ignore them. One thing obvious is that your body is innocent. Your body does not know how to deal with your metaphors and desires. You know how, but your body doesn't. When you realize that your body has this trusting innocence and depends upon your judgment, it sharpens your sense of responsibility. For example, when you cross a street, you take certain precautions. Have you noticed how much more careful you are if you are supervising a child crossing the street? You see how natural it is to respond to the trusting innocence of a child. If you look at your body as this trusting, innocent living creature that depends upon your judgment, you see how natural it can be to take this position of respect and protection toward your body. What you are doing is so radically changing your philosophy of living that you are taking a new point of view toward your body. You are viewing it as this trusting little creature that counts on your judgment, and as a consequence of that you are changing your eating behavior rather than fighting calories.*

Now I am going to give you those three points as a reminder, and before you go would you like to get a visual preview of what you can look like when you have lost your weight?

(The patient is given an opportunity to view himself in a modern variant of the old "fun house" mirror which makes him look much more slender. This usually ends the session on a hopeful and amusing note.)

CONCLUSION

The patient has had an opportunity to put an old problem in a new perspective, that of his relationship to his body. He has been urged to use his trance capacity as a way of concentrating on this new relationship, just as the trance experience itself may have provided an opportunity for him to experience his body in new ways. He has been urged to eat with respect for his body, and to eat "like a gourmet." He has been advised to plan an appropriate diet day by day, and to view additional food as a "poison" for his body. This makes it possible to dissociate an urge to eat for biological or symbolic reasons, from the necessity to act on that urge. He then has the choice of making use of this information as he wishes. Therapy is an opportunity which leaves a patient with clarified choices and the awareness that he is making them.

The approach described here was tailored for an Odyssean patient. If the patient scored lower on the HIP, more emphasis would be placed on the cognitive aspects of the treatment, the idea of taking a new approach to an old problem, use of the nine-point puzzle, the dialectical aspects of the mind–body relationship, etc. The patient would be encouraged to work at the exercises more, which appeals to an Apollonian cognitive framework and gives recognition to his lower trance capacity.

A Dionysian would be encouraged to utilize the self-hypnosis exercise religiously every one to two hours, and the more emotional aspects of the exercise would be emphasized. Such patients are often particularly struck by the analogy between their body and an infant which must take into it anything given it, even if it is damaged by it. They often refer quickly and easily to feelings they had as a parent. This emotional connection is quite helpful in getting across the message of respect for their body.

In our experience hypnotizability itself is not a major factor in follow-up success. In general, those patients who were already within 10 percent of their ideal weight do best in the long run.

FOLLOW-UP DATA ON OBESITY CONTROL

Obesity is an endemic disease in this affluent culture, and interest in its control has grown markedly as evidence has mounted that excess weight is related to damage of the cardiovascular system. In a detailed review of obesity and its treatment, Stunkard (1975) estimated that within four years the behavior modification approach had resulted in a doubling of treatment effectiveness. Many aspects of the program he has employed overlap with our self-hypnosis technique—for example, the emphasis on enjoying the taste of food. However, these elements are incorporated into a more extensive and intensive treatment program, with detailed record-keeping of food ingested and a point system of rewards for good behavior. Stunkard also points to promising work done by self-help groups such as TOPS (Take Off Pounds Sensibly), and commercial groups such as Weight Watchers, in influencing a large segment of the population.

Stuart (1967) made an important contribution in demonstrating the effectiveness of behavior modification approaches, and he reported a ripple effect as well. He found no symptom substitution, but rather that some patients improved their social relationships and others adapted the weight control regimen to stop smoking.

There are several clinical reports in the literature of the successful use of hypnosis in the treatment of obesity (Crasilneck and Hall 1975; Stanton 1975; Wick et al. 1971; Hanley 1967; Glover 1961; Oakley 1960). Brodie (1964) reported successful use of the concept of enhancing the enjoyment of food while losing weight, mingled with an analogy between fat and cancer. These approaches require four or more visits and generally involve a mixture of suggestion that appetite will decline, with emphasis on enjoying the taste of food. In an intriguing clinical article, Erickson (1960) described three successful cases in which he used hypnotic time distortion to extend the pleasurable experience of eating for one patient, and paradoxical techniques to give the other two patients the feeling of defiant overeating as they actually ate less.

Clearly there is much overlap between behavioral and hypnotic techniques in the treatment of obesity. Elements of our restructuring approach have been successfully employed under both rubrics. The concept of hypnosis as a *facilitator* is most important in this issue. Identification of trance capacity and utilizing it to launch a patient on a course of self-generated eating with respect for his body makes minimal demands on a therapist's time. More extensive behavioral techniques may be more useful for patients who are not hypnotizable, who do not respond to a one-session approach, or who require a more authoritarian and structured treatment strategy.

Anorexia Nervosa

In essence, the same strategy that is used for diet control applies to anorexia nervosa, with some additional considerations. In the first place, the profile is critically important to differentiate the kind of person who has the anorexia. If the profile is soft or decrement, the odds are that the basic condition is schizophrenia or a serious character disorder, in which case the anorectic symptoms are secondary to the treatment modality for containing the primary psychiatric illness. In our clinical experience, anorexia nervosa is a situation in which differential diagnosis, aided by the score on the HIP, is especially important. For borderline or schizophrenic patients with decrement profiles, the disturbed eating pattern represents a somatic delusional system acted out, and psychotropic medication along with structured milieu and rehabilitative treatment is of great importance (Bruch 1973).

If the profile is intact, and especially if it is mid-range or high, then the instructions are basically in terms of: 1) overeating and undereating are insults to body integrity, in effect they become a poison to the body; 2) you need your body to live; and 3) to the extent that you want to live, you owe your body this respect and protection.

Among anorectic patients scoring high on the profile, anorexia is more consistent with a diagnosis of hysterical character disorder than with schizophrenia. These patients may be using their eating disorder in a dramatic conflict with other people in their lives or as a way of acting out a message from members of their family that they do not deserve to live. The somatic consequences can be serious in both cases; but for the latter group, structured psychotherapeutic intervention (along the lines discussed later for the highs) is appropriate. Intervention with the living situation of the patient is very important in the event that the patient is acting out a message being conveyed by other members of the family. If significant depression is a factor, antidepressant medication can be of adjunctive benefit. It is especially important to treat, if necessary, the affective disorder and then to take into account any secondary gain and loss factors in the patient's environment.

Thus, we add to the traditional treatment for anorectics an emphasis on sorting out those for whom the affective component rather than the thought disorder is of primary importance, and then utilizing the techniques described later in the book for treating the highly hypnotizable person (see chapter 22).

Case Example. M.L. was a 31-year-old divored woman who requested help with hypnosis for weight control. She complained of epi-
sodic binge eating, several medical problems including lupus, and a
history of some social isolation for the preceding three years. It was
quickly obvious, however, that she was seriously underweight rather
than overweight, and that her preoccupation with occasional episodes
of excessive eating camouflaged her more serious problem of damaging
herself by undereating. She had a history of amenorrhea for the preceding three years and it turned out that she was also seriously
depressed. Her profile was a 3 soft, consistent with this depression.

She was taught an exercise that emphasized helping her learn to
eat with respect for her body and which included cutting down on the
eating binges but eating more regularly. She was also started on a tricyclic antidepressant. Within a month her depression began to lift and
she began to examine some unresolved issues in the break-up of her
former marriage and in coping with her parents. At the six-month
follow-up her weight was in the normal range, her depression had
lifted considerably, and her social isolation had diminished.

Thus, hypnosis has a peripheral and differential diagnostic application in this serious form of weight disturbance. Its main use is to help
sort out the serious underlying psychiatric disorder, and especially to
help identify the important field forces that influence outcome in a
subgroup of these patients who are highly hypnotizable.

15

Anxiety, Concentration, and Insomnia

Anxiety and Concentration Problems[*]

From the point of view of therapeutic strategy, we view anxiety and concentration difficulty as related aspects of the same overall treatment problem. Both involve some pathological distraction of attention from necessary day-to-day functions, and both involve a negative feedback cycle between psychological preoccupation and somatic discomfort. It is particularly important to employ the dissociative capacity of the patient, to help him separate his focal attention from somatic sensations of discomfort and restlessness. Because these problems of anxiety and concentration difficulty are so closely related, the treatment strategy for them is virtually the same.

It is particularly important to provide the patient with a tool for interrupting the snowball effect of developing anxiety. Very often, an individual who suffers from periodic attacks of anxiety becomes more and more fearful of the cycle following an initial signal that something is wrong. He may find himself preoccupied with a situation that makes him anxious and then begin to recognize the physical concomitants of anxiety: tightness of the stomach, shortness of breath, parathesias, or other signs. He then begins to respond to the physical signals with

[*] There have been reports of the successful use of hypnosis for performance anxiety (Lodato 1968; Hammer 1954; Goldburgh), although Egan and Egan (1968) reported that hypnosis was not helpful in improving academic performance. Hypnosis has been applied to the problem of anxiety in various ways. Isham (1962) found hypnotic techniques equally as effective as psychotherapy. There are numerous other clinical reports of useful anxiety-reducing techniques (Perin 1968; Meares 1956; Moss 1958; Schneck 1975; Frankel 1974).

worry, which then provokes even more physical discomfort. This sets up a feedback cycle, which escalates into a major and immobilizing state of anxiety.

A history is taken and in particular some effort is made to elicit information about the psychological or social setting in which the anxiety attacks are likely to occur. The patient is administered the HIP. Presuming the psychiatric history, mental status examination, and results of the HIP indicate that the anxiety is of a moderate and neurotic type, and that the patient has intact trance capacity, the following instructions are given. The patient is told to put himself into an hypnotic trance, and then is told:

> *While you imagine yourself floating, in your mind's eye visualize a huge screen. It can be a movie screen, a TV screen, or, if you wish, a clear blue sky that acts like a screen. On that screen you project your thoughts, ideas, feelings, memories, fantasies, plans, while you float here. You establish this clear sense of your body floating here, while you relate to your thoughts and ideas out there. Once you have established this screen, you can further separate out a main screen and a split screen or, if you wish, you can insert a screen within the main screen. Allow the spontaneous flow of thoughts and feelings to continue as they proceed onto the main screen, but exert your own selectivity by focusing aspects of the main screen onto the split screen. By focusing on the split screen, you now can engage in the kind of technical virtuosity of fast-forward, or fast-backward; or slow-motion forward, or slow-motion backward; or you can freeze a frame and examine it carefully. You can even use a psychological zoom lens in which you focus with great detail on an aspect of something that occurs on the split or insert screen.*
>
> *With this as an art form, you now have several options open. The first one is that as you learn new material, you can put yourself in a trance state and visualize this new material on the screen, especially the split screen. Then as a practice session later, you can reinstitute the trance state and learn the art of retrieving the memory of what previously was imprinted on the screen. By doing this in a systematic way, you are accumulating and processing those feelings and thoughts on the screen. At the same time you have a practice effect of learning the art of retrieving what was there before. While doing that, it is even possible to use a retrieval experience of whole memories of the past that come into focus at will.*
>
> *When your main goal is to focus on anxiety control, the emphasis in this training is to concentrate on the floating, floating, floating. Sometimes you can make it more vivid by imagining that you're floating in water. Or if it's more helpful, imagine that you're like an astronaut, floating above the field of gravity. The focus on floating leads to an inevitable sense of muscle relaxation; with the muscles more relaxed, anxiety itself is reduced. It is very difficult to instruct the muscles to relax through intellectual means, but to feel yourself floating is a direct communication with the muscle to shift into a state of buoyant repose. An indirect consequence of this buoyant repose is that thinking and feeling out there on the imaginary screen happens with greater ease.*
>
> *When the focus is on concentration, floating is still the theme although the main emphasis now is on imprinting new feelings, new thoughts, new content, onto the screen, especially the split or insert screen. Have practice sessions in the beginning, maybe four or five times a day, to learn the art of retrieving what was imprinted on the screen. The art form is in essence this two-way arrangement of both imposing the imprint of the thought or feeling on the screen, and at the same time, feeling equally comfortable*

with reestablishing the screen, so that retrieval is available as the floating constantly goes on. It is especially helpful to use the slow-motion and zoom lens technique in retrieval processes, to be sure that the art of remembering on command, in response to questions, or in stress situations occurs by training and not as a surprise. This is a very useful preparatory experience for anticipated examinations.

Case Example. K.U. was a 44-year-old, well-trained psychiatrist with four years of psychoanalytic training, who had failed her board examinations two years in a row. This was especially disturbing because she was well informed and her colleagues knew her as a competent psychiatrist and analyst. Yet something happened in the examination process that led to blocking and intellectual paralysis. For use in that setting, she inquired about learning self-hypnosis to discipline her concentration. She was taught the procedure for self-hypnosis after determining that she had an intact grade 2 to 3 profile. She responded immediately after the first practice session with this observation: "It's a nice, relaxing sensation—something I have not experienced in a long while." She practiced this exercise about ten times a day. In fact, a week or so later she made a phone call to check up on the procedure and to be sure that she was doing it correctly. She conscientiously prepared for the next board exam by imprinting the review information on her private imaginary screen. After a four-month preparation period using the exercise, she again took the examination and passed. She successfully passed the oral exam as well. A year after the treatment session she wrote the following letter:

"It is probably unforgivable that one receive a thank you a year after the event. But one of my first thoughts on learning that I had passed Part 2 of the boards in psychiatry was to thank you. The trial session of hypnosis last October helped me considerably with both rest and study. My single 'buoyant' left arm was, I think, a great asset."

The patient is taught the self-hypnosis exercise and is given instructions to practice it every one to two hours during the first few weeks, until he becomes confident of his own ability to invoke this relaxed, dissociated state whenever necessary. It is particularly important to instruct patients suffering from anxiety to use the exercise every time they feel an anxiety attack coming. This gives them a sense of something to resort to at a time when they are prone to feel especially helpless, and it facilitates their development of a sense of mastery over the symptom.

The treatment strategy is designed not merely to counter a sense of anxiety or distraction in concentration, but to provide the patient with an alternative strategy for working through psychological problems or for doing intellectual work. In particular, the patient suffering from anxiety is encouraged to use the trance experience of thinking with the screen to work through psychological problems as he maintains a sense of relaxed floating in his body. It is also helpful to have the patient practice visualizing situations on a screen which do in fact provoke anxiety; to have him freeze the action on the screen when he begins to sense the physical signs of anxiety in his body, and reestablish a sense of floating before proceeding with the scene on the screen. This method enables a patient to contain his somatic responses so that he can more clearly think through the psychological pressures and conflicts with which he is coping. At times this provides an occasion for a necessary insight-oriented explanation as to the causes of the anxiety. The following case example illustrates this point.

U.L. was an accomplished accountant who was highly respected by his peers and employer. He went into analysis and, despite efforts at working through many of his private problems in analysis over a four-year period, he failed the CPA exams six consecutive times. At the suggestion of his analyst, he came to learn about the possibilities of using self-hypnosis to prepare for the next exam. He profiled as an intact 1 to 2. He was taught the screen technique and he practiced it diligently. He even looked forward to taking the next exam. When it was over, he had a sense of elation that at last he had learned the art of concentrating and responding directly to the questions—but that evening he was shocked to realize that he had totally overlooked an entire question on the exam. This resulted in yet another failure, which became a major issue in his analytic work for several months. He explored the significance of the obsessive style of undermining even a newly acquired talent and of feeling the exuberance of mastering a new technique at the same time.

He had unconsciously sabotaged the exam-taking process by overlooking one entire question. Much of this resonated well with other issues that had been previously dealt with in his analysis. The next time he took the exam, he was able to pass it not only successfully, but with a high grade. Mastering this problem, recognizing the trap that he had set for himself, and understanding its meaning in relation to other events in his life led to the termination of his formal analysis. On follow-up eight years later, he was practicing successfully in his profession.

In this case the hypnosis worked well in tandem with the psychoanalytic therapy. There came a point where his premises needed to be challenged before he could pass the examination. His experience with self-hypnosis and his subsequent performance on the sixth examination proved to him that he could indeed pass it, which sharpened the focus on the question, "Since I can, why won't I pass the exam?" This issue was then fruitfully explored in analysis and he did finally allow himself to succeed.

The technique for using self-hypnosis in dealing with anxiety and concentration difficulties is basically the same, regardless of the HIP score, as long as it is in the intact range. As is true with other problems, it is often helpful to emphasize the intellectually intriguing aspects of the approach with Apollonians, discussing the nature of dissociation and the mind–body question, and emphasizing the importance of discipline in performing the exercise regularly. For Dionysians, the compliance aspects are emphasized and the patient is encouraged to explore his newly found facility at bringing on a sense of floating. All patients are encouraged to use this state creatively, to meditate on issues that concern them, and to use it to think through difficult situations. They are also taught to take their anxiety or concentration difficulties as a message; not to be frightened or overwhelmed by their difficulties, but to use them as an occasion to examine what it is that is bothering them. In the last example, anxiety was an important message to the patient about his self-destructive impulses. In other instances anxiety may have more shallow roots and simply reflect a habitual or socially reinforced response to a difficult situation. In any event, the patient is encouraged to use this experience as an occasion to widen his sense of mastery.

Insomnia

Insomnia is a widespread and annoying problem, but it is rarely serious in and of itself. Patients who have difficulty sleeping often complicate the situation considerably by worrying about what the loss of sleep means and by taking vast quantities of hypnotic drugs. (In this instance, the Greek root "hypnos" is correctly used.) The pattern of sleep disturbance is worth noting, since certain types of insomnia are among the most reliable indicators of a depression that will respond to somatic treatment. This pattern usually involves early morning awakening. The patient finds himself unable to return to sleep after waking up earlier than he needs to in the morning, typically at five or six A.M. He usually finds himself particularly devoid of energy early in the day, with improvement later on. An accompanying loss of appetite and a feeling of depression is common to this syndrome.

By contrast, a much more prevalent pattern of insomnia which is usually associated with anxiety or situational stress involves difficulty falling asleep or, in a more serious form, waking throughout the night. Patients toss and turn, find themselves ruminating about problems, and become increasingly frustrated and tense about their inability to fall asleep. It is instructive to determine major events in the patient's life at the time the insomnia became a problem. It is worth bearing in mind that it may be more important to treat the underlying depression or anxiety, if it is prominent in the history and examination of mental status.

It is also important to be aware of the widespread use and abuse of sedative and hypnotic drugs, predominantly the benzodiazepenes and barbiturates. These drugs have potential for habituation and addiction. Some patients may have to be tapered and observed for signs of withdrawal which, in the case of barbiturates, can be fatal if not managed properly. Drugs of this class also hamper trance capacity because of their sedative properties. It may be necessary for the patient to cease using these drugs before self-hypnotic techniques become reasonably effective.

In addition, there is evidence that chronic use of sedative and hypnotic drugs interferes with sleep, especially REM sleep during which dreaming occurs (Dement and Guilleminault 1973). There is some evidence that deprivation of REM sleep over an extended period of time can have acute but reversible psychopathological consequences (Dement and Fisher 1963).

Several closely related concentration techniques have been reported to be effective in treating insomnia. Included among these techniques are Jacobson's progressive relaxation (1938, 1964), Schultz's autogenic training (1949), and various self-hypnosis techniques. Nicassio and Bootzin (1974) found progressive relaxation and autogenic training equally effective and more useful than simply instructing the patients to set aside time to relax. Graham et al. (1975) reported progressive relaxation to be somewhat more effective than hypnosis in treating insomnia, although they explained that the finding was related to differences in expectancy of outcome for the two groups. Although they administered the Harvard Group Scale of Hypnotic Susceptibility (Shor and Orne 1962), they failed to correlate outcome with hypnotizability, which would have done more to clarify the role of hypnosis in the clinical result. In any event, there is evidence that various concentration techniques are helpful in treating insomnia.

Once we have determined that insomnia rather than serious depression or anxiety is the primary problem, we begin by reassuring the patient that the problem is annoying but not dangerous. We then apply a puzzle form in the Weldon sense: the patient projects his preoccupying thoughts onto an imaginary screen and allows his body to float, since muscle tension is an enemy of sleep. Rather than forcing himself to sleep and fighting his thoughts, the patient is instructed to allow himself to sleep by concentrating on creating a dissociation between his mental activity and his physical relaxation. He is instructed in using the self-hypnotic mode to avoid the paradox of "forcing himself to relax."

Case Example. T.M. was a 36-year-old writer and married mother of one child, who came for help with a lifetime pattern of insomnia which had worsened during the previous six years, the time since her marriage. She had tried a variety of sedative and hypnotic drugs without effect. Her profile score was a 2 to 4 increment. An edited transcript of the treatment encounter with her follows:

DOCTOR: *Look up, close your eyelids. Now, take a deep breath. Three, exhale, let you eyes relax, your body float, permit one hand or the other to feel like a buoyant balloon, and let it float upward. As it does, your elbow bends, your forearm floats into an upright position; this becomes your signal to enter a state of meditation in which you concentrate on this imaginary floating and at the same time concentrate on this:*

In your mind's eye imagine a huge screen, a movie screen; or if you wish, a TV screen; or if you wish, a clear, blue sky that acts like a screen. On this screen you project your thoughts, ideas, feelings, memories, and plans. So while you are floating here, you can now relate to your thoughts and feelings, memories, and plans out there on the screen. By doing this you're now able to enhance your communication with your own thoughts and fantasies, and sharpen your access so that you can retrieve your thoughts and feelings more readily. This is in a way like setting up a private theater in which you can absorb yourself in the drama of your own life. Now, this means that when you're trying to fall asleep and your engine is working, your thoughts are going. Instead of trying to fight your thoughts, to turn them off, which you can't do, what you can do is to become a traffic director and learn to direct your thoughts, feelings, and fantasies out there on your screen while you are floating here. The function of that is to enable your muscles to relax.

To simply tell your muscles to relax is too intellectual and is not in the mode of your muscle understanding. But when you feel yourself floating, then you're in a much better position to bring about muscle relaxation. Muscle tension is an enemy of sleep. When you are trying to fall asleep, a change of guard takes place. In your autonomic nervous system there are two controls. When you are awake the sympathetic headquarters takes control; when you fall asleep the parasympathetic takes over. Muscle tension interferes with this change of guard. By learning to float while you are at the same time accounting for the thoughts, feelings, and ideas that are going around in your mind, by allowing them to occur out there on the screen, you don't have to fight them; you let them occur while you are floating here. The change of guard takes place and the parasympathetic takes over and you naturally fall asleep.

Now, I propose that you prepare yourself for this during the daytime by doing this exercise, in the beginning every one to two hours. Each time the exercise takes only about twenty seconds. And the exercise is as follows. Sit or lie down, and to yourself you count to three. One, you do one thing; two, you do two things; and three, you do three things. One, look up to the top of your head. Two, while looking up, you close your eyelids and take a deep breath. Three, you exhale, let your eyes relax, and let your body float. As you feel yourself floating, you permit one hand or the other to feel like a buoyant balloon and let it float upward, as your left hand is doing now. When it reaches this upright position, this becomes your signal to enter a state of meditation in which you concentrate on this imaginary feeling and at the same time on this concept: floating here with your thoughts, feelings, and ideas out there on the screen. Lock this concept in your mind so that it becomes a posthypnotic signal that you retain. Then when the time to sleep comes, you now have something that you can invoke rather quickly. Each time you do the exercise, you bring yourself out of the state of concentration this way: three, get ready; two, with your eyelids closed, roll up your eyes, do it now; one, let your eyelids open slowly. Then when your eyes are in focus, slowly make a fist with the hand that is up, open your fist slowly, let it float down, and that is the end of the exercise. Now, stay in this position and describe what physical sensations you're aware of.

PATIENT: My hand goes up like that, comes down, and does whatever you tell me to do. And the same with my eyes. But I don't know that I'm totally relaxed.

DOCTOR: *You're not totally relaxed, but it's learning to shift from one level to another. Then as you practice your art form, you get more and more relaxed. Have you ever noticed when you are falling asleep at night that at times you get a startle reaction and shortly thereafter you are asleep?*

PATIENT: Yes.

DOCTOR: *Isn't that a contradiction? You would think that if you have a startle reaction, it would wake you up.*

PATIENT: Yes, but I fall asleep.

DOCTOR: *Yes. Do you know what that is? A change of guard takes place. Right now you are under sympathetic control, but when the change takes place, the parasympathetic takes over. Usually it occurs so gradually that you don't feel it. But should it happen faster than usual, that is when you really feel it. But you know that you're going to sleep after that, because the switch has already taken place. Now, have you noticed that when you try to fall asleep your sympathetic machinery is working?*

PATIENT: Yes.

DOCTOR: *You simply cannot turn your mind off in that way. That is like telling yourself, "Don't think about purple elephants." What happens?*

PATIENT: I think about them.

DOCTOR: *So, since that doesn't work, why use it? But what you can do is turn it around and you know this: It is much more human to make peace with the rhythm of the way you think. You can float here with your thoughts, feelings, and ideas out there on the screen. And by doing that, it enables the change of guard to take place. Now, during the daytime you don't prepare yourself for this, you don't do this to fall asleep. All that you are doing is preparing the art form; it is just like practicing a dance step. If you practice it enough, then when the time comes to dance it just happens automatically. That is the point of practicing during the day, not to go to sleep.*

Now when bedtime comes, you can do one of two things. Either while you are lying in bed look up, close your eyelids, take a deep breath, exhale, eyes relaxed, body float, let one hand come up, visualize a screen floating here, project your thoughts and feelings on it, and watch your own TV program. By learning to float in this way, your muscles relax, a change of guard takes place, and you fall asleep. One thing you can do is stay in this formal trance state until the change of guard takes place, and with this shift into natural sleep you end hypnosis. Natural sleep automatically cuts off self-hypnosis.

There is another way of doing it. Where do you like to sleep, what position do you usually sleep in?

PATIENT: On my side.

DOCTOR: *All right, then, here is how you do it. Do the exercise first lying on your back. Then give yourself a posthypnotic signal. You are going to turn over on your side or on your stomach. You will continue to float, but relate to the screen. Now you are responding to a posthypnotic signal that you have given to yourself; by relating to your own screen out there, you are in effect in hypnosis, but it is a posthypnotic state that you have structured for yourself. Then just wait until natural sleep takes over.*

PATIENT: So, do the exercise and turn over.

DOCTOR: *Turn over, that is right. Before you come out of it, you give yourself a posthypnotic signal. But you are going to turn over and continue to float and continue to look at your screen. So that you are now responding to your own structure. And when you are turning over, you can even imagine yourself floating as you turn over.*

PATIENT: What happens if I wake up?

DOCTOR: *Then you do the same thing all over again. Restructure the screen, float, and turn back over. If you fight insomnia, all you do is make your insomnia worse. That is like telling yourself not to think about purple elephants. But if you learn to float and have your thoughts and feelings out there, then the floating enhances the shift, the changing of the guard. Any questions?*

PATIENT: During the day if I hear noises should it bother me?

DOCTOR: *In general, to be annoyed by this is understandable. Noises are an enemy for they disturb tranquillity. The most you can do is to get so absorbed in doing your exercise that you ignore the noise. But if you have nothing to do, and you start fighting the noise, then you make a bad situation worse. So that the best you can do is to learn to ignore it by doing your routine: floating, relating to your own thoughts and feelings.*

PATIENT: Now you see I feel very relaxed. Now, when I'm standing up I feel more floating than I did when I was sitting down.

DOCTOR: *Okay, you have it. Now, you see that I didn't do this to you. This was a capacity you brought with you to the room. Learn to develop this art form so it is with you all of the time.*

Follow-up one year later revealed that she was "sleeping very well" and "feeling sensationally good."

As in other symptom-oriented treatment, emphasis is placed on using self-hypnosis, on practicing the exercise frequently, and on using the dissociated state of the trance to separate psychological tension from somatic discomfort. The patient is instructed not to fight his pressured thoughts, but to project them onto an imaginary screen and to allow his body to float. In this way he is taught to allow himself to sleep rather than fruitlessly attempting to force himself to sleep.

16

Phobias

Introduction

The treatment of phobias has been one of the more encouraging areas in clinical psychiatry in the past several decades. Such diverse approaches as behavior modification, psychoanalysis, and hypnosis have been used with generally good results. There is widespread agreement that a firm but gentle approach can be effective in directing the phobic patient toward a step-by-step confrontation with overcoming the phobic situation. Therapists employing behavior modification often construct a hierarchy of more or less frightening aspects of the phobic situation. They then employ relaxation techniques which are virtually indistinguishable from self-hypnosis to help their patients gradually cope with the elements of increasing anxiety on the hierarchy (Wolpe 1958). Some therapists go so far as to accompany patients to the rooftop or elevator of which they are fearful.

In a recent report, phobics were more highly hypnotizable as a group, than a matched control group who came for smoking control (Frankel and Orne 1976). This study at least suggests that phobics are a good population to treat using hypnosis.

Flying Phobia

Flying phobias are the most common type of phobia seen in our practice. Our treatment strategy is easily adaptable to other phobic situations, since it involves both cognitive and behavioral elements. The cognitive element involves taking a new point of view with regard to the feared situation. The dissociative and relaxing aspects of the self-hypnotic trance state are employed behaviorally to reinforce the cognitive message and to give the patient a feeling of mastery when confronted with anxiety.

After the clinical history has been taken, a cluster questionnaire given, and a profile performed, the patient is taught to induce self-hypnosis and is instructed to put himself into a trance. When he is in the trance state, he is told the following:

Behind the fear of flying, you are unconsciously fighting the plane. This is absurd. The plane is a mechanical instrument that is neither for you nor against you. You can correct this misconception by feeling yourself floating with the plane; float with the plane, feel the plane as an extension of your body, and by floating with the plane you are correcting the fear.

All of man's instruments are in effect an extension of his body. For example, if you want to pound something into the ground you can use your fist. You can also use a hammer; in that sense a hammer is an instrument that is an extension of your body, your hand, your arm. If you want to point, you can use your finger and arm. Another way you can do it is to use a wooden pointer; in that sense the wooden pointer is an instrument that is an extension of your body. If you want to go from here to there, one way to go is to walk; another way to go is to use a bicycle; in that sense the bicycle is an instrument that is an extension of your body, your legs. Still another way to go is to use an automobile. In that sense the automobile is an instrument; an extension of the legs. Still another way to go is to fly. The airplane is an instrument that in effect is an extension of the body. You can make this correction by feeling yourself floating with the plane. Float with the plane. In the course of floating with the plane, you are simultaneously ignoring and dissolving the fight with the plane, and as a consequence, the fear.

You practice the exercise as preparation several times a day, every one or two hours. Each time it takes about twenty seconds in which you simply shift into the state of self-hypnosis and reimprint that concept; float with the plane, float with the plane. Then bring yourself out of the trance state and go about doing what you ordinarily do. You can repeat the exercise in the car while you are going to the airport. If you are driving, do it at a red light, which usually lasts a minute. The exercise itself takes only twenty seconds. While you are waiting at the airport, sit down and do the exercise again. And while you are getting on the plane, even though you know you are walking onto the plane, instead feel yourself floating onto the plane. If you have a chance, take a look at the cockpit and the pilot as well, so you have a fresh image of what the cockpit looks like.

Now go to your seat, tighten your seat belt, and you have three options. The first option is to put yourself in a trance state, lock in this concept of floating with the plane, and stay in the trance until the plane lands. A second option is to put yourself into the trance and stay in it until the plane is in the air, give yourself a posthypnotic signal that you will continue to float with the plane even though you are out of the formal trance state, bring yourself out, and feel yourself floating with the plane during the flight. Then go back into

*the formal trance state when the plane is about to land and bring yourself out
of it after the plane lands. The third and preferred option is this: go in and
out of the trance state several times, each time giving yourself the signal to
remain floating when you are out of the trance state. This keeps reinforcing
the concept of constantly floating with the plane. Make it a point to be in the
formal trance state when the plane takes off, go in and out several times
during the flight, put yourself into the formal trance state when the plane is
about to land, and bring yourself out after the plane lands.*

*As a variation during the flight you can sometimes imagine that you are
sitting alongside the pilot in the cockpit and imagine yourself relating to the
instruments on the panel board. The pilot is an agent, your agent, he mediates
your control over the plane; so that instead of fearing that the plane is not
controlled, by feeling the pilot as your agent and feeling that he mediates
your control, then your hand through the pilot's hand on the instruments is in
effect controlling the plane.*

The patient is instructed to meditate on this approach for a moment
and then to bring himself out of the trance state. The following discussion ensues:

*A basic consideration in getting your orientation is to keep in mind the dis-
tinction between a possibility and a probability. Of course there is a possibility
that the plane will crash, but it is highly improbable. The sign of a phobia is
that you deal with a possibility as if it were a probability. You confuse normal
anticipatory anxiety with fear. For example, you got here to the office despite
the possibility that your auto might have been wrecked on your way, but since
you assumed it was only a possibility, in probabilistic terms you had a chance
to make it here safely and you did. You are sitting here in your chair and
there is a possibility that the boiler in the basement underneath will blow up,
but since you accept that as only a possibility, the probability is that it will not
happen, and therefore you can sit here and pay attention to me. There is a
possibility that when you leave the office and walk down the street a loose
air conditioner may fall on your head, yet you will walk down the street.
There again, you are already making the decision between a probability and
a possibility and you are free to walk on the street. The same principle applies
in your decision about flying. To ask for an absolute positive guarantee means
that you are in a trap. It is impossible to get that, but what you can do is
extend your usual mastery technique in making choices and apply it to your
decisions about flying, as you do with everything else.*

The patient is warned that the common practice of drinking heavily
or taking tranquilizers in large doses will interfere with his ability to
concentrate and employ this strategy. Intoxication can lead to panic
rather than prevent it.

Often the session is ended by surfacing the fundamental anxiety
about death with a sense of humor. The patient is asked to send a card
or call after his first flight experience. Then the patient is told: "However, if the plane crashes and you are killed, don't bother writing." The
therapist's humorous manner of verbalizing the common fear about
being killed on a flight places the fear in a different perspective. The
message to the patient is that it is expected that one will be afraid—
just do not take the fear too seriously.

The crucial aspects of the treatment strategy for plane phobias are
"floating with the plane" and learning to view the plane as an extension

of one's body. The effort is to reintegrate the person within his body and within the plane, and establish a sense of control. This restructuring of the experience of flying takes advantage of the natural state of buoyancy often experienced in the dissociated state, and makes use of it. This can best be seen in the context of the nature of the anxiety often experienced by people who are significantly fearful of flying.

THOUGHTS ABOUT THE FEAR OF FLYING

Our model for formulating the nature of this anxiety is similar to those used for other problems. An individual's experience of his fear of flying is usually a composite of avoidance and obsession; some people may primarily avoid any contact with airplanes or any thought about their fears; others may become obsessed, and many people alternate between the two. But the act of flying has a meaning which stimulates both avoidance and obsession. The fantasy of flying and the fear of falling have long been essential to human religion and mythology. They have often been related in complex ways to the wish for transcendence over life and death and to the moral state of an individual. Ludwig Binswanger explores this theme in his fascinating essay "Dream and Existence":

It is true of both ancient and modern literature, and true of dreams and myths of all periods and peoples: again and again the eagle or the falcon, the kite or the hawk, personify our existence as rising or longing to rise and as falling. This merely indicates how essential to human existence it is to determine itself as rising or falling. This essential tendency is, of course, not to be confused with the conscious, purposeful wish to rise, or the conscious fear of falling. These are already mirrorings or reflections in consciousness of that basic tendency. It is precisely this unreflected, or in psychoanalytic language— unconscious factor that, in the soaring existence of the bird of prey, strikes such a sympathetic note within us.

> Innate in each of us
> Is that rising in the heart
> When the lark, lost in skyey space above us,
> Gives forth his pealing song;
> When above the jagged trees
> The eagle hovers, his wings outspread,
> And when above the flatness of the earth and seas
> The crane compels himself toward home.
> (Binswanger [Needleman, trans.] 1967)

He makes it clear that the conscious fear of flying is not the same as but is clearly related to fundamental hopes and fears about the state of one's being. The opportunity of actually flying suggests levels of unimagined escape and transcendance. First, it literally suggests transcendence of the pull of gravity, transcendence of the physical limitations of the body. It suggests the possibility of escape of difficult situations, of rising above one's troubles. Thus flying, even in common language, is connected with escape and avoidance.

But the very extremity of the hope often provokes its extreme (and not unrelated) counterpart: intense fear and anxiety. One can become obsessed with the sense of falling, of the "rug being pulled out from under." People fearful of flying feel trapped in the plane like a sardine in a can, utterly bound and unable to escape. Perhaps their wishes to escape are stronger than those of other people who accept flying with more equanimity. In any event, they feel utterly trapped and bound to fall—they are obsessed.

The individual is seeing himself in terms of the literal need to do something, either to escape and transcend or to fall. The therapeutic strategy employed here is an attempt to help the person restructure his situation by relating to himself in a different way which takes into account all the aspects of his situation. He is encouraged to enter his own natural state of dissociation, the trance state, which already indicates that he can revise his relationship to himself and his body. It is recommended that he "float with the plane." Floating is like flying, but more passive; it implies less moving. One goes, but gently, letting the plane carry him. This helps the patient cope with the obsessional anxiety by saying, "yes, you are carried by the plane, but you can go along with it." Furthermore, the idea of perceiving the plane as an extension of one's body helps to alter the person's perspective about who is in control. Is the plane carrying him off, or is he not in fact using the plane to get something done, to extend his body? In this sense he is in control. The symbolic fear or wish of escaping from everything is replaced in part by the literal fact of using the plane to get somewhere faster. A certain amount of transcending is made real, not denied, yet its limitations make clear that one must float *with* the plane. With less extravagant (even if unconscious) goals, the fear of falling seems more manageable. The suggestion is that the individual does indeed decide the course of the plane; that is why he chose it. His unconscious fears and wishes are not likely to carry him farther than he chooses to go, or to drop him along the way.

In this manner a person is taught to relate to his situation and to himself in a new way, to re-examine his controlling part in the drama of flying, and to keep it in perspective. He cannot escape, but he is not entirely trapped. He is indeed at risk, but it is a limited and calculated risk which is undertaken with a defined and limited goal in mind.

OUTCOME STUDIES

We found that almost half of those patients with intact profiles reported significant improvement several years after this single-session treatment. This and our follow-up data relating hypnotizability as measured by HIP scores to clinical improvement are reported in the Appendix. These data are consistent with a report of Horowitz (1970) in a controlled study of various treatment approaches to snake phobias. She found a .39 correlation between hypnotizability as measured by the SHSS, and scores of the patients' capacity to approach a live snake after treatment. She also found that several different approaches such as relaxation, fear arousal, and suggestion were more or less equally effective in comparison with a control group.

There has been considerable interest in the behavior modification literature in treating phobias. Wolpe (1958, 1973; Wolpe and Lazarus 1966) and other authors (Malleson 1959; Bandura 1969) reported considerable success in utilizing systematic desensitization and reciprocal inhibition. Lang and Lazovik (1963) reported significant success utilizing systematic desensitization to treat patients with snake phobia in a controlled study. The therapy consisted of eleven sessions. Of the eleven experimentally treated subjects who responded, six were able to hold a snake at the end of the last treatment session. Four of those six were still able to do it at six-month follow-up. The authors dismissed any role of hypnosis in this treatment with two specious arguments: the first was that no significant changes were observed in association with an undefined "pretherapy training program." They went on to note that "hypnosis and general muscle relaxation were not in themselves vehicles of change" (p. 524). This is of course true; but hypnosis may well be a facilitator of change, given the utilization of any treatment strategy. They then went on to comment that there was no difference in SHSS Form-A scores between the experimental and control groups. All this fact demonstrates is that the groups were comparable.

Their argument would have been more convincing if they had demonstrated no relationship between hypnotizability and treatment response in the experimental group. Given our data for flying phobias and the data of Horowitz (1970) on snake phobias, it would be surprising if Lang and Lazovik did not find a correlation between hypnotizability and treatment responsiveness, even though the treatment strategy was systematic desensitization. Since hypnosis occurs whether or not a formal induction ceremony is performed, it is likely that the desensitization technique tapped hypnotic capacity in those individuals who had it. Certainly nothing in their study disproves this assertion.

In a carefully designed crossover study, Marks et al. (1968) addressed this problem somewhat more satisfactorily. Members of a group of 28 patients having a variety of phobias were randomly assigned to treatment with systematic desensitization or hypnosis, the latter involving simple direct suggestions of improvement of the symptom and relaxation. Patients who failed with the first technique were switched to the other. The treatment program took three months. They found that desensitization techniques produced more improvement than hypnosis intervention, but that in general the differences were not statistically significant. They employed a rather crude body-sway measure of suggestibility that correlated at .34 with treatment response for subjects treated with hypnosis. They did not report on the hypnotizability of subjects given desensitization treatment, and they employed the outmoded hypnotic "depth" concept in discussing the low but positive correlation of suggestibility with outcome. They speculated that hypnosis may be more effective than desensitization among highly anxious subjects. Taken as a whole, the study purported to demonstrate that behavioral techniques were superior to hypnosis in the treatment of phobias, but, given the simplicity of the hypnotic intervention and the crudeness of the measure of hypnotizability, the outcomes for the two approaches proved surprisingly comparable.

Dog Phobia

A morbid fear of dogs is not an uncommon complaint and can be a surprisingly disabling symptom. Such individuals find themselves tailoring their lives around the avoidance of encounters with dogs; they plan their walks on the street at times when people are less likely to be walking their dogs, carry big shopping bags to protect themselves should a dog approach them, or avoid going outside at all. They may disrupt social occasions with their panic resulting from a chance encounter with a dog.

The patient with this problem is taught a restructuring strategy which acknowledges that some fear of animals is reasonable but which seeks to help the patient incorporate the distinction between tame and wild animals. The patient does not fight the fear; rather, he accepts it as natural, seen in the proper perspective. The patient is put in a self-hypnotic trance and told the following:

1. A fear of animals is normal for all sensitive humans.
2. There is a vast difference between wild and tame animals.
3. By all means, keep your fear of wild animals.
4. Learn that tame animals are not only not harmful, but dogs especially are people-oriented and would prefer to have a warm relationship with humans.

The patient is then given instructions to find a friend who has a dog and make this contractual agreement with the friend. Under no circumstances will the friend use tricks or deception. At the patient's request, he will have the dog on a leash in a room, and the patient will enter the same room as the dog. The patient can repeat the experience at his or her own pace, and try moving toward the dog. As these practice sessions continue, the patient develops a growing desire to cuddle the dog. Eventually, at his own pace, he goes toward the dog, touches it, feels the fur. The patient then sits or stands in the room and, at his request, the friend brings the dog on the leash toward the patient, and finally comes all the way up to the patient. When the patient is ready, he takes the leash, holds the dog, and cuddles it. As an ultimate act of closeness, the patient opens the palm of his hand and allows the dog to sniff or lick the palm.

This step-by-step sequence is spelled out but at the same time the patient is informed that the time intervals between training sessions are a matter of personal choice. The whole procedure can take place in a day or a month, depending on convenience, cooperation, and desire.

This approach has elements of the systematic desensitization technique used by behavior therapists in dealing with phobias (Wolpe 1958). A hierarchy is established, allowing the patient to experience situations which in the past were increasingly anxiety-provoking. Given the generally good results which behavior therapists report for phobias, this overlap is not surprising. However, in the restructuring approach the sequence and timing are determined by the patient rather than the therapist. The self-hypnotic trance is taught to the patient so that he can more quickly incorporate a new perspective toward dogs and at the same time cope with anxiety. The hierarchy also is not imagined; rather, it is acted out using the self-hypnosis exercise for anxiety containment during the process.

Case Example. S.M. sought help at age thirty for a lifelong dog and cat phobia. This fear had been shared by her mother, brother, aunts, and cousins. She had come to feel that her life was crippled by this fear; she avoided walking outside and did so only when there were likely to be few dogs in the street. Finally she had decided that she wanted to "clean house."

Her profile score was a 2 to 3, and she responded to the cluster questions with mid-range Odyssean answers. After one session she carried out the training sessions, and got to the point where she was able to touch her friend's dog. However, she had a setback when her father visited during a training session and said, "Don't be afraid." This repetition of a statement she had heard so often in the past shook her confidence and her overwhelming fear of dogs returned. This setback underscores the fact that interactional problems are often related to the perpetuation of such symptoms, and that fighing the symptom is almost invariably immobilizing. Her father's admonition not to be afraid was processed by her as a command to pay attention to the fear, and it returned. She returned for a second session during which she was consoled about her father's intrusion and the technique was reviewed. She then resumed her progress in overcoming the fear.

A month after the initial visit, she phoned to say, "I'm cured. I let the dog lick my hand, and what a tremendous relief." She subsequently wrote a brief autobiography. The following excerpts are included because they capture the flavor of her sense of being trapped by the symptom and her exuberance in overcoming it.

THE INVISIBLE PRISON

Just as a prism held in front of the eyes distorts everything one sees, so did my thirty-year phobia of dogs distort my life style and relationships, before I conquered it.

From the beginning until the spring of my thirtieth year, I existed, frozen, immobilized by deep feelings of fear, shame, and embarrassment, because of my phobia and phobic behavior.

Every waking hour of my life was spent planning my strategy of survival. As a child, if unaccompanied by an adult in the street, I searched out doorways and other escape routes from unleashed dogs. I waited on each landing until it was safe to run into my apartment. Childhood memories of afternoons without friends. Memories of the embarrassment of being different. Mocked by the kind of cruelty only children are capable of. Party dresses, but no parties. Suppose there was a dog at the party? I couldn't bear the consequences. So, alone, I sought solace and safety in close family ties, books, and classical music. I lived within my intellectual interests to define the reality of my life and to gain a perspective to maintain my sanity. Fantasies of what I could *if*. What I would *be*. Separating out the me who might be *if*—from the me who was. STUCK!

I was the personification of the silent student who knows the answer but never raises her hand in class. The satisfaction of knowing I knew had to be enough because I was too frightened to bring any attention to myself.

I was a shadow person, an observer but never a participant. Consequently my marks never reflected my knowledge. The information was frozen in my mind because I had to concentrate my energies on plotting the walk between home and school.

I developed counter-animal instincts and compensatory antennae. I could tell if an unleashed dog would remain on one side of the street or cross over. I knew which streets had the least number of unleashed dogs. I knew the streets with the most accessible doorways for ducking into for momentary safety.

My family and relatives were protective and usually understanding of my phobia during my childhood. As I grew into my teens, they were still protective but not as understanding. They were embarrassed by my behavior and fright on encountering an unleashed dog. They would tell me that I had nothing to be afraid of and that the dog was more frightened of me than I of it. These were worthless palliatives because I knew intellectually that the dog would not harm me but I could not deal with it emotionally.

Graduation from high school signified the beginning of seeking a structural change in my life. I felt I could no longer remain dependent upon my family. I had to find my own way. I was reluctant to attend college in the conventional way because I wanted to get away from a peer group I had little in common with and could not socialize with because I felt embarrassed by my phobia.

I graduated in 1957 and from that summer until 1964 I attended Hunter College, New York University, and the New School for Social Research as a nonmatriculated student.

My fear of becoming an emotional cripple wah almost equal to my fear of dogs. I forced myself to go to Mexico alone. I wanted to see if I could function independently in a place unknown to me and I unknown to it. I stayed in my hotel room most of the time and left only to take taxi excursions to museums, but it was the beginning of living on my own with my handicap.

As a result of this experience I decided to go to secretarial school. I felt that the business world would provide a "safe" area in which I could keep my phobia a secret.

At the age of twenty-one I got my own apartment and my first job as a secretary. My apartment was on the third floor, so I was able to avoid the use of the elevator by using the staircase to avoid dogs. I created my own safe world from office to home in the Village.

FROM PHOBIA TO PRISON

My biological date of birth is December, 1939, but I also consider my birthdate to be May, 1970.

I am the undisputed and grateful daughter of my parents, but my brother was the emissary of my emancipation from fear.

My brother and I had often discussed the source of my phobia. I "inherited" it from my mother. I learned to be afraid of dogs from the beginning of my life. On seeing a dog in the street, my mother would run with my carriage. My fear of dogs was perpetuated and reinforced by other family members sharing the same fear. I delved into this family phobia and traced its origin to Rumania and my maternal grandmother. I was told that dogs were used punitively to ghettoize the Jews. My grandmother left Rumania when she married my grandfather and brought the fear with her.

I revealed this and other relevant information to Dr. Spiegel. I was highly motivated and excited about the prospect of overcoming my phobia.

I proved to be hypnotizable and during the first session Dr. Spiegel put me in the trance state and explained the method and technique with which I could cure myself.

While I was in the trance state, Dr. Spiegel explained my phobia to me as a normal progression considering my family background. He explained that I had never learned about domesticated animals. He taught me auto-hypnosis and a set of suggestions and steps I could take in my own time to overcome my phobia. He taught me the technique to gain *executive control* over my phobia and, consequently, my life. Through autohypnosis I was able to open up a part of my mind previously closed to receptivity about dogs.

The plan was for me to arrange to work with a dog and follow a number of steps for which I would prepare myself daily through autohypnosis. The poodle next door, Dolly, became my co-therapist. For two days prior to my first planned encounter with Dolly I used autohypnosis ten times a day. I began each trance state with the following suggestion: "My natural feeling of love and protection will enable me to overcome my fear of dogs." I asked Dolly's owner to hold her on a tight leash with the dog facing away from me. I was afraid of approaching her face-to-face so I started by stroking her back. It took me more than ten minutes to cross the room and touch her.

Each day thereafter I programmed myself through autohypnosis. The next steps were to stroke her whole back and head. It took me one week to accomplish this goal.

Around that time my father visited my home. I was eager to demonstrate my ability to pet the back of a leashed dog. Just as I was about to do so, he uttered encouragingly the dreaded words of my youth, "You have nothing to be afraid of." I froze. I was unable to resume the first simple step. Once again, I knew intellectually he was right but his statement devastated me. The next day I saw Dr. Spiegel and he reinforced the hypnotic suggestions.

It became increasingly difficult to arrange dog time with my neighbors, so my ex-husband bought me a puppy whom I named Spiegel. I was faced with still another problem. How could I live alone in an apartment with this dog? The solution was a home-made playpen for the puppy. The sides were made out of chicken wire and were over four feet high! We then put locks on the kitchen door to make sure this little puppy who might jump four feet high would be stopped at the door. It is amusing in retrospect, but at the time I was further traumatized by being under the same roof with a dog, even though I knew it would facilitate my cure.

The following steps in my progressive cure were: to have Spiegel lick my hand, to put my arms around Spiegel, to allow Spiegel to come to me— unleashed—for that final, all-encompassing hug of acceptance. I invented a few tricks of my own to help me toward these goals. I stroked my Persian lamb jacket because it felt like poodle hair. My ex-husband licked my hand in a simulated dog lick so I could practice the feeling.

I was cured of a thirty-year phobia within one month.

> One must be a prisoner just once to hear
> the lock twist into his gut.
> After all that, one is free to grasp at the
> trees, the stones, the sky, the birds that
> make sense out of air

(Anne Sexton)

I no longer had the phobia but I still retained the habits of a phobic, for example, I had to learn to walk in the street without seeking escape routes. I learned "dog etiquette"—how and when to approach dogs—because I wanted to touch and play with all of them! For the first time in my life I walked the streets, parks, beaches, country roads or anywhere without fear of dogs.

This patient's comments are quoted at length because they indicate not only her sense of being trapped by the symptom and her exhilaration at overcoming it, but also the variety of complex unconscious and interpersonal issues that were negotiated and influenced even though they were not worked through consciously. It is obvious from the history and to the patient that her mother's fear of dogs was an important influence on her. Her setback, when her father commented that she had nothing to fear, makes it clear that her fear of dogs had some important symbolic meaning in relation to her feelings about her father. Certainly, ambivalent feelings about her father could hardly have been more clearly expressed than by using the therapist's name for a dog.

But the emphasis in the therapy was on mastery rather than insight. It is interesting that this patient, a 2 to 3 on the profile, with an induction score of 8.5, went on to consolidate her gain and demonstrate a ripple effect in other areas of her life. Seemingly, the symptom was resolved without resolution of underlying unconscious conflicts that may have related to its emergence, if not its perpetuation. The subsequent events in her life, as reported by the patient herself, are revealing.

I will spare the reader my cliché-ridden descriptions of my feelings (then and now) by limiting the changes to the following examples.

Pre-cure, I was obsessive about order and cleanliness in my home: I was "Mrs. Craig Clean." As I gained control and mobility in my personal life, I needed less control and regimentation in my home. I had also been obsessive about paying bills before they were due.

Pre-cure, I was *preoccupied* with literature, movies, plays, and art about concentration camp victims and survivors; doom and death were my catharses.

My eating habits changed. Pre-cure, I ate mostly refined carbohydrates for energy. Eating was a joyless chore, because I had a knotted, nervous stomach. I remember my father scrambling half an egg in an effort to get something other than a chocolate cupcake down my throat. To this date, I am working on reversing the nutritional damage done to my body during childhood and early adult years.

To this date, too, I have not completely reversed the thirty years of tension and tautness in my body. My body had been my instrument of escape, always tensed, ready for flight. My tolerance for stress and ability to function under a lot of pressure are unusually high because of my pre-cure conditions.

Pre-cure survival had been a challenge. Reinterpretating my handicap to my advantage became a challenge.

"To live is to suffer, to survive is to find meaning in the suffering" (Dr. Victor Frankl).

I have sought to sketch my two worlds within and without the veil of fear. Thus the *modus operandi* of my transcendence from phobia to freedom can be loosely defined as pragmatic and experiential.

I believe that problems and obstructions that individuals face can be solved if the individual has the motivation and the mechanism with which to bring about change.

I believe that one can discover the meaning in suffering and derive a sense of responsibility from its existence and reinterpretation.

This patient made a decision to finish her college education, which had been neglected, and study for a Master's degree in social work. She was exuberant about her new independence and direction in life. As her story makes clear, she was immobilized as much by the humiliation of having the fear as she was by the fear itself, and her sense of mastery seems to have given her courage to overcome other fears and limitations in her pattern of living. As she notes at the end of her comments, the two critical factors which seem to have worked were "motivation and mechanism." She was highly motivated to eliminate the major secondary loss which the symptom posed for her life, and she found a mechanism that facilitated change—a dynamism which did not humiliate her further, but which gave her a sense of mastery.

Other Phobias

The treatment techniques for other types of phobia are similar to that described for the plane phobia. The patient is taught a self-hypnosis exercise which emphasizes his restructuring of the old situation. What follows are several adaptations of the technique for other specific kinds of phobia.

ACROPHOBIA

The patient is told to put himself in a trance state and then is given the following three-point message:
1. Gravity can be my security.
2. My feet lock me into this magnetic gravity.
3. This downward pull stabilizes my movement.
The patient is instructed to repeat this exercise every one to two hours, as in previous strategies. The reinforcement signal simply is to stroke the side of his forehead to remind himself of this commitment toward the stabilized pull downward.

AGORAPHOBIA

For this type of phobia, which can be socially crippling, the patient in the trance is given this three-point message:
1. Objective space is infinite.
2. My subjective space is my choice.
3. I choose to limit my space to my private plastic dome. Through this private, imaginary dome, I can relate to the world around me.
The patient is told that the plastic dome is a product of his imagina-

tion in which, by design, he can establish a territory around his own body. By choosing to focus upon this territory, he separates the individual experience of relating to space from this often frightening sense of the infinite. The "plastic" nature of the dome enables him to see and relate through this imaginary shell that he puts around himself to affirm his relationship with his own private territory.

CONCLUSION

There are numerous other phobias, and it is not unusual for a patient to have more than one. In our experience, mastery over the primary phobia is sufficient to lead to resolution of the other satellite phobias. The treatment strategies presented for these four—flying phobia, dog phobia, acrophobia, and agorophobia—provide the general framework for dealing with other phobias.

The trance state is used not only for anxiety reduction and to help the patient acknowledge the old fear, but also to place it in a new perspective. He is encouraged to examine the difference between a probability and a possibility and to exist with his fear, but to rearrange it so that it is no longer overwhelming. The patient is given the sense of having something to resort to if he should become frightened, and is encouraged to concentrate on the aspects of the situation that reinforce his own sense of being in control. For example, he views a plane as an extension of his body; or recognizes that dogs prefer friendly relations with people.

Phobic symptoms in patients with intact profiles seem especially responsive to brief intervention utilizing hypnosis. Although phobias have been successfully treated by a number of other approaches, including behavior modification and antidepressants, the role of hypnosis as a facilitator and accelerator of therapy is especially clear among patients who have phobic symptoms. Techniques employing hypnosis to treat phobics deserve primary consideration because cure is often possible in one or two sessions.

17

Pain Control

Pain, like anxiety, has an important signal function. It is a message to the psyche that something is wrong with the soma, and it constitutes an urgent call for action. But like anxiety, pain can get out of hand, become the problem itself, or interfere with corrective action. The message becomes the medium: in our mechanistic way we are inclined to dichotomize the pain experience, to insist that pain is "real" only if with diligent medical exploration we find some plausible physical dysfunction to account for it. Conversely, pain is often described as unreal or hysterical if no plausible organic explanation is found or, even worse, if pain relief follows the administration of a placebo. This constitutes a sad misunderstanding; many individuals who have pain associated with serious organic disease are quite capable of responding to placebos or hypnotic pain relief, and many individuals with so-called functional pain do not respond to placebos.

It is useful to think of pain perception as a complex interaction between the physical stimulus that causes the pain and the psychological reactive component to it, which we can call the "hurt." In most clinical pain situations, the physical component fortunately is not so severe that it saturates the entire perceptual channel, leaving no room for the reactive component, the hurt. When the physical stimulus causing pain is that intense, it often leads to surgical shock or other kinds of unconsciousness. Should the patient retain consciousness with an overwhelming physical insult—for example, passing a renal stone, suffering acute pancreatitis, or receiving a crushing blow to a limb—psychological factors are of minimal importance in controlling the pain. However, in most clinical pain situations the reactive component is important and provides great flexibility in the perception of the pain.

In a classic study we have referred to earlier, the last point was well made by Beecher (1966), who compared the pain experiences of a group of soldiers wounded on the Anzio beachhead during World War II, with a matched group of surgical patients in Massachusetts General Hospital. He found that the soldiers reported minimal pain and rarely requested pain medication, whereas the surgical patients demanded drugs for pain-relief. The soldiers were grateful to be alive and wished to remain as alert as possible, in order to continue being alive. They processed their pain stimulus very differently from the surgical patients, to whom the pain represented an interference in the flow of their lives. Beecher disconnected the severity of the injury from the hurt experienced by the patient. He went on to demonstrate that relief from pain also is not so mechanical. In a later study (1959) he demonstrated that one-third of a group of patients in pain responded to a placebo medication, two-thirds responded to morphine, and one-third did not respond to morphine. In other words, half the morphine responders were really placebo responders, and a third of the population responded to neither.

On the other hand, the subjective reportage of pain is neither arbitrary nor capricious. Hilgard (1975) found, when using the cold-presser test as a laboratory measure, that subjective reporting of discomfort correlated better with the temperature of the water than with such physiological measures as an increase in heart rate and blood pressure. Hilgard's book (1975) offers an excellent recent review of the role of hypnosis in pain control. Because of the importance of the reactive component in the pain experience, and especially because of the sense of physical threat implied by clinical pain, it must be borne in mind that the laboratory experience with paid volunteers is of a very different order. Thus laboratory data, though interesting, is not directly applicable to the clinical situation.

Numerous clinical reports cite the usefulness of hypnosis in dealing with pain. It has been shown to be effective in treating patients with terminal cancer (Butler 1954, 1953; Cangello 1961; Sacerdote 1965, 1970), in obstetrics (Kroger and DeLee 1967; August 1961; Spiegel, H. 1963), in surgery (Crasilneck and Hall 1966; Bowen 1973), and in dentistry (Thompson 1963). Bowen's report is particularly intriguing; a psychiatrist, he used self-hypnosis as the sole anesthesia during his own transurethral resection. He reported on his structuring of pain relief and on his sense of comfort during the procedure—and on the surprise and discomfort of his colleagues.

The Technique

After an appropriate history is taken, and the clinician is convinced that no further medical explanation as to the cause of the pain is required, the cluster questionnaire and the profile are performed. The results of the profile are particularly important for this approach, since there is considerable evidence in the literature that responsiveness to hypnotic pain-relief intervention is related to hypnotizability (Bowers 1976, p. 34; Kroger 1975, p. 198). Furthermore, different strategies are relevant and useful to the highly hypnotizable subjects as compared to the low and mid-range subjects. As an overview, patients who score 3 and above on the profile often respond well to trance induction instructions that the painful part of their body will become numb. Patients in the 2 to 3 range often respond well to instructions that alter the perception of the pain, converting it to a tingling numbness or an ache, for example. The low-hypnotizable patients in the 1 to 2 range respond best to a distraction technique in which they are instructed to pay attention to some other sensation and, by inference, to ignore the pain.

If trance capacity is not assessed, an individual with good ability to restructure pain perception using hypnosis may be misunderstood as a treatment failure when, in fact, the wrong strategy was employed. For example, a 45-year-old man with syringomyelia and chronic, associated pain sought help with hypnosis for pain relief. The hypnotist employed the naive direction: "When I touch your body, the pain will go away." Such an approach might temporarily have worked with a grade 5, but it left this patient still in pain and, in addition, disgusted. Several months later the same patient was examined with the HIP and he scored in the 1 to 2 range. He was taught an exercise which mobilized both his intact but low trance capacity and his critical cognitive style. Distraction from the pain was established by using the trance state to help him remember (rather than experience) the sensation of being in a dentist's chair and receiving novocaine anesthesia. He was encouraged to actually apply an icebag to his extremities to intensify his experience of setting up a filter between himself and the pain. He quickly mastered this method, and acquired such expertise in controlling his pain that in one teaching session with medical students he aptly referred to himself as a "co-therapist for the pain."

Restructuring Strategies

Before inducing the actual trance for hypnotic pain relief, it is often useful to put the patient through a little lesson in pain perception. This exercise impresses upon the patient the fact that he can control his perception of pain by controlling both muscle tension and the amount of attention that he pays to the pain. The patient is told:

If in addition to the original pain you have, you react by tensing muscles around the painful area, the muscle tension alone can produce more pain. You are thus inadvertently producing even more pain than existed in the first place, as you try to cope with the original pain. To make this clearer, make a tight fist, stretching out your arm straight. Now, make a fist three times harder than that, and concentrate on the pain you feel as a result of this muscle tension. Now, let the fist open and notice how the pain from the muscle tension dissipates.

The second part of the lesson is to ask the patient to produce pain in a different manner. The instructions are:

Now pinch the web of skin between your thumb and forefinger until you feel pain. All right, now stop, and let the pain go away. Now try it again, the same way. Only this time, look at that painting over there on the wall and tell me what you think the artist was trying to say.

The patient gives some bemused explanation, and then you ask him to think in which of these two experiments he experienced more pain, the first or the second. The patients as a rule observe that they felt more pain the first time. The second time they experienced less hurt because they were distracted by focusing attention on the painting. This is the second lesson: when absorbed in something else, the hurt is less.

THE DIONYSIAN PATIENT

The patient is now taught to put himself in a trance, and if he is a high (3 or above) scorer, this technique or a variant thereof can be used:

Imagine yourself sitting in a dentist's chair. Picture the lights in the room, the feeling of the chair, the smells and sounds of a dentist's office. Remember the time when he took out that large needle and injected novocaine into your gum. Try now to re-create that feeling of the pressure in your gum and the gradual numbness spreading throughout your jaw and your cheek. Feel your cheek getting more and more numb, that numbness spreading throughout cheek and mouth; and then when you are ready, let your hand float up and touch your cheek and feel how numb it is, and as you feel that numbness, let the numbness spread from your cheek to your fingers, so that your hand begins to feel numb. Then let your hand float over to touch the part of your body in which you feel some discomfort and let that numbness spread. This numbness becomes a filter through which you experience pain, and you learn in this manner to filter the hurt out of the pain.

The patient is instructed not to fight the pain, but to focus upon the numbness instead, and in this manner he is simultaneously distracting himself from his awareness of pain. The subject uses intense hypnotic concentration to focus on a comforting sensation. At the same time, he uses the constriction of peripheral awareness to ignore the hurt associated with the pain. This concept of combined awareness of numbness and pain, of filtering the hurt out of the pain, is a formula which enables the patient to acknowledge the presence of the pain and at the same time to be aware of something else—the numbness. This is a kind of parallel or dual awareness. Furthermore, the instructions include the notion of a sense of mastery and pride when the patient is able to supersede the pain with a sense of numbness. The patient is taught to do this exercise every one to two hours, or whenever he feels a sense of discomfort.

The capacity to dissociate hurt from pain in a highly hypnotizable individual is so great that, if necessary, major surgery can be performed with self-hypnosis as the sole anesthetic agent. Dr. E. E. Rockey of New York Medical College diagnosed a right lower lobe carcinoma of the lung in a 50-year-old patient with chronic, obstructive pulmonary disease. A lobectomy was indicated; but because of the obstructive disease he was a poor candidate for inhalation anesthesia. A decision was made to perform the surgery using hypnotic anesthesia after a profile performed on the man indicated that he was a grade 4.

The patient was highly motivated and understood the risks of conventional anesthesia. He had experienced hypnosis in the profile, but was given no extensive training prior to the operation. In the operating room, Dr. Rockey instructed him to: "Feel yourself floating in ice water, surrounded by ice cubes."

His conscious memory after the procedure follows:

"First I felt as though my windpipe were frozen. Then I felt him marking my chest with a pencil (the scalpel) and wondered why. Anyway, from then on I don't remember a damned thing. The next thing I remember is coming into a recovery room and ripping the pipes out of my mouth, you know. And that is the whole story."

He was then rehypnotized, and he regressed to recall what had gone on during the three-hour procedure. Then he said:

"I can remember a sort of crunching sound—I expect my ribs were being cracked. I could hear it. Then I remember floating in the Arctic, watching an iceberg with seals and penguins and things like that. I was trying to make a joke of the whole thing. That was the idea, to create a chilly situation—seals and penguins go along with the Arctic."

Ironically, at the conclusion of the postsurgery interview, the patient added, "I'm a coward when it comes to pain." His dissociation was so profound that he could not give himself credit for it; it was as though someone else had undergone the pain. The surgical procedure was completed successfully, and the patient required no analgesic medication in the postoperative period.

THE ODYSSEAN PATIENT

The mid-range patient is often asked what somatic sensation for him is associated with pain relief. Usually an alteration in temperature, either coldness or warmth, provides some relief and becomes a metaphor for the self-hypnotic exercise. It is of interest that in the spinal cord, pain fibers run with temperature fibers through the lateral spinothalamic tract to the thalamus, and these are the only major sensory fibers which do not run in the posterior columns. Thus alterations in temperature often do provide some kind of pain relief and the metaphor of temperature change is an effective one when used with hypnosis. The neurophysiology is intriguing. There have been speculations that temperature is crucial to a central nervous system pain-and-pleasure reinforcing system (Chin et al. 1976).

The mid-range patient is put in a trance and is given these instructions:

While your hand is in the air, imagine yourself floating, and as you feel yourself floating, make it more vivid by imagining that you are floating in water—make it ice water. As a matter of fact, make it so icy that you feel the cubes if ice floating in the water and as it gets colder and colder you can even feel an imaginary tingling numbness coming from the cold. This tingling numbness gives you a protective coating around the pain area, so you learn to filter the hurt out of the pain. Practice this exercise every one to two hours— the exercise itself takes about twenty seconds—and each time you bring yourself out of this state of self-hypnosis, give yourself a posthypnotic signal to retain this feeling of induced numbness, even when you're out of the formal trance state. Eventually, with practice, you can retain a constant state of numbness around the clock, which gives you a chance to modify your pain perception. That is, even though intellectually you know that the pain is there, by making your commitment to the imposed numbness, you feel the numbness more than the pain. That is, you filter the hurt out of the pain.

The patient is then instructed to bring himself out of the state of self-hypnosis by counting backwards from three to one. Further instructions are:

By doing this exercise every one to two hours, you establish a private signal system between yourself and your body, so that you're ever alert to this com- mitment to maintain the tingling numbness. Now, if you find that you're more aware of the pain between exercises, give yourself a private signal, like clench- ing a fist, stroking your arm, or stroking the pain area. Each time you do this, it becomes a reminder of your commitment to cover the pain area with a blanket of tingling numbness. This gesture becomes a reinforcement signal that reminds you of your commitment to maintain this blanket of numbness which filters the hurt out of the pain.

THE APOLLONIAN PATIENT

The person who scores lower on the profile, in the 1 to 2 range, is less likely to respond to these metaphors. Even with focal concentration, his peripheral awareness is never so withdrawn that it enables him to ignore the painful stimulus. Rather, he is encouraged to focus as much as possible on a distracting stimulus. The patient is put in a trance state and told, for example:

Each time you begin to feel the discomfort, focus instead on the exquisite sensations you can feel in the fingers of your left hand. Rub your fingers, one against the other, and describe to yourself the texture, the temperature, the sensation that you feel. Each time you are tempted to concentrate on the sense of discomfort elsewhere in your body, rub your fingers together gently, and discipline yourself to pay attention to the sensations in the fingers in your left hand. This becomes an exercise through which you filter your perception of the pain and concentrate instead on what you choose to.

It is often helpful to remind the patient that this is an exercise which requires work, but that through it mastery of the pain experience is possible.

A 62-year-old professor recovered from a cerebrovascular accident which left him with a painful spastic paralysis of the left wrist and hand. He was otherwise intact and alert, and wanted very much to resume his teaching and writing. The one major obstacle was the sedation he experienced as a side effect of the analgesic drugs that were prescribed, and because of this he sought help with hypnosis.

He scored a grade 1 on the profile. Given this low but intact hypnotic capacity and his high motivation, he was instructed to put himself in a trance and feel an icy-cold numbness in the affected hand. Because he was low-hypnotizable, he was urged to practice placing an ice bag on his hand and wrist to intensify his ability to remember the sensation during the self-induced trance. He succeeded, but noted that the pain tended to return after lunch. It turned out that he was accustomed to take a nap after lunch, and that the intense concentration required for hypnotic pain relief was impaired by fatigue. He was encouraged to sleep immediately after lunch and to resume his hypnotic exercises upon awakening.

Such was his success that he was able to use his spastic hand on his electric typewriter. He took analgesic medication only in the evening as a preparation for sleep, after his day's work had been completed. He maintained this pain control for the remaining years of his life.

Since most pain medications are sedating, they interfere with trance capacity. Therefore, whether to prescribe pain medication often becomes an uncomfortable choice for the patient and the therapist. One patient (a 2 to 3) noted that she could not do the hypnotic exercise, which provided her with relief of atypical facial pain, within two hours of taking the minor tranquilizer which had been prescribed for her. However, as soon as the sedative effect had worn off she was able to reinduce the hypnotic analgesia. Often the most useful way to wean patients from their pain medications is to tell them to do the hypnotic exercise just at the time they would ordinarily take another pain pill, in an effort to prolong intervals between medication. In this way they are likely to be freer of sedative side effects and are able to gradually acquire a sense of mastery over the pain, thereby diminishing their use of consciousness-clouding pain medication.

Patients under acute stress—for example, in trauma—often spontaneously go into a trance state. They are frightened, are concentrating intently, and are especially receptive to any intervention which will relieve them of pain and anxiety. The following case example illustrates.

A man in his thirties was brought into the emergency ward of Massachusetts General Hospital within hours after his left hand was severed in an industrial accident. Numerous members of the medical and nursing staffs attended him at first, preparing him for an attempt at surgical restoration of the hand (an effort which ultimately failed). A few minutes later the entire staff left him alone in the emergency operating room as preparations continued to admit him to the hospital.

I (D.S.), at the time a medical student, remained in the room, not having a special duty to perform. My initial impulse was to leave as well, since the man was in considerable discomfort, and had lost a hand, which aroused considerable anxiety in those around him. Fortunately, I asked the patient if he was in pain. The man responded that he was, and I suggested an exercise as something that might help with the pain. The patient readily agreed.

I instructed him to concentrate on developing a sense of floating after rolling up his eyes and closing them. He communicated his response to each suggestion by a nod of the head. I then asked him whether he could remember having been in a dentist's chair, to which he assented, and whether he could remember the feeling of having a novocaine injection, recalling to him the initial discomfort and pressure of the fluid being injected in the gum. He nodded and was asked to re-create that feeling in his mouth, which he apparently did. I then asked him to first remember and then re-create the feeling of numbness spreading through his mouth and cheek. After he nodded positively, I suggested that the numbness would spread down his mouth, through his jaw, to his shoulder and to his injured arm. I also explained that he could reinforce this feeling as we had done together, by closing his eyes, floating, and re-creating the numbness; and that it would last for some time after he came out of the state of concentration.

At the end of this procedure, which lasted about five minutes, the patient said he felt less pain. One other relevant piece of data about the utility of the procedure is that it enabled me to stay in the room with the patient in the face of his serious injury and the sense of helplessness it engendered. Furthermore, it gave me the sense that I could be of help to the patient without doing anything mechanical to him such as giving medication. One wonders how often medical procedures are performed for the purpose of treating the quite legitimate anxiety of the helping person rather than the needs of the patient. The procedure was helpful to both me and the patient and further, it had no side effects.

Hypnosis can also be extremely helpful to patients enduring the anxiety and stress of painful hospital procedures. K.S. was a 45-year-old, mother of three, who had undergone a mastectomy for carcinoma of the breast eight years previously. She developed metastases of the lung and spine, and a gastric ulcer. She found the necessary gastroscopy impossibly painful and sought help with hypnosis. Her profile was 2 to 3 intact, and she was taught to use the trance state to telescope time, making an experience seem much shorter than it actually was. She utilized the self-hypnotic exercise during the gastroscopy, and reported the following by phone:

"I was totally relaxed. I remember this from the last time as one of the most painful things I have ever experienced. I was absolutely right. The last time it seemed like it took four hours, but this time is was different—it felt like I was only there two or three seconds. It was actually ten minutes in all. I maintained my arm position but was in total agony, sweating, gagging. However, I did my best to concentrate on my balloons. I even felt like screaming. While the agony was total, I was still completely able to cooperate with him. When he took out the tube, it was so short a period that I thought something had gone wrong and they would have to do it over again. I am impressed with the power of the mind. This is the greatest thing that has ever happened to me. It has made my hospital stay almost enjoyable. I know I have some kind of control in myself that I was never aware of."

The woman's description is particularly helpful in clarifying the distinction between hurt and pain. She makes it clear that the discomfort was there, but her sense of suffering was diminished and her sense of control enhanced. She so effectively telescoped her time sense that she actually thought the procedure had not been completed. One month later she underwent abdominal surgery, and reported minimal preoperative anxiety and postoperative discomfort, which was confirmed by her attending physician. It is notable that this woman with terminal carcinoma found considerable satisfaction in enhancing her sense of mastery over the treatment procedures.

The overall strategy involves making optimum use of the dissociative state to direct focal concentration toward some pleasant sensation in the painful area, such as the tingling sensation; or to interpret the input sensation in an alternative way, such as icy numbness; or to redirect the focal attention to a different sensory input. The major concept is to help the patient set up a psychological filter so that he learns to process the pain experience in a new way. He learns to recognize and exploit the difference between hurt and pain. He does not deny that the painful stimulus is there; rather he learns, in varying degrees, to ignore it. This process should always be carried out in a medically suitable atmosphere, so that the secondary anxiety, which of course can enhance pain, is realistically allayed. That is, the pain as a message has been attended to, and the patient can be assured that whatever medical procedures are necessary will be carried out.

Migraine

The technique for treating migraine is somewhat more specific, because of the well-known observation that during the migraine attack the patient feels warmth in his head and coldness in his hands. There has been speculation that migraine headaches are related to some vasodilatation in the head. Peripheral vasoconstriction with a drop in the temperature of extremities has also been associated with migraine attacks. Therefore, the strategy is designed to provoke psychological and even somatic reversal of this presumed pathophysiological event. There have been reports that hypnosis can facilitate vasodilatation as measured by observation of capillary blood flow, increase of temperature in the hands by several degrees (Grabowska 1971), and vasoconstriction (Dubin and Shapiro 1974). Thus the trance instructions may provoke circulatory changes.

After the profile has been performed, the patient is told to put himself in a trance state and the following instructions are given:

While you are floating, at the same time visualize a huge cake of ice, suspended above your head. There is a large hole in the center, large enough for your head to fit into. The ice is now slowly descending from above, covering your entire head, all the way down to your shoulders; and as this happens, you may even develop a shivering sensation. At the same time, in the front part of this cake is an opening, a channel of air, an air tube, that permits fresh air to come in so you can breathe. As the air comes through this ice channel, you breathe this cool, icy air and feel it entering your nostrils and your sinuses. It is so cold that you develop an icy feeling inside your head, as well as the icy feeling outside your head. This tingling numbness now enables you to filter the hurt out of the pain, by focusing more on the numbness than on the pain.

At the same time, imagine that you are wearing asbestos gloves on both hands, with tiny wires in the lining of the gloves. The wires are attached to a battery; the battery sends a charge through the wires and warms them up like an electric blanket, and these asbestos gloves are warming your hands. You now have a contradictory experience: the ice is cooling your head, but the gloves are warming your hands; cooling your head, warming your hands. This contradictory experience neutralizes the extreme sensations that take place with the migraine, and by doing that, you bring about a sense of relief. Again, you do the exercises every one to two hours by maintaining this imposed sense of coolness in your head and warmth in your hands, and in this way you can develop a new sense of mastery in regard to the headaches.

Regardless of the degree to which these migraine patients can actually alter blood-flow intracranially or in their extremities, the combination of this possible physiological effect with the more predictable psychological effect seems to provide considerable comfort to these patients. They can learn to abort headaches in the early stages, using this self-hypnotic exercise, and eventually wean themselves off their various analgesic medications.

Case Example. A 57-year-old, mother of four had suffered with migraine headaches since the age of six. The headaches had become increasingly severe since the age of thirty. The typical presentation was a throbbing, left-sided headache followed by nausea and at times vomiting without paresthesias or visual changes. She had obtained little relief from a complete array of analgesics, including the ergot alkaloids and codeine. She had received intensive neurological evaluation and medical care. Eventually she was referred for hypnosis.

Her responses to the cluster survey were Odyssean, and her profile score was a 1 to 4 increment. She was taught the self-hypnosis exercise and she practiced it diligently. She was somewhat perfectionistic and insisted on a modification of the exercise, preferring to employ the image of dental anesthesia rather than ice, with the concurrence of the therapist. One month later she sent the following letter:

"I am making the most marvelous progress, and I can't tell you how happy I am to be able to make this report to you.

I am trying the self-hynosis technique every two or three hours and I think it is very effective. To be able to relax at odd moments of the day is very intelligent and I can also see that the method is very successful.

It has been very hard for me to find the time to relax as I am always enormously busy. Sometimes too much so, and then I can feel the tension mounting and my head aching more and more. Recently I played golf for the first time ever without a headache. I have also been playing bridge without any head pain. The only time my self-hypnosis doesn't work is when I wake up with a headache such as 2 to 3 A.M.

I feel there has certainly been a great deal of benefit in a short time and I am certainly enjoying life much, much, more. I feel very optimistic about getting rid of these headaches completely.

Because of this wonderful improvement I am taking much less medication. In the meantime I am gloating, and floating, and getting more and more numb."

During the ensuing six years the patient had occasional migraine attacks which she controlled with self-hypnosis, but she considered herself markedly improved for the first time in her life.

Acupuncture

From our point of view, the acupuncture ceremony is simply another way in which the person in pain can distract his attention from the painful stimulus by accepting the belief that the acupuncture needle serves to neutralize pain. The conviction that this ceremony eliminates pain serves the same purpose as the physiological imagination of numbness. It is the ritual that counts, and there seems to be nothing unique or specific about the needle itself.

This is still a somewhat controversial position, but it is supported by a number of studies using acupuncture in the treatment of pain: the efficacy of using correct and incorrect acupuncture points were compared, and response was found related to hypnotizability rather than acupuncture per se. Katz et al. (1974) employed acupuncture for various kinds of chronic, clinical pain and found that acupuncture indeed relieved pain. However, when these same patients were administered the HIP, positive response to acupuncture was clearly related to the profile scores. For example, of the 30 patients reporting almost complete pain relief, 19 scored in the 4 to 5 range on the HIP and none scored in the 0 to 1 range. By contrast, among those reporting no relief five were in the 4 to 5 range and 12 were in the 0 to 1 range on the HIP. Moore and Burke (1976) divided patients suffering from chronic shoulder pain into two groups: one treated with classic acupuncture and one with an acupuncture placebo in which the needles did not penetrate the skin. They also varied the psychological tone of the treatment settings, one being positive and encouraging and the other negative. All of the patients were administered the Hypnotic Induction Profile. Some 43 percent experienced moderate to excellent pain relief, but there were no significant differences between responses to classic acupuncture and to the placebo. The emotional tone of the treatment setting made no significant difference. However, there was a clear relationship between higher hypnotizability and pain relief.

Kepes et al. (1976) reported similar results. They found no difference in response to placebo or real acupuncture points with and without electrical stimulation, in cases of clinical pain. However, they did find a relationship between pain relief and HIP scores. Gaw et al. (1975) performed a similar study among patients with osteoarthritis. He administered acupuncture at classic and placebo points. There was no difference between the acupuncture and placebo group; both groups showed a significant improvement in tenderness and the experience of pain.

These studies raise serious questions regarding the specificity of acupuncture points. At the same time they demonstrate that the acupuncture ceremony as a whole is effective in producing pain relief. Furthermore, some of them demonstrate a correlation between this effectiveness of the acupuncture ceremony in producing pain relief, and hypnotizability.

As an integration of the apparent success of acupuncture with more mechanical, Western notions of pain and the perception of pain, the "gate control" theory of Melzak and Wall has been widely invoked (Melzak and Wall 1965). It is worth noting that one of the original observations which led Melzak and Wall to formulate the gate control theory was the observation by Pavlov that after a certain period of time the same noxious stimulus failed to elicit an obvious pain response in his dogs. They looked for mechanisms whereby central inhibition could occur in the pain experience. Wall has taken the position that acupuncture is largely an alternative hypnotic ceremony: "My own belief is that in this context acupuncture is an effective use of hypnosis. This in no way dismisses or diminishes the value of acupuncture but it does place it in a class of phenomena with which we are partly familiar" (Wall 1972, p. 130). It is also worth noting that a Japanese form of acupuncture called acupressure or shiatsu works along similar principles, but without needles and without breaking the skin.

The wide area of common ground between hypnosis and pain relief is reported at least as far back as Esdaile's nineteenth century description of achieving surgical anesthesia with hypnosis in India (1846). The several-thousand-year-old Chinese tradition of employing acupuncture for pain relief, among other medical purposes, is hardly surprising when the phenomenon of pain itself is not viewed in a purely mechanical manner. Neither hypnosis nor acupuncture work with all patients; both involve a significant component of belief and training, and active cooperation on the part of the subject. Both can be artfully employed to invoke the reactive component to pain in such a manner as to reduce the pain perception. Both have fewer side effects than pain medication or general anesthesia. The ceremonial relief of pain is more widely practiced in China than is hypnosis in the United States.

It is not necessary to revise our knowledge of neurophysiology in order to incorporate the acupuncture experience into the realm of Western medicine. What we must constantly keep in mind is that the higher cortical component of the pain experience is of critical importance: the strain in pain lies mainly in the brain.

18

Psychosomatic Disorders and Conversion Symptoms

The following case descriptions are samples of the vast array of disorders with psychological and emotional components. It is neither practical nor useful to attempt to review treatment of each type of disorder, since the main point of treatment is that it be addressed to the person who has the disease rather than to the symptom. The psychiatric assessment and the information gathered from the HIP provide a picture of the patient's major problems and personality style. The treatment approach can be constructed taking these into account, and helping the patient restructure his relationship to his body.

Ortega commented that, "the metaphor is probably the most fertile power man possesses" (Marias 1970, p. 283). Altering metaphors can be a powerful tool in therapy, just as unrecognized somatic metaphors can cause major disruption in a patient's life. We consider the psychosomatic disorders and conversion symptoms to be on a spectrum, from those with a major somatic component and minimal psychological contribution—such as peptic ulcer, ulcerative colitis and hypertension—to those with little or no somatic involvement and major emotional input, e.g., conversion paralysis and hysterical seizures. These illnesses are at the crux of the mind–body problem, and provide one of the most difficult diagnostic challenges in medicine. The presence of a plausible psychological explanation for somatic distress is by no means proof of causation. Likewise, relief of a somatic symptom, such as pain, with psychological means has been widely misinterpreted as implying that the cause of the pain is functional.

Many such problems can be explained in terms of somatic vulnerability to stress that patients acquired genetically or environmentally, as in asthma and ulcer disease. On the other hand, we argue that some individuals have a psychological vulnerability to the use of somatic metaphor. Highly hypnotizable people seem to be especially prone to the use of somatic metaphors in expressing interpersonal or intrapsychic stress. They are also especially flexible in altering these metaphors (Erickson 1967). The situation is complicated by the fact that even a pure conversion symptom, such as hysterical paralysis, can lead to objective somatic changes, such as muscle atrophy.

Asthma

There are numerous reports in the literature of the successful use of hypnosis in the treatment of asthma. It is not clear whether the pathophysiological condition is caused by or causes the often described emotional difficulty and interpersonal problems; but this seems fairly irrelevant to the effectiveness of a psychological intervention in the disease process. Whether the triggering stimulus is atopic or emotional, a feedback cycle is set up: the patient feels bronchial constriction, which results in anxiety, and which in turn results in more bronchial constriction, and so on.

In a rather thorough review of the literature, Kelly and Zeller (1969) reported on a number of studies which indicated the effective use of hypnosis in the treatment of asthma. There seems to be wider agreement that teaching a patient self-hypnosis improves his subjective experience of the illness, than hard data that the pathophysiological condition improves. The studies of Smith and Burns (1960) and White (1961) support this subjective–objective distinction, indicating clear subjective improvement with no demonstrable objective effect. On the other hand, several other studies reported positive subjective and objective findings, including complete remissions (Brown 1965; Edgell 1966; Edward 1960, 1964; McLean 1965; Moorefield 1971).

Maher-Loughnan (1970) reported on a series of studies in which patients using self-hypnosis exercises which emphasized confidence-building did better than control subjects who simply did breathing exercises. There was a clear difference in subjective response, favoring the patients taught self-hypnosis, although both groups improved. There was a smaller but significant difference in measured vital capacity. They found age difference to be of no significance in the responders. The nature of the triggering stimulus was irrelevant to patients' responsiveness to self-hypnosis. They also found an extremely low incidence of symptom substitution, which they estimated at 1.5 percent, and new symptoms were mild and transitory. It is noteworthy that Maher-Loughnan found that the group taught self-hypnosis did significantly better than a group which used only an inhalant bronchial dilator.

Collison (1968, 1975) reported good to excellent improvement in two-thirds of a group of asthmatic patients taught self-hypnosis. Using a clinical estimation of so-called trance depth, he found that patients capable of a deeper trance proved more responsive to treatment. Also, responsiveness declined with age, which persisted even when corrected for the fact that, in general, hypnotizability is higher earlier in life.

There is considerable evidence that self-hypnotic exercises can be of significant benefit to patients suffering from asthma. In many of the previously cited studies, patients were taught rather lengthy self-hypnotic exercises which lasted from fifteen to sixty minutes, and which emphasized a general sense of building self-confidence. Our approach differs somewhat in that we emphasize brief and frequent self-hypnotic exercises, every one to two hours for one or two minutes, and whenever anxiety or wheezing increase.

After the appropriate history is taken and the HIP is performed, the patient is taught to put himself in a trance and is given the following instruction:

As you feel yourself floating, imagine that the tubes in your lungs are slowly opening up, and cool, fresh air is entering them. As you feel yourself floating with these cool breezes coming into your lungs, you develop a tingling numbness inside your lungs, and an opening of the bronchial tubes. By concentrating on this floating sense and on the feeling of a cool breeze in your lungs, you enable your lungs to open up. In this way you will find that each breath is a little deeper. Every time you take a new breath, you find that you're able to inhale a bit more deeply, and you feel your lungs opening up and getting wider and wider.

The patient is taught to do this exercise for himself, and it is emphasized that it is something he can do when an attack is coming on. This exercise provides both relaxation and distraction for the patient. He is encouraged to use this exercise as a first resort, before reaching for the isoproteronol inhaler.

Case Example. Carol was first seen when she was sixteen years old and had been admitted to the hospital for the third time in as many months in *status asthmaticus*. She had a history of asthma and various atopic sensitivities from the age of six months. She had been maintained on a standard anti-asthmatic regimen, including decongestants and isoproteronol inhalers. She led a somewhat limited but active life, but during the preceding several months she had clearly decompensated.

Prior to this particular admission, Carol had been twice unresponsive to subcutaneous epinephrine. When examined by the author (D.S.) she was wheezing audibly and was quite uncomfortable. The standard medical treatments had all been tried, short of intubation and general anesthesia. Because she had a high (3) eye roll, a rapid induction was performed without formal testing of trance capacity. A simple instruction was given that with each breath the patient would find that she could breathe a little deeper and more easily. She was told to develop a sensation of floating. Within five minutes she was resting in her bed rather than sitting upright and her wheezing, though still audible, had diminished.

It is not incidental that this approach was taken in the face of the failure of medical treatment. The author, at the time a medical student, could not think of any useful additional medical procedure. It is still not clear whether the trance induction did more to relieve the therapist's anxiety or the patient's. It is clear that she responded and that we avoided the danger of more heroic medical treatment, which can often occur in response to the anxiety of the physician.

Carol, who turned out to be a mid-range subject (an Odyssean), was taught self-hypnosis, and she regularly practiced an exercise similar to the one just described. She was released from the hospital several days later, and had one remission shortly thereafter, but had none in the following seven years. She felt that the self-hypnosis was quite helpful, used it more or less daily, and thought of it as a first resort before turning to isoproteronol inhalers.

It is difficult to evaluate the role of hypnosis in this patient's improvement as compared with medication, because she had also been intermittently on prednisone and an experimental drug called Intal, which seems to prevent release of histamine and similar bronchioconstricting agents from mast cells on antigenic challenge. The least we can say is that the use of self-hypnotic exercises did not interfere with her medical regimen, and it gave her a sense of mastery over her illness— to the extent that she trained to be a respiratory therapist. It seems likely that her resorting to self-hypnosis when she felt her chest getting tight also cut down on her use of isoproteronol, which in recent reports has been implicated in occasional episodes of sudden death (Lockett 1965; McManis 1964; Goodman and Gilman 1975, p. 494).

Self-hypnosis seems to be particularly useful in aborting the "snowballing" effect of the anxiety which follows an initial physiological danger sign. An asthmatic may sense a bit of constriction due to an atopic or emotional stimulus. Then he reacts with anxiety about the consequences, which serves to enhance the constriction, and so on. The hypnosis exercise is a way of acknowledging the initial problem while avoiding panic. The patient shifts his attention toward floating and re-establishing mastery over his body in a gradual manner. The exercise, properly taught, thus expands the repertory of choices available to an individual with a psychosomatic problem such as asthma.

Pigmentary Glaucoma

Case Example. This case description provides an illustration of two basic themes related to hypnotizability: an individual's considerable capacity to influence physiological events, and the ripple effect.

Joann asked to be seen by the author (D.S.) with a rather unusual complaint. She had been diagnosed as having pigmentary glaucoma some eighteen months before coming for an evaluation of her hypnotizability. She had been warned by the physician who first made the diagnosis that she could go blind, and that the loose pieces of pigment in her eye could do more damage if her ocular pressure was elevated. Joann was frightened by this, and quickly became aware that her eye pressure seemed to increase when she was upset. She had been in group therapy for the previous six months, and had found it helpful. She had learned from it that she tended to focus on her eyes when she became upset, and then to worry about that, setting up a vicious cycle. She had tried yoga, which she said was helpful in reducing her ocular pressure. In spite of that, she had been quite upset during the preceding few months, and her increasing pressure had forced her to resort to medication to lower it. In this context she wanted to see if self-hypnosis could help her control the pressure.

The Hypnotic Induction Profile was performed, and she scored 3 to 4. She was amused and surprised by her capacity for entering a profound trance state. As we discussed her trance capacity, an interesting history began to emerge. Joann had always considered herself quite unstable emotionally, an opinion which she felt was shared by many of her friends and people in her family. In the past she had had many physical ailments, including joint pains which lasted for months, a period in college of what she described as anorexia when she ate very little in an extreme effort to lose weight, and a period of partial deafness. The latter occurred when the doctor who diagnosed the pigmentary glaucoma mentioned that ear trouble often accompanies it. As Joann described it: "I suddenly started feeling pressure in my ears, as though they were filled with fluid. I couldn't hear low voices, and thought I was going deaf. The doctor insisted it was strictly functional." By this time it was becoming clear that Joann seemed to be describing a capacity to spontaneously shift into trance modes and soak up other peoples' speculations as though they were instructions. She was able to transform the concern of others into a physical experience.

As an experiment, Joann entered the trance state and I suggested that she would have difficulty hearing anything except my snapping fingers, which would signal the end of the period of difficulty. On coming out of the trance state, Joann noted that things did indeed sound dimmer, although she could still hear them. She went on to say: "I don't know why—it may be related to your suggestion. Things did sound sharper when you snapped your fingers. I felt myself going into my old state. You know, I had had a confrontation with my sister after five years of not seeing her. She said some things I didn't want to hear— that I had no right to be happy." She went on to agree that she tended to use "body language" to express things; in this case, the combination of not wanting to hear what her sister said, along with not wanting to hear and at the same time accepting in the extreme her doctor's rather blunt bad news.

She went on to describe herself in this way: "I pick up suggestions. When that doctor suggested I might go blind, I went into a depression worrying about it. Then he mentioned ear trouble. I am generally more anxious than depressed. I look for people to rely on. I like to please them. It is hard for me to say no." She described an incident in college when a close friend died of a particularly grim disease which necessitated amputation of both legs prior to the girl's death. Joann began to feel pains in her legs, and was certain for a while that she had the same illness.

What she described about herself was quite consistent with the way other Dionysians describe themselves. She mentioned the desire to please, the capacity to pick up suggestions, and her proneness to use body language in a literal sense. Her vulnerability to anxiety and depression was also consistent.

She was taught an exercise in self-hypnosis which involved two parts. The first part was an exercise in floating and developing the sense that with each breath she exhaled a bit more tension out of her body. But the primary focus was on the floating. The second part involved seeing a movie screen in front of herself on which she could visualize any problems, people, or events which were on her mind. In this way she could continue to think and feel freely about what concerned her, but at the same time could leave her body in a state of restful floating. She was instructed to do the exercise every one to two hours.

She returned several weeks later, and said that she had been doing the exercise about five times a day: "Sometimes it doesn't work, but often it does. It is a different feeling from meditation [which she also practiced]. I get a tingling in the back of my neck like when I'm going to have an anxiety attack, but I don't have one. I feel I have control." A follow-up three months later revealed that her eye pressure had returned to normal from its previous level of approximately 50 percent above normal, and her doctors were planning to discontinue topical medication. The ophthalmologist had commented: "Your pressure is surprisingly good. When you're relaxed, things go better." Although the role of the medication could not be discounted, both Joann and her physician seemed to feel that her capacity to control her state of mind had had a positive influence on controlling her ocular pressure.

A ripple effect began to appear. Joann found herself speaking out with people around her in a way she had not before. She gave one particularly notable example: "I've always had skin trouble. But one day I noted that my skin was particularly itchy and that I had a rash. I decided to try the exercise to stop it, and sure enough, within ten minutes it wasn't itching. But then I noticed something else. I began to feel angry. I realized that I had been angered by something one of the people I live with did, and I told the person off. The rash no longer itched, and the anger went where it should." Thus Joann was learning to control and translate her "body language" into English; to make more direct use of her affective responses, with less concern about pleasing people and less preoccupation over her somatic problems.

Joann was seen only three times altogether for the work with hypnosis. She continued in group therapy. She learned self-hypnosis easily, and utilized it not only to control her somatic problem, but also to gain a new perspective on her style of relating to herself, her body, and her friends. This brief encounter seemed to have the effect of enhancing her capacity to reflect rather than to comply with others; and also to give her a sense of mastery over her somatic representations of her feelings. She clearly remained quite hypnotizable, and had learned something about utilizing her capacities—choosing when and when not to use them.

Follow-up of Joann's treatment with hypnosis revealed that four years later she is having no significant problem with her vision. She still uses eye drops but at a reduced amount and has only occasional episodes of soreness in her eyes and interference with her vision. She interrupted her regular treatment with doctors because they were so critical of her use of hypnosis and other techniques such as meditation and yoga in controlling her eye pressure. She reported that her sense of tension and pressure around her eyes and her overall state of relaxation is much better. She had stopped formally using self-hypnosis for several years but recently has resumed using it as a relaxation exercise. She noted that after she uses self-hypnosis she feels, "very lighthearted."

She also commented on the perspective of herself that she gained in recognizing her high hypnotizability: "It helped me understand a lot of the reactions in my marriage. It was really a central insight. I seem to be attracted to people who are cool and rational, often to a person who denies a lot of his feelings. I also find that I haven't somatized my feelings very much recently but when I have, it has been useful."

In summary, Joann made good use of her three visits, both to achieve considerable control over her physical symptom which was related to her general level of tension and anxiety, and also to view in a new perspective her tendency to somatize feelings and seek out relationships with people with Apollonian characteristics.

Pruritis

Case Example. K.H. was a 27-year-old married salesman. He had a 21-year history of itching and scratching on his hands and legs, with consequent chronic dermatitis. Eczema had been diagnosed at age seven, for which he had been given intermittent medication. He had been treated by a dermatologist and the dermatitis had improved, but the pruritis remained.

He happened to be at the dermatology clinic on the day of the hypnosis course at Columbia University, and was invited to be seen in front of the students for consultation and treatment. His profile score was an intact 3. He was taught self-hypnosis, and in trance was instructed to imagine a tingling numbness, and to concentrate on that as a means of transforming the sensation of itching into one of tingling numbness. As he was in the trance, he reported that he could feel the tingling and with surprise commented: "I hear bells ringing!" After he came out of the trance, he interrupted a general discussion of the treatment approach with: "Do you realize what has happened here? My itching is gone!" Four-year follow-up revealed that the itching was still being controlled using the same exercise, and that the dermatitis had disappeared.

Bruxism

Case Example. S.N. was a 42-year-old businessman, separated from his wife. He had a thirty-year history of intermittent facial tics, and a one-year history of bruxism (teeth grinding) which had produced serious dental problems. His profile score was a 2 to 3 intact, and during the first and only treatment session he was taught the "movie screen" technique. He was instructed to float and relate his thoughts and feelings on an imaginary screen, thereby allowing the muscles throughout his body, including his jaws, to relax. Even though the bruxism occurred primarily during sleep, his hypnotically induced relaxation with the screen technique during the day enabled him to eliminate the muscle tension during sleep over a period of two months. A five-year follow-up revealed that he was still free of the symptom. He referred to the treatment as "instant Yoga."

Psychogenic Urinary Retention

In the case to be described, the patient was taught to maintain a sense of floating relaxation and thereby avoid the metaphor of fighting her body or of forcing herself to urinate. Instead, she was invited to float, relax, and allow it to happen. The patient had reported that the place where she was best able to urinate was her own bathroom at home. Therefore, part of the instruction was that in the trance state she would picture herself in her bathroom at home. This principle has general application in constructing a strategy: it is very useful in taking the history to find out the "home remedies" which seem to work best for the patient. These remedies often provide the therapist with metaphors that are particularly appealing to the patient and which may be incorporated in the trance approach. For example, the fact that this patient had reduced anxiety when in her own bathroom was used to create an atmosphere, wherever she was, that was most conducive to relaxing her urinary sphincters.

Case Example. Beth was a 26-year-old married woman who was seen once by the author (D.S.) for the treatment of chronic urinary retention. Her difficulty was most acute in strange and especially large public bathrooms. She had gone for as long as twenty-four hours without voiding, and had required catheterization several times. Previous medical work-ups indicated no organic disturbance. She took no medication.

Beth had suffered with this problem in one degree or another for twenty years. She attributed its beginning to a warning from her mother during a vacation trip not to sit on strange toilet seats. At this time she watched her mother urinate while squatting, and developed an inability to urinate away from home. She remembered having to call her father to pick her up from a friend's house so that she could urinate at home, but she also remembered times when he did not come to get her until the next day, leaving her in considerable discomfort. As she grew up she developed an ability to urinate in unfamiliar bathrooms, as long as they were not large and public. She was also unable to urinate on camping trips.

Beth was an only child. She reported being rather "repressed" around the issue of masturbation, but recalled getting pleasure as a girl from "rubbing my thighs together with a full bladder." She had been married for a year, after having lived with the man for several years before that. She said they got along well, and that their sex life was very good. She noted that her husband was understanding about her problem on trips, although he showed some displeasure when they had to cut short or avoid a trip because of her inability to urinate. She was a college graduate, and denied any other significant psychiatric problems.

Three years previously, she had had several sessions with a psychologist who had used hypnosis with her. Although she could not remember the details of the procedure, she said it did result in "significant improvement."

Beth was evaluated by another psychiatrist, and referred for treatment utilizing hypnosis. She was seen once. The Hypnotic Induction Profile was performed, and indicated that she was an intact 1 to 2. This score made it clear that she was on the Apollonian side. She was taught to hypnotize herself, and was given a two-part exercise to do every 1 to 2 hours at first, and to do it as well when she was in the bathroom. She was to picture herself in her own bathroom at home, where she was comfortable urinating. She was also to concentrate on the sensation of her hand floating in the air: the idea of this part was to get her off the endless transformations from avoidance of urinating to the paradox of forcing herself to let go. The concentration on her hand floating emphasized her mastery over her body and how such mastery felt without the sense of forcing herself.

Immediately after the exercise, she said: "I think this will be helpful —I feel more relaxed." She then provided a fascinating description of her bathroom at home. She said that at first she had thought of her parents' bathroom during the exercise, but then had pictured her own: "It's like a zoo, full of stuffed animals." The unconscious sexual and dependency implications of her symptom seemed intriguing; but she had no interest in pursuing them, and so we did not press the issue.

A phone call one month later brought a report of "no problems." She had taken several short trips and had urinated without major difficulty. She had been doing the exercise several times a day, and said that she had been able to bring about a feeling of relaxation. She also recalled at this time that whenever she had had such problems as a child, she had to return home to void, but that she had modified the difficulty when she went to college. She said she was planning a long trip with her husband, and that this would be the real test. She wrote a letter after this trip, which occurred three months after her visit. It is reprinted in entirety:

Sorry I didn't write sooner, but I have been pretty busy. The trip went very well. It almost seemed as if I never had had a problem. It just takes the right kind of effort now (but in most circumstances, it does take active effort to allow myself to go.) Basically that's what it boils down to—whether or not I let myself go (or *can* let myself.) In any case, *now* I am in much more control, and much more comfortable than I've ever been. It took ten years, total, to alleviate the problem one step at a time.

Yes, your exercise was positive, but I never used it specifically the way you told me to. I never had to. I would use it mostly in the car, and also got into the habit of giving myself a subconscious (in the hypnotic state) pep talk every so often—part of the practice. I think that was the most helpful thing of all. The right frame of mind is paramount, but now I have the right frame of mind. That's about it, I guess. Now I hope this will be some help to you in treating others. My sincere thanks for your willingness to help me.

Several things are notable about this letter besides the obvious improvement in the symptom. The key things are her emphasis on control and her predictable modification of the exercise. Both of these elements are characteristic of Apollonians. Someone highly hypnotizable might accept the exercise in its entirety and do it to the letter, but Beth extracted what she wanted from the protocol. She assimilated the exercise, critically evaluating which parts were useful to her and which were not. It also is interesting to note that in spite of the dramatic change which she describes, she is careful to report it as gradual ("It took ten years, total, to alleviate the problem one step at a time"), and related her success to past more than present efforts. Thus she demonstrates the past–future time orientation so characteristic of Apollonians.

She gave no evidence of symptom substitution, but rather seemed to feel proud and happy. She had experienced a sense of mastery: this aspect of the technique cannot be overemphasized. People with functional physical disturbances often are treated gruffly by physicians and family members, who imply that the person is faking the illness in some way and should just "snap out of it." This position has just enough truth to it to make the patient angry and defensive. If he were simply to stop having the problem, he then would feel somewhat sheepish; the implication being that he should have done it a long time ago and saved everyone much trouble and expense. But this learning model involves teaching the patient something new. It thus provides a face-saving way out of his dilemma. Indeed, the patient is learning something new, that he has more control over his body than he thought, if less than he (and others) would wish. Thus the patient can overcome the problem with a sense of mastery, as illustrated here, rather than embarrassment.

In this context, secondary gain must be mentioned. Beth showed relatively little evidence of secondary gain. She had taken the position, especially as she got older, of fighting the problem rather than giving in to it. She had compromised with it, but had refused to allow it to interfere in a major way with her education away from home, or with her social life. Thus she was ripe for further change. There are people for whom the secondary gain factors make changes more difficult. Beth's husband's attitude seemed particularly helpful; he was at once understanding and openly annoyed when the problem began to interfere with their activities.

This case illustrates that a restructuring strategy that helps the patient strengthen his relationship to himself and his body by making the problem part of this relationship is useful to people with little trance capacity. Such people extract and make good use of the parts of the exercise which are meaningful to them.

Dysphonia

We now proceed further along the spectrum toward the more clear-cut conversion symptoms, in which somatic dysfunction is minimal and the psychological or metaphoric component is primary.

Case Example. K.U. was a 52-year-old, single businesswoman who lived with two sisters, a brother, and a nephew. She developed a dysphonia and was sent to New York by her company for evaluation and treatment. The president of the company was personally concerned. He was willing to underwrite the cost because he valued her as an employee, and feared that retirement would be necessary if her problem was not resolved. She was seen by the author (H.S.) for thirty sessions over a six-week period after medical examination revealed no organic pathology.

The patient noted increasing difficulty in speaking over an eighteen-month period. When she sought help it had progressed to the point where she could barely whisper. It had not progressed to the point of being an aphonia but, as the patient described it, she needed help to "get the noise out." She had consulted with a psychoanalyst for two months, but became discouraged and stopped treatment when he told her that the dysphonia was a sign of sexual frustration.

During the first session, her profile revealed her to be an intact 2 to 3. She was highly motivated and insisted on daily treatment sessions. During the second session, a two-pronged treatment strategy was undertaken, involving restructuring of metaphors and further data gathering. She was asked to lie on the couch, and she was placed in a trance and told the following:

1. You seem to regard speech as noise.
2. The symptom is a statement that you are in despair about something.
3. As humans, we all have our share of faults and virtues.
4. You seem to be out on a limb—here is your chance to come down to earth.
5. We will start by pretending you are a little girl—let's sing songs together.

The therapist spent the remainder of the session singing nursery rhymes and the ABC's with the patient. During this first session, she produced very little phonation other than a whisper. She was told that this exercise would be continued at each session and was encouraged to practice. She left feeling somewhat disappointed and she cried that night.

The subsequent two sessions were devoted to this kind of regression (metaphorical or pretended, rather than an actual hypnotic regression, as one would expect with a 4 or a 5) and she began to report dreams. The first dream was the following:

I went to a party, didn't know the people there. They served cocktails. I wondered if I should take any since I was on medication. I suddenly discovered that the home of the party was on a precipice, that the only way down was by steep steps, and that my only phobia was height—I couldn't look down. I wondered how I would get down.

She associated to that: "I enjoyed the party until I was aware of the steps—then I was scared to death."

At the fifth session she reported this dream:

I had gone home and learned that our pet dog was put away by the vet. He was fourteen years old. My sister said, "we got a new pet—it's in the bathroom." I went there and saw a snake in the bathtub. I felt I didn't care what happened, but we had to get rid of it.

She awoke with a feeling of revulsion, and reported thinking, "I don't think a snake would hurt me, but I don't want to be near one."

The therapist chose not to discuss this dream further, but took it as a warning to keep away from the sexual theme. This dream seemed to be a clear enough message regarding the patient's first experience in psychotherapy. She commented later that she had made her peace with her spinsterhood, and added, "If I wanted to pick up a man I could certainly do it."

The singing continued, and she gradually developed islands of phonation which grew in duration. By the eighth session, she said "I now accept this symptom as emotional." At the ninth session she experi-

enced the first clearly phonated sounds in eighteen months while singing the ABC's. This transition was followed by another dream:

> I was home Sunday morning, then went to church. I thought I was outside
> the door of a nursery. People came with a baby. People fussed over the baby,
> but it did not respond. Then I went to the baby. It responded to me and
> reached for me. I awoke and felt wonderful.

Her associations to the dream were: "I am secure in church and I
often visit the nursery. The babies like me—there are very few children
who can't make friends with me." By this point the patient had accepted
the symptom as a statement of an emotional conflict, and was making
progress, but the message was not yet clear.

What soon emerged was that the key conflict was not sex but power.
She had been promoted in her company from elevator operator through
a series of positions to one of considerable managerial responsibility.
There were two men working under her who had exploited her dili-
gence and reputation for being kind and considerate. She had found
herself doing increasing amounts of their poorly completed tasks in
order to protect them and to represent the work of the department well.
As she put in more and more overtime, she was increasingly enraged
at them, but unable to express her anger.

It was in this context that the meanings of the first and third dreams
became clear. Her fear of heights was a metaphorical statement about
her anxiety concerning her high position at work. She did indeed fear
what was beneath her—these two employees. The third dream expressed
both a wish to be liked by those under her, and her confusion of that
wish with her acceptance of herself. Feeling unlikeable, she had hesitated to say anything which would arouse overt dislike from her employees. The regression and singing exercises had put her in touch
with a warmer, more accepting feeling about herself. From this new
position of security, she was able to acknowledge her fear and anger
toward those two men beneath her in the organization.

This impression was confirmed by the Rorschach report, which was
read to the patient. It included statements about "exaggerated guilt in
relation to any aggressive or sexual impulse, depression, and denial."
The tester went on to note: "She also is guilty and anxious because she
sees herself as competing with the mother and other feminine objects.
In order to avoid this aggressive competitive relationship, the patient
tends to regress and to adopt the role of the little girl who need not
face adult problems. At the same time, there certainly is considerable
ego strength here."

The patient began to focus on her problem at work. She came to
accept responsibility for what happened there, and formulated a plan
for doing something about it. As she left the office for the last time,
she commented in a clear voice: "There are a few gentlemen back
home who will not be glad I have my voice back."

She wrote a month later, indicating that she had been home and
at work for four weeks and was feeling fine. "Nothing is changed except

me." She was promoted at work, and retired several years later. Follow-up fourteen years later revealed that she continued to do well and had no symptom recurrence.

This treatment required some thirty sessions over a six-week period, and thus was considerably longer than our usual symptom-oriented treatment approach. In this case, defining the problem and then applying the proper puzzle form was a complex issue. The nature and timing of the symptom suggested that its metaphorical meaning required attention for rapid resolution to occur.

Facial Tics

Case Example. J.D., an infantryman overseas, was startled by a loud mortar explosion in combat and became unconscious. When he was evacuated to a clearing station and treated for his minor surgical wounds, he also noticed that he had developed a diffuse facial tic in which his eyes closed, presumably without control, and his shoulders hunched up. The facial movements, eye closure, and hunched shoulders all suggested a constant repetition of his defensive gesture against the explosive noise. This tic continued for several weeks as he was being evacuated to the States. He was given a medical discharge and permitted to return home, but he refused to leave the hospital because of the embarrassment of these tic movements. He said he would be unable to face his family, especially his girlfriend. With that new set of motivations, he was re-admitted to the hospital and assigned to another treatment unit, where he was found to be hypnotizable.

In the trance state he was given this message: that although it was still important for him to carry the defense against this threat to his life, because of the distance from it, he could now transform this traumatic event into a hyperactive movement of his left big toe. In order to demonstrate this kind of control, he was given the opportunity over several days to come out of the trance state and first move the tics only to the right side of his face, and then to the left side of his face. Then on other occasions he moved the tics from his face and shoulders down to his abdomen and legs; then to the right leg, and then to the left leg; and finally, to the left big toe. The concept was that he could control the tics by shifting the locus and then moving them downward to his toe, which gave him a sense of mastery. The thesis behind it was that by establishing control over the defensive symptoms he would be able to totally master all movements, even the symbolic movements of his left big toe. In fact, this is what happened.

One year later he wrote a letter saying that he was employed as a civil servant in the Veterans' Administration and had married. He included the interesting observation that although he felt well, every once in a while when he had periods of anxiety, he got peculiar movements in his big toe. The way he mentioned this in the letter indicated that he had an amnesia for the structure of the whole treatment program, but had accepted the gradual phasing out of the exaggerated movement to a symbolic minimal statement. With his new level of security, he was able to phase out the symptom entirely except for occasional episodes of anxiety.

Although this patient was seen many years before the HIP was developed, in retrospect we estimate that he would have scored high and was probably a grade 5.

The case demonstrates the importance of secondary gain and loss. When he was about to leave the army and go back to civilian life with an honorable medical discharge, he confronted himself with the potential embarrassment of the tics. He consciously or unconsciously no longer wanted to extract whatever secondary gain factor was present while in the military. Thus he demanded treatment for control of the symptom before returning to his family and his girlfriend, where he would have encountered significant secondary loss if the symptom had persisted. Because the timing was so appropriate, showing him how to shift the symptom from one part of his body to another taught him a sense of mastery over the symptom which eventually enabled him to control the symptom entirely and thus abandon secondary gain and avoid the secondary loss in self-respect.

Hysterical Paralysis

Two Cases. D.L. was a 40-year-old divorced mother who was hospitalized with a spastic paralysis of her left leg following surgery for repair of presumed disc disease. Two years earlier one of her two sons had developed pancreatitis, and died a year later after a painful and debilitating illness. Friends commented that the patient shed no tears at the funeral, but that she remained withdrawn. In an effort to cheer her up some months later, they invited her to a party in her honor. At the party she slipped and fell, apparently injuring her back. A surgeon diagnosed disc disease, and a laminectomy was performed. When taken out of traction, her left leg was paralyzed and rigidly inverted. A variety of treatments were employed without benefit. She was hospitalized on the orthopedic service when a psychiatric consultation was requested.

Her profile was an intact 4. In the trance she was instructed to develop tremors in both legs, which commenced and continued after the trance. This movement helped to diminish the edema in her left leg, which was two inches greater in circumference than the right. After three months the edema disappeared, leaving her left leg one inch smaller in circumference than the right leg, due to muscle atrophy. Her movement gradually returned with physiotherapy, and after adhesions in her ankle were repaired she was able to resume walking normally in another six months. During this time muscle exercises were performed daily in a self-induced trance state, and she was also encouraged to express her grief at having watched her son slowly weaken and die without having been able to do anything to alter the course of his illness.

Her metaphorical wish that she could have taken his suffering upon herself was expressed somatically. This ventilation of feeling, in addition to insight regarding the metaphorical significance of her disability and a renewed interest in caring for her other child, enabled her to overcome the symptom.

In the following case also, recognizing and interpreting the metaphorical significance of a conversion symptom was crucial in establishing and maintaining its resolution. S.L. was twenty-eight years old and a married mother of two, who was referred for consultation by a surgeon who had seen her for a spastic inversion of her left foot. This spastic condition had developed gradually over the preceding three months. One year previously she had had a similar spasm of the right foot operated on successfully, but the surgeon hesitated to undertake a second operation because the organic findings which had been present in the right leg were not found.

Her profile was an intact 2 to 3, and a two-pronged approach was taken. She was instructed to develop tremors in her left leg, which led to a gradual but consistent increase in flexibility of her muscles. Within two weeks she was able to straighten out her foot and walk. The second aspect of the treatment involved an exploration of her family situation. She was engaged in a struggle with her husband, a temperamental and authoritarian man whom she felt had usurped her authority in running the home. She had learned when her right foot was disabled that such a condition precluded sexual involvement with her husband. The paralysis of the left became an unconscious means of witholding sexual intimacy and indirectly fighting him. She was encouraged to recognize her anger and be more direct in insisting of her prerogatives in the marriage. Her husband accepted and accommodated to her new assertiveness, and much of the resentment was resolved. She was seen for a total of ten sessions over a two-week period. Follow-up during the next ten years revealed her to be exuberant about the new direction she was taking in her marriage. She had occasional periods of rigidity in her foot, but quickly mastered them using the self-hypnotic exercises.

Conversion Symptoms Presented as Neurological Disease

The following two cases involve highly hypnotizable individuals who were initially diagnosed as having serious neurologic disorders. Their cases are presented to emphasize the chameleon-like quality of the highs, and their extreme capacity to employ and become trapped by somatic metaphors. As previous cases have illustrated, less hypnotizable individuals are also vulnerable to conversion; but in a probabilistic sense conversion symptoms are much more prominent among the highs.

Case Example I. T.J. was forty-five years old, a married housewife with two adolescent children. She developed severe convulsive seizures occurring eight to twelve times a day, sometimes during sleep, over a two-year period. The seizures themselves lasted fifteen to twenty minutes. She was never incontinent, never hurt herself or bit her tongue, and exhibited extension rather than contraction of her anti-gravity muscles during the seizure. All of her extensive laboratory and EEG studies proved to be negative. Despite all evidence to the contrary, she was diagnosed as epileptic and placed on anticonvulsive medications, without effect. During this period she was seen by seven different doctors and all concurred with the diagnosis. The seventh doctor implied that her case was hopeless, and referred to a "hospital for the incurable." This frightened her and her husband into seeking further help, which led to a psychiatric consultation.

The author (H.S.) examined her with her husband present. She scored a 4 to 5 on the HIP with a cluster score revealing Dionysian traits. Eight years previously, at the age of thirty-seven, she had had a hysterectomy. A note in the hospital chart indicated that she had had seizure movements postoperatively, but it was attributed to the anesthesia. One year later she had a brief attack of an inability to open her eyes. During the first interview she was instructed to re-enter the trance state and to let a seizure come on. The seizure which followed was so intense that she slipped out of the chair and onto the floor. When she was brought out of the trance, the therapist said, "Good, I have something to show you that will help you." This was the first time in her entire experience with doctors that she had not received a message of despair or fear but rather one of hope and approbation at the production of the symptom. In the presence of her husband, she was instructed to re-enter the trance state and start another seizure, which she did. After a while, she was told, "Since you started it, now you can learn to stop it." She was given instructions to make a fist, and then by opening the fist to terminate the seizure and leave the trance state. She was advised to practice entering the trance five times a day, bringing on a small seizure and then stopping it. In the event that a seizure occurred spontaneously, she could then invoke her new skill to stop it. The exercise had a double effect; it reduced the probability of a spontaneous attack, and if one did occur she had a method for controlling it.

In five sessions over a two-month period, she succeeded in reducing the seizures to the point that they became occasional minor episodes lasting a few seconds. The family rejoiced at her newly-found control. They had been so concerned that her husband and children had actually signed up for shifts to watch her during the previous two years, so that she would not have a seizure alone. Because this restructuring approach using self-hypnosis became a learning and discovery experience, she was not humiliated by overcoming the symptom; rather, it emerged as a victory for the whole family. Her husband's loving concern and support was especially helpful in avoiding any recriminations or setbacks. There was no discernible secondary gain.

This case differs from several presented previously in that no clear message emerged from the symptom. Although she had received additional attention and concern from her family, there were no obvious family problems. From a dynamic point of view, much could be made of the importance of her hysterectomy as an unconscious factor, but, typical of the Dionysians, the patient evidenced no curiosity at all about the causes of the disorder. At twelve-year follow-up she and her family were doing well and there had been no recurrence of the symptom.

Case Example II. K.N. was a 24-year-old New York born female who was diagnosed as having multiple sclerosis two and a half years prior to coming to the author's attention.* Her initial symptoms included weakness, pain, and tingling in her left leg. Over the next several months she complained of blurred vision, diplopia, urinary frequency, increasing weakness in her lower extremities, ataxia, slurred speech, and other transitory symptoms.

The patient was first seen in Madrid, where she lived. Later she came to New York for further neurological testing. The objective findings were: slight ataxia in the lower extremity, slight hyperreflexia of the left biceps and left patella, and questionable minimal temporal pallor of the left optic disc. After the New York work-up she went to a southern medical center for further treatment. She had skull X-rays, electro-encephalograms, a brain scan, echo-encephalogram, and cerebro-spinal fluid studies, all of which were within normal limits. She also had a myelogram with foramen magnum studies which were normal but she developed a pulmonary embolus postmyelogram.

She received Coumadin, intrathecal steroids, intravenous ACTH, and a course of immuno-suppressive drugs (Imuran). While on Imuran she got pregnant and obtained a therapeutic abortion because of the medication. Approximately one year after the onset of the illness she was again admitted to a New York hospital and received another course of intrathecal steroids, with a resulting chemical meningitis. She also developed an allergy to ACTH. She got progressively worse and was finally confined to a wheelchair.

The patient's past medical history was essentially negative, except

---

* Barbara DeBetz, M.D., provided this case report.

for seven episodes of thrombophlebitis when in nursing school. She was a middle child in a family or seven siblings. One brother had an episode of blindness at the age of eighteen which had lasted for one month. Although he was diagnosed as having multiple sclerosis, he had since been well for over ten years. One first-degree female cousin had a diagnosis of multiple sclerosis and was nursed by the patient for a while. The patient's father had chronic disc disease and had multiple operations for it. Her mother had had several episodes of thrombophlebitis.

The patient came from a middle-class family and described her childhood as relatively happy and uneventful. At the age of eight, a few days after her mother returned from the hospital with a new baby, she developed "brain fever" and was hospitalized. She remembered thinking at that time how nice it would be to receive attention while being in the hospital. During high school she had dysmenorrhea which was conveniently used to avoid taking tests. She had frequent colds and episodes of thrombophlebitis while going to nursing school. After graduation her phlebitic episodes stopped completely. She worked as a psychiatric nurse, felt very competent, and had no physical complaints.

As a nurse, she met her husband, a Spanish lawyer getting graduate training in the States. After he finished his training they got married and moved to Madrid. The patient was faced with adjusting to a rather different way of living. His family did not readily accept an American as their son's wife; also, they constantly criticized her for not having a maid, for being too independent, and for not becoming pregnant right away. Her husband started his law practice and had less and less time for her. At about that time her first symptom appeared. Two and a half years later, she returned to New York for further hospitalization. One of the neurologists started to have doubts about the dignosis because of the lack of objective findings throughout the illness. Psychiatric consultation was done and the patient was found to be a grade 5. Psychological testing showed no organicity, but evidence of the dynamics of a hysterical conversion reaction with depressive features. She was discharged from the hospital and referred to the author for appropriate psychotherapy.

The patient was seen for a total of eleven therapy sessions over a period of two months. The treatment strategy consisted of the following steps. First, several basic questions had to be clarified, such as: "What got her into the situation of using a conversion mechanism to express her conflict? What cues did she get from her environment to act in this specific way? Why did she use somatic metaphors as means of communication? What was the secondary gain element?

In summary, the clarification of these questions follows: K.N. had married into a family which did not really want her, with a different language, culture, and value system. When in New York she was in charge and on top of the situation; in Spain, her husband was. His family put pressure on her to be something she could not be, a "Spanish wife." Initially, she rebelled against them, but the pressure increased and the message she received was: "You'd better be a helpless, submissive dependent woman, if you want to make it with us." She got the message and became progressively more debilitated, needed a maid, could not ride her bicycle anymore, and needed an escort even to leave the house. Now she was helpless and dependent. She had fulfilled and caricatured their expectations.

The patient used a body metaphor because it had worked for her before, i.e., when she was eight years old and had that strange "brain fever" to get more attention than the newly arrived baby. In high school dysmenorrhea had been convenient and in nursing school thrombophlebitis had been useful. Her family had always responded to illness. The secondary gain factor was that when she was totally disabled, her husband and his entire family got very involved with her. After all, who would be rejecting towards someone who has such a tragic disease as multiple sclerosis? Not only did she receive attention at home, but also as a patient. In any hospital she rapidly became the favorite patient, the most interesting and most presented patient. One of the many doctors throughout her illness was so fascinated by her as a patient that he wanted her to leave her husband and stay with him.

After these issues were clarified with her, therapy consisted of a restructuring of her metaphors. She progressed rapidly and learned to recognize her vulnerabilities and how to master them. She learned that she had alternatives and a right to use them. Therapy did not include gaining analytic insight in a longitudinal way, but was rather present and future-oriented. The transference between patient and therapist was left completely untouched. Since treatment 2½ years ago the patient has been symptom-free, has delivered her first child, and has maintained a full schedule of physical and intellectual activities.

Although we have focused attention on the use of the HIP in identifying individuals with high scores who are prone to the use of somatic metaphor, it can be equally useful in contributing to the diagnosis of organic disease which masquerades as a functional disturbance.

Case Example III. F.J. was a 41-year-old teacher who noticed a gradual onset of difficulty in breathing while talking to his class. He then began emitting noises which made him sound as though he were about to cry, which he attempted to stifle. At unexpected moments, his voice would begin to quiver, and he would feel on the verge of tears. He came to the point that he made excuses to avoid lecturing. He had concluded an apparently successful analysis some ten years before, and he returned to his analyst in an effort to understand the emotional meaning of this embarrassing new symptom. After two months with no insight about the problem, which had not abated, he was referred for treatment with hypnosis.

His profile was a 2-soft, and his cluster questionnaire responses were on the Apollonian side. This configuration was inconsistent with the assumption that the symptom was an hysterical conversion. A high-intact profile would have been consistent with a tendency to employ somatic metaphor in this manner. Because a neurological deficit might account for the soft pattern on the profile, he was referred to a neurologist, who diagnosed the symptom as an unusual variant of the Giles de la Tourette syndrome. He was placed on haloperidol, which contained the symptom, and at four-year follow-up he was still in good control.

Iatrogenic Anxiety

In dealing with a highly hypnotizable patient, there exists a fine line between an inquiry about a symptom and an instruction to have it. Some patients are capable of listening to a doctor's doubts and concerns, and keeping them in proper perspective as speculation. Other patients, often those who are highly hypnotizable, are more inclined to lose this perspective and pick up on the doctor's affect of anxiety rather than the content of his concern.

A psychiatrist, Dr. A., was the informal consultant for a large family circle, through a patient he had known for a number of years. He had even done a profile on her, knowing her to be a grade 4 to 5 with most of the typical Dionysian features. She had recently begun complaining of chest pain and had consulted an internist about this problem. He gave her a thorough work-up, including a stress test and an electrocardiogram. Although there were no positive findings, he reported to the patient that she might have some heart trouble and that he wanted her to return in six months for another examination. This was hardly reassuring to the patient, who immediately impressed upon her family the message that there was something drastically wrong with her heart. Dr. A. was called in as a result of the ensuing family turmoil. The patient's husband was especially handicapped, confused, and asked for guidance.

In that setting, the psychiatrist then phoned the internist for clarification. The internist was shocked when the psychiatrist told him that "someone scared the daylights out of her." The internist stated that he found some nonspecific changes but no evidence of coronary artery disease. He then went on to say "her symptoms sound so real." She had convinced him to ignore his own findings. The psychiatrist informed the internist that the patient had a long history of dramatically exaggerating minor somatic complaints. She had interpreted the internist's minor concerns and methodical approach as indicating a probability of heart disease, rather than a rather remote possibility. The psychiatrist prevailed upon the internist to give the patient a clear message that she was in good physical health. The patient was given this message by the internist, and her anxiety and that of the family diminished markedly. At a two-year follow-up, the patient still had no signs of coronary disease.

An Apollonian patient might have accepted and understood the meticulous concern of this internist much better. The careful plan for retesting would have reduced such a patient's anxiety, rather than increasing it. In this case, the patient was so sensitive to emotional cues that she more or less ignored the context of the communication. Taking this into account, the psychiatrist was of help in clarifying the basic communication between the internist and the patient, with the resulting decrease in everyone's anxiety.

It is hoped that these considerations can help to refine a time-honored but often forgotten clinical maxim; that what is said is not necessarily what is heard. .Patients with different personality styles and problems listen selectively, and a clinician can be far more effective if he takes into account enough of the patient's personality style that he can design a communication which will convey what he intends rather than what the patient fears or expects. Information about a patient's hypnotizability, even if only probable such as the eye roll, may alert the clinician to possibilities of misunderstanding and to a preferred mode of communication.

CONCLUSION

These case examples demonstrate that hypnosis can be an effective tool in evaluating and treating a variety of psychosomatic and conversion disorders. Whether the primary etiology is organic or functional, significant symptom mastery can be obtained with this psychological intervention. Intact hypnotizability, whether low or high, is all that is necessary to signal the clinician that hypnosis may be helpful. Treatment with low-hypnotizable patients usually requires a synthesis of self-hypnosis exercises with interpretation of the meaning of the somatic metaphor, if one can be discerned. More highly hypnotizable patients often obtain dramatic symptom mastery with a relative disinterest in insight or explanation, which is consistent with their Dionysian characteristics.

The importance of the assessment of hypnotizability as a diagnostic probe deserves emphasis. The difficulties of differential diagnosis of functional versus organic disease can be mitigated somewhat by a disciplined measure of the propensity and style of the patient's use of somatic metaphors. We have found the HIP to be a feasible clinical instrument for evaluating the significance of the reactive component in a somatic complaint. In this sense, the assessment of hypnotizability can help the clinician distinguish between the dramatic subjective reportage of the Dionysian and the stoicism of the Apollonian. Just as we are inclined to think metaphorically when we hear a somatic complaint from a Dionysian, we are inclined to think organically when we hear a similar complaint from an Apollonian. Likewise, the same statement from a concerned physician may be heard entirely differently by patients with contrasting personality styles.

This situation is no less confusing for the patient. Widespread reports of cures with faith healing, psychic surgery, cult treatments such as

Laetrile, and accusations of overmedication and unnecessary surgery (Knowles 1977), all serve to undermine confidence in our health care system. As helpful as technological advances have been, they do not suffice. The fact is that some patients are helped by witch doctors, faith healers, and shrines, with metaphorical illnesses which are mistakenly diagnosed as organic diseases. This confusion will continue as long as we do not bring a more disciplined approach to understanding the relationship between psychological and somatic aspects of illness.

19

Miscellaneous Behavior Disorders

Hair Pulling (Trichotillomania)

This problem is interesting because of the complex interaction between the underlying dynamics and the secondary gain and loss factors which rapidly intervene. Many patients who habitually pull out their hair become quite embarrassed about the symptom and go to great lengths to hide their "secret," including the wearing of wigs, the use of artificial eyebrows and eyelashes, and social withdrawal. Nonetheless, the problem can often be dealt with successfully.

After the appropriate medical and psychiatric history is taken, the profile is administered. Presuming that the patient has some trance capacity—that is, that the patient is within the intact range on the HIP—the following procedure is employed:

DOCTOR: *Let your body float. Concentrate on this imaginary floating and, at the same time, permit one hand or the other to feel like a buoyant balloon and let it float upward. As it does, your elbow bends, and your forearm floats into an upright position just like a balloon. This is the beginning of the treatment for hair pulling. Now when your hand reaches this upright position, this becomes your signal to enter a state of meditation in which you concentrate on this imaginary floating, and at the same time concentrate on these three critical points. The first point is: for your body, hair pulling is an insult. You are composed of a number of components, the most important of which is your body. Hair pulling is not so much an insult to you as it is to your body specifically. The second point is that you cannot live without your body; your body is a precious physical plant through which you experience life. The third point is: to the extent that you want to live your life to its fullest, you owe your body this commitment to respect it and protect it. This includes protecting it from the insult of pulling out its natural adornment.*

Now I propose that you do this exercise every one or two hours. Each time it takes about twenty seconds. During this twenty-second period you repeat these three points. Later I will show you a camouflaged way of doing it if you don't have privacy. Each time you do the exercise you bring yourself out of the state of concentration this way. On three, get ready, two, with your eyes closed, roll up your eyes, do it now; and one, let your eyes open slowly. When your eyes are in focus, slowly make a fist with the hand that is up. Open your fist slowly, let it float down, and that is the end of the exercise.

Now allow a few moments for the patient to react to the impact of the message, and then discuss it with her. By way of review, let the patient watch the therapist go through the entire exercise and repeat the three points aloud. The patient is taught a camouflaged way of performing this exercise so that she can do it in the presence of others. The patient is also taught a reinforcement sign, usually that of letting the hand float up to stroke the eyebrow, as a somatic way of reinforcing the concept of respecting and protecting her body. In this case the signal is particularly appropriate, since the patient is taught to caress rather than destroy that same part of her body. The discussion with the patient is tailored to his or her personality style. The major themes involve avoiding negative injunctions to the patient and emphasizing the patient's respect for his body. The following examples indicate the response of two patients with opposite personality styles and HIP scores.

Case History I: An Apollonian. The first patient was a young woman, who used a phenothiazine during her treatment and felt that the combination of self-hypnosis and medication was useful.

M.T., 23 years old and separated from her husband, was referred for treatment by her group therapist. She had begun pulling out her hair approximately three years previously: "I had to prove an easy math theorem. I got mad at my brain. It was a way of getting at my knotty nerves." She talked about feeling lonely and depressed in the face of a bad marriage, and of considerable loneliness while studying far away from home. M.T. had bought a wig in an effort to stop the hair pulling, hoping that this would keep her from touching her hair. It had the opposite effect of hiding the results; having bought the wig, she found herself missing "50 percent" of her hair. She described herself as "doing it every day—all the time." She said that she felt desperate and at times suicidal, and had become convinced "that there is no such thing as free will."

She had been in group therapy for about a year. She had gotten some help in arresting the hair pulling by taking trifluoperazine HCl 15 mg/day, but she did not like being on medication and after several months had stopped it and resumed pulling out her hair. Her therapist viewed her as a depressed and obsessional but nonpsychotic and nonsuicidal young woman. He said she had been working in the group on her relationships with people, but that she was particularly interested in stopping the hair pulling now because she was planning a trip home in three months and her parents did not know of her self-destructive habit.

M.T. was extremely talkative during all three of her visits. Initially she was argumentative, stating that one could really make no choices. She was quite skeptical about hypnosis. She assented to cooperating with the Hypnotic Induction Profile on the first visit, and was graded as special zero (induction score 6.5) with a zero roll and one levitation. During the second session M.T. apologized for the first: "I became sad at the idea that I hurt people, for example you, by laughing and calling your technique 'simple-minded.' " She then stated that she thought I had constructed the induction procedure especially for her to prove that she was in control and to "prove something about choice." As she said this, she smiled her unchanging sad smile. Nonetheless, she responded to a suggestion that we set aside the debate and get on with the treatment. She was taught an exercise in self-hypnosis in which she was to repeat the following three points to herself:

1. For my body hair pulling is an insult.
2. I need my body to live.
3. To the extent that I want to live and do productive work to help others, I owe my body this commitment to respect it.

It was further proposed that if she felt an impulse to pull her hair, her hand would float up and stroke it instead, as if caressing it.

She returned approximately two weeks later, equipped with graphs documenting her improvement. She estimated an overall "60 percent" improvement, meaning that she was pulling out her hair only sixty percent as much as she had prior to treatment. She added that she pulled her hair ". . . when I think it isn't worth it—that nothing is. I have a feeling I have to have the courage to follow a thought through to its conclusion." The graph documented a cycle of ups and downs in her hair pulling. On some days she pulled virtually none at all, and on others she pulled out the same amount, or in one instance more hair than before.

A follow-up by phone three months later produced the information that M.T. had effected a "90 percent reduction": "I tried the hypnosis again, but with a different emphasis—it was best to concentrate on relaxing and that is very effective." She mentioned that she had resumed taking trifluoperazine HCl, this time 5 mg/day, and she said that the combination was useful: "I am surprised that the effects are so good." She said that she would be returning home shortly and might have to tell her parents about her hair pulling, but thought that soon she would no longer need to wear a wig.

M.T.'s story provides a number of interesting points. The restructuring technique seemed moderately useful, although the patient preferred utilizing the trance state primarily for the relaxation it gave her. She initially came to the therapy prepared to argue, and the issue of control seemed primary. She was both afraid that she would hurt the therapist by failing, and prepared to prove that the technique was laughable. With the help of her work in group therapy, it was largely possible to bypass this competitive and angry side of her and make the hair-pulling issue her problem rather than that of the therapist. Characteristic of people who are low on the hypnotizability spectrum and who are primarily obsessional, she put great emphasis on talking out the strategy, examining it on her own terms, and employing only the parts of it which she decided were useful to her. For M.T. to make a change in her behavior took a great deal of effort. She had to examine it cognitively and test out how much her change would involve some kind of compliance or submission to the therapist's will. Only when she satisfied herself that she could accept and reject parts or the whole did she finally, cautiously, and in graded steps utilize the technique along with medication to reduce her symptom.

Case History II: A Dionysian. The case of J.R. provides an interesting contrast to that of M.T. Both young women presented the same chief complaint, that they were habitually pulling out their hair. Yet their trance capacities, personality structures, and manners of response to treatment were quite different.

J.R., a single woman in her late twenties, was brought to the clinic by her boyfriend because of her hair pulling. She had been pulling out strands of hair on a daily basis for about a year, and had several bald spots on the back and sides of her head as a result of this practice. She had taken to wearing a wig constantly in public, and her boyfriend was the only person who knew about the problem prior to her seeking help. J.R. was at first quite shy and embarrassed about the problem, and came for help only with the insistence of her boyfriend. The Hypnotic Induction Profile was performed on the second visit, and she scored high with an induction score of 9. She was taught self-hypnosis, and an exercise similar to the one given M.T.

She performed the exercise regularly, and within several weeks had completely stopped pulling out her hair. She also requested continued psychotherapy to help her assess various aspects of her life, including her relationship with her boyfriend, her job, and her view of herself. For her, the initial problem was one of being "acceptable" to the therapist so he would continue treatment. She made the problem into one of being good enough that he would be interested in treating her. She showed a classic aspect of those with hysterical features—sexualizing the non-sexual. It took several sessions before she would allow the therapist to examine the part of her head where she had pulled out hair, and then she agreed only with blushing and the expectation of ridicule. As the weekly sessions proceeded, she developed a sexualized transference to the therapist.

She made numerous changes in her life during the 18 months of treatment. During the period of her most intense positive transference, she began the break-up of her seven-year relationship with her boyfriend. He was a bright but quite disturbed young man who had attacked her with a knife during a psychotic episode several years previously. After this change the transference changed also, from hopeful longing to angry disappointment that the therapist would not take the boy-friend's place in her life. She always put the problem in terms of what was wrong with her—was she not attractive or bright enough? J.R. felt herself to be in competition with the therapist's real or imagined woman, and she also sought to control him by forcing him to change occupations—from therapist to boyfriend. (In the case of M.T., anger and confrontation had been overt, with the hostile attack perhaps serving to provoke an intense involvement and to deny positive feelings.) In this case sexualized advances were the overt method of relating, with competitive anger beneath them.

The other side of the hysterical coin, the desexualization of the sexual, was revealed in discussions of the significance of hair pulling, which occurred several months after the symptom abated. J.R. began talking about a local hairdresser she had frequented before she began pulling out her hair. He was a handsome married man in his thirties, who had commented repeatedly on how beautiful her hair was. He had often done her hair for no fee, and in exchange she allowed him to use pictures of her hair as advertisements of his work. She smiled as she confessed how much she had enjoyed his loving care of her hair, and she related that she had resisted his attempts to seduce her. She recognized that her destruction of her hair was in some way a retreat from her strong sexual response to him.

J.R. made numerous changes in her life during therapy, which included achieving orgasm with a man, although she had not specifically dealt with this problem in therapy. She was also promoted at work, and took the opportunity to reassess her career choices. These changes provide an illustration of the ripple effect: she ended a difficult and in many ways unsatisfactory relationship with a man, improved her sexual satisfaction, and did better at her job. She began rethinking her relationship with her family. The only signs of anything like symptom substitution was a brief period of bruxism (teeth grinding), which she mastered in a week with a similar self-hypnotic exercise. Right at the end of therapy she briefly resumed pulling her hair, in an almost symbolic recapitulation of the presenting situation, but again she quickly mastered it.

It should also be noted that resolution of the problem did not prevent the patient from exploring aspects of its symbolic meaning. In fact, she seemed far less resistant to such exploration because she could examine the behavior as part of her past, and not as something which still dominated her.

COMPARING THE TWO CASES

Finally, it may be useful to review ways in which J.R.'s responses contrast with those of M.T., an Apollonian. J.R. responded quickly and dramatically, stopping her hair pulling completely. She felt that the help of the therapist was indispensable, and made it her project to convince the therapist that she needed more treatment with him. In contrast, M.T. stopped quite gradually, and not completely. Although it was true that she was in group therapy, she showed no particular interest in pursuing treatment with the therapist who taught her to use hypnosis. She insisted on making corrections in the treatment, and in modifying it. She felt that she had thoroughly ridiculed the therapist in the first session—whereas J.R. felt she had displeased him. J.R. showed the characteristic core of self-doubt seen in people who are quite hypnotizable. The problem for such people becomes that of complying, so that others will overlook their "obvious" shortcomings.

Furthermore, J.R. immersed herself in the "here and now" of the treatment, quickly adopting it as an important part of her life. M.T. was skeptical from the outset, cautiously comparing the treatment approach with her own set of philosophical beliefs. She evaluated the results as a percentage of her past tendencies. She came for help not out of current distress, because she felt she had mastered a way of living with the problem, but in anticipation of a future problem when she returned home several months later. Thus her time perspective was not present-oriented, but past and future oriented. Furthermore, her approach was rational and critical, as compared with the affective immersion of J.R.'s relationship with the therapist. M.T. assimilated the new experience; choosing parts of it, graphing her response on paper, evaluating the philosophical background. J.R. affiliated with the approach, emphasizing compliance as opposed to rational review. For M.T., hostility covered sexuality; for J.R., sexuality covered hostility. M.T. thought before feeling; J.R. felt before thinking. Intensive therapy for J.R. involved getting her to step back and take a critical look at an intense personal involvement in which she had gotten little in return for much support of her partner. Group work for M.T. was focused around getting her to loosen up and relate more emotionally to people.

Thus in many ways these two women were transformations of one another. They presented the same initial problem, self-mutilation by hair pulling. They both suffered from a lack of self-esteem and could not easily express hostility other than by hurting their bodies. And yet their styles of living and of responding to the therapy were quite different. Where one emphasized thought, the other gave preference to affect. Where one criticized, the other accepted. What is interesting is that both were given a basically similar restructuring approach utilizing self-hypnosis, and each gained quite different things from it. M.T. picked certain aspects, modified them, and even then complied only partially with them. J.R. uncritically complied, and made her problem the response of the therapist to her.

This contrast suggests that the technique is broad enough to offer something to people with styles which differ considerably. They listen in their personal language, and take what they understand. Subsequent psychotherapy aimed at centering (see chapter 21) may involve an attempt to broaden the language and increase the realm of conscious choice about such issues as uncritical compliance or hypercritical withdrawal. However, the initial symptom approach seems useful to people of both high and low hypnotizability. The manner of response is both diagnostically revealing and useful in itself if further exploratory treatment is planned.

Stuttering

There are many kinds of stuttering, but the common denominator in the problem seems to be some defect in sensing or using an internal sense of rhythm when speaking. Although the humiliation of stuttering is often associated with painful pauses in speech, the fact is that many stutterers actually rush into their speech, which alternates between being too rapid and too slow—the natural cadence is missing. Stutterers alternate between a rushing and a frozen sense of time in their speech, which points to the appropriate therapeutic strategy—helping them to develop a more flowing, rhythmic sense of time while speaking.

This approach using hypnosis is an adaptation of the speech therapy technique developed by Brady (1971). Using the trance state as a means of eliciting intense concentration, the following instructions are given with a metronome providing cadence for the therapist's speech. The therapist models the verbal exercise of timing speech to the beat throughout the instruction period:

When you imagine yourself floating, keep in mind that the major deficit in stuttering and stammering is the tendency to rush into speech out of synchrony. This can be corrected by talking, thinking, and feeling in terms of the beat, always the beat. It is well known that stutterers rarely stutter when they sing. It is not because of the melody, it is because of the beat, the beat, the beat, always the beat. When most people who speak fluently are speaking, they are unconsciously or consciously in tune with their beat, the beat, the beat, always the beat.

It is useful at the beginning to have a metronome set at the beat of the resting heart, which is around 65 to 70 beats per minute. In this context, it is possible to now re-establish contact with your natural rhythm, your natural beat, the beat, the beat, always the beat. Sometimes, if you wish, you rest or pause but always in tune with the beat. Sometimes you can bunch up your words and speak quick phrases bunched together, but always in terms of the beat. You can function just like a conductor who controls the rhythm of the orchestra, making some variations from time to time but always in tune with the beat. Sometimes, if you wish, you may syncopate the beat. But always in tune with the beat, the beat, always the beat.

At first, if it is necessary have the metronome around so you hear it day and night. You can have it at your bedside, allow yourself to fall asleep in tune with the beat, the beat, always the beat. Once you make this commitment to speak and think in terms of the beat, even pause in terms of the beat, the correction becomes fixed and you are now able to make up for a deficit, you are now able to speak with the same sense of rhythm that fluent people use. In a way this is very much like approaching the problem the way you would the problem of diabetes. The deficit in diabetes is that the body does not produce enough insulin. The correction is to simply provide something that is missing. In that case it is insulin. In this case it is the beat, to re-establish contact with the beat, starting with the beat of your own heart.

I propose you do this exercise every one to two hours. Each time the exercise takes about twenty seconds in which you simply reinforce the concept of float-ing and at the same time remind yourself to speak and think and talk and feel in terms of the beat, the beat, the beat, always the beat. When you come out of this self-induced exercise, give yourself the posthypnotic signal that you will continue to think and talk in terms of the beat, the beat, the beat, always the beat.

If you do not find this helpful enough you can resort to a more extreme correction by buying a metronome that is battery powered and looks like a hearing device. You can insert it behind your ear and hear the beat while nobody else does. Until you find yourself able to correct the problem on your own, this device may be of use.

Case Example. R.E. was a 20-year-old single college student who was seen by the author (H.S.) for stuttering and a "speech block" which was prominent when the patient had to speak on the phone. This prob-lem had begun at age three and did not respond to speech therapy. He had suffered from encephalitis at age ten, and developed possibly un-related migraine at age twelve. In spite of these problems, he was an excellent student.

He was taught the exercise described above after being profiled at the intact 2 level. Follow-up six years later revealed that his speech was almost always in control and he was now an active and successful lawyer.

This case underscores the fact that hypnosis is not treatment. The approach developed by Brady for the specific problem of speech path-ology is the treatment strategy; hypnosis is the facilitator.

20

Spontaneous Trance, Amnesia, and Abreaction

Trance states may occur with or without the benefit of a formal induction ceremony. Such occurrences can be disciplined or undisciplined, exciting or frightening, helpful or destructive. It takes relatively little external pressure to elicit a spontaneous trance, traumatic amnesia, or abreaction in a highly hypnotizable person. It takes a good deal more environmental stress or stimulation to bring about such phenomena in a low-hypnotizable person. Thus the clinical assessment of trance capacity provides a measure of the probable amount of external pressure involved in a given situation, as well as guidelines for therapy.

Spontaneous Trance

O.H. was a 34-year-old physician and married father of three who developed a spontaneous dissociative state while voluntarily participating in a psychodrama demonstration. The workshop leader had asked O.H. to act the role of his wife, who was not present. During the interaction, issues about loyalty and faithfulness emerged. He returned to the audience and then rushed from the room, following me (H.S.) onto the street. He literally grabbed my arm, pleading: "Help me! Help me!"

I had left the meeting to attend to another emergency case, and I took O.H. with me in a taxi. The man was unable to give his name, seemed quite upset, and then I remembered seeing him participate in the psychodrama demonstration. In seemed that he was in a spontaneous trance. When we arrived at my office, O.H. was quickly examined and found to have a 4 eye roll. He was formally placed in a trance and instructed to sit quietly with his left hand in the air and think about what he wanted to tell me when I returned. In the meantime, I attended to the other emergency case. Forty-five minutes later, O.H. was found sitting in exactly the same position with his arm in the air. In response to an inquiry as he was still in the trance, he talked about his longstanding concerns over his wife's faithfulness. Given the pressure of time, he was told the following:

1. Imperfection is a part of being human.
2. Granted, your wife has faults.
3. So do you.
4. Consider the balance between compassion and forgiveness.
5. At the same time, be aware of limits for yourself and your wife.

In trance, he was told to think this over and prepare for the next session, scheduled for the following day. He was told that after he came out of the trance he would know who he was and would remember everything that happened. He was obviously relieved, and said, "Thank you, I feel better." In a subsequent session, it turned out that he as well as his wife had been unfaithful. He was taught precautions against entering spontaneous trance states, which involved instructing him to find someone with whom to discuss problems of guilt or anger when these feelings arose, rather than trying to deny them. He did well, and a five-year follow-up revealed that his marriage was also going well.

Spontaneous trances are not always so traumatic. P.A. was a 34-year-old doctor who felt a sudden paralysis in her right arm when driving home from a hypnosis course. At first she thought she had had a stroke. However, she was able to return her hand to the steering wheel. When she reached again for the cigarettes in her purse, she realized what had happened. The self-hypnosis technique for smoking control had been demonstrated that day in the class. She had been ruminating about the word "poison" and her two-pack-a-day habit. What she had not realized was that she had spontaneously entered a trance when the technique was demonstrated, and her body was responding in its own way to the message of being poisoned and not to any specific instruction in the demonstration. She was later profiled as an intact 4. During the ensuing eight years she has not resumed smoking.

The biggest danger in spontaneous trance states is that they often go unrecognized. This danger is compounded when trance is elicited by nonclinicians who are unable to recognize and deal with dissociated states, which can be a form of spontaneous trance. R.O. was a 35-year-old married woman with no children, who had been in psychotherapy for two years because of marital difficulties. One night she volunteered to be the subject for a stage hypnotist in a nightclub. As part of the act she was asked to imagine that she had a bird in her hand, which she did, along with others on the stage. She talked with this imaginary bird, and then was given a seemingly innocent enough instruction by the hypnotist: "Now let the bird fly away." R.O. later remembered shaking her hand, but the imagined bird would not leave. The audience laughed, and she was dismissed from the stage. She appeared dazed and confused, and her escort took her out of the club. As he was hailing a taxi, she strayed onto the street and was nearly hit by a car.

She was seen on an emergency basis that night, and it was apparent that she was still in the trance. I (H.S.) gave her a clear-cut cut-off signal and she came out of the trance. Her profile was grade 4 to 5. This experience was used in the course of her therapy to define a theme: she viewed herself as a bird in a golden cage, the cage of her marriage. She had become so absorbed in her identification with the hallucinated bird that she had failed to respond to the stage hypnotist's cut-off signal. It is clear from this case that a highly hypnotizable individual may respond quite intensely to what appears to be rather benign external influences.

Amnesia

Hypnosis is associated with spontaneous amnesia for traumatic and nontraumatic occurrences, as well as with intensifying the recall of forgotten memories. Sometimes the enhancement of recall for a traumatic event can have important legal or financial consequences.

U.Y. was a 16-year-old boy who was involved in an automobile accident in which his father was killed. He had recovered from a concussion, having regained consciousness in the hospital. They had been involved in a collision with a truck, whose driver claimed that he had stopped at the intersection where the accident had occurred. On this basis, and in the absence of any other witnesses, the insurance company was refusing to pay damages. U.Y. had no memory for a period of ten minutes prior to the accident, and was sent for evaluation with hypnosis to me (H.S.)

His profile score was 5. He was able to regress to the past and live it in the present tense. Initially, age regression was performed to neutral (nonemotionally charged) times, such as his tenth birthday and the age of one month. He was then brought to the night of the accident, and he was able to relive in sequence entering the car with his father, dropping off his aunt at the gas station, climbing from the back to the front seat to sit next to his father, seeing a light coming from the right, hearing his father say, "The truck will stop—there is a stop sign," then seeing his father quickly turn the car to the left before blacking out. He came out of the trance state with a sense of despair because he had not been able to recall the accident itself. Such was his motivation and honesty that he presumed he had failed, not knowing that his concussion had to have resulted in a period of retrograde amnesia lasting a few seconds before the accident. What had been uncovered was the traumatic amnesia; what could not be recovered was the few seconds of memory during the impact, which had not been neurologically processed because of his concussion. His recall was so authentic that the insurance company settled the claim rather than going to court, realizing that he would be a credible witness.

Hypnotic uncovering techniques are also helpful with less hypnotizable individuals. The approach is often more indirect, since regression to the past as though it were the present is not possible. E.J. was a 50-year-old married mother of four, who had assumed responsibility for her brother's financial affairs during his service in the Korean War. Several years later her brother was audited by the Internal Revenue Service and the sum of ten thousand dollars was unaccounted for. Accountants had been unable to solve the mystery, and the IRS was pressing charges of tax fraud. With the trial date set for a Monday, she desperately sought help with hypnosis on the preceding Thursday.

Her Profile was a 1 to 2, and she seemed predominantly Apollonian. She was initially disappointed that she was not capable of regression and dramatic recall, but she was taught to use the screen technique. She was instructed to try to sensitize herself to marginal thoughts and memories on the screen, and to be especially alert to any dreams that might occur. She volunteered to have a pencil and paper near her bed. Thus an effort was made to mobilize all of her conscious and unconscious resources. On Saturday morning at breakfast her husband asked her if she had remembered anything. With disappointment, she replied that she had not. She then related a dream she had had that night. In the course of the dream, she referred to a "Jack Miller" several times. Her husband asked, "Who the hell is Jack Miller?" She then recalled that he was a teller at a bank that she had used to handle her brother's affairs. She finally located him by phone the next day. He was now the vice-president of a Midwestern bank. She said to him, "I feel a little silly, but I feel I need to talk to you. Do you remember me?" He replied, "Weren't you the lady who took care of your brother's business when he was in Korea? As I recall, the last time we met I sold you several thousand dollars' worth of Series E savings bonds!" The mystery was solved, and the IRS dropped the charges.

Abreaction

Abreaction can occur spontaneously or with guidance. It is a sudden and dramatic outpouring of emotions, often tied to a specific traumatic event in the past. It can often occur as a "mini-abreaction" in the course of intensive psychotherapy. Usually the structure of the therapy situation is sufficient to contain and guide the intensity and direction of the abreaction. Occasionally, however, it may be so intense in a highly hypnotizable patient that both the patient and the therapist can become frightened.

This occurred in the case of B.I., a 19-year-old single woman who was in analysis for interpersonal problems and depression. Her childhood and adolescent years had been stormy. As the analysis proceeded, she would spontaneously and intensely regress when associating to dreams. She developed such extreme abreactions that her analyst, a very competent therapist, felt he lost contact and control. He identified this as a spontaneous trance state and referred her to me (H.S.) for evaluation. Her profile score was initially a 4, and she passed the additional three criteria for being rated a grade 5. She had typically Dionysian responses to the cluster questions. With this information the analyst agreed to suspend further analysis, and the treatment strategy shifted to one of ego support and guidance. For details of this treatment approach, the reader is referred to the section on long-term treatment strategies (Chapter 22). With this approach the spontaneous abreactions were controlled and she responded well to treatment.

Spontaneous abreactions can be disruptive, but they also can be used therapeutically in a structured setting. In the following case, abreaction was used to help a woman resolve a crisis brought on by a rape. Although she was low-hypnotizable (in the 2 range), the intensity of the external pressure, the rape, made abreaction possible.

Case Example I. G.E., a 40-year-old woman real estate agent, who had lived alone since being separated from her husband the year before, was brought for consultation by friends who wanted to hospitalize her because she had been confused, tearful, and "panicky," especially during the preceding twenty-four hours.

One week prior to this, a man entered her apartment and attempted to rape her. She screamed and he ran out of the window of her ground-floor apartment. The police found evidence of how the intruder escaped, but could not discover who he was. The patient was shaken and horrified by this experience, but with the sympathetic encouragement of her neighbors and friends she managed to go to work the next day and tried to regard the matter as a "nightmare that is all over." Although she worked each ensuing day, she gradually became more irritable and frightened.

By the sixth day after the event, her frequent bursts of tears and feelings of growing confusion so disabled her that she was sent home from the office. A neighbor tried to comfort her, but her restlessness, confusion, and tearfulness mounted; and in that condition she was brought to my office. As she cried she told how embarrassed she felt by all this—"after all, it happened a week ago and I got over it all right and now suddenly I feel like a wreck." I asked her to tell me what had happened and she replied, "Well, there wasn't much to it. I came home after work, I was tired, I took off my clothes, washed, then lay on the bed to rest before preparing supper. Next thing I knew there was a man in bed trying to rape me. I screamed and he ran out of the window. I called the police, but they could not find him. Oh, what did I do that a thing like this should happen to me?" Because of the revealing pauses in her account, which are difficult to convey in this report, it occurred to me that she was trying to remember more of this, but because of her anxiety had difficulty grasping it. I told this to her and proposed that she try hypnosis. She answered, "I don't know if I can be hypnotized, but I'll try anything."

She went into a trance and I then asked her to recall much more data. The affect connected with the recall was much more specific and intense. We learned that between the time she fell asleep on her bed and the time that she recalled screaming, much had transpired. Enough had occurred to enable her to sense "his desperate need for me. He touched me in such a way that I felt his gentleness. He made me feel so alluring and so desirable and so lovely and wonderful."

What became apparent was the nature of a strong conflict in her fantasy and memory of this event. On the one hand, she did yield to him somewhat and by her sensuous excitement was reminded of her own need for physical and sexual closeness. Yet, on the other hand, she experienced the horror of this, including the surprise and defenselessness of her position in living alone. As days passed, she gradually realized that her temporary acceptance of this physical and sensuous excitement so offended her sense of moral decency, that she berated herself for allowing this feeling to occur, and feared she was degraded and perverted. This accounted for her delayed symptoms.

While she was in trance, I reminded her that in spite of her horror she had without choice been forced to accept his presence for a while. And even though yielding to him to the extent that she did was an accidental reminder of her deprivation, it was also a reminder that she was unable to accept her attacker. In fact, she did scream and frighten him away. By establishing the perspective that her transient sensuous experience was merely an accidental uncovering of an understandable human feeling that had been dormant, it became clear to her that her fears that she was degraded were not founded upon fact, but merely represented a confusion of issues.

She was told that when she was out of the trance she would remember as much of this experience as she would be able to endure. She shifted from the trance on signal and wiped her tears. We reviewed the events again and she experienced a great sense of relief when she was able to tell me that her sexual excitement was understandable, but it in no way indicated that she desired such an experience in such a setting or that she condoned this man's intrusion. She lit up a cigarette, sighed several times, and jokingly referred to what an ordeal she had been through. Within a matter of another five or ten minutes she became composed and with a kind of gaiety remarked several times how unbelievable it was that she could feel so relieved within the course of an hour and a half. When she walked into the waiting room and her two friends looked at her, the expressions on their faces indicated their amazement and pleasant surprise at the drastic change that had occurred. She said to her friends, "Let's go home and have a drink."

Three days later I saw her a second and final time. We reviewed the events of the first session. She seemed quite satisfied with the formulation, and by that time was back at work. Follow-up nine years later confirmed that the issue had been resolved.

*Case Example II.** D.R. was a 43-year-old black career Army supply sergeant who was separated from his wife. He was brought to the hospital after a near-fatal attempt to drive his car off a mountain road. On admission he was acutely depressed but nonpsychotic. He had seen his estranged wife with another man that day which seemed to be the acute precipitant of the suicide attempt, but he made it clear that he had not been the same since his service in Vietnam. During a five-year period he had been hospitalized ten times in Army, Veterans' Administration, and state institutions. He had been diagnosed variously as paranoid schizophrenic, psychopathic, and depressed.

Prior to this period, he had served for twenty-two years as a noncommissioned officer in the Army without any psychiatric difficulties. He had been wounded in combat in Korea, and served for three and a half years in Vietnam, where he learned to speak fluent Vietnamese, helped to construct an orphanage for wounded Vietnamese children, adopted a Vietnamese child, and performed his duties as a special dietician.

A report that he had suffered a fugue state after witnessing a rocket attack destroy the orphanage he had helped to build, with his adopted son inside, led us to speculate that he might be highly hypnotizable, and also that this trauma and loss might be unresolved and contributing to his current depression.

The HIP was administered. He scored 4 and with further testing met all the criteria of a grade 5. In an effort to uncover details of his experiences in Vietnam, and to help him put them in perspective, hypnotic regression was employed to help him relive several important episodes. The emotional intensity with which he did so constituted an abreaction, not merely a regression. He relived his arrival in Vietnam with shock and sadness, seeing soldiers casually sitting on caskets, and malnourished children everywhere.

The scene then shifted to a time several years later, when he saw the orphanage destroyed by a Vietcong rocket attack. Inside the building was his adopted Vietnamese son, a young boy who had been badly burned earlier, and whom D.R. had named "Chi Town" after his home town, Chicago. When he regressed to this extent in the trance, he screamed: "The rockets are coming! The rockets! They can't do that. They can't do that—we got the Geneva Convention! Why do they gotta kill kids?" He experienced defending what was left of the hospital and

* We gratefully acknowledge the assistance of Leslie E. Becker III, M.D., resident in psychiatry, Stanford University School of Medicine, who was co-therapist in this case.

being told that his son had been killed. He then relived the fugue state that had followed, in which he commandeered an ambulance and went out into the jungle alone to find and fight Vietcong. He had no conscious memory of this incident.

The regression then involved his tearful burial of his son: "If I'd just been with you in my hut! If I hadn't gone away!" He was asked what the boy would have said to him about that. With a tearful smile, he mimicked the boy's voice: "It's okay Sargie. You number one Sargie." We shifted to an earlier time when he had thrown a birthday party for the boy as he was coming out of his bandages. His affect suddenly switched from anguish to a warm happiness. He relived giving Chi Town an electric train set, and showing him his birthday cake.

He was then given a self-hypnosis exercise to perform in which he pictured on a screen in his mind the grave on one side, and the cake on the other. He was told that this symbolized both the profound loss which the boy's death represented to him, and at the same time the joy they had given one another. He was helped to see that he had in fact kept the boy alive for a number of years. This latter point was especially important; he had undertaken an impossible task, that of creating a loving and safe environment in the midst of a brutal war. He blamed himself for failing at this, when in fact he had succeeded beyond any reasonable expectation.

As he came out of the trance, he seemed a bit dazed, remembered little of what had transpired (forty-five minutes seemed like five to him), but said he had a visual image of a grave and a cake. He practiced the exercise several times a day, and within several weeks his suicidal ideation disappeared and his depression began to resolve. He was also treated with a tricyclic antidepressant and was discharged a month later, continued weekly psychotherapy and medication for several months, and then the therapy was terminated.

D.R. had suffered a pathological grief reaction leading to chronic depression. The resolution of this traumatic neurosis was delayed by D.R.'s Dionysian sensitivity to his Army environment, which conveyed to him the message that his efforts to build and defend an orphanage for Vietnamese children made him a traitor. The combination of the loss of his son ("Fifteen years in the Army and he was all I had") and criticism by others of his efforts at helping Vietnamese children had kept him depressed. He had no anchor point, and his efforts to do the right thing left him grieving and ostracized. The external criticism reinforced his own self-doubts and consequently he blamed himself more than he should have for the loss of his son, so that the depressive dynamism was constantly reinforced. The abreaction using hypnosis enabled us to identify this dynamism and interrupt it, helping him to mourn his losses and gain perspective on what he had done in Vietnam. The ensuing psychotherapy involved helping the patient develop "ego-scaffolding" to enhance mastery of his Dionysian characteristics. These issues are discussed in Chapter 22 on the psychotherapy of the grade 5 patient.

CONCLUSION

Abreactions are most likely to occur spontaneously, and are often therapeutic in a crisis intervention setting when therapist support can reinforce executive self-control (Caplan 1964). An individual who has just been through a trauma is most prone to abreact. The sooner it occurs, the more likely it can avoid the emergence and crystallization of a traumatic neurosis (Kardiner and Spiegel 1947). The abreaction may help the patient come to terms with a sudden change in his life. It may involve earthquakes, fires, physical accidents, mourning the death of a relative, coping with physical assault, or putting into perspective some heated exchange with a family member. Highly hypnotizable individuals are especially prone to abreact under even fairly mild stress. The same degree of emotional outburst in an Apollonian should alert the therapist that significant trauma must have occurred.

Such trance phenomena often occur in association with dissociative features such as fugue, when the patient believes himself to be in a different time and place. They are not harmful and can be helpful to the patient if handled properly. It is mainly important to recognize the event as a trance phenomenon rather than as a sign of psychosis, organic brain disease, or intoxication. A simple measure of trance capacity can assist in this differential diagnosis. Then if the clinician maintains a firm but supportive manner in guiding the patient through the experience and extracting what meaning can be found in it, rapid resolution of the crisis often can be achieved.

TREATMENT STRATEGIES: LONG TERM

21

The Spectrum of Therapies

We have now reviewed a series of short-term treatment strategies which are designed to help the patient restructure his approach to a problem using self-hypnosis in one treatment session. We prefer to abide by the principle of parsimony, utilizing short-term treatment wherever possible, assessing the results, and hoping that a ripple effect may occur, in which the initial mastery of a symptom leads to mastery of other problem areas. Thus even a small intervention can have a sizable impact on a patient's life, at times comparable to the effect of more intensive psychotherapy. An example is the patient who found, after overcoming her dog phobia in two sessions, that she was able to make major changes in her life, including ending a failing marriage, going back to school and fulfilling educational aspirations that she had had for most of her life, losing weight, and in general feeling much happier about herself and her new social life. For many patients like this one, brief intervention is enough formal psychotherapy.

When the question is raised by a patient about whether short-term or long-term therapy is necessary, we propose a trial of short-term therapy with a subsequent re-evaluation. If the symptom is not quickly resolved, then we reappraise the problem. The initial failure may indicate that more intensive psychotherapy is necessary. It may also involve obtaining additional history and reformulating the problem. Sometimes the success of brief intervention stimulates the patient's curiosity about how the problem evolved. Intensive treatment may be undertaken in an effort to prevent the emergence of such problems in the future.

Our approach is in line with a definition of the correct dose of a medication, which was provided by a pharmacology professor of the "old school." His definition was "enough." Although we have emphasized the use of hypnosis in brief psychotherapy, we in no way discount the value of the various long-term psychotherapies.

Determining the Mode of Treatment

Hypnosis is useful for both diagnostic and ancillary treatment purposes in intensive therapy. We will first turn our attention to the diagnostic uses of the HIP in selecting the appropriate intensive therapy. We have found that the results of the HIP are extremely useful in supplementing the clinical impression, the results of the mental status examination, the clinical interview, and psychodiagnostic testing. In the process of selecting an appropriate intensive therapy, none of these factors alone provides an absolute answer to the question of what the best treatment is. We have found, however, that the profile provides an initial direction as to areas in which we can ask futher questions to arrive at a treatment strategy that is relevant and aesthetically appealing to the patient. Although the profile has all of the limitations inherent in any brief clinical instrument, it offers a starting point in assessing a patient's capacity for change.

THERAPIES FOR SOFTS AND DECREMENTS

Data cited earlier indicates that there is a significant association between relatively severe psychopathology and a decrement or soft pattern on the profile. (See Figure 8–2). If a soft or decrement performance cannot be accounted for by such transient factors as sedation from medication, then the clinician's index of suspicion should be raised concerning the presence of serious psychopathology. These patterns of performance on the HIP convey a message in probabilistic terms of impaired capacity to respond to a therapy which is self-generating. This association is supported by the follow-up data on single-session treatment using self-hypnosis for flying phobias (see Appendix). The percentage of patients in the intact group responding to the treatment was twice as high as that from the soft and decrement group.

Thus when a patient has a soft or decrement profile, we are inclined to review the history, mental status examination, and psychodiagnostic testing if available, for evidence of a thought, character, or affective disorder. Patients who score in the nonintact zone on the HIP often convey a message of a kind of helplessness in regard to their internal ability for disciplined concentration. Because of this internal deficit, treatment intervention for this group is largely external and supportive, such as social or milieu support, or medication. As we have discussed previously, included in this group are a large proportion of patients with schizophrenia, depression, sociopathy, and manic-depressive illness.

At the least, a soft or decrement profile suggests that self-hypnosis is not likely to be of help in implementing a treatment strategy. Our thinking in terms of treatment then turns in the direction of anti-psychotic medication for schizophrenics, antidepressants for patients with serious depression with somatic signs, lithium for those with cyclical affective disorders, and various occupational and rehabilitative programs, including family and social support, for those patients with character disorders and schizophrenia. Some of these patients regain their intact capacity to concentrate when they recover, especially those with de-pression who respond well to antidepressant medification. In this con-text, the profile has proven useful as a measuring stick for clinical change.

F.D., a 25-year-old married college student, requested help with hyp-nosis because he had difficulty concentrating on his studies. His profile was a 2 to 3 soft. Further history elicited the fact that his marriage was going quite badly, his wife, who was of a different nationality and religion than his own, felt very unhappy with his family and with the prospect of their returning to his home country at the end of his studies. He seemed moderately depressed and acknowledged that his marital problems were making him quite unhappy. A month later he returned, stating that he had sorted things out with his wife, and that he was feeling much better as a result. His profile then was an intact 2 to 3. In this case his clinical improvement was mirrored by the improvement in his trance capacity, most likely in relation to the resolution of his reactive depression. It then became possible to use his recovered trance capacity as an aid in concentration.

Centering

This brings us to the concept of centering. We conceive of an individual's position on the Apollonian–Odyssean–Dionysian (AOD) spectrum to be a kind of biological and psychological anchor point (see Figure 21–1). If an individual decompensates, he is likely to do so in certain char-acteristic directions. Apollonians are likely to develop obsessional fea-tures; or, given a concurrence of biological, psychological, and social factors, they may decompensate into schizophrenia. On the other ex-treme, Dionysians are prone to develop hysteria and affective disorders.

However, these same individuals also are prone to recompensate in

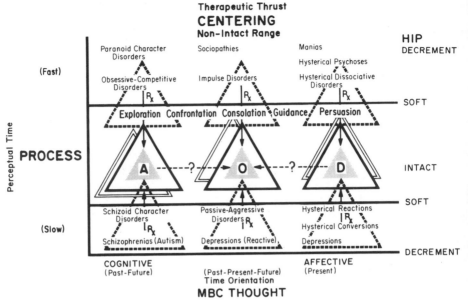

Figure 21–1

characteristic directions. In the case just cited, F.D. recovered from a reactive depression (he had a 2 to 3 soft profile at the time) to a milder action–despair syndrome with a 2 to 3 intact profile. He graduated from clinical depression to brooding about the direction of his career and marriage. This is an example of centering; he recovered his biological and psychological anchor point from a decompensated position. It is hoped that the appropriate psychotherapeutic approach, whether pharmacotherapy, family therapy, vocational rehabilitation, electroconvulsive therapy, or inpatient care, will help the more disturbed patients center on their healthier anchor points. For example, we expect that a schizophrenic in remission would show some Apollonian features, perhaps harboring some obsessional preoccupations bordering on delusions, but functioning well. We would not expect him to develop the dramatic emotional and interpersonal style of a Dionysian.

Likewise we anticipate that a manic controlled on lithium would recompensate to a Dionysian position, perhaps with some hysterical features. In the case of H.L. reported earlier, lithium only partially contained her mood swings and, given her 3 to 4 profile score, self-hypnosis was helpful in further containing them. There were certain dramatic and hysterical features to her instability on lithium which were addressed by a restructuring approach using self-hypnosis.

As Figure 21–1 indicates, it is hoped that a certain amount of centering will occur when Apollonians and Dionysians are given psychotherapy. Such patients are unlikely to exchange places on the spectrum, but it is hoped that they will gain perspective about their vulnerabilities and modify them.

PATIENTS WITH INTACT PROFILES

We take the presence of an intact profile as indicative of a patient's relative mental health and of an intact capacity to concentrate in a disciplined manner. Such a person is in tune with his biological capacity to concentrate and does not show major interference in this ability, as do individuals with soft and decrement profiles. In clinical practice we have employed the profile score as a factor in selecting an appropriate intensive psychotherapeutic approach for patients in the intact range who request or have need of such treatment. The intactness of the profile is evidence of a patient's capacity for change. The score itself— high, mid-range or low—suggests something about personality style and probable type of neurotic decompensation, which in turn has implications for the type of psychotherapy which may be appropriate.

We have divided the intensive psychotherapies along a continuum from exploration to persuasion, with three gradations between: confrontation, consolation, and guidance. (See Figure 21–2). As the diagram indicates, we are inclined to emphasize exploratory psychotherapy for neurotic Apollonian patients who frequently suffer from obsessive–competitive disorders. On the other extreme, the Dionysians who decompensate, frequently with some form of hysterical neurosis, often do best with a more persuasive psychotherapy which helps the patient discover what to do rather than why he does it. Odysseans who require psychotherapy frequently have periods of depression, an exaggeration of the action–despair syndrome, and we have found that some of the more existential therapies emphasizing confrontation and consolation seem

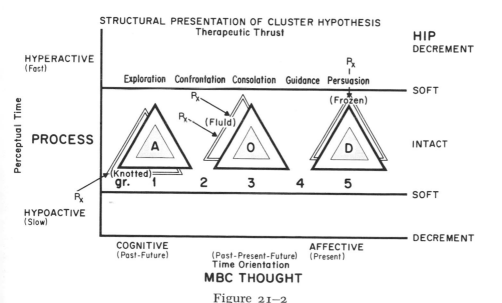

Figure 21–2

most appropriate. With this broad overview in mind, let us examine the spectrum of psychotherapies in more detail.

THERAPIES FOR APOLLONIANS

Perhaps the archetypal exploratory psychotherapy is the early client-centered therapy described by Carl Rogers (1951). In his approach no assumption about the nature of man is made and the patient structures the premises with which the treatment unfolds. The therapist's role is a responsive one, in which he reflects back to the patient the premises and guidelines that the patient has set down. At times and in specific ways, the therapist may confront the patient with contraditions, inconsistencies, or self-defeating operations, but this must be done in a well-prepared way and with a suspension of critical judgment toward the patient, which Rogers terms unconditional positive regard.

Another therapy of this general type is classical psychoanalysis and several modern variations on the psychoanalytic method. Of this subgroup, the Sullivanian approach is more like Rogers' style than like classical analysis because, like Rogers, Sullivan does not make an assumption about the nature of man. His analytic technique is essentially an operational one in which he focuses on trying to understand the interpersonal phenomena between patient and doctor. In the course of understanding this interaction, he hopes to construct a direction which leads to conflict or anxiety resolution. Together with the patient, the therapist identifies and explores parataxic distortions and their sources, utilizing the therapy relationship as an experiential laboratory for identifying and delineating the sources of interpersonal misunderstanding.

These approaches require a patient who is introspective and intellectually curious, one who wants to know why he is doing what he is doing. They also require a patient who is sufficiently disciplined to persist with what can be a painstaking and difficult process. Sullivan enjoyed working with obsessionals and noted with some amusement that it was rare that an hysteric survived his first interview to return for a second. This is consistent with our general impression that obsessional patients, who are frequently decompensated Apollonians, are the most appropriate candidates for this type of exploratory psychotherapy. They have the requisite intellectual curiosity and are inclined to structure an encounter to such an extent that they almost require a therapist who is relatively passive and nondirective. He becomes more of an advisor or consultant, eliciting information to satisfy the intellectual curiosity of the patient and aiding him in delineating the problem area. Once this is done there may be some occasion when the therapist may resort to confrontation, but only after careful preparation.

It is our clinical impression that if psychoanalytic therapy is the method of choice for any group, it is for these stressed or decompensated Apollonians; patients with obsessive–competitive disorders who can affiliate readily with a model of therapy which emphasizes talking and exploration in the service of freeing bound affect. Although many of

Freud's early explorations of psychoanalytic technique were performed with hysterics rather than obsessionals (Breuer and Freud 1893–95), we have observed that the very malleability of the hysterics makes them prime candidates for proving the efficacy of almost any psychotherapeutic intervention.

The approach employed by psychoanalysts, which is quite rational and cognitive, with emphasis on replacing irrational conflict with reason, is very much in tune with the cognitive rational style of an Apollonian. They tend to genuinely participate in the exploration as both an intellectual and a therapeutic process of untying cognitive knots, unlike the Dionysians, who tend to turn the psychoanalytic approach into an exercise in compliance with the inferred wishes of the analyst. The goal of analytic psychotherapy, "where id was, ego shall be," is consonant with the style of an Apollonian who needs to learn to use his reason in the service of unbinding and freeing his affect.

Furthermore, this therapeutic approach is consistent with the time sense and style of incorporating new approaches that characterize the Apollonians. It is a long, step-by-step therapeutic strategy. Change comes slowly, interpretation by interpretation. It is not even a stated goal of pure psychoanalysis; rather, the purpose is to enhance the individual's understanding of the roots of his personality structure, a goal which is bound to intrigue an obsessional and not unduly frighten him with its prospect of some great transformation. Psychoanalysis deliberately focuses a great deal of attention on how the past influences the present personality structure. This likewise appeals to Apollonians, who tend to focus more on past and future than on the present.

Psychoanalysis does make assumptions about the nature of man, unlike the client-centered approach. The power and social-drive theories derived from psychoanalysis (Adler 1927; Rank 1929; Reich 1972), and theories about man in relation to the cosmos (Jung 1964) all involve inferences about man, and thus are not as "pure" as Rogers' premise of starting at zero expectation. Because of this implication, that the therapist in these neo-Freudian approaches has some awareness of the desired direction for the patient in terms of a contextual concept of man, there are apt to be more occasions for confrontation in these therapies. The data from the patient gives the therapist the opportunity to perceive contradictions in comparison to his own theory of personality and the resulting interpretation can be a confrontation as well as an exploration.

It has been our experience that obsessional patients in general demonstrate somewhat constricted affect, consistent with their tendency to isolate and displace feelings and overinvest their cognitive processes with importance. When they suffer emotionally, it is usually with a sense of despair, rather than with an intense depression. These patients require assistance in disentangling the cognitive knots in which they find themselves bound (Laing 1970) (see Figure 21–2). They become immobilized by their anxious desire to understand everything, to reason through emotional problems, to put everything in their life in order. They need to be guided in the use of their reason in a manner which respects their desire to understand but which gently loosens their need to rationalize.

THERAPIES FOR ODYSSEANS

Patients who suffer with clinically obvious depression often respond well to a psychotherapeutic approach which emphasizes an alternation between confrontation and consolation, mirroring the patient's fluctuation between periods of activity and despair. Approaches such as Gestalt therapy (Perls 1969, 1970), with its emphasis on facing the here and now and confronting people in one's real or unconscious world, can be quite helpful. The Gestalt approach can be quite effective in mobilizing affect in an individual who is unsuccessfully attempting to ignore it. The importance of "insight" is minimized in Gestalt therapy.

Often group therapies are very helpful for these patients. They confront an individual with his withdrawal and depression and at the same time provide a series of supportive relationships when consolation is in order. In his study of curative factors in group psychotherapy, Yalom (1970) found that the most important curative factors listed by group patients involved a mixture of insight, catharsis, interpersonal learning, and an existential recognition of responsibilty for oneself (pp. 67–69). These patients felt that they had been helped most by coming to terms with parts of themselves which they had been unaware of or had not accepted, by learning to express feelings, by coming to terms with other group members' opinions of them, and by accepting more responsibility for their own actions.

These factors have an important affective and interpersonal component: the group members stressed the importance of self-acceptance and self-expression at least as much as any particular content or insight gained about themselves. Acceptance was at least as important as discovery of insight. Thus exploration is only one of the many factors operative in group therapy. This approach provides a mixture of exploration, confrontation, and consolation, which seems especially helpful to patients with reactive depression in what we call the Odyssean group. We have found that Apollonian patients are often frightened of group therapy. In particular, obsessional patients are often sufficiently rigid in their interpersonal contacts that they often have difficulty in learning from a group experience (Yalom 1970, pp. 366–367).

We have also found that the existential psychotherapies are particularly relevant to Odysseans. The logotherapy of Victor Frankl (1966), for example, places a strong emphasis on consolation—on the therapist's learning to share the despairing world of the patient and thereby counter the patient's sense of isolation and depression. The goal of such psychotherapy is genuine connectedness with another person rather than insight. Understanding of what a person is, is viewed as a reification of personhood. Insights are processed as necessary obstacles to be overcome. Knowing what someone is, is seen as a substitute for experiencing him as he is (Havens 1974). To borrow from the philosophical model, the exploratory psychotherapies are more idealist; they make understanding the essence of a person, that is, insight, the primary criterion for change. The existential therapies, on the other hand, make existing with the patient coincidental with an understanding of his essence. To truly be with the patient—bracketing one's preconceptions of him—is to allow for the possibility of change.

The emotional encounter at times requires confrontation; for example Minkowski's (1970) famous outburst of frustration at a psychotic patient with whom he had lived. He later felt this was a crucial step in his process of contacting this autistic patient. At the same time consolation is very important. Frankl (1964, pp. 56–57) reports having treated an older man with an acute reactive depression subsequent to his wife's death. Frankl asked him to think about the pain his wife would have gone through if he had died first. The patient reportedly radically altered his perspective on the situation and was consoled in his grief. Such approaches, however, require patients who are sufficiently attuned to the importance of interpersonal relating as opposed to strictly intellectual process; that is, they are willing to engage in a therapy that values relatedness above insight. It has been our clinical impression that depressed patients with Odyssean characteristics meet this criteria and are good candidates for such therapeutic approaches as Gestalt, group therapy, and existential psychotherapy.

THERAPIES FOR DIONYSIANS

A third group of psychotherapies emphasize persuasion and guidance over such factors as insight, confrontation, and consolation. In this type of psychotherapy the psychotherapist becomes more authoritarian and directive, emphasizing "what" rather than "why." The therapist seeks to provide a cognitive structure for the patient rather than to develop a pattern of meaning. The strength of the relationship with the patient becomes especially important because this therapy involves an active intervention in the patient's life. Some of the behavior modification approaches fall within this group in that they focus on directing behavior with relatively little interest in insight. Many kinds of counseling and consolation also fall within this group, and the therapist is freer about giving advice and support than he would be in a more exploratory approach.

It has been our clinical experience that this type of psychotherapy is especially relevant to decompensated Dionysians who have some of the varied and shifting symptoms of hysteria. The association between hysteria and hypnotizability is hardly new. In *Studies on Hysteria* Breuer noted, "What we should be doing would be first to assign the phenomena of hysteria to hypnosis, and then to assert that hypnosis is the cause of those phenomena" (Breuer and Freud 1893–95, p. 248). Highly hypnotizable people with symptoms such as conversion reactions, fugue states, dissociative states, and interpersonal difficulties are often quite dependent and demanding and yet relatively disinterested in insight. Recalling the compulsive triad diagram (see Figures 5–1 and 21–2), they are frozen into a pattern of compulsive compliance. They display amnesia to the various signals to which they are complying and a relative disinterest in rationalizing, but they are capable of producing dramatic and incongruous rationalizations, that is, trance logic. Dionysians' tendency to please, their willingness to suspend critical judgment, and their absorption in the here and now make them eager for a psychotherapy situation which provides them with structure. Such an approach is complementary to their dependence, emphasis on affectivity and relatedness, and tendency to comply.

THE GRADE 5 PATIENT AND INSIGHT THERAPY

We will discuss the structured psychotherapy of the highly hypnotizable patient in more detail in the next chapter. In view of the widespread use of exploratory psychotherapy with such individuals, it is worth noting that many highly hypnotizable patients find themselves befuddled by cognitive, insight-oriented psychotherapy. When a Dionysian patient is presented with the inquiring "Why?" his typical response is not "What a fine occasion to gather more understanding about myself," but "My God, what does he expect me to say? What am I supposed to think?" In such a situation, innocent inquiry on the part of the therapist can set off anxiety or panic in the patient because of the urge to comply. A sense of inferiority often is experienced by the grade 5 patient.

A case example of this was a brilliant, troubled young man (T.C.), who entered intensive psychoanalysis after a casual remark that he "must be homosexual" left him so anxious that he had difficulty concentrating on his studies. He felt more despairing and disjointed after a year of therapy than when he had begun. During the analyst's month-long vacation the patient felt much better—his old gloom was gone—until the doctor's return. His emotional difficulties led to his being granted a leave of absence from his college, but the Selective Service then informed him that his student deferment status was valid only if he remained in school. His analyst wrote to the Selective Service on the patient's behalf. Not surprisingly, the young man opened the letter and read that he was, among other things, "psychotic." The man had the self-protective sense to ask the doctor, "When you called me psychotic, did you really mean that, or did you say it in order to get me a medical deferment?" The doctor responded with silence, whereupon the patient grew anxious and raised the question again. The analyst said, "Why do you ask?" The patient of course pressed further, and finally the doctor replied, "Well, if you noticed, I didn't say that you were irreversibly psychotic."

Such an approach might have been useful in treating an Apollonian, but it created appalling anxiety in this young man. His mother intervened during his psychoanalysis, seeking help for her son. Examination revealed him to be a grade 5 and this new insight altered the therapeutic approach to his problem. The patient shifted into a new treatment setting and within a few weeks, using the knowledge of his grade 5 characteristics, his clinical picture was transformed from one of chronic panic to an acceptance of responsibility for his actions. In a few months he was able to return to his pre-illness level of excellent academic work. He has since completed his schooling successfully, is well launched upon his chosen career, and is married and a father.

Often grade 5 patients have to be literally salvaged from the confusion and abrasiveness of "why" therapy. They require a transition period in which they can re-orient themselves and experience the relief and support of establishing guidelines for a new therapeutic perspective.

There is a growing accumulation of clinical data which suggests that introspective psychoanalytic therapy is contraindicated for the grade 5 patient, and in some instances may seriously aggravate the patient's turmoil without concurrent clinical insight or benefit. One can argue that after the crisis period is alleviated there may be a limited role for introspective therapy in such cases, provided it does not exceed the pace of the patient's curiosity. At the same time, it is interesting to observe how little curiosity these patients have about themselves once their crisis is resolved.

This is consistent with our centering concept (see Figure 5-5). Once the patient is able to recognize and control his frozen tendency to comply with external cues, he can perceive more alternatives and enhance the use of his cognitive resources. For example, in the case example just presented, the young man was able to alter his perspective on the homosexual anxiety which had brought him to treatment in the first place; he realized that he was disturbed by the comment, not because it represented some deep truth about himself, but because he was so prone to uncritically accept cues from others. With this new security and perspective, he became able to modify his Dionysian tendencies. In fact, he became quite interested in understanding these aspects of himself and in studying the psychotherapeutic approaches relevant to different types of people. By adding this cognitive framework to his Dionysian make-up, he began a process of centering.

COMPLIANCE IN THERAPY

At times, as the previous case illustrates, the grade 5 patient copes with his anxiety and uncertainty in the therapy situation by picking up cues from the nature of the inquiry by the therapist and using them to provide a response which he surmises will fulfill the therapist's expectations. The therapeutic interaction is reduced to a charade in which the patient artfully elaborates on the therapist's theme rather than uncovering information about himself. It is not unlikely that the reason why many analysts regard hysterics as good patients is because they are so responsive. In the absence of careful examination, the therapist and the patient come to operate on the assumption that the information produced is an accurate recall of real events or fantasies, rather than convenient rationalizations to cope with pressure for compliance provoked by the analytic process of inquiry. This problem plagued even Freud, who was misled in the development of his theories of infantile sexuality by data supplied by compliant hysteric patients to the effect that as children they actually underwent episodes of sexual seduction by their parents:

> I thus overestimated the frequency of such events (though in other respects they were not open to doubt). Moreover, I was at that period unable to distinguish with certainty between falsifications made by hysterics in their memories of childhood and traces of real events.
>
> (Freud 1906, p. 275)

Since highly hypnotizable patients are so compliant, this compliance can be utilized in a therapeutic technique which emphasizes guidance and persuasion. Such patients are likely to present themselves in severe emotional and interpersonal distress and are not likely to see their problem in a cognitive framework, or to be terribly curious about reducing it to such a framework. The burden falls upon the therapist to help the patient isolate and define specific treatable problems; that is, to apply the "puzzle form" to the vague problem areas and dysphoria in the patient's life. The therapist acknowledges the patient's need for cognitive structure and supplies it directly rather than indirectly, as in the exploratory psychoanalytic approach.

Organizing and Utilizing the Therapeutic Strategies

This spectrum of psychotherapies from exploration to guidance is quite brief and simplified. It is hardly a comprehensive listing of the myriad of psychotherapeutic strategies. It provides one possible framework for organizing various psychotherapeutic approaches in relation to the psychopathologies and personality styles of the patients seeking therapy. Our overall approach is to match the style of the therapy to the personality style and inclinations of the patient. More "head-oriented" patients seem to do better with cognitive-oriented, exploratory psychotherapy. Highly hypnotizable patients with hysterical problems seem to prefer a therapeutic strategy which emphasizes the importance of the relationship between the patient and the therapist, and the provision of cognitive structure rather than exploration.

Some may argue that a given therapy belongs in a different place on the schema. For example, Karasu (1977) recently published an article classifying the psychotherapies into three groups: dynamic, behavioral, and experiential. He categorizes Rogers' client-centered therapy in the same group with the existential psychotherapies of Binswanger, Boss, and Frankl. In his framework the dynamic psychotherapies consist of psychoanalysis and all the neo-Freudian movements. The behavioral group consists primarily of variations on the behavior modification theme, including social-learning psychotherapy and biofeedback training. There are considerable areas of overlap between his more comprehensive listing of the psychotherapies and our categorization. His tendency is to classify these psychotherapies into discrete units. Our preference is to place the psychotherapies on a continuum with the cognitive psychotherapies on one side, and to shift gradually toward those therapies which emphasize affect and relatedness rather than insight.

The reader may object that this formulation makes it too "easy" for the patients; that a good psychotherapy challenges a patient to overcome his limitations; that an intellectualizing obsessional should seek a therapy situation which forces him to relate intensely to the therapist; and that a compliant hysteric should learn to utilize his cognitive capacity to understand his life situation more. As we see it, the issue involves making the best use of the patient's resources in the hope that he will become more balanced and perhaps later be able to use less characteristic strategies. For example, it is quite possible that after a given problem is resolved and from a new vantage point of security, the highly hypnotizable patient may raise some questions about how he happens to be so vulnerable to manipulation and dependency relationships. This may be an occasion when a more explorative and cognitive approach can be used to develop what amounts to "ego scaffolding" or ego strengthening procedures which can reacquaint this patient with the value of cognitive consolidation. In this sense, the treatment procedure can shift in the direction of consolation and confrontation. Similarly, when an Apollonian in brief symptom-oriented treatment or in an intensive insight-oriented psychotherapy has reached a point of achievement, the freeing of his affect from the constrictions of isolation and displacement may provide him an occasion to move toward the mid-range, in which a more emotive affect-oriented psychotherapy would be important. In this sense, a kind of centering may occur after the initial phase of therapy, and patients on either extreme may move toward the Odyssean mid-range (see Figure 5–5).

Thus, after any patient consolidates at a new level, it may become necessary to alter the treatment strategy to take into account this new integration. If with persuasion and guidance, a Dionysian has managed to make significant life changes or has overcome a troubling symptom, he may request and benefit from a therapy which is more confrontational. On the other hand, an obsessional Apollonian, having utilized his cognitive capacities to allow himself to experience more affect, may develop a reactive depression which is best treated with consolation. We view the resilient therapist as thinking in ever-shifting terms, making use of such categories as Apollonian, Odyssean, and Dionysian as points of departure and orientation to therapy, rather than as fixed prescriptions for therapy.

22

The Grade 5 Syndrome: Special Considerations in Treating the Dionysian

Highly hypnotizable individuals who also suffer from psychological problems present special difficulties for the psychotherapist. As has been discussed in the previous chapter, a well intentioned exploratory effort can be turned into a futile exercise in compliance by a patient who seeks to provide answers that the therapist wants, rather than engaging in active mutual exploration. Earlier in the book we described the highly hypnotizable individual in terms of personality style and characteristics such as a relative proneness to trust, a reliance on feeling rather than reasoning, a tendency to live in the present, and a capacity for intense focal concentration. When severe psychological decompensation occurs, these normal attributes are exaggerated and the individual becomes the victim of his own capacities rather than the master of them. A proneness to trust becomes a pathological compliance with people in his environment; a preference for feeling over reason becomes an unwillingness to think through the consequences of action; a tendency to live in the present becomes a denial of past precedents and future consequences; and the capacity for intense concentration becomes transformed into dissociative episodes such as fugue states.

These patients, when stressed, often present hysterical symptoms, conversion reactions, dissociative episodes, or interpersonal difficulties

The material in this chapter appeared, in a different form, in Spiegel, H. 1974. The grade 5 syndrome. The highly hypnotizable person. Int. J. Clin. Exp. Hypn. 22:303–319.

including classic hysterical sexualizing of the nonsexual, and desexualizing of the sexual in relationships. The initial clinical impression can be confirmed or challenged by the patient's score on the HIP. This discussion is meant to describe patients who score in the 4 to 5 range on the HIP. In this chapter we will describe some of the behavioral and personality attributes which we have observed in this relatively rare group of patients. We go on to discuss what seems to us to be the most appropriate and effective psychotherapeutic strategy when these patients require intensive treatment.

Configuration of Traits and Characteristics

High HIP Score. These individuals usually score in the 4 to 5 range on the HIP with a high eye roll, immediate hand levitation, and a profound sense of differential control between the hypnotized and nonhypnotized hand. They are usually capable of experiencing age regression in the present tense, sustained posthypnotic motor alterations and hallucinatory responses in compliance with a cue, and/or global amnesia for the entire hypnotic episode. If the individual is capable of all these experiences, he is considered a grade 5; if only one or two, a grade 4 to 5; and if none, a grade 4.

Posture of Trust. In an interpersonal situation, the grade 5 patients exude an intense beguilingly innocent expectation of support from others in a somewhat atavistic, prelinguistic mode. This incredibly demanding faith can well be described as a posture of trust, in that the faith or trust goes beyond reasonable limits to become postured and demanding. They demand that all attention and concern be focused upon them. This demand is often so tenacious as to feed any latent grandiosity a therapist may have. The therapist must therefore know where he ends and where the subject begins in order to avoid entrapment. Undoubtedly, this is the patient Bernheim (1889) had in mind when he admonished his students that it is a wise hypnotist who realizes who is hypnotizing whom.

In conjunction with the feeling of trust, the grade 5 patients have an enduring feeling of hope combined with a lack of cynicism. Whatever the difficulties of their therapy, they retain faith, hope, trust, and the conviction that therapy is "good" for them; that the therapist has real concern for their well-being.

Suspension of Critical Judgment. A third predictable trait of grade 5 patients is a willingness to replace old premises and beliefs with new ones, if necessary, and without the usual cognitive review of the Apollonian. During the trance experience an apparent suspension of the usual level of critical judgment is consistent with the posture of trust. Tenacious clinging to the past is absent.

This receptivity is an asset in applying a treatment strategy. It is postulated that all of us live with a more or less organized (conscious and unconscious) premise system—a combination of assumptions, beliefs, convictions, myths, biases, prejudices, and knowledge, which forms the cloud through which we perceive our world—a myth–belief constellation, or possibly a metaphor–belief cluster, or simply a metaphor mix. We are able to cope with some aspects of these metaphors better than others. Grade 5 individuals especially are able to shift the components of their metaphor mix to reach new treatment goals.

As mentioned earlier, Ortega y Gasset maintains that "The metaphor is probably the most fertile power that man possesses." Since we use it, we may as well use it with more knowledge. If metaphors were ignored, our language would be largely ineffective (Marias 1970). If we as therapists avoid metaphors, we miss one of our best therapeutic devices (Spiegel and Shainess 1963).

Affiliation with New Events. The grade 5 has an incredible ability to affiliate with new events—either concrete events or perspectives—with an almost magnetic attraction to them.

Dorothy, a grade 5, said that even though she had overcome a major crisis in her life, she still remained a grade 5 (once a 5, always a 5); but she had learned the advantage of artfulness in using the associated traits. The sight of a friend crying would evoke tears before she even knew the cause of the sadness, such was her receptiveness to others. With therapy, she became aware of her empathic sensitivities and that she need not relate others' symptoms to herself. Her ability to affiliate led to receptiveness to treatment, especially when in the state of intense concentration called hypnosis.

Relatively Telescoped Sense of Time. Grade 5 time perspective is unusual. They seem to have a relatively telescoped time sense, focused almost exclusively in the present, rather than the past or the future. The paradox is that only grade 5 people can regress as they do. Typically, when a grade 5 person regresses to a first or fourth birthday, it is actually experienced in the present tense as a first or a fourth birthday. When anybody less hypnotizable similarly regresses, he may get some fragmentary experience, but he is always aware of the actual present time and that he is recalling an event of the past. Although a grade 5 patient's regression may uncover a spectacular and revealing memory, he does not relate the memory to present considerations or understanding. Layer upon layer of memory is available to him, but he keeps them dormant and does not apply them to current decision making.

Trance Logic. Such patients are strikingly unaware of even extreme logical incongruity. This is the phenomenon that Orne (1959) identified as trance logic. Although more or less evident in everybody, it is less subtle and even more dramatically observed in grade 5 patients. Those below grade 5 tend to relate to fragments of past memories in a judgmental way. Because they are prone to assay critically each new life experience as it unfolds, they usually retain a judgmental distillate of the event rather than the entire detailed sequence and its effects. They focus more on derivation than on affiliation; hence past time perspective remains intact.

In the incongruous world of today, it might be less jarring to all of us if we shared more of this feature which is so extreme in the grade 5 individual. For example, we were told by the military in Viet Nam that in order to secure a village we had to destroy it. We might be able to understand and accept without disturbance the Army logic of the statement if we were all Grade 5. For most of us, of course, it is very difficult to sufficiently immerse ourselves in the military premise system so that we can make peace with that kind of "logic," because it violates so many other premises.

On the other hand, trance logic can be comfortable, making it easy for the subject to produce and accept changes. A delightful example of this logic can be found in one of Sholem Aleichem's stories. Tevya, a milkman, listening to two friends arguing—one is taking the "a" position, and the other the opposite "b"—is called upon to decide who is right. Tevya listens to "a" and says "You're right." He then listens to "b" and says "You're right." A third man protests this judgment as impossibly illogical, and Tevya says "You're right, too."

Excellent Memory. A somewhat less discernible trait of the grade 5s is the possession of an excellent memory: their great capacity for total recall makes regression feasible to them. They are especially talented in rote and eidetic (visual) memory, and when highly motivated to learn something, they can do so almost the way a sponge absorbs water. This learning is uncritical; they take in everything. Critical judgment does occur later, calling upon the information already incorporated.

One example of this kind of memory was provided by a grade 5 student. He said that after seeing an anatomy diagram he could so vividly recall his visual experience that, when answering exam questions on the subject, he felt as though he was actually copying from the diagram. So strong was his memory that he sometimes found himself with a minor moral problem: Was he cheating?

Capacity for Concentration. Grade 5 people have an intense capacity for concentrating, and for dissociating while doing so. This ability caused Jackson Pollock to comment, "When I paint, I have no knowledge of what I am doing. Only after a moment of returning consciousness do I become aware of what I have been doing. Then, however, I have no hesitation about making changes or destroying images because the painting has a life of its own. My mission is to bring forth that life." This is an eloquent description of such involvement with the creative experience that only after it is over is one able to assess the creation objectively. It is almost as if the creation were on another plane from the creator.

A similar example comes from a New York playwright who learned this hypnotic method of concentration and visual imagination. He visualized a stage, and having decided for example to work upon Act 1, Scene 2, he entered a trance state. He placed three actors on his imaginary stage and in effect said to them: "Go ahead; I'll listen." After about five minutes he would bring himself out of the trance state and write down what "they" had said and done.

In the intense state of concentration that everyone experiences from time to time, there exists a more or less concomitant state of dissociation, which the grade 5s experience vividly. Many times painters or writers, and novelists especially, say of a finished work: "That character fascinates me. It's as if I didn't write him; he created himself, and I kept getting more and more amazed at what he was doing as we went along in the story." This intense concentration is what makes the creator able to be with his creation and alongside it at the same time; to relate to that concentration in a guided, disciplined, yet dissociated way. It is also the critical feature that characterizes the perceptual alteration common to all hypnosis: the observed motor phenomena are secondary to the perceptual shift.

Fixed Personality Core. Underneath this wonderful, malleable overlay is a narrow, hard, fixed core—a dynamism so fixed that it is subject to neither negotiation nor change. This core corresponds to "imprint learning" or perhaps a "foundation experience" (Spiegel 1965). It is a special kind of learning that occurs at critical times and remains relatively intact throughout the subsequent development of sophisticated, associative forms of learning. Aspects of this kind of learning can be found within all grade groups, but it is especially prominent and clinically significant in the grade 5 group.

It is expressed linguistically in a primitive, paleological mode. An amusing illustration in a sociological aspect was provided by a Haitian native. When asked what the distribution of the different religious beliefs in Haiti is, he replied without hesitation: "70 percent Catholics, 20 percent Protestants, and 95 percent Voodoo." In sum, this is an illustration of the hard-core nonnegotiability.

Another example of hard-core nonnegotiability was a 38-year-old woman with a psychogenic urinary retention. She was unable to initiate urination despite all forms of medical and surgical treatment. Her condition was discovered when her bladder became so distended that it kinked her ureters and she had to be catheterized. This woman was so profoundly hypnotizable that her score was virtually beyond a grade 5. Under hypnosis it was found that her perceptual alteration is so precise that when she was regressed to age four, she perceived the illusions of the Titchener Circle Illusion Test as any 4-year-old child would; that is, with the subtle perceptual accuracy that many very young children but few adults have. Despite her hypnotizability, repeated therapeutic counseling, and her ability to urinate when in formal trance and under firm hospital control, the patient refused to assert control over her bladder on her own. The apparent basis for this refusal lay in secondary gain factors. She was engaged in a complicated sibling rivalry situation.

The patient was married to a man whom she felt was inadequate. Her younger sister's husband was visibly successful and also prosperous. She discovered that her physical difficulty made it impossible for her to engage in sexual relations with her husband, a situation she apparently preferred. Moreover, the patient had learned how to catheterize herself with the intricate use of a mirror, and she was thus able to accommodate her bladder invalidism. A secondary "advantage" was gained by the extra caretaking and affection she received from her sister and brother-in-law. Rather than give up these secondary gains for bladder control, she stubbornly insisted upon maintaining her symptoms, however discomforting they were. For several months her family was unwilling to alter their behavior to reduce the secondary gains. Although her neurologist and urologist were both certain that her bladder control mechanisms were intact, the patient requested and was about to receive further surgical manipulation of the bladder sphincter. At that point, her entire family became enough alarmed to alter their prospective radically, thus removing all possible gains from her invalidism. She then re-established bladder control. What had been nonnegotiable in one setting became negotiable in another.

The problem seemed resolved for about six months because of relative discipline by the family and the patient. Then the family relaxed its guard and, surprisingly, the bladder symptom returned. Since that time the bladder has served as a fairly accurate indicator of the family–patient relationship.

Another such patient was the woman (T.J.) discussed in Chapter 18 with hysterical seizures. Once she perceived that these seizures could be induced and terminated by hypnotic signal, she insisted on retaining a certain cycle of response. She would predictably take about a minute to come out of the seizure after having been signalled to do so. This minute was gradually reduced, but she insisted on holding to a little hard-core refractory period.

These cases reveal that the surface malleability, flexibility, and ability to change that grade 5 patients possess can provide a remarkable area to work within therapeutically. However, totally resolving the hard-core dynamism is highly unlikely.

Role Confusion. The paradoxical relationship between hard-core dynamism and chameleon-like malleability, which is so sensitive to both supportive and antithetical field forces, can provoke role confusion and a reactive sense of inferiority. If the shifts and internal permutations of the metaphor occur too frequently because of environmental fluctuations, a profound and chronic sense of embarrassment may evolve along with inferiority. For example, even when the grade 5 individual performs so competently or creatively that he evokes praise from others, he is so dissociated from the performance that there is little recognition that he did it: "It just happened."

The medical student mentioned earlier who felt embarrassed and guilty about his ability to recall an anatomy diagram is a case in point. Because he felt that he had simply copied the diagram from his eidetic memory, it seemed to him that he had done nothing himself. Praise for his work by his professor merely increased his guilty sense of separation from the act—hence, his role confusion. This self-evaluation was

basically honest in a subtle way, because his affiliation with rote knowledge was not authentic knowledge. He appeared to know more than he
actually did.

Sluggishness in Reorientation to Internal Cues. These individuals are
often exquisitely responsive to external cues, but also painfully slow in
freeing themselves of external pressure and in applying their own principles or beliefs to adjusting to new situations. A healthier person's
plasticity and willingness to engage with other people in their own
environment becomes in these patients a pathological suspension of
their own critical judgment. This is rooted in the sense of inferiority
we described earlier and also in a sluggishness of their processes of
cognitive scrutiny. Many of these patients experience great difficulty in
applying what they know to what they do.

For example, Sally was a grade 5 with a diagnosis of "multiple personality syndrome." She found herself in a repetitive conflict with her
family regarding finances. They tended to rely on her to help out with
their unending financial difficulties more than was appropriate. Although Sally knew that the situation was unfair to her, she had im-
mense difficulty setting limits on her family's financial expectations of
her. She would leave therapy sessions determined to "stick to her guns"
and refuse the next request when the phone bill came due, but she
repeatedly gave in. It was as if, when external pressure was applied,
it took her a long period of time to bring her own internal scrutiny to
bear. By that time the money was gone and she would go through a
period of depression and self-recrimination.

Thus these individuals often become victims of their own profound
trance capacity. They form dependent and at times mutually destructive interpersonal relationships. They are naively trusting, self-dis-
paraging, and intermittently depressed as a consequence. Often they
actively seek situations in which another individual provides structure
which they feel they cannot provide for themselves. One such patient
described herself as "a disciple in search of a teacher." This search sets
the tone for treatment considerations in the intensive psychotherapy
of this group of patients.

Treatment Considerations

In our experience, the most effective form of intensive psychotherapy
for patients with the grade 5 "syndrome" largely involves guidance in
perceiving alternatives and in exercising choice. The therapist affiliates
with their willingness to comply and their comparative disinterest in
reason and explanation. He focuses instead of persuasion, using this
compliance in the service of defining and following reasonable goals.
These patients usually have to be pushed, especially at the beginning,

to think out appropriate long-term goals, since their tendency is to float along with whatever external pressures happen into their lives. Thus the therapist initially plays the part of Apollonian to the patient's Dionysian, with the hope that the patient will internalize some of this cognitive structure as the therapy progresses, or at least become more aware of and expert in using his own capacities for dissociation and compliance. The therapist attempts to thaw the patient's frozen pattern of compliance and to stimulate movement toward the mid-range (see Figure 5–5). This therapeutic change constitutes a centering process in which the patient acquires perspective on his extreme responsiveness and learns to modify it.

Central Versus Peripheral Values. Because of the grade 5 patient's proclivity for affiliating with new premises, without the critical scrutiny they would ordinarily apply when not in a state of high motivation and intense concentration, it is very useful to learn about their life values. The relevant areas of their knowledge can thus be explained to them, so that they recognize more clearly where their expertise and best critical judgment lie. In other words, they must understand clearly the difference between peripheral and basic decisions.

A colorful example of differential decision making is seen in the case of a brilliant research scientist, a man with an IQ exceeding 180 and a HIP of grade 4 to 5. He was an outstanding scientist, thoroughly conversant with the literature of his field. In addition, he was an expert at his hobby, the commodities market. This specialty was highly complicated and he was very successful at it. In these two fields he could not be misled. However, there was a catch: this man might go to a department store and let an enthusiastic salesperson convince him that what his family needed most was a new refrigerator and he would, without particular thought, order one. His wife was routinely left with the chore of returning such items. This illustrates the conflict in decision-making processes. Whatever cleverness and confidence grade 5 people have within their central areas of competence, in more peripheral areas they are likely to be guileless.

Another instance of this behavior was evidenced by an actor who made a good deal of money, if not as much as he liked to imagine. People would invariably "touch" him for money for various charities, and he readily wrote checks to comply. Admonitions from his financial advisors had little impact on him. Finally an answer was found: he agreed to have his business manager countersign all his checks. Then when people approached him for donations, he could still sign a check, but he also informed them: "Now you have to go to my manager," and he would shake the person's hand, adding, "and I wish you luck." Because the theater remained his central interest and his check writing was to him a peripheral issue, he had no interest or enthusiasm for learning how to internalize this discipline. Therefore his manager served as an external and surrogate disciplinary support.

In other words, for vulnerable people the best defense against exploitation is to offer as surrogate another person with better judgment than their own. This "re-enforcement" is apparently essential and is an important factor of the treatment program.

Protection from Negative Field Forces. Because they so urgently need direction, certainty, and faith, grade 5 individuals are likely to be receptive to all kinds of forces, even those antithetical to their best interests. They are uncritical and thus have difficulty in distinguishing between what is and is not good for them. The therapist must help the patient to distinguish and deal with conflicts between the two.

Secondary Gain and Loss. The critical factor of secondary gain and secondary loss is related therapeutically to the last item. Assuming a disability on the part of the patient, any resultant secondary gain must not go unchallenged; enormous damage may be done before the secondary loss manifests itself. The therapist must anticipate this secondary loss and prevent any potential dangers from being obscured by the secondary gain. He can then prepare the patient to avoid the secondary-gain syndrome before secondary loss develops. Timing of the therapeutic intrusion is critical.

An example of this secondary gain and loss situation follows. A 15-year-old boy injured his knee in a bicycle accident. Surgery was required. After three months his surgeon and physiotherapist agreed that full leg movement should have returned; nevertheless, partial paralysis remained in the leg. After a year the boy was still using a crutch, despite no physical damage. Use of the crutch interfered with some of his school work and his social life, and was of great concern to his parents. When the parents complained about the situation in the boy's presence, it became evident that the boy was enjoying their concern about the situation.

The boy was a grade 5, a trance state was induced, and during it he was very responsive. At this point, remembering Al Capone's observation that "You can get much further with kindness and a gun that you can with kindness alone," the therapist decided to confront the young man with some options. He told him that he was perfectly able to discard the crutch, and they both knew it. The parents, of course, knew nothing of this discourse and the therapist promised that he would not disclose it. He then offered the following choices: either the young man could walk out of the office without his crutch, or he could discard it within the next few days. However, if the boy was still using it when the father called the following Tuesday, the therapist would tell the father that the paralysis was a posture and a fake.

When he emerged from the trance state, the boy claimed to have no memory of the experience. The therapist simply announced his conviction that the boy knew how to re-establish mastery over his leg and that the boy would look forward with great joy to discarding his crutch.

Two days later the boy's father asked the therapist whether it would be all right to honor his son's request to go to school without his crutch, providing that he be allowed to use it when he came home (if he felt it necessary). The therapist agreed with alacrity, and when the young man returned he announced that he did not need his crutch anymore. His happy parents congratulated him.

Here the trance mode was employed as a facade behind which the patient could salvage his self-respect and avoid total exposure and humiliation. In this case the secondary gain and loss factors were prominent, though not openly discussed. The boy needed a way to be honorably released from the situation he had created, which the therapy gave him. Thus the secondary gain from the extra attention he had been getting, having been superseded by the secondary loss, was no longer useful.

Action Compliance. Grade 5 people do not simply derive and formulate new abstractions; they require immediate action to retain their value. They also tend to look at a simple proposal as a demand, and to concretize it without appreciating its full metaphorical meaning to the point that they may mistakenly use a metaphor as a concrete command to perform. An example of this cited earlier is that of the young man who responded to his doctor's metaphorical admonition to leave home and go to Alaska by literally traveling there.

Supportive Guidance. The most useful therapy involves a great deal of guidance and direct support, with emphasis on guidelines to help the patient perceive the metaphor mix in his life. By clarifying the relative importance of his values, the patient's goals become clear. In other words, he learns what can and cannot be changed in his life, and the therapist is able to encourage the patient in his choice. He needs not only to recognize his options, but to develop the sense that he has the right to exercise them.

A humorous approach is sometimes invaluable: What better way to perceive the irony or the uncertainty of what one is doing? Often by laughing with (never at) the patient, it becomes possible to offer alternatives which otherwise would be inconceivable.

In the case of S.M., a woman whose treatment for a dog phobia was described earlier, the use of humor was important. The therapy began with one simple concept, presented with casual humor, that the fear of animals is natural and understandable. I (H.S.) admitted that I, too, was afraid of animals. She was startled by my confession and looked ready to leave the office, asking, "Then what am I doing here?" I pointed out that the fear of animals is a sensible fear; however, there is a substantial difference between being afraid of tame animals and being afraid of wild ones, and we laughed together. I also reminded her that when a dog sees a frightened person it senses the fright; a dog feels more secure in the presence of secure humans. This gave her the option, not previously realized, of offering a dog security and comfort rather than dwelling on her own anxieties. She left the office muttering to herself, "Dog, friend; dog, friend." That single concept, presented with humor, was enough to help her overcome a lifelong fear.

Duress-Evoked Hysteria. Under duress, grades 4 to 5 may develop a syndrome that today is called hysteria. It is a transient, mixed state, often of frightening appearance—even mistakenly thought to be a psychosis. The duress and confusion may intensify to such an extent that they lead to hysterical psychosis. However, grade 4 and 5 people rarely become schizophrenic. When the treatment strategy alleviates stress, clarifies somatic metaphors, and accounts for secondary gain and loss, these patients usually go rapidly back to their previous states.

All too often such people are misdiagnosed and hospitalized as schizophrenics. It is not surprising to find people with high eye rolls and high intact profile scores in the back wards of many hospitals. Unfortunately, they have been conditioned by society and the hospital milieu to behave as though insane. This misdiagnosis has even been repeatedly reinforced in the field. Furthermore, the old-fashioned notion of hysterical phenomena as being limited to women is sheer nonsense: it occurs equally in men. The old theory that an aberration of the uterus is a necessary prerequisite to the illness explains the use of the Greek root *hyster*, meaning uterus. It has about as much relevance to the disease as *hypnos* does to hypnosis.

Differential Diagnosis. Another feature of grade 4 to 5 people is their dramatic surface malleability, which can falsely appear as a psychiatric syndrome, from relatively healthy to severely ill. Under situational stress they may simulate the critical characteristics of the various psychotic categories. Thus, differential diagnosis of the condition is crucial. It is like the role of syphilis in internal medicine; many internists believe that if a diagnostician can understand the differential diagnosis of its symptoms, with all their subtleties, he has mastered the field of diagnostic medicine.

The same situation prevails in psychiatry when dealing with the grade 5 syndrome and hysteria. An understanding of the chameleon-like quality of the grades 4 to 5 especially under duress, and the multiple forms of their hysteria, enables the clinician to differentiate with more precision the stressed grade 5 patients from authentic schizophrenics, psychopaths, character disorders, those with mental retardation and neurological deficits (Williams et al. 1978), and others who are likely to have decrement profiles. With this clarification, treatment choice can be more precise.

An illustration of this is a doctor who, after an unhappy experience with surgery, was carelessly given too much Demerol. He left the hospital a Demerol addict. At the time of his treatment he had been addicted for three years, and was vividly aware that if he did not overcome the habit he would be discovered. He thus was strongly motivated.

Examination revealed him to be a grade 4 to 5. Hard work enabled him to reorient his metaphor mix, learn more about the clinical assets and liabilities of a grade 5, and subsequently overcome his problem. The therapist and the patient freed themselves from the discouraging "addict" connotation; instead, the patient was seen as a grade 5 caught in a series of blunders. With appropriate therapy he extricated himself from the situation, and since then has been drug-free.

CONCLUSIONS

The high eye roll and the high-intact profile tend to be found in a trusting person who easily suspends his critical judgment, readily affiliates with new metaphors, emphasizes the present without too much concern for past and future perspectives, is comfortable with incongruities, has an excellent memory, is capable of intense concentration, and may have a hard-core stubbornness surrounded by a malleable overlay—which may provoke role confusion and a sense of inferiority.

Because of these traits, the treatment strategy delineates specific areas of competence and thereby clarifies peripheral areas where critical judgment is weaker. It arranges for external supports, increasing sensitivity to and protection from exploitative or antithetical field forces; brings out awareness of secondary gain and loss factors; clarifies patient's beliefs and metaphor mix with guidelines for acting upon them; and provides ample opportunity, especially in the supportive guidance atmosphere of the treatment situation, to perceive alternatives and to appreciate and exercise the patient's right to use those alternatives.

Under duress grade 5 patients can assume symptoms of hysteria and, under severe distress, hysterical psychosis, which may be misdiagnosed as schizophrenia. Because of the highly favorable therapeutic potential of this group, an accurate differential diagnosis is crucial.

Specifically, grade 5 individuals must be identified so that if they do come for help they can be offered appropriate therapy of the "what" rather than "why" variety, at least during the crisis period.

The reader may wonder at the absence of any reference to hypnosis in the treatment of these highly hypnotizable patients. In general, the problem is not of putting them into trance states, but of keeping them out of trance. They are victimized by their trance proneness, and if anything need to be taught how to be nonhypnotized rather than hypnotized. Thus, with the exception of occasional uses for anxiety control or abreaction, hypnosis has little place in the intensive psychotherapy of the highly hypnotizable patient. It is the identification of this profound hypnotic capacity which is critical to their therapy.

Epilogue

Review of the Main Themes

We consider the various concepts and labels in this book valid only to the extent that they are challenging and useful in the ongoing process of therapy and research. We view them as true not in any absolute sense, but only in an operational sense. It is in this spirit that throughout the book we have differed with certain traditional concepts of psychotherapy and hypnosis. We take an eclectic view of the psychotherapies, advocating only that the type of therapy should be selected with the needs and capacities of the patient in mind. Furthermore, we have demonstrated that the systematic assessment of hypnotizability with the Hypnotic Induction Profile can help the clinician in selecting the most appropriate psychotherapy. We have utilized the Hypnotic Induction Profile as a way of learning more about brain–mind interaction and of identifying configurations of response on the HIP which are useful to the clinical investigation.

We have employed several criteria in refining parts of our theoretical approach. Many of the constructs initially came into being because in some intuitive sense they seemed to fit, and they also seemed acceptable when presented to patients. This intuitive sense of appropriateness might be characterized as a Dionysian criterion. In the Apollonian sense, they fit with philosophical, anthropological, and psychological knowledge—especially existential philosophy, structuralism, and the more empirical statistical psychological approaches which we used to test the theory. The theory continues to be altered in the back-and-forth process of generation and clinical testing which continues.

A major portion of our empirical testing has been to determine whether or not the constructs are useful in the service of a therapeutic strategy. Our approach has been based on the principle of parsimony. We have tried to carry the minimal theoretical baggage necessary to achieve a therapeutic goal.

Hypnotizability as a Test

We have presented a description of the Hypnotic Induction Profile, a ten-minute clinical assessment procedure of hypnotizabiilty. (Reliability and validity data for the HIP will be found in the Appendix.) We believe that the HIP measures two factors: a biological data point—the eye-roll sign—and the reactive sensorimotor phenomena in their relationship to this biological sign. The eye-roll sign shows constancy over time and can be observed when the subject is not in the trance state. In this sense it is a measure of biological hypnotic potential. The reactive or performance items in the test measure the degree to which the biological capacity can be utilized to experience hypnosis. The profile, we believe, indicates the integrity or lack of integrity present in this biological, psychological reactivity area. By inference, it gives information about both mental health and personality style. For example, when the sensorimotor reactive components are consistent with the biological sign (the eye roll), this becomes a prediction of relative mental health. We have also presented evidence that when the reactive sensorimotor components collapse downward and do not fulfill the potential promised by the biological measurement, this indicates a break in the ribbon of concentration and is a strong clinical indication of biological or psychological dysfunction. In other words, the eye roll has a pivotal role in interpreting the presence or absence of hypnotic responsivity.

The Cluster Hypothesis

We have presented evidence to suggest that certain typical personality styles are associated with different levels of hypnotizability as measured by the Hypnotic Inducton Profile. For example, the high-hypnotizable Dionysians tend to be capable of such extreme absorption and inward concentration that they lose contact with their usual spatial orientation. Their time sense is primarily the present; past, present, and future are telescoped into "now." The major premises in their life (myth–belief constellation) tend to value affect rather than cold logic. They are relatively prone to accept control from others and to trust others, to suspend critical judgment as they affiliate with new information; and to have a rich imagination.

The low-hypnotizable Apollonians, on the other hand, tend to value "brain" over "heart." Even with intense concentration they do not relinquish their spatial awareness; and their time perception is primarily past or future, often to the extent of ignoring the present. They prefer to control others; are less prone to trust; constantly utilize critical judgment in the assimilation of new information; and are more likely to find satisfaction in implementing rather than generating new ideas. They value their sense of responsibility, and tend to stick to commitments once they make them.

The mid-range group, or Odysseans, have personality features that represent a mixture of the less extreme attributes of the Dionysians and Apollonians. They negotiate a middle way between the Scylla and Charybdis of life during their odyssey of living. Their spatial sense, time perception, and affective–cognitive balance tend to be mid-range. When learning new information, they accommodate with a balance between fixity and uncritical acceptance. This group also has a tendency to oscillate between action and inaction, which under stress conditions becomes action and despair.

Another promising evolution of this clinical test of hypnotizability is its correlation with current split-brain research and lateralization phenomena. For example, we have found that a dominant hand clasp and low eye roll are strongly associated with what is now described as left hemispheric functioning or what we call Apollonian attributes. Alternatively, a high eye roll and a nondominant hand clasp are, at least in right-handed subjects, associated with right hemispheric or what we call Dionysian themes.

Of more clinical importance are collapses of hypnotic performance on the HIP from the biological plateau, the eye roll, which indicate pathological conditions. The low-hypnotizability group tends under stress to evolve obsessive personality disorders, paranoid character disorders, and schizophrenia. Theoretically, those with high profiles under duress tend to exhibit the affective disorders; that is, hysterias, depressions, and manias. The mid-range group under stress tends to develop impulse disorders, borderline character disorders, and reactive depressions. We have demonstrated that a drop-off or decrement response on the HIP, in which the behavioral measure is at the zero level and the biological measure is at a higher level, is consistent with serious impairment of mental health along the lines of thought, character, and affective disorders. In this sense the HIP can be seen as a useful addition to the mental status examination, in that it may help confirm or refute a tentative diagnosis of serious emotional disorder.

Restructuring

All the individuals in those groups which are in the intact zone of hypnotizability on the HIP are likely to make good use of a brief symptom-oriented approach which emphasizes restructuring their view of themselves and their lives. Our overall approach to symptom-oriented treatment using hypnosis involves eliciting the maximum response from the patient with the minimal amount of time and effort necessary from the therapist. Most of our treatment strategies involve one or two visits with the therapist in which a brief history is taken, the problem area is defined, the Hypnotic Induction Profile is performed and evaluated, a decision is made to proceed with the symptom-oriented treatment, and the patient is taught a self-hypnotic exercise relevant to his problem.

All of the strategies are directed at making the best use of a given patient's hypnotic capacity and associated personality style in the service of a clearly defined therapeutic goal. This restructuring strategy is designed to invite rather than coerce the patient. It emphasizes commitment to a new way of relating to himself and his body, rather than submitting to a series of instructions given by the therapist. The patient is invited to clarify the choices he is making and to decide whether a reorientation is consistent with goals that are important to him, such as the respect for and protection of his body.

We have presented treatment strategies for such problems as smoking and obesity, anxiety, insomnia, phobias, pain, stuttering, asthma, and other functional and psychosomatic disorders. We have emphasized the fact that hypnosis per se is not treatment; but that, in the service of a good therapeutic strategy, hypnosis can be a useful facilitator.

We have outlined a therapeutic strategy that employs dialectical principles in helping a patient use his symptom as an occasion for reassessing and changing his relatedness to himself and his body. In particular, we have found that the most effective therapeutic strategies used in association with the trance state are those which help the patient to explore and develop a sense of relatedness to his body and to adopt a respectful and protective stance toward it. These therapeutic approaches avoid obsessional activity or denial about the nature of the problem, and they avoid putting the patient and the therapist in a position of fighting the symptom. Rather, they emphasize the idea that in the course of exploring the sense of dialectical relatedness to his body, the patient will naturally place the symptom in a new perspective and overcome it. The trance state—with its natural sense of dissociation and comfortable sense of floating relatedness to one's body—provides an added leverage in making this concept physically as well as psychologically real to the patient.

The element of surprise is also important. A patient often comes to someone who uses hypnosis expecting to be controlled and manipulated.

It is this very occasion that can be turned around to demonstrate to the patient how easily he can enhance and expand his own sense of control of himself and his body. The clarification of this misconception about hypnosis can be employed to enhance a patient's own sense of mastery.

Uses of the HIP in Personal Exploration

We have also presented evidence that the choice of appropriate treatment strategy can be facilitated by information gained from the Hypnotic Induction Profile. For example, patients with intact profiles have an intact capacity for mobilizing their resources and for committing themselves to change. Thus appropriate psychotherapeutic intervention is of primary importance.

If intensive psychotherapy rather than brief symptom-oriented treatment is indicated, the Apollonians have a style which makes them most likely to accept and benefit from the various introspective, analytically oriented psychotherapies. The mid-range group prefers somewhat less emphasis upon analysis as such and responds better to consolation and confrontation from the therapist in the Gestalt or existential mode. The Dionysians eschew "why" therapy and prefer "what" therapy. They want firm guidelines to enhance their capacity to generate their own decisions and directions. If arbitrarily pressed into self-investigation, they can even become confused and the therapy is converted into an exercise in compliance rather than an unearthing of insight.

Once appropriate goals for the treatment are established, the Dionysians prefer to affiliate with the therapeutic model and can readily accept guidance to enhance internal discipline. In summary, low-hypnotizable patients do best with a therapeutic strategy which employs reason to free and mobilize affect; high-hypnotizable patients do best with a therapy which employs affective relatedness to the therapist in the service of enhancing rational control. Those in the mid-range respond to an approach which employs a balance of rational and affective factors in helping the patient confront and put in perspective his own tendency to oscillate between periods of activity and despair. Ultimately, with all three modes, the treatment can culminate with a puzzle that the patient can identify with and respond to with a restructured sense of mastery.

However, the type of treatment for the nonintact, soft, and decrement groups is chosen at a different level. Such individuals do not easily maintain a disciplined response of concentration when tested, and they are less likely to accept psychological or emotional commitments to a treatment goal. Therefore, the various external treatment modalities such as drugs, electroshock therapy, family, social, or institutional containment; or direct supportive care are more relevant for this group.

We hope to have demonstrated that the systematic clinical assessment of hypnotizability can provide a great deal of information about a patient in a brief period of time. It can also indicate the most appropriately and aesthetically attractive style of therapeutic intervention for a given patient.

Implications for the Future

The emergence of modern psychotherapy has been characterized by the development of many modes of therapy and many divisions among the various schools so that the adherents of one are often unaware of the value of others. Because of the ambiguity which is necessarily inherent in this entire field of psychotherapy, it is understandable that therapists are in a constant quest for a sense of certainty. Sometimes the urgent need for certainty leads to a premature closure, and an overcommitment to the premises and specific contents of a given treatment mode.

A new way of developing a sense of certainty is the use of a disciplined probe to facilitate a clinical evaluation in a relatively short time. Such a diagnostic probe can elucidate data about the personality style, the nature of the problem, and the type of therapy most appropriate for a person at a given time. This approach promotes a wider appreciation of all the therapeutic modes, and it also provides both the patient and the therapist with opportunities for informed choice. The use of a clinical instrument (HIP) which is subject to reliability and validity studies adds a new dimension to the art of clinical assessment. The HIP hopefully will lead the way toward a more scientifically disciplined approach to clinical evaluation.

Studies are continuing and even expanding into the disciplined psychosomatic research areas involving the interface between neurophysiology and psychological phenomena. The HIP promises to serve as a bridge between laboratory observations and rich and diverse clinical data. These broad fields have remained isolated from each other too long.

The categories that we have presented are meant to be operational hypotheses for generating new hypotheses on the basis of accumulated data. They are in no way meant to be absolute. The purpose is not to reduce people to categories, but rather to use systematic information to enhance their capacity to make choices. As noted in the preface, "if you can measure it, it is science, everything else is poetry." Yet, assessment techniques have limitations. In the therapeutic odyssey, the clinician is best guided by both the science of Apollo and the poetry of Dionysos.

Hypnosis is a fertile phenomenon for exploration by both the researcher and the clinician. It is a style of concentration, not a therapy; a capacity, not just a mystery. When the therapist employs trance and treatment, he is making maximum use of his patient's hypnotic capacity and motivation for change.

APPENDIX

Interpretation and Standardization of the Hypnotic Induction Profile

A Two-Factor Theory of Clinical Hypnotizability

There are hypotheses associated with most profile configurations. In general, intact profiles indicate that the biologically based hypnotic potential, represented by positive ER score, has been expressed (i.e., CD and Lev scores are nonzero). It is thought that this constitutes evidence of clinical hypnotizability. The special intact profile may indicate particularly strong motivation to benefit from or to experience hypnosis. Among the nonintact patterns, the potential suggested by the positive ER scores is not expressed, suggesting little or no hypnotizability. The zero profile indicates an absence of biologically based, hypnotic potential. (ER is scored zero.)

These hypotheses are set in the context of a two-factor theory of clinical hypnotizability (Spiegel et al. 1976), which was developed to account for some of the findings to be reviewed here. It is hypothesized that the two factors are measured by ER and the induction score. The eye-roll sign is thought to be a measure of potential hypnotic

This section is reproduced from a draft of the following paper: Stern, D., Spiegel H., and Nee, J. In press. The Hypnotic Induction Profile: Normative Observations, Reliability and Validity. Am. J. Clin. Hypn. The research summarized here as well as the writing of this paper were supported in part by the Charles E. Merrill Trust and the Merlin Foundation.

capacity. This potential is conceived of as biologically based, and probably inborn. The induction score indicates whether or not potential hypnotic capacity can be expressed.

The profile configuration is a method of representing the *type* of relationship between potential hypnotic capacity and its expression. Several combinations are possible:

1. No potential, no expression of potential (regular zero profile)
2. Some potential, little or no expression of potential (soft and decrement profiles)
3. Some potential, some expression of potential (regular and special intact profiles)

The factors which determine when hypnotic potential is not expressed as usable hypnotizability are related to impairments in concentration such as those in severe psychopathology. Thus a disproportionate number of patients who score the soft and decrement profiles are characterized by relatively severe psychological disturbance. This clinical observation was evaluated by an investigation (Spiegel, Stern, and Lipman 1977) summarized in the section on the validity of the HIP as a test for severity of psychopathology.

A second inference made from the HIP score is whether the patient can benefit from psychotherapy in which hypnosis plays a significant part. According to the two-factor theory, clinically usable hypnotizability should be present only when there is evidence of both hypnotic potential and its expression. Hypnotic potential without hypnotizability (soft and decrement profiles) should predict poor clinical outcome when psychotherapy includes hypnotic strategies. A zero score on the measure of potential (zero profile) should predict poor outcome no matter how the patient scores on the measure of usable capacity. Both the nonintact and zero profile types should predict poorer treatment response than the intact profile (i.e., profiles showing evidence of potential and capacity). These hypotheses also will be examined here in the light of preliminary data.

Note that the theory (as well as the validity of ER) hinges on the zero profile; although no restriction says that the induction scores of those earning zero profiles cannot be high, they should not respond to treatment as well as intacts, because of the zero ER. And although zero-profile types can and often do fail the CD and Lev items (like the soft and decrement types), the zero profile should have less value in the identification of severe psychopathology than the nonintact profiles, again because of the zero ER.

Clinicians having prior experience with the HIP will notice some changes in the categories of the profile configuration and in the way the configuration is conceptualized as a nominal scale, versus its prior presentation as an ordinal scale. However, all data presented in this Appendix were derived by applying the scoring criteria exactly as we describe here and in the HIP manual (Spiegel, in press). Earlier normative observations and statistical evaluations of reliability of the profile pattern (Spiegel et al. 1976) are no longer applicable and should be replaced by those to be described here. The earlier standardization data on the induction score and ER (Spiegel et al. 1976) may still be used.

Normative Observations

All data in this section are based on the HIP scores of 4,621 private psychiatric patients seen and tested by H. Spiegel between 1969 and 1976. Approximately 500 of the patients seen in 1969 and 1970 received the items of the profile scale but were not administered one of the induction scale items, "Float," which had yet to be devised. Other than these 500 patients, who are not included, the normative sample is a consecutive series.

Four demographic variables were included in the early data analyses: sex, age, educational level, and marital status. The only effect (or interaction) for marital status was a mild depressing effect on the scores of widowed persons, who made up a very small proportion of the sample. It was decided that the small clinical gain that might be involved in presenting these data was not worth the complication.

It was soon clear that age was by far the most important of the three remaining demographic variables. However, because there were some smaller significant effects for educational level, sex, and some of the two-way interactions between the three factors, these data are also presented.

Evaluation of interactions required analyses of measures of central tendency; therefore, the data had to be presented in that form. But we also wanted to present the distributions of the HIP scores in a more direct way. The solution we arrived at was to present the data both ways, and to present the distribution of scores by age level.

The combined frequency distributions of age, sex, and educational level in the normative clinical sample appear in Table A–1. The sample is obviously heterogeneous, underlining the need for norms specific to subject characteristics. The immediately apparent aspects of the sample are its heavy concentration of patients in young to middle age (74 percent were between 25 and 54 years old), the high proportion of women (56 percent), and the very high educational level (74 percent had at least some college). Males had a higher educational level than females but, contrary to most large samples, males were slightly older than females.

Most of the patients (60 percent) sought treatment for cigarette smoking. Of the others, a common complaint was of being overweight. The rest came for a consultation regarding any one of the wide range of problems seen in the practice of a private psychotherapist.

TABLE A-1

Distribution of the Normative Clinical Sample by Age, Sex, and Educational Level.

| Age in Years | Highest Educational Level Attained | | | | | Total | Percent of Female Sample |
	Elementary School	Secondary School	Some College	College Degree	Graduate Training		
FEMALES							
Under 25	5	66	91	50	27	239	9.2
25-34	6	137	197	214	154	708	27.3
35-44	4	162	168	172	133	639	24.6
45-54	4	195	173	113	87	572	22.0
55-64	10	128	83	54	40	315	12.1
Over 64	9	44	38	28	4	123	4.8
Total	38	732	750	631	445	2,596	
Percent of female sample	1.5	28.2	28.8	24.3	17.1	—	100.0
MALES							Percent of Male Sample
Under 25	3	51	62	33	22	171	8.4
25-34	5	51	81	121	171	429	21.2
35-44	5	83	96	159	200	543	26.8
45-54	12	125	76	173	145	531	26.2
55-64	13	72	51	65	55	256	12.7
Over 64	6	21	19	16	33	95	4.7
Total	44	403	385	567	626	2,025	
Percent of male sample	2.2	19.9	19.1	27.9	30.9	—	100.0

The HIP was always administered in the first treatment session, and most patients were seen only once. The reason for collecting this information was to facilitate the treatment (or referral) process. The idea of conducting quantitative research was conceived later; thus, the standardization studies, as well as the other investigations to be summarized here, were retrospective in design.

EYE-ROLL SIGN

Table A–2 shows the distribution of ER by age. By reading across the stepwise changes in each row of the table, it is clear how large an effect age has on ER. For instance, the frequency of ER = zero increases from 1.5 percent in the youngest group (less than 25 years) to 16.5 percent in the oldest group (over 64 years). There was no one in the oldest group who scored an ER of 4.0, although 6.1 percent of the youngest group performed in this range. (Approximately 10 percent of the total sample had a positive squint score. The squint scores are not presented separately, but are incorporated in the scores for ER.)

The clinical use of these findings depends upon how they are viewed.

TABLE A-2

Normative Observations for the Eye-Roll Sign:
the Effects of Age on the Distribution of Scores. *

Score on Eye-Roll Sign	Percent of Age Group					
	Less Than 25 Years	25-34 Years	35-44 Years	45-54 Years	55-64 Years	Over 64 Years
0	1.5	1.1	1.9	4.1	4.8	16.5
1.0	5.4	8.7	9.2	11.8	23.1	23.0
1.5	9.5	10.4	12.2	14.0	15.0	21.6
2.0	23.7	26.7	28.8	31.0	28.2	22.9
2.5	20.8	22.9	20.4	19.1	16.4	10.1
3.0	22.7	19.0	17.6	13.9	10.9	5.0
3.5	10.3	7.1	6.2	3.8	1.1	0.9
4.0	6.1	4.1	3.6	2.3	0.7	0.0
Total	100.0	100.0	100.0	100.0	100.0	100.0

*N = 4,621. If desired, the raw data can be retrieved by multiplying the entry in this table by the appropriate marginal frequencies in Table A-1.

The most parsimonious interpretation is that the decline in ER represents a decrease with age in the flexibility and strength of the extraocular muscles. The less simple explanation—that a decline in ER reflects a decline in the hypnotic potential that this measure is said to represent—should not be favored unless there is some reason to reject the former hypothesis.

If the simpler way of understanding this finding is tentatively accepted, then the meaning of the ER score varies according to age. Very roughly speaking, the low and high ranges of ER can be defined as follows: At 44 years old or younger, a low ER score is 1.5 or less and a high score is 3.5 or 4.0. At 45 to 54 years old, the low range is 1.0 or less and the high range includes some people who score 3.0. At age 55 to 64, zero is the only score which can with certainty be included in the low range, and the high range includes people who score 3.0. Over 64 years, the high range drops even further to include some people scoring 2.5, with the low range restricted to zero. These remarks are only guidelines, since the data cannot be broken down in a way that assigns an equal proportion of each age group to the low and high range. Spiegel (1974, 1977a) has suggested that the range of ER is related to certain broad personality styles which the clinician needs to identify in order to provide the most appropriate treatment strategy.

Table A-3 shows expected mean ER scores for groups formed on the basis of age, sex, and educational level. The entries on the table were computed according to the following equation, which resulted from a multiple regression analysis performed on the ER scores:

Mean expected ER score = 2.791 − .242 (Age) + .046 (sex) + .037 (age × sex) − .050 (education) + .020 (education × age) + .023 (education × sex).

TABLE A-3

Normative Observations for the Eye-Roll Sign:
The Effects of Age, Sex, and Educational Level on Mean Expected Score. *

Educational Level	Sex	Age in Years					
		Less than 25	25-34	35-44	45-54	55-64	Over 64
Elementary school	M	2.6	2.4	2.2	2.0	1.8	1.6
	F	2.5	2.3	2.1	1.8	1.6	1.3
Secondary school	M	2.6	2.4	2.3	2.1	1.9	1.7
	F	2.5	2.3	2.1	1.9	1.6	1.4
Some college	M	2.6	2.5	2.4	2.1	2.0	1.8
	F	2.5	2.3	2.1	1.9	1.7	1.5
College degree	M	2.6	2.5	2.3	2.2	2.0	1.9
	F	2.5	2.3	2.1	1.9	1.7	1.6
Graduate training	M	2.6	2.5	2.4	2.2	2.1	1.9
	F	2.4	2.3	2.1	2.0	1.8	1.6

*Entries in this table are derived by computation from a regression equation (see text). Standard error of estimate = .804. $N = 4,621$. For cell n, see Table A-1.

In this equation, and in other equations presented here, age, sex, and educational level are entered as:

Age in Years	Sex	Educational Level
less than 25 = 1	Female = 0	Elementary school = 0
25-34 = 2	Male = 1	Secondary school = 1
35-44 = 3		Some college = 2
45-54 = 4		College graduate = 3
55-64 = 5		Graduate or professional
more than 64 = 6		training = 4

Thus the following equation would be calculated for a 48-year-old woman with a college degree:

Mean expected ER score = $2.791 - .242 \, (4 = \text{age}) + .046 \, (0 = \text{sex}) + .037 \, [(4) \times (0)] - .050 \, (3 = \text{education}) + .020 \, [(3) \times (4)] + .023 \, [(3) \times (0)] = 1.92$

All the main factors and interactions in the equation reached accepted levels of statistical significance. The nonlinear effects of age and education were also examined. Although the nonlinear effects of these two variables were statistically significant, they contributed very little of the variation of ER score. Therefore they were not included in the final regression equation. The regression analysis can be interpreted in the following way. As stated above, the strongest effect is age. Beyond that, male ER scores were .2 higher than females, even with age controlled.

However, this effect was due largely to the age × sex interaction. Ignoring the effect of education, at age = 1 (less than 25 years) the male–female difference was .14; whereas at age 2, 3 . . . 6, the differences were, respectively, .18, .23, .27, .31, and .36. In other words, the deterioration of ER due to age was faster among women than men. Presently we can offer no satisfactory interpretation of this effect.

Surprisingly, educational level had some effect on ER. The group with the highest level of education was .11 higher than the group with the least education. Although statistically significant, this effect was weak in comparison to the education × age interaction. The interesting finding here was that ER deterioration due to the age effect was halved among people with graduate or professional level education. These data suggest that highly educated subjects age more slowly than subjects with less education.

INDUCTION SCORE

The induction score, an actuarial index, was constructed on the basis of the intercorrelations and factor analysis of the HIP items presented by Spiegel et al. (1976) and reproduced here as Table A–4. To the surprise of the investigators who carried out the analysis, hypnotizability as measured by the HIP was not a unifactorial dimension. This finding led to the establishment of the two HIP scores and to the development of the two-factor theory of clinical hypnotizability. It was factor B in Table A–4 which suggested that the induction score might

TABLE A-4

Correlations Between Ten Components of the Hypnotic Induction Profile, and Rotated Factor Analyses (N = 1,674).

		1	2	3	4	5	6	7	8	9	10
Correlations											
1.	Up Gaze	—									
2.	Eye Roll	.77	—								
3.	Preparatory Arm Levitation	.37	.37	—							
4.	Tingle	.03	.05	.11	—						
5.	Dissociation	.09	.12	.21	.27	—					
6.	Signaled Levitation	.17	.21	.40	.20	.43	—				
7.	Control Differential	.06	.11	.28	.22	.58	.59	—			
8.	Cut-Off	.10	.10	.21	.20	.48	.42	.70	—		
9.	Amnesia	−.05	−.05	−.02	.02	.03	−.05	.02	−.01	—	
10.	Float	.14	.16	.27	.20	.46	.48	.57	.43	.07	—
Factor Loadings											
	Factor A	.90	.92	.54	.00	.05	.22	.03	.03	−.12	.13
	Factor B	.03	.08	.31	.40	.76	.70	.88	.77	.12	.73

TABLE A-5

Normative Observations for the HIP Induction Score:
The Effect of Age on the Distribution of Scores. *

Induction Score	Percent of Age Group					
	Less Than 25 Years	25-34 Years	35-44 Years	45-54 Years	55-64 Years	Over 64 Years
0	3.4	2.8	4.2	6.5	9.3	17.4
.25-1	1.2	2.0	3.9	4.1	6.2	8.3
1.25-2	1.7	2.4	3.4	3.6	4.6	7.8
2.25-3	2.4	2.3	2.5	3.3	3.5	4.1
3.25-4	2.6	2.8	3.1	2.7	3.5	2.3
4.25-5	2.7	5.7	6.8	6.6	6.7	6.4
5.25-6	6.9	9.3	9.9	13.2	12.5	14.7
6.25-7	14.2	17.7	16.0	16.2	16.2	15.6
7.25-8	27.4	26.1	25.8	22.7	20.2	14.7
8.25-9	24.7	20.2	18.0	16.4	13.8	7.3
9.25-10	12.7	8.6	6.4	4.7	3.5	1.4
Total	100.0	100.0	100.0	100.0	100.0	100.0

*N = 4,621. If desired, the raw data can be retrieved by multiplying the entry in this table by the appropriate marginal frequencies in Table A-1.

be a useful and feasible way to organize the data. (The sample in this analysis consisted of the 1,674 consecutive patients who had been administered all induction items at the time of the earlier paper.)

The individual items of the induction score are all "easy." Except for the Lev item, which was passed (score greater than zero) by 73 percent of the sample, the induction items were passed by 83 to 85 percent of the sample. Failing an item was thus more informative than passing it. The absence of semi-difficult and challenging items made it likely that the induction score would not be highly sensitive to small differences within the range of hypnotizability.

Table A–5 shows that the effect of age on the frequency distribution of the induction score is quite similar to the effect of age on the distribution of ER (Table A–2). For instance, scores of zero increased from 3.4 percent of the youngest group to 17.4 percent of the oldest group, and scores above 9.0 declined from 12.7 percent of the youngest group to 1.4 percent of the oldest group. Here, though, the interpretation is not so muddied by nonhypnotic considerations. Clearly, the finding should be viewed as an indication that hypnotizability declines with age. It is a constant decline, particularly steep in later years, but observable in each decade of adult life. This finding closely parallels results of several recent investigations (Berg and Melin 1975; Morgan and Hilgard 1973; Gordon 1972), all of which employed the Stanford Hypnotic Susceptibility Scale (Weitzenhoffer and Hilgard 1959).

Table A–6 presents the expected mean induction scores for all combinations of age, sex, and educational level. These figures again were

TABLE A-6

Normative Observations for the HIP Induction Score:
The Effects of Age, Sex, and Educational Level on Mean Expected Score. *

Educational Level	Sex	Age in Years					
		Less than 25	25-34	35-44	45-54	55-64	Over 64
Elementary school	M	6.9	6.5	6.1	5.8	5.4	5.0
	F	6.9	6.4	5.9	5.4	4.9	4.5
Secondary school	M	7.1	6.7	6.3	5.9	5.5	5.1
	F	7.0	6.5	6.0	5.6	5.1	4.6
Some college	M	7.2	6.8	6.5	6.1	5.7	5.3
	F	7.2	6.7	6.2	5.7	5.3	4.8
College degree	M	7.4	7.0	6.6	6.2	5.9	5.5
	F	7.3	6.7	6.4	5.9	5.4	4.9
Graduate training	M	7.5	7.2	6.8	6.4	6.0	5.6
	F	7.5	6.9	6.5	6.0	5.6	5.1

*Entries in this table are derived by computation from a regression equation (see text). Standard error of estimate = 2.561. N = 4,621. For cell n, see Table A-1.

computed by an equation which was the result of a multiple regression analysis:

Mean expected induction score = 7.34 − .480 (age) − .060 (sex) + .098 (age × sex) + .160 (education)

As in the case of ER, each of the main factors and interactions in the equation reached statistical significance. The variables were entered into the equation according to the same code used in the regression analysis of the ER scores.

In general, the effects of age, sex, and education on the induction score followed the same pattern that was observed for ER. However, these effects were much smaller for the induction score than for ER. About 10 percent of the variance of ER was explained by these three variables and their interactions; but only 6 percent of the variance of the induction score could be accounted for in the same way. Age was the most important predictor; age alone explained 5 percent of the variance. Among females, the increase in age from one level to the next was associated with .5 decline of the induction score. Among the males, this effect was .4. Males generally had higher induction scores than females, but this effect was highly dependent on age. At age 1 (less than 25 years), the difference was .07. The differences increased with each age level to .18, .29, .40, .51, and .61. People with more education had higher induction scores. Each successive increase in educational level was associated with a .16 point increase in induction score. There was no apparent education × sex interaction, nor an education × age interaction.

PROFILE CONFIGURATION

Because the profile pattern is a nominal score, a regression analysis like that performed on the ER and induction scores could not be carried out. However, the effects of the demographic variables can be reviewed in tabular form. Again the age effect is very strong (Table A–7). From the youngest to the oldest age group, frequency of the two "zero" categories increases tenfold. This finding is to be expected on the basis of the declines with age for ER and induction scores already described. Age also has a large effect on the incidence of the decrement. The interpretation consistent with the two-factor theory is that hypnotic potential not only declines with advancing age, but more and more people cannot express the potential they do possess.

The frequency of the soft profile is not affected by age. The incidence of the special intact profile is constant up to age 64 and then suddenly drops. As a result of these findings, the regular intact profile decreases in frequency with age.

Only the age effect is presented in Table A–7. Sex has a much smaller effect, not large enough for clinical significance: women obtain a larger proportion of decrement patterns than men (15.4 percent versus 13.3 percent), a larger proportion of soft patterns (20.0 percent versus 16.7 percent), a larger proportion of regular zero profiles (2.2 percent versus 1.3 percent), and a larger proportion of special zero profiles (1.3 percent versus 0.9 percent). The frequency of three of these four categories increases with age (Table A–7), which means, because the males in our sample had a higher mean age than the females, that sex differences would probably be larger if age were controlled. This topic obviously deserves future investigation.

TABLE A-7

Normative Observations for the HIP Profile Configuration:
The Effects of Age on the Frequency of Each Profile Category.*

Profile Configuration	Percent of Age Group					
	Less Than 25 Years	25-34 Years	35-44 Years	45-54 Years	55-64 Years	Over 64 Years
Intact (regular)	68.3	64.6	62.9	56.4	52.1	42.2
Special intact	4.0	3.4	3.4	4.1	4.4	1.8
Soft	16.9	19.4	18.0	20.1	18.5	14.7
Decrement	9.5	11.4	13.9	15.5	19.9	24.3
Zero (regular)	.5	.4	1.0	2.6	2.5	11.9
Special zero	1.0	1.0	1.0	1.6	2.8	5.0
Total	100.0	100.0	100.0	100.0	100.0	100.0

*N = 4,621. If desired, the raw data can be retrieved by multiplying the entry in this table by the appropriate marginal frequencies in Table A-1.

Educational level does have a small effect on profile scores (more education is associated with a decline in the proportion of intact profiles), but this association is also dwarfed by the association between profile pattern and age. Furthermore, the educational level is severely contaminated by age: younger patients have had more years of schooling. The effects of these two variables could be extricated from one another in the regression equations, but not in the case of the profile configuration.

In practice, a subject's profile configuration should be compared to the age norms in Table A–7.

Reliability

EYE-ROLL SIGN

When two independent examiners scored the same patient's ER, the intraclass correlation coefficients representing the degree of relationship between the two sets of scores were .80 among a group of 53 psychiatric clinic outpatients (Spiegel and Haber 1976), and .73 among a group of 43 private psychiatric patients (Spiegel and DeBetz 1977). Wheeler et al. (1974) reported that the product–moment correlation between two sets of ER scores, each collected by a separate examiner, was .75. In a group of 75 private psychiatric office patients seen twice by one of the authors (H.S.) after intervening periods of a few months to three years, the correlation between first and second ER scores was .90. This represents excellent test–retest reliability.

INDUCTION SCORE

Among a group of 75 private psychiatric patients, level of test–retest reliability was reported to be .76 (Spiegel et al. 1976). Degree of inter-rater agreement for the induction score was calculated to be .75 for the group of 53 psychiatric clinic outpatients (Spiegel et al. 1976). These coefficients indicate adequate reliability for the induction score.

PROFILE SCORE

In an earlier paper (Spiegel et al. 1976), degree of reliability of the profile score was represented by a correlation coefficient. Unfortunately, the same simple strategy could not be followed here. Because the profile score is now considered a nominal scale, degree of agreement had to be determined separately for each of its categories. The statistic used for estimation of reliability was *kappa* (Fleiss 1971). *Kappa*, a statistic ranging from 0 to 1.0, indicates the degree of agreement (in two sets of nominal scores) which is above the degree of agreement expected by chance. It is directly comparable to the intraclass correlation coefficient which makes it possible, in the case of the present data, to estimate on the same scale the reliability of ER, induction score, and profile configuration.

Table A–8 presents test–retest results for 167 patients seen by H.S. in private psychiatric practice. They constituted a consecutive series of patients who were administered a second HIP. The intervening time period ranged from a few weeks to six years. Of the 99 patients who scored a regular intact profile the first time, 90 (91 percent) also obtained a regular intact profile on their second testing (*kappa* = .70). Ten of the 14 patients (71 percent) who first scored the special intact pattern obtained the same pattern on retest (*kappa* = .68). For the broader category of intact profiles, test–retest reliability was excellent: of 113 patients whose initial HIP fell in the intact range, 108 (or 96 percent) also scored an intact profile on the second examination.

The decrement pattern also showed acceptable stability over time (*kappa* = .63), but two-thirds of the patients who were initially "softs" scored a different pattern on retest (*kappa* = .34).

The trend was toward a regular intact profile on retest: 59 percent (99) of the sample scored a regular intact pattern on the initial testing, and 70 percent (117) scored a regular intact pattern on the second testing. This may have been a phenomenon of regression to the mean; that is, CD and Lev were so "easy" that subjects who failed them once tended to pass them on the second try. However, there is at least one reason to doubt the completeness of this interpretation. Despite its lower test–retest reliability, the data below indicate that the soft score predicts the same relatively poor response to treatment as does the decrement profile. (Both scores predict poorer therapeutic outcome than the intact profile.) This fact makes it seem worthwhile to retain the soft score and look for the source of its low stability in what it does

TABLE A-8

Test-Retest Reliability of the Six HIP Profile Configurations.

Profile Configuration Obtained on First Examination	Total	Profile Configuration Obtained on Second Examination					
		Intact (regular)	Special intact	Soft	Decrement	Zero (regular)	Special zero
Intact (regular)	99	90	5	3	0	0	1
Special intact	14	3	10	0	0	0	1
Soft	21	14	0	7	0	0	0
Decrement	29	9	0	6	14	0	0
Zero (regular)	1	0	0	0	0	1	0
Special zero	3	1	0	0	0	0	2
Total	167	117	15	16	14	1	4
Kappa		.70	.68	.34	.63	1.00	.57

measure, rather than viewing the instability as a sign that the score should be discarded.

Table A–9 presents data from the two studies of inter-rater reliability of the profile configuration. Study I (Spiegel et al. 1976) was performed in the outpatient department of the Payne Whitney Clinic, Cornell Medical School, by one of the authors (H.S.) and a colleague. The two testers administered the test independently and without knowledge of prior test findings. Order of the examiners was systematically varied; there was no evidence of an order effect. All these comments also apply to Study II, except that it was performed in a private psychiatric setting for clinical purposes, and the testers were H.S. and a second colleague. In Study I the colleague was male; in Study II the colleague was female. In Study I the intervening time between testing was only a matter of hours; in Study II the intervening period ranged from one day to several years.

Since the direction of the findings of the two studies was similar, they will be collapsed for the purpose of discussion. (The larger proportion of decrement profiles in Study I is to be expected. It represents the fact that the clinic sample was more severely disturbed than the sample drawn from private practice. The decrement pattern seems to predict the presence of severe psychopathology.) The results were that the regular intact category showed good reliability: 30/37, or 81 percent of the subjects who scored a regular intact pattern on the first examination also did so on the second (*kappa* = .65). Also as before, the general intact category showed a high degree of inter-tester agreement (35/40, or 88 percent). However, *kappa* was low (.32) for inter-rater reliability of the special intact pattern.

A relatively low proportion of initially soft profiles (7/15, or 47 percent) remained soft on the second tester's examination (*kappa* = .50). The decrement pattern showed a much higher degree of inter-rater agreement: 20/23 or 87 percent remained in the decrement category

TABLE A-9

Inter-rater Reliability of the Six HIP Profile Configurations: Two Studies. *

		Second Examiner					
First Examiner	Total	Intact (Regular)	Special Intact	Soft	Decrement	Zero (Regular)	Special Zero
Intact (Regular)	37	12 *18*	2 *0*	1 *0*	3 *1*	0 *0*	0 *0*
Special Intact	3	1 *1*	0 *1*	0 *0*	0 *0*	0 *0*	0 *0*
Soft	15	4 *3*	0 *0*	5 *2*	1 *0*	0 *0*	0 *0*
Decrement	23	1 *2*	0 *0*	3 *0*	14 *3*	0 *0*	0 *0*
Zero (Regular)	0	0 *0*	0 *0*	0 *0*	0 *0*	0 *0*	0 *0*
Special Zero		0 *0*	0 *0*	0 *0*	0 *0*	0 *0*	2 *0*
Total	80	42	3	11	22	0	2
Kappa		.65	.32	.50	.71	—	1.0

*Data from Study I are printed in roman type. Data from Study II are printed in italics.

on second testing (*kappa* = .71). By collapsing soft and decrement profiles to form the group of nonintact profile patterns, we found that 28/38 or 74 percent of patients who were nonintact on initial examination were also nonintact on second examination.

The reliability of neither the special zero nor the regular zero patterns could be evaluated on the basis of these data.

In summary, the regular intact profile and the intact profiles as a whole showed a high degree of test–retest and inter-tester reliability. The nonintact patterns had a much lower degree of reliability. Of the two nonintact patterns, the decrement pattern was the more stable. This finding coincides with the observation made by one of the writers (H.S.) that the decrement profile is earned by persons who show a definite "break in the ribbon of concentration," and the soft pattern is obtained by persons with less severe psychopathology, who present a kind of "wavering" back and forth across the boundary between intact and mildly impaired concentration.

Validity

VALIDITY AS A MEASURE OF CLINICALLY USABLE HYPNOTIZABILITY

Estimates of the degree of relationship between the HIP scores and scores on laboratory tests of hypnotizability will soon be available. It will simplify matters, of course, if the correlations are high enough to permit the conclusion that the HIP and these previously standardized measures are tests of the same phenomena. However, because the HIP purports to measure clinically usable hypnotizability, the clearest test of its validity is the degree of association between the scores and the outcome in psychotherapy in which hypnosis is employed.*

The usual problems in carrying out this kind of study include controlling for the content and length of therapy across groups and deciding on a suitable measure of outcome. These problems do not exist in the case of follow-up data on the single-session treatment of smoking, which is a standardized approach varying only slightly from patient to patient (Spiegel 1970a; 1970b).

° At publication time we received word of the results of one of the two investigations in which the HIP was correlated with laboratory measures. In this study (Crawford, Spiegel, D., & Hilgard, E. R., in preparation), the relationship between the two tests was characterized as "mild." The correlations between the Stanford Hypnotic Susceptibility Scale (SHSS), Forms A and C, and the HIP induction score were low and nonsignificant. None of the persons scoring in the low range of the induction score (0–6.0) though, scored in the highest range of SHSS (11–12). The mean SHSS A score was significantly lower among nonintacts than among intacts; the same difference was observed for SHSS C, though it did not reach the .05 level.

The Stanford study was conceived as a supplement to one undertaken earlier by Martin T. Orne and his colleagues and staff with the aid of Herbert Spiegel. In the "Pennsylvania study," the laboratory measures were administered prior to the HIP; in the "Stanford study," the HIP was administered first.

TABLE A-10

The HIP Profile Configuration and Clinical Outcome
(At 10 Days Post-Treatment) in the Single-Session Treatment of Smoking.

Profile Configuration	N	Clinical outcome by Self-report			
		% Successful (No Smoking)	% Unsuccessful (Still Smoking)	% No Response to Follow-up	% of Respondents Who report Success
Special intact	78	47.4	21.8	30.8	68.5
Regular intact	2,155	38.8	29.9	31.3	56.5
Soft	692	27.5	38.3	34.2	41.8
Decrement	542	22.1	41.9	36.0	34.5
Special zero	69	27.5	40.6	31.9	40.4
Regular zero	85	17.6	44.7	37.6	28.3

The earlier follow-up reports on this technique of treating smokers (Spiegel 1970a; 1970b) were concerned with a sample of about 600 patients. We currently are beginning the questionaire follow-up of a group of 3,600 smokers. At this point, information on the induction score is not available, but we do have preliminary data on the profile configuration (Table A–10).

The data in Table A–10 are limited to ten-day follow-up because at the next follow-up period (six months) profile types began to show so much difference in the "no response" column that differences in the positive and negative outcome columns could not be clearly interpreted. That is, the groups with the lowest success rates also had the lowest response rates, raising the possibility that profile types differed mainly in percentage of responders and not in percentage of successful outcomes. This pattern can be seen even in the ten-day data in Table A–10. At ten days, though, the between-group differences in rate of no-response were much smaller than the differences in success rates. Therefore, the data in Table A–10 are probably a reflection of real differences in the proportion of successful outcomes associated with various profile patterns.

Data for six-month, one-year, and two-year follow-up will be presented in the future. For the present purpose, we followed the conservative course of comparing the proportion of successful outcomes to the proportion of patients who responded. Since it is our impression from an unsystematic canvassing of nonresponders that most members of the group were unsuccessful, our method of analysis is counter-intuitive, minimizing what we think may be larger differences. However, adopting this method of analysis buttresses the validity of any of the predicted differences which are observed.

The following hypotheses regarding clinical hypnotizability and profile configuration are supported by the data in Table A–10. (All differences are based on responders only and were significant beyond the .01 level.)

1. The success rate of intacts (56.9 percent) was higher than that of non-intacts (38.7 percent), softs (41.8 percent), and decrements (34.5 percent).
2. The success rate of intacts was higher than that of zeros (35 percent).
3. The success rates of zeros and nonintacts, the two profile types hypothesized to indicate little or no hypnotizability, were both low and differed by only four percentage points.
4. The rate of success for the special intact profile (68.5 percent) was higher than that for the regular intact profile (56.5 percent), consistent with the notion that the special intact profile indicates strong motivation.

These findings support the validity of interpreting the intact profiles as evidence of positive clinical hypnotizability, and the nonintact and zero profiles as evidence of significantly less usable hypnotizability. Because a number of nonintacts and zeros responded favorably to treatment, we cannot conclude that these profile types predict an absence of clinical hypnotizability. However, if a clinician has a limited amount of time, the results suggest that the best short-term response is obtained from intacts, particularly from those relatively rare people who obtain the special intact pattern.

The soft profile showed such poor reliability (Tables A–8 and A–9) that in terms of measurement theory, it should be discarded. Such a recommendation would be based partly on the supposition that a score with such low reliability would also have little validity. Yet Table A–10 indicates that certain interpretations from the soft profile are valid. These seemingly discrepant findings might be integrated in the following way: the soft and decrement profiles require failure of the CD and/or Lev item. These items were, respectively, passed by 85 percent and 73 percent of the normative clinical sample. Failing one of these items even once during two testings is an unusual occurrence, and a significant indication of low hypnotizability.

The second possibility, which cannot be discounted by anything in the present data, is that the "validity" of the soft profile is an experimenter effect. That is, did patients respond to what may have been the tester's expectation that soft profiles indicate poor clinical response? Neither Spiegel nor those who have observed his work can determine any difference in his treatment of patients which might lead to differential outcomes, but this issue awaits more rigorous investigation (i.e., a therapist blind to HIP score). It may be noted here that differential therapist expectations are a potential contaminant of all the data reported in this section.

A second source of data concerning the validity of the HIP as a test of hypnotizability is follow-up information on a group of 97 patients who consulted H.S. between 1968 and 1974 for flying phobia. A paper on this data is in preparation but preliminary findings will be reported here. Fifty-two percent of the sample was female; 87 percent had attended at least some college; mean age was 40.5 years. The only criterion for inclusion in this study was that the patient had sought treatment employing hypnosis for fear of airplane travel. Follow-up data were collected by postcard. On the card, the patient was asked to answer: "At this time have you successfully mastered this problem?" The patient could check *Yes, No,* or *Partially.* Time intervening between treatment and last follow-up contact ranged from two to nine years. It was always the last follow-up information which was selected for use, although only 14 patients' reports changed over time, and of these, ten changed *Partial* to *Yes,* or vice versa. Only four changed from *Yes* or *Partial* to *No.* Treatment in all cases consisted of a single, standardized session.

The relationship between the profile configuration and clinical outcome for these patients is presented in Table A–11. The information is preserved in its original form since there is, of course, no way to be certain what each person exactly meant by *Yes, No,* or *Partially.* Nevertheless, making the assumption that *Yes* and *No* mean what they seem to mean, the data are a second source of support for the validity of inferences made about clinical hypnotizability from the profile configurations. (Because of the low N, the special and regular intacts were combined, the softs and decrements were combined, and the special and regular zeros were combined.)

Of all the intacts who responded, 37 percent (19) reported mastery of the phobia. The proportion of *Yes* answers among the nonintact responders was 23 percent (3) and among the zero responders, 25 percent (1). Though the direction of difference followed the prediction, the magnitude of difference between the intact and the nonintact success rates and between the intact and zero success rates was not statistically significant. If a *Partially* response is taken to mean that the patient derived some benefit from treatment, then the proportion of responders who felt helped by the contact (*Yes* responses plus *Partially* responses) was 61 percent (31) among the intacts, 31 percent (4) among the nonintacts, and 25 percent (1) among the zeros. Analyzing the data on this basis leads to a significant difference between the

TABLE A-11

HIP Profile Configuration and Clinical Outcome in the Single-Session Treatment of Flying Phobia.

Profile Configuration	"At this time, have you successfully mastered this problem?"				
	Yes	Partially	No	No response to Follow-up	Total
Intact (Regular and Special Types)	19	12	20	16	67
Nonintact (Soft and Decrement)	3	1	9	10	23
Zero (Regular and Special Types)	1	0	3	3	7
Total	23	13	32	29	97 = N

success rates of intacts and nonintacts ($x^2 = 3.8$, $df = 1$, $p < .05$). The number of zeros was too small to yield a significant difference between their rate of success and the rate of intacts, though the direction of difference was as predicted.*

Is there an advantage to retaining two HIP scores? Does the induction score add anything to the predictive accuracy of the profile configuration? In reference to the flying phobia data, the answer to this question seems to be "no." That is, among the intacts there was little difference between the mean induction scores of patients who responded *Yes* ($n = 15$, $\overline{X} = 7.79$), *Partially* ($n = 10$, $\overline{X} = 8.25$), and *No* ($n = 15$, $\overline{X} = 7.92$). (The number of patients with induction scores was slightly lower than the number with profile patterns because the induction score had not been devised in the early stages of this study.) In fact, all except four of the nonintacts and zeros had scores of 7.0 or below. With this much overlap, why not retain the induction score and jettison the more complicated profile pattern? The only reason not to take this step would be that the two types of profiles which seem to indicate low hypnotizability—nonintacts and zeros—are different according to some nonhypnotic criterion. According to the two-factor theory, the nonintact profile predicts the presence of relatively severe psychopathology, whereas the zero profile does not.

VALIDITY AS A MEASURE OF SEVERITY OF PSYCHOPATHOLOGY

On the basis of the clinical observation that patients with severe psychopathology seem to obtain low (o to 6) induction scores and nonintact profile patterns, it appears that the HIP can also be used to identify relatively disturbed patients. A preliminary study (Spiegel, Stern, and Lipman 1977) was undertaken to evaluate more formally the validity of this inference. Subjects in the study were 105 of 110 consecutive private psychiatric patients who had been administered both the HIP and a battery of psychological tests, including the Wechsler Adult Intelligence Scale and a number of projectives. (The other five patients did not have complete records.) The HIP and the psychodiagnostic examination were always part of the patients' treatment:

---

* At publication time, findings concerning the relationship of demographics, the profile pattern, and the clinical outcome of the treatment of flying phobia became available. Briefly, these findings are as follows: Patients with high education (graduate or professional school) and/or relatively high age (over 54 years) showed a higher incidence of positive treatment outcomes (20/35 or 57%) and a higher proportion of intact profiles (27/35, or 77%) than did patients with lower levels of age and education (16/62, or 26% positive outcomes: 40/62, or 64% intact profiles). These findings raised the possibility that the association depicted in Table A–11 between treatment outcome and the profile pattern could be equally well predicted by age and education.

However, among the group with high education and/or high age, the intact profile was still a much better predictor of reports of positive outcome (19/28, or 68%) than the nonintact and zero profiles (1/7 or 14%). Among the group with less education and lower age, there was a much smaller association between the profile pattern and treatment outcome (29%, or 12/42 reports of positive response from intacts; 18% or 4/22 reports of positive outcome from non-intacts and zeros).

Sex had no effect. Also note that the incidence of intact profiles rises with age in this sample, which is contrary to the normative data in Table A–7.

These findings will be explored, of course, in much more detail in the forthcoming paper, which will also present the standardized treatment method used for these patients. Finally, the rates of positive outcome reported here are based on the assumption that the *Yes* and *Partially* post card responses (see text) indicated that the patient felt some gain from treatment, and the total groups include those who were treated but did not return follow-up information.

neither the patient, the therapist, nor the examining psychologist were aware that the test results would be used for research purposes. The psychologist was also unaware of the patient's HIP scores.

The 105 patients were assigned to one of two groups on the basis of an independent psychiatrist's rating of the psychologists' test reports. The rater was also blind to HIP scores. The first group ($N = 56$) included patients whose psychopathology was rated as mild or moderate neurosis. The second group ($N = 49$) consisted of patients with psychopathology rated as more severe—severe neurosis, probable psychosis, and obvious psychosis. The groups performed on the HIP in the predicted ways, and all predicted differences reached statistical significance: the proportion of the intacts with severe psychopathology was 29 percent (20/69); the proportion among nonintacts was 81 percent (29/36). Low induction scores (0 to 6) were earned by only 16 percent (9) of the group with mild to moderate psychopathology, but comprised 49 percent (24) of the patients whose psychopathology was more severe. Of the 16 high induction scores (9.25 to 10.0), 15 (94 percent) belonged to subjects in the mild to moderate group.

These findings provide clear support for the validity of the HIP as a test of severity of psychopathology. It should be noted that, given the low test–retest reliability of the soft score (Table A–9), soft and decrement profiles were equally accurate in predicting degree of psychopathology.

There was also an opportunity in this study to evaluate the meaningfulness of ER. If it is specifically the contrast between positive ER and zero scores on other items which predicts the presence of severe psychopathology, then—for ER to be meaningful—profile patterns which are the same as nonintact ones in all ways except for zero ER should not show an association with severe psychopathology. This hypothesis was borne out: only 25 percent (2) of the patients selected for this second study were rated as showing evidence of severe psychopathology. The difference between this proportion and the 81 percent of nonintacts rated as showing relatively severe psychopathology reached statistical significance. Thus a zero score on CD and/or Lev predicts severe psychopathology only in the presence of positive ER. In conjunction with the rest of the HIP, the eye-roll sign appears to be useful in predicting the severity of psychopathology.

The following conclusions can be drawn from bringing together the evidence concerning the HIP as a test of hypnotizability and a test of severity of psychopathology. Inferences can be made from the profile pattern concerning both clinical outcome and the presence or absence of severe psychopathology. These inferences are valid in a probabalistic sense for groups, but not for individuals. Those familiar with statistical analysis of course know this, but it should be pointed out to other test users that the evidence for validity that we have presented does not necessarily mean that any one individual's nonintact profile pattern indicates the presence of severe psychopathology.

The fact that only one of the two types of low hypnotizability, the nonintact profile, predicts severe psychopathology suggests that the profile configuration, for all its complexity, should be retained. It offers something new to the field of hypnosis; that is, the capacity to differentiate two independent sources of low hypnotizability.

The little data available at this point do not indicate that the induction score adds to the predictive power of the profile pattern. However, the evidence is not strong enough to support a decision to discard it. The fact that it is an ordinal scale also makes the induction score amenable to parametric statistical analysis, a potential advantage to researchers. Therefore both the profile configuration and the induction score will be retained for the time being.

DISCUSSION

The reliability indices for the induction score, ER, and intact profile patterns are high enough to fall within most test users' limits of acceptability. Reliability of the zero profiles has not yet been adequately tested. Reliability of the decrement profile and particularly of the soft profile is probably not high enough, from a psychometric point of view, to merit their use. However, a mitigating circumstance is that these two profile patterns are valuable in identifying patients whose psychopathology can be characterized as relatively severe.

The profile configuration and the induction score are equally good predictors of clinical outcome in therapy in which hypnosis is used. The profile pattern offers the added advantage of identifying two types of low hypnotizability, one associated with relatively severe psychopathology, as just stated, and one associated with zero ER or, according to the hypothesis, low inborn potential for hypnosis. This finding is evidence that ER is meaningful in the assessment of hypnotizability.

The relationship between ER and usable hypnotizability is not direct —even the correlation between ER and the HIP induction score is low (Table A–4). Rather, it seems likely that the relationship between scores on tests of hypnotizability and clinical outcome is mediated by ER. This is at least the case for the HIP; positive CD and/or Lev scores are better predictors of positive outcome when ER is scored positive than when it is scored zero. This indirect relationship may be part of the reason for the negligible correlation recorded between ER and laboratory measures of hypnotizability (Eliseo 1974; Switras 1974; Wheeler et al. 1974). On the other hand, a high correlation between ER and laboratory tests is not to be expected. Spiegel (1972), in introducing ER, described it as a "clinical 'soft focus' observation." Given the data collected to date, that seems to have been an accurate way to put it.

The distinction between zero ER and nonzero ER appears to be most meaningful. However, we decided to test the possibility that the lack of correlations between ER and other measures might partly be due to not taking the indirectness of the relationship into account. This test could be accomplished by comparing the correlations between ER and induction score in groups with and without severe psychopathology. The correlation should be low or negligible among the "severe" group because people in this group seem to have difficulty in expressing whatever hypnotic potential they do have. That is, induction scores should be low no matter what the score is for ER. However, among the group without severe psychopathology, there should be less interference with expression of potential, and thus more relationship between ER and induction score. Of course, the finding that nonintact profiles are more common among people with severe psychopathology led us to expect that our hypothesis would be confirmed. What we did not know was what the magnitude of difference would be.

The result was a highly significant association ($r = .52$, $p < .001$) among the "healthy" group ($n = 56$) and a nonsignificant correlation ($r = .15$, $p > .10$) among the more disturbed group ($n = 49$). The difference between the correlations was significant ($z = 2.3$, $p < .05$). The two samples were the same ones described by Spiegel, Stern, and Lipman (1977).

The age effect observed in the normative data, consistent across all three HIP measures, is notable. What makes this consistency more intriguing is that these findings were wholly unexpected.

This Appendix presents the opportunity to gather in one place all standardization data currently available. It is fragmentary in some spots, a regrettable but unavoidable consequence of the fact that some of the most interesting studies are in process. In conclusion, the encouragement of future research should be underlined in red. Clinical investigation is notoriously difficult because patient care takes priority. Replication of the findings must come from the clinic but the institution of manipulative designs and control groups, design features we wish we could use but cannot, must come from the laboratory.*

* The authors would like to thank Barbara DeBetz, M.D. and Jerome Haber, M.D. for their contribution as examiners in the two test-retest studies of profile patterns. Others whose help in the collection of the data was invaluable are Laurie Lipman, Michelle Aronson, and Brian Maruffi.

REFERENCES

Abrams, S. 1964. The use of hypnotic techniques with psychotics: a critical review. *Amer. J .Psychother.* 18:79–94. Jun 64

Adler, A. 1927. *Understanding Human Nature.* New York: Greenberg.

Agras, W. S. 1972. Ed. Behavior Modification: *Principles and Clinical Applications.* Boston: Little Brown & Co.

Arieti, S. 1962. Psychotherapy of schizophrenia. *Arch. Gen. Psychiat.* 6: 112–122.

Arieti, S., and Chrzanowski, G., eds. 1975. *New Dimensions in Psychiatry.* Vol. I. New York: John Wiley and Sons.

——— and ———, eds. 1977. *New Dimensions in Psychiatry.* Vol. II. New York: John Wiley and Sons.

Aristotle. 1961. *Physics.* Trans. R. Hope. Lincoln, Nebraska: University of Nebraska Press.

Ås, A. 1962. Non-hypnotic experiences related to hypnotizability in male and female college students. *Scand. J. Psychol.* 3:47–64.

———, and Lauer, L. W. 1962. A factor-analytic study of hypnotizability and related personal experiences. *Int. J. Clin. and Exp. Hypn.* 10:169–181.

August, R. S. 1961. *Hypnosis in Obstetrics.* New York: McGraw-Hill.

Bakan, P. 1969. Hypnotizability, laterality of eye-movements and functional brain asymmetry. *Percept. Motor Skills* 28:927–932.

———, and Svorad, D. 1969. Resting EEG alpha and asymmetry of reflective lateral eye movement. *Nature* (London) 223:975–976.

———. 1970. Handedness and hypotizability. *Int. J. Clin. Exp. Hypn.* 18: 99–104.

Bandura, Albert, 1969. *Principles of Behavior Modification.* New York: Holt Rinehart & Winston.

Barber, T. X. 1956. A note on "hypnotizability" and personality traits. *Int. J. Clin. Exp. Hypn.* 4:109–114.

———, and Glass, L. B. 1962. Significant factors in hypnotic behavior. *J. Abnorm. Soc. Psychol.* 64:222–228.

———, and Calverley, D. S. 1964. Hypnotizability, suggestibility, and personality: two studies with the Edwards Personal Preference Schedule, the Jourard Self-Disclosure Scale, and the Marlowe-Crowne Social Desirability Scale. *J. Psychol.* 58:215–222.

———, Karacan I., and Calverley, D. S. 1964. "Hypnotizability" and suggestibility in chronic schizophrenics. *Arch. Gen. Psychiat.* 11:439–451.

Bateson, G. 1972. *Steps to an Ecology of Mind.* New York: Ballantine Books, Inc.

Beecher, H. K. 1956. Relationship of significance of wound to pain experiences. *JAMA* 161:1609–1613.

————. 1959. *Measurement of Subjective Responses: Quantitative Effects of Drugs*. New York: Oxford University Press.

Bender, L. 1946. *Visual Motor Gestalt*. New York: American Orthopsychiatric Association.

Benedict, R. 1934. *Patterns of Culture*. Boston: Houghton Mifflin Co.

Benson, H. 1975. *The Relaxation Response*. New York: William Morrow and Co.

Bentler, P. M. 1963. Interpersonal orientation in relation to hypnotic susceptibility. *J. Consult. Psychol.* 27:426–431.

Berg, S., and Melin, E. 1975. Hypnotic susceptibility in old age—some data from residential homes for old people. *Int. J. Clin. Exp. Hypn.* 23, 3:184–189.

Bergson, H. 1911. *Creative Evolution*. Trans. A. Mitchell. New York: Henry Holt and Co.

————, 1960. *Time and Free Will*. New York: Harper and Row.

Berkowitz, B. Ross-Townsend, A., and Kohberger, R. In press. Hypnotic treatment of smoking: the single treatment approach revisited. Am. J. Psychiat.

Bernheim, H. 1889. *Hypnosis and Suggestion in Psychotherapy: A Treatise on the Nature of Hypnotism*. Reprint. Trans. C. A. Herter, New Hyde Park, New York: University Books, 1964.

Binswanger, L. 1967. Dream and Existence. In *Being in the World*. Trans. J. Needleman. New York: Harper Torchbooks.

Bleuler, E. 1950. Trans. J. Zinkin. *Dementia Praecox or The Group of Schizophrenias*, Monograph Series on Schizophrenia No. 1. New York: International Universities Press.

Bowen, D. E. 1973. Transurethral resection under self-hypnosis. *Amer. J. Clin. Hypn.* 16:132–134.

Bowers, K. S. 1976. *Hypnosis for the Seriously Curious*. Belmont, California: Wadsworth Publishing Co.

Brady, J. P. 1971. Metronome-conditioned speech retraining for stuttering. *Behav. Ther.* 2:129–150.

Brenman, M., and Gill, M. M. 1947. *Hypnotherapy: A Survey of the Literature*. New York: International Universities Press.

Breuer, J., and Freud, S. 1893–95. *Studies on Hysteria*. Vol. II. Stand. ed., trans. J. Strachey and A. Freud. London: Hogarth Press, 1955.

Brodie, E. I. 1964. A hypnotherapeutic approach to obesity. *Amer. J. Clin. Hypn.* 6:211–215.

Brown, E. A. 1965. The treatment of asthma by means of hypnosis as viewed by the allergist. *J. Asthma. Res.* 3:101–119.

Bruch, H. 1973. *Eating Disorders: Obesity, Anorexia Nervosa and the Person Within*. New York: Basic Books.

Butler, B. 1954. The use of hypnosis in the care of the cancer patient. *Cancer* 7:1–14.

Campbell, P., and Mullen, G. 1975. The effects of hypnotic susceptibility on reducing smoking behavior treated by hypnotic technique. *J. Clin. Psychol.* 31:498–505.

Cangello, V. W. 1961. Hypnosis for the patient with cancer. *Amer. J. Clin. Hypn.* 4:215–226.

Caplan, G. 1964. *Principles of Preventive Psychiatry*. New York: Basic Books.

Chin, J. H., Pribram, K. H., Drake, K., and Greene, L. O., Jr. 1976. Disruption of temperature discrimination during limbic forebrain stimulation in monkeys. *Neuropsychologia* 14:293–310.

Collison, D. R. 1968. Hypnotherapy in the management of asthma. *Amer. J. Clin. Hypn.* 11:6–11.

———. 1975. Which asthmatic patients should be treated by hypnotherapy? *Med. J. Aust.* 1(25):776–781.

Copeland, M. D., and Kitching, E. H. 1937. Hypnosis in mental hospital practice. *J. Ment. Sci.* 83:316–329.

Crasilneck, H. D., McCranie, E. J., and Jenkins, M. T. 1956. Special indications for hypnosis as a method of anesthesia. *JAMA* 162:1606–1608.

———, and Hall, J. A. 1968. Use of hypnosis in controlling cigarette smoking. *J. South. Med. Assoc.* 61:999–1002.

———, and ———. 1975. *Clinical Hypnosis: Principles and Applications.* New York: Grune & Stratton, pp. 147–175.

Davis, L. W., and Husband, R. W. 1931. A study of hypnotic susceptibility in relation to personality traits. *J. Abnorm. Soc. Psychol.* 26:175–183.

Day, M. E. 1967. An eye-movement indicator of individual differences in the physiological organization of attentional processes and anxiety. *J. of Psychol.* 66:51–62.

Deckert, G. H., and West, L. J. 1963. The problem of hypnotizability: A review. *Int. J. Clin. Exp. Hypn.* 11:205–235.

Dement, W. C., and Fisher, C. 1963. Experimental interference with the sleep cycle. *Can. Psychiat. Assoc. J.* 8:400–405.

———, and Guilleminault, C. 1973. Sleep disorders: The state of the art. *Hosp. Practice,* 8:57–71.

Derman, D. and London, P. 1965. Correlates of hypnotic susceptibility. *J. of Consult. Psychol.* 29:537–545.

Dick Read, G. 1944. *Childbirth Without Fear.* New York: Harper.

Doyle, J. C., Ornstein, R., and Galin, D. 1974. Lateral specialization of cognitive mode: II. EEG frequency analysis. *Psychophysiology* 2:567–578.

Dubin, L. L., and Shapiro, S. S. 1974. Use of hypnosis to facilitate dental extraction and hemostasis in a classic hemophiliac with a high antibody titer to factor VIII. *Amer. J. Clin. Hypn.* 17:79–83.

Duke, J. D. 1968. Failure of inner/other directedness to correlate with waking indices of hypnotizability. *Psychol. Rep.* 23:270.

———. 1969. Relatedness and waking suggestibility. *Int. J. Clin. Exp. Hypn.* 17:242–250.

Eagan, R. M., and Egan, W. P. 1968. The effect of hypnosis on academic performance. *Am. J. Clin. Hypn.* 2:30–34.

Edgell, P. G. 1966. Psychiatric approach to the treatment of bronchial asthma. *Mod. Treat.* 3:900.

Edwards, G. 1960. Hypnotic treatment of asthma: Real and illusory result. *Brit. Med. J.* 2:492–497.

———, 1964. Hypnotic treatment of asthma. In *Experiments in Behavior Therapy,* ed. H. J. Eysenck. Oxford: Pergamon Press, pp. 407–431.

Eliseo, T. S. 1974. The Hypnotic Induction Profile and hypnotic susceptibility. *Int. J. Clin. and Exp. Hypn.* 22:320–326.

Ellenberger, H. F. 1970. *Discovery of the Unconscious: The History and Evolution of Dynamic Psychiatry.* New York: Basic Books, pp. 90–91.

Erickson, M. H. 1960. The utilization of patient behavior in the hypnotherapy of obesity: Three case reports. *Amer. J. Clin. Hypn.* 3:112–116.

———. 1967. *Advanced Techniques of Hypnosis and Therapy,* ed. J. Haley. New York: Grune & Stratton.

————, Rossi, E. L., and Rossi, R. 1976. *Hypnotic Realities: The Induction of Clinical Hypnosis and Forms of Indirect Suggestion*. New York: John Wiley and Sons.

Erlichman, H., Weiner, S. L., and Baker, A. H. 1974. Effects of verbal and spatial questions in initial gaze shifts. *Neuropsychologia* 12:265–277.

Esdaile, J. 1846. Reprint. *Hypnosis in Medicine and Surgery*. New York: Julian Press. 1957.

Evans, F. J. 1963. The Maudsley Personality Inventory, suggestibility and hypnosis. *Int. J. Clin. Exp. Hypn.* 11:3, 187–200.

Eysenck, H. J. 1943. Suggestibility and hysteria. *J. Neurol. and Psychiat.* 6:22–31.

————. 1964. *Experiments in Behavior Therapy*. Oxford, England: Pergamon Press.

Fairbairn, W. R. D. 1954. *Object-Relations Theory of the Personality*. New York: Basic Books.

Faw, V., and Wilcox, W. W. 1958. Personality characteristics of susceptible and unsusceptible hypnotic subjects. *Int. J. Clin. Exp. Hypn.* 6:83–94.

————, Sellers, D. J., and Wilcox, W. W. 1968. Psychopathological effects of hypnosis. *J. Clin. Exp. Hypn.* 16:26–37.

Festinger, L. 1957. *A Theory of Cognitive Dissonance*. Stanford, California: Stanford University Press.

Fleiss, J. L. 1971. Measuring nominal scale agreement among many raters. *Psychol. Bull.* 76:378–382.

————. 1973. *Statistical Methods for Rates and Proportions*. New York: John Wiley and Sons, Sec. 9.2, 92–99.

Flor-Henry, P. 1976. Lateralized temporal-limbic dysfunction and psychopathology. *Annals of the N. Y. Acad. of Sci.* 280:777–795.

————. 1977. Neuropsychological and power spectral EEG investigations of the obsessive-compulsive syndrome. Presented to the annual meeting of the American Psychiatric Association, May 1977, in Toronto, Canada. (To be published.)

Frank, J. 1962. *Persuasion and Healing*. Baltimore, Maryland: Johns Hopkins University Press.

Frankel, F. H. 1974(a). Trance capacity and the genesis of phobic behavior. *Arch. Gen. Psychiat.* 31:261–263.

————. 1974(b). The use of hypnosis in crisis intervention. *Int. J. Clin. Exp. Hypn.* 22:188–200.

————. 1976. *Hypnosis: Trance as a Coping Mechanism*. New York: Plenum Publishing Co.

————, and Orne, M. T. 1976. Hypnotizability and phobic behavior. *Arch. Gen. Psychiat.* 33:1259–1261.

Frankl, V. E., 1964. *The Philosophical Foundations of Logotherapy, in Phenomenology: Pure and Applied*. Ed. E. W. Straus. Pittsburgh, Penn.: Duquesne Univ. Press, pp. 43–59.

————. 1966. Logotherapy and existential analysis: A review. *Am. J. Psychother.* 20:252–261.

Freud, S. 1906 [1905]. *My Views On the Part Played by Sexuality in the Aetiology of the Neuroses*. Vol. VII. Stand. ed., trans J. Strachey and A. Freud. London: Hogarth Press, 1953.

————. 1915. *Papers on Metapsychology*. Vol. XIV. Stand. ed., trans. J. Strachey and A. Freud. London: Hogarth Press, 1963.

————. 1917. *Introductory Lectures on Psycho-analysis*. Vol. XVI. Stand. ed., trans. J. Strachey and A. Freud. London: Hogarth Press, 1953.

————. 1925 [1924]. *An Autobiographical Study*. Vol. XX. Stand. ed., trans. J. Strachey and A. Freud. London: Hogarth Press, 1959.

Fromm, E., and Shor, R. E., eds. 1972. *Hypnosis: Research Developments and Perspectives*. Chicago: Aldinne-Atherton Publishers, Inc.

Fromm-Reichmann, F. 1950. *Principles of Intensive Psychotherapy*. Chicago: University of Chicago Press.

Furneaux, W. D., and Gibson, H. B. 1961. The Maudsley Personality Inventory as a predictor of susceptibility to hypnosis. *Int. J. Clin. Exp. Hypn.* 9: 167–177.

Gainotti, G. 1972. Emotional behavior and hemispheric side of the lesion. *Cortex* 8:41–55.

Galbraith, G. C., and Cooper, L. M. 1972. Hypnotic susceptibility and the sensory-evoked response. *J. Comp. Physiol. Psychol.* 80:509–514.

Gale, C., and Herman, M. 1956. Hypnosis and the psychotic patient. *Psychiat. Quart.* 30:417.

Galin, D., and Ornstein, R. 1972. Lateral specialization of cognitive mode: an EEG study. *Psychophysiology* 9:412–418.

————, and ————. 1974. Individual differences in cognitive style-I reflective eye movements. *Neuropsychologia* 12:367–375.

————. 1974. Implications for psychiatry of left and right cerebral specialization: A neurophysiological context for unconscious processes. *Arch. Gen. Psychiat.* 31:572–583.

————, and Ellis, R. R. 1975. Asymmetry in evoked potentials as an index of lateralized cognitive processes: Relation to EEG alpha asymmetry. *Neuropsychologia* 13(9):45–50.

Gaw, A. C., Chang, L. W., and Lein-Chun Shaw. 1975. Efficacy of acupuncture on osteoarthritic pain. *N Engl. J. Med.* 293:375–378.

Glover, F. S. 1961. Use of hypnosis for weight reduction in a group of nurses. *Amer. J. Clin. Hypn.* 3:250–251.

Goldberger, N. I., and Wachtel, P. L. 1973. Hypnotizability and cognitive controls. *Int. J. Clin. Exp. Hypn.* 21:298–304.

Goldburgh, S. J. 1968. Hypnotherapy, chemotherapy, and expressive-directive therapy in the treatment of examination anxiety. *Amer. J. Clin. Hypn.* 11:42–44.

Goodman, L. S., and Gilman, A. 1975. *The Pharmacological Basis of Therapeutics*, 5th ed. New York: The Macmillan Co.

Gordon, M. C. 1972. Age and performance differences of male patients on modified SHSS. *Int. J. Clin. Exp. Hypn.* 20:152–155.

————. 1973. Suggestibility of chronic schizophrenic and normal males matched for age. *Int. J. Clin. and Exp. Hypn.* 21:284–288.

Grabowska, M. J. 1971. The effect of hypnosis and hypnotic suggestion on the blood flow in the extremities. *Polish Med. J.* 10:1044–1051.

Graham, K. R., Wright, G. W., Toman, W. J., and Mark, C. B. 1975. Relaxation and hypnosis in the treatment of insomnia. *Amer. J. Clin. Hypn.* 18: 39–42.

Greene, J. T. 1969. Hypnotizability of hospitalized psychotic patients. *Int. J. Clin. Exp. Hypn.* 17:103–108.

Greenberg, I. M. Unpublished manuscript. A General Systems Theory of Trance State.

Greenson, R. R. 1965. The working alliance and the transference neurosis. *Psychoanal. Quart.* 34:155–182.

Grinker, R., Sr., Werble, B., and Drye, R. 1968. *The Borderline Syndrome*. New York: Basic Books.

Group for the advancement of psychiatry. 1962. *Medical uses of hypnosis.* Symposium 8:641–706.

Gur, R. C., and Gur, R. E. 1974. Handedness, sex and eyedness as moderating variables in the relation between hypnotic susceptibility and functional brain asymmetry. *J. Abnorm. Psychol.* 83:635–643.

———. 1975. Conjugate lateral eye movements as an index of hemispheric activation. *J. Pers. and Soc. Psychol.* 31:751–757.

———, Gur, R. E., and Harris, L. J. 1975. Cerebral activation, as measured by subjects' lateral eye movements, is influenced by experimenter location. *Neuropsychologia* 13:35–44.

Gur, R. E., and Rehyer, J. 1973. Relationship between style of hypnotic induction and direction of lateral eye movements. *J. Abnorm. Psychol.* 82:499–505.

Haley, J., ed. 1967. *Advanced Techniques of Hypnosis and Therapy: Selected Papers of Milton H. Erickson, M.D.* New York: Grune & Stratton.

Hall, J. A., and Crasilneck, H. B. 1970. Development of a hypnotic technique for treating chronic cigarette smoking. *Int. J. Clin. Exper. Hypn.* 18:283–289.

Hammer, E. F. 1954. Post-hypnotic suggestion and test performance. *J. Clin. Exper. Hypn.* 2:178–185.

Hanley, F. W. 1967. The treatment of obesity by individual and group hypnosis. *Canad. Psychiat. Assoc.* 12:549–551.

Havens, L. L. 1973. *Approaches to the Mind: Movement of the Psychiatric Schools from Sects Toward Science.* Boston: Little, Brown & Co.

———. 1974. The existential use of the self. *Am. J. Psychiat.* 131:1–10.

Hayflick, L. 1965. The limited *in vitro* lifetime of human diploid cell strains. *Exper. Cell Res.* 37:614–636.

Heath, E. S., Hoaken, P. C. S., and Sainz, A. A. 1961. Hypnotizability in state hospitalized schizophrenics. *Psychiat. Quart.* 34:65.

Hegel, G. W. F. 1961. *The Phenomenology of Mind.* Trans. J. B. Ballie. New York: The Macmillan Co.

Heidegger, M. 1972. *Being and Time.* Trans. J. Macquarrie and E. Robinson. New York: Harper & Row.

Hess, E. H. 1959. Imprinting, *Science* 130:133–141.

Hilgard, E. R., and Lauer, L. W. 1962. Lack of correlation between the California Psychological Inventory and hypnotic susceptibility. *J. Consult. Psychol.* 26:331–335.

———. 1965. *Hypnotic Susceptibility.* New York: Harcourt, Brace, & World.

———, and Hilgard, J. R. 1975. *Hypnosis in the Relief of Pain.* Los Altos, California: William Kaufmann, Inc.

———. 1975. Hypnosis. *Ann. Rev. Psychol.* 26:19–44.

Hilgard, J. R. 1970. *Personality and Hypnosis: A Study of Imaginative Involvement.* Chicago: University of Chicago Press.

Hoppe, K. D. 1977. Split brains and psychoanalysis. *Psychoanal. Quart.* 46:220–244.

Horowitz, S. L. 1970. Strategies within hypnosis for reducing phobic behavior. *J. Abnorm. Psychol.* 75:104–112.

Irvin, F. S. 1972. *Sentence Completion Test.* Jacksonville, Illinois: Psychologist and Educator Corp.

Isham, A. C. 1962. Hypnorelaxation therapy for tension state. *Amer. J. Clin. Hypn.* 5:152.

Jacobs, L., and Jacobs, J. 1966. Hypnotizability of children as related to hemispheric reference and neurological organization. *Amer. J. Clin. Hypn.* 8:269–274.

Jacobson, E. 1938. *Progressive Relaxation*. Chicago: University of Chicago Press.

——. 1964. *Anxiety and Tension Control*. Philadelphia: Lippincott, Inc.

Janov, A. 1970. *The Primal Scream: Primal Therapy, The Cure for Neurosis*. New York: Dell Publishing Co.

Johnston, E., and Donahue, J. R. 1971. Hypnosis and smoking: A review of the literature. *Amer. J. Clin. Hypn.* 13:265–272.

Joseph, E. D., Peck, S. N., and Kaufman, M. R. 1949. A psychological study of neurodermatitis with a case report. *Mt. Sinai Hosp. Jl.* 15:360–366.

Jung, C. G. 1964. *Man and His Symbols*. New York: Doubleday.

Kant, I. 1965. *Critique of Pure Reason*. Trans. N. K. Smith. New York: St. Martin's Press.

Kanzler, M., Jaffe, J. H., and Zeidenburg, P. 1976. Long and short-term effectiveness of a large-scale proprietary smoking cessation program—a four year follow-up of smoke-enders participants. *J. Clin. Psychol.* 32:661–669.

Kardiner, A., and Spiegel, H. 1947. *War Stress and Neurotic Illness*. New York: Paul Hoeber, Inc.

Katz, R. L., Kao, C. Y., Spiegel, H., and Katz, G. J. 1974. Acupuncture, and Hypnosis. *Adv. in Neurol.* 4:819–825.

Kelly, E., and Zeller, B. 1969. Asthma and the psychiatrist. *J. Psychosom. Res.* 13:377–395.

Kepes, E. R., Chen, M., and Schapira, M. 1976. A critical evaluation of acupuncture in the treatment of pain. *Adv. in Pain Res. Ther.* 1:817–822.

Kernberg, O. 1975. *Borderline Conditions and Pathological Narcissism*. New York: Jason Aronson, Inc.

Keutzer, C., and Lichtenstein, E. 1968. Modification of smoking behavior: A review. *Psychol. Bull.* 70:520–533.

Kierkegaard, S. 1954. *Fear and Trembling and the Sickness Unto Death*. Trans. W. Lowrie. Garden City, New York: Doubleday.

Kinsbourne, M. 1972. Eye and head turning indicates cerebral lateralization. *Science* 176:539–541.

——. 1974. Direction of gaze and distribution of cerebral thought processes. *Neuropsychologia* 12:279–281.

Kline, M. V. 1970. The uses of extended group hypnotherapy sessions in controlling cigarette habituation. *Int. J. Clin. Exp. Hypn.* 28:270–282.

Knowles, J., ed. 1977. *The Responsibility of the Individual, in Doing Better and Feeling Worse*. New York: W. W. Norton, pp. 57–80.

Koestler, A. 1967. *The Ghost in the Machine*. New York: The Macmillan Co.

Kotin, J., and Goodwin, F. K. 1972. Depression during mania: Clinical observations and theoretical implications. *Am. J. Psychiat.* 129:679–684.

Kramer, E., and Brennan, E. P. 1964. Hypnotic susceptibility of schizophrenic patients. *J. Abnorm. Soc. Psychol.* 69:657–659.

——. 1966. Group induction of hypnosis with institutional patients. *Int. J. Clin. Exp. Hypn.* 14:243–246.

Kroger, W. S., and DeLee, S. T. 1957. Use of hypnoanestesthesia for caesarian section and hysterectomy. *JAMA* 163:442–444.

Laing, R. D. 1965. *The Divided Self: An Existential Study in Sanity and Madness*. Middlesex, England: Penguin Books, Ltd.

——. 1970. *Knots*. New York: Vintage Press, Random House, Inc.

Lange, P. J., and Lazovik, A. D. 1963. Experimental desensitization of a phobia. *J. Abnorm. Soc. Psychol.* 66:519–525.

Lavoie, G., and Sabourin, M. 1973. Hypnotic susceptibility, amnesia, and IQ in chronic schizophrenia. *Int. J. Clin. Exp. Hypn.* 21:157–168.

Lazarus, A. A. 1971. *Behavior Therapy and Beyond.* New York: McGraw-Hill.

———. 1973. Multimodal behavior therapy: Treating the basic id. *J. Nerv. Ment. Dis.* 156:404–411.

Leichter, H. J., ed. 1974. Some perspectives on the family as educator. In *The Family as Educator.* New York: Teachers College Press, Columbia University, pp. 1–43.

———, and Mitchell, W. E. 1967. *Kinship and Casework.* New York: Russell Sage Foundation.

———, and ———. 1978. *Kinship and Casework: Family Networks and Social Intervention.* New York: Teachers College Press, Columbia University.

Levi-Strauss, C. 1963. *Structural Anthropology.* Trans. E. Jacobson and B. G. Schoepf. New York: Basic Books.

———. 1969. *The Raw and the Cooked.* New York: Harper & Row.

Levitt, E. E., Brady, J. P., and Lubin, B. 1963. Correlates of hypnotizability in young women: Anxiety and dependency. *J. Personality* 31:52–57.

———, Lubin, B., and Brady, J. P. 1965. The personality pattern associated with insusceptibility to hypnosis in young women. *Dis. Nerv. Syst.* 26:506–7.

Lockett, M. F. 1965. Dangerous effects of isoprenaline in myocardial failure. *Lancet* 2:104–106.

Lodato, F. J. 1968. Hypnosis: An adjunct to test performance. *Amer. J. Clin. Hypn.* 2:129–130.

London, P., Hart, J. T., and Leibovitz, M. P. 1969. EEG alpha rhythms and susceptibility to hypnosis. *Nature* 219:71–72.

McGlashan, T. H., Evans, F. J., and Orne, M. T. 1969. The nature of hypnotic analgesia and the placebo response to experimental pain. *Psychosom. Med.* 31:227–246.

McManis, A. G. 1964. Adrenaline and isoprenaline: A warning. *Med. J. Aust.* 2:76.

Machover, K. 1949. *Machover Draw-A-Person Test (Machover Figure Drawing Test).* Springfield, Illinois: Charles C. Thomas.

Mack, J. 1975. *Borderline States in Psychiatry.* New York: Grune and Stratton.

McLean, A. F. 1965. Hypnosis in "psychosomatic" illness. *Brit. J. Med. Psychol.* 38:211–230.

Maclean, P. D. 1977. On the evolution of three mentalities. In *New Dimensions in Psychiatry.* Vol. II, eds. S. Arieti and G. Chrzanowski. New York: John Wiley and Sons.

Maher-Loughnan, G. P. 1970. Hypnosis and autohypnosis for the treatment of asthma. *Int. J. Clin. Exp. Hypn.* 18:1–14.

Malleson, N. 1959. Panic and phobia: A possible method of treatment. *Lancet* 2:1225–1227.

Mann, J. 1973. *Time-Limited Psychotherapy.* Cambridge: Harvard University Press.

Marias, J. 1970. *Jose Ortega y Gasset, Circumstance and Vocation.* Trans. F. M. Lopez-Morillas. Norman, Oklahoma: University of Oklahoma Press.

Marks, I. M., Gelder, M. G., and Edwards, G. 1968. Hypnosis and desensitization for phobias: A controlled prospective trial. *Brit. J. Psychiatry* 114: 1263–1274.

Martin, G. M., Sprague, C. A., and Epstein, C. J. 1970. Replicative life-span of cultivated human cells. *Lab Investig.* 23:86–92.

Meares, A. 1956. Recent work in hypnosis and its relation to general phychiatry. *Med. J. Aust.* 43:1–5.

–––––. 1960. *A System of Medical Hypnosis*. Philadelphia: W. B. Saunders.

Melzack, R., and Wall, P. D. 1965. Pain mechanisms: A new theory. *Science* 150:971–979.

Merleau-Ponty, M. 1962. *Phenomenology of Perception*. New York: The Humanities Press.

Metzig, E., Rosenberg, S., Ast, M., and Krashen, S. D. 1976. Bipolar manic-depressives and unipolar depressives distinguished by test of lateral asymmetry. *Biol. Psychiatry* 11:313–323.

Minkowski, E. 1970. *Lived Time: Phenomenological and Psychopathological Studies*. Trans. J. Needleman. Evanston, Illinois: Northwestern University Press, p. 72.

Moore, M. E., and Berk, S. N. 1976. Acupuncture for chronic shoulder pain. *Ann. Int. Med.* 84:381–384.

Moorefield, C. W. 1971. The use of hypnosis and behavior therapy in asthma. *Amer. J. Clin Hypn.* 13:162–168.

Morgan, A. H., McDonald, P. J., and Macdonald, H. 1971. Difference in bilateral alpha activity as a function of experimental task, with a note on lateral eye movements and hypnotizability. *Neuropsychologica* 9:459–469.

–––––. 1973. The heritability of hypnotic susceptibility in twins. *J. Abnorm. Soc. Psychol.* 82:55–61.

–––––, and Hilgard, E. R. 1973. Age differences in susceptibility to hypnosis. *Int. J. Clin. Exp. Hypn.* 21:78–85.

–––––, Johnson, D. L., and Hilgard, E. R. 1974. The stability of hypnotic susceptibility: A longitudinal study. *Int. J. Clin. Exp. Hypn.* 22:249–57.

–––––, MacDonald, H., and Hilgard, E. R. 1974. EEG alpha: Lateral asymmetry related to task and hypnotizability. *Psychophysiology* 11:275–282.

Moss, C. S. 1958. Therapeutic suggestion and autosuggestion. *Int. J. Clin. Exp. Hypn.* 6:109–115.

Mullahy, P. 1970. *Psychoanalysis and Interpersonal Psychiatry: The Conceptions of Harry Stack Sullivan*. New York: Science House.

Murray, H. A. 1943. *Thematic Apperception Test*. Cambridge: Harvard University Press.

Nemiah, J. 1961. *Foundations of Psychopathology*. New York: Oxford University Press.

Nicassio, P., and Bootzin, R. 1974. A comparison of progressive relaxation and autogenic training as treatments for insomnia. *J. Abnorm. Psychol.* 83:253–260.

Nietzsche, F. [Golffing, F. trans.] 1956. *The Birth of Tragedy*. New York: Doubleday.

Nowlis, D. P., and Rhead, J. C. 1968. Relation of eyes-closed resting EEG alpha activity to hypnotic susceptibility. *Percept. and Motor Skills* 27:1047–1050.

Nuland, W., and Field, P. B. 1970. Smoking and hypnosis: a systematic clinical approach. *Int. J. Clin. Exp. Hypn.* 18:290–306.

–––––. 1970. A single-treatment method to stop smoking using ancillary self-hypnosis: Discussion. *Int. J. Clin. Exp. Hypn.* 18:257–260.

Oakley, R. P. 1960. Hypnosis with a positive approach in the management of "problem" obesity. *J. Am. Soc. Psychosom. Dent. Med.* 7:28–40.

Orne, M. T. 1959. The nature of hypnosis: Artifact and essence. *J. Abnorm. Soc. Psychol.* 58:277–299.

―――. 1966. Hypnosis, motivation and compliance. *Am. J. Psychiatry,* 122:721–726.

Ortega y Gasset, 1957. *On Love: Aspects of a Single Theme.* Trans. T. Talbot. New York: Meridian Books/The World Publishing Co.

Pederson, L., Scrimjeour, W., and Lefcoe, N. 1975. Comparison of hypnosis plus counseling, counseling alone, and hypnosis alone in a community service smoking withdrawal program. *J. Counsel. Clin. Psychol.* 43:920.

Perin, C. T. 1968. The use of substitute response signals in anxiety situations. *Amer. J. Clin. Hypn.* 10:207–208.

Perls, F. S. 1969. *Ego, Hunger and Aggression: The Beginnings of Gestalt Therapy.* New York: Random House, Inc.

―――. 1970. *Gestalt Therapy: Verbatim.* New York: Bantam Books, Inc.

Perry, C. 1977. Is hypnotizability modifiable? *Int. J. Clin. Exp. Hypn.* 25:125–146.

Piaget, J. 1954. *The Construction of Reality in the Child.* New York: Basic Books.

―――. 1971. *Psychology and Epistemology: Towards A Theory of Knowledge.* New York: Viking Press.

Plato. 1956. Meno. In *Great Dialogues of Plato.* Trans. W. H. D. Rouse. New York: Mentor Books, p. 42.

Polak, P. R., Mountain, H. E., and Emde, R. N. 1964. Hypnotizability and the prediction of hypnotizability in hospitalized psychotic patients. *Int. J. Clin. Exp. Hypn.* 12:252–257.

Pribram, K. 1961. Limbic System. In *Electrical Stimulation of the Brain,* ed. D. E. Sheer. Austin, Texas: University of Houston Press, pp. 311–320.

―――. 1969(a). *The Neurobehavioral Analysis of Limbic Forebrain Mechanisms: Revision and Progress Report.* In *Advances in the Study of Behavior.* Vol. II. New York: Academic Press, pp. 297–332.

―――. 1969(b). Neural servosystems and the structure of personality. *J. Nerv. Ment. Dis.* 149:30–39.

―――, and McGuinness, D. 1975. Arousal, activation and effort in the control of attention. *Psychol. Rev.* 82:116–149.

Rank, O. 1929. *The Trauma of Birth.* New York: Harcourt, Brace.

Reich, W. 1972. *Character Analysis.* Trans. V. R. Carfagno. New York: Simon and Schuster.

Reider, N. 1976. Symptom substitution. *Bull. Menn. Clinic.* 40:629–640.

Ricoeur, P. 1970. *Freud and Philosophy.* Trans. D. Savage. New Haven: Yale University Press.

Roberts, A. H., and Tellegen, A. 1973. Ratings of "trust" and hypnotic susceptibility. *Int. J. Clin. Exp. Hypn.* 21:289–297.

Rogers, C. 1951. *Client-Centered Therapy.* Boston: Houghton Mifflin Co.

Rorschach, H. 1954. *Psychodiagnostic Plates,* 5th ed. New York: Grune & Stratton.

Rosenhan, D. 1969. Hypnosis and personality: A moderator variable analysis. In *Psychophysiological Mechanisms of Hypnosis,* ed. L. Chertok. New York: Springer-Verlag, pp. 193–198.

Sacerdote, P. 1965. Additional contributions to the hypnotherapy of the advanced cancer patient. *Amer. J. Clin. Hypn.* 7:308–319.

————. 1970. Theory and practice of pain control in malignancy and other protracted or recurring painful illnesses. *Int. J. Clin. Exp. Hypn.* 18:160–180.

Sarbin, T. R., and Slagle, R. W. 1972. Hypnosis and psychophysiological outcomes. In *Hypnosis: Research Developments and Perspectives*, eds. E. Fromm and R. E. Shor. Chicago: Aldine-Atherton, pp. 185–214.

Sartre, J. P. 1969. A psychoanalytic dialogue with a commentary by Jean-Paul Sartre, *Ramparts* 8:43–49.

Scagnelli, J. 1974. A case of hypnotherapy with an acute schizophrenic. *Amer. J. Clin. Hypn.* 17:60–63.

————. 1976. Hypnotherapy with schizophrenic and borderline patients: Summary of therapy with eight patients. *Amer. J. Clin. Hypn.* 19:33–38.

Schneck, J. M. 1975. Prehypnotic suggestion in psychotherapy. *Amer. J. Clin. Hypn.* 17:158–159.

Schulman, R. E., and London, P. 1963. Hypnotic susceptibility and MMPI Profiles. *J. Consult. Psychol.* 27:157–160.

Schultz, J. H., and Luthe, W. 1959. *Autogenic Training*. New York: Grune & Stratton.

Schwartz, G.E., Davidson, R. J., and Maer, F. 1975. Right hemisphere lateralization for emotion in the human brain: Interactions with cognition. *Science* 190: 286–288.

Shader, R., ed. 1975. *Manual of Psychiatric Therapeutics: Practical Pharmacology and Psychiatry*. Boston: Little, Brown and Co.

Shakow, D. 1969. On doing research in schizophrenia. *Arch. Gen. Psychiat.* 20:618–642.

————. 1971. Some observations on the psychology (and some fewer on the biology) of schizophrenia, *J. Nerv. Ment. Dis.* 153:300–316.

————. 1972. The Worcester state hospital research on schizophrenia (1927–1946). *J. Abnorm. Psychol.* 80:67–110.

————. 1974. Segmental set: A theory of the formal psychological deficit in schizophrenia. *Arch. Gen. Psychiat.* 6:1–7.

Shapiro, A. K., and Morris, L. A. 1978. Placebo effect in medical and psychological therapies. In *Handbook of Psychotherapy and Behavior Change: An Empirical Analysis*, 2nd ed. A. Bergin and S. Garfield, eds. New York: John Wiley and Sons.

Shapiro, D. 1965. *Neurotic Styles*. New York: Basic Books.

Shor, R. E. 1960. The frequency of naturally occurring "hypnotic-like" experiences in the normal college population. *Int. J. Clin. Exp. Hypn.* 8:151–163.

————, and Orne, E. D. 1962. *The Harvard Group Scale of Hypnotic Susceptibility, Form A*. Palo Alto, California: Consulting Psychologists Press.

————, Orne, M. T., and O'Connell, D. N. 1962. Validation and cross-validation of a scale of self-reported personal experiences which predicts hypnotizability, *J. Psychol.* 53:72.

————, Orne, M. T., and O'Connell, D. N. 1966. Psychological correlates of plateau hypnotizability in a special volunteer sample. *J. Pers. and Soc. Psychol.* 3:80–95.

Sifneos, P. E. 1972. *Short-Term Psychotherapy and Emotional Crisis*. Cambridge: Harvard University Press.

Silver, M. J. 1973. Hypnotizability as related to repression-sensitization and mood. *Amer. J. Clin. Hypn.* 15:245–249.

Skinner, B. F. 1938. *The Behavior of Organisms*. Century Psychology Series. New York: Appleton-Century Crofts.

――――. 1948, 1976 reissued ed. *Walden II.* New York: The Macmillan Co.

――――. 1957. *Science and Human Behavior.* New York: Free Press.

Smith, J. M., and Burns, C. L. 1960. The treatment of asthmatic children by hypnotic suggestion. *Brit. J. Dis. Chest* 54:78–81.

Spiegel, D., and Shader, R. 1975. *Hypnosis.* In *Manual of Psychiatric Therapeutics: Practical Psychopharmacology and Psychiatry,* ed. R. Shader. Boston: Little, Brown and Co., pp. 295–298.

Spiegel, D., and Fink, R. 1978. *Hysterical Psychosis and Hypnotizability.* (Submitted for publication.)

Spiegel, H., Fishman, S. and Shor, J. 1945. An hypnotic ablation technique for the study of personality development: A preliminary report. *Psychosom. Med.* 75:273–278.

――――. 1959. Hypnosis and transference: A theoretical formulation. *Arch. Gen. Psychiat.* 1:634.

――――. 1960. Hypnosis and the psychotherapeutic process. *Compr. Psychiat.* 1:174.

――――, and Shainess, N. 1963. Operational spectrum of psychotherapeutic process. *Arch. Gen. Psychiat.* 9:477–488.

――――. 1963(a). Current perspectives on hypnosis in obstetrics *Acta. Psychother.* 11:412–429.

――――. 1963(b). The dissociation-association continuum. *J. Nerv. Ment. Dis.* 136:374–378.

――――. 1965. Imprinting, hypnotizability, and learning as factors in the psychotherapeutic process. *Am. J. Clin. Hypn.* 7:221–225.

――――. 1967. Is symptom removal dangerous? *Am. J. Psychiatry* 123:1279–1283.

――――, and Linn, L. 1969. The "ripple effect" following adjunct hypnosis in analytic psychotherapy. *Am. J. Psychiatry* 126:53–58.

――――. 1970(a). Termination of smoking by a single treatment. *Arch. Environ. Health* 20:736–742.

――――. 1970(b). A single-treatment method to stop smoking using ancillary self-hypnosis. *Int. J. Clin. Exp. Hypn.* 18:235–250.

――――. 1972. An eye-roll test for hypnotizability. *Amer. J. Clin. Hypn.* 15:25–28.

――――. 1973. *Manual for Hypnotic Induction Profile: Eye-Roll Levitation Method,* rev. ed. New York: Soni Medica.

――――. 1974. The grade 5 syndrome: the highly hypnotizable person. *Int. J. Clin. Exp. Hypn.* 22:303–319.

――――, Fleiss, J. L., Bridger, A. A., and Aronson, M. 1975. Hypnotizability and mental health. In *New Dimensions in Psychiatry: A World View,* ed. S. Arieti. New York: John Wiley and Sons, pp. 341–356.

――――, Aronson, M., Fleiss, J. L., and Haber, J. 1976. Psychometric analysis of the Hypnotic Induction Profile. *Int. J. Clin. Exp. Hypn.* 24:300–315.

――――. 1977. The Hypnotic Induction Profile: A review of its development. In *Conceptual and Investigative Approaches to Hypnosis and Hypnotic Phenomena.* Annals of the New York Academy of Sciences, Vol. 296, pp. 129–142.

――――, and Spiegel, D. Forthcoming. *Manual for the Hypnotic Induction Profile.* Revised and enlarged edition. New York: Basic Books.

――――, and Lipman, L. 1978. Hypnotizability and the hand clasp sign. (Submitted for publication.)

――――, Stern, D. B., and Lipman, L. S. The Hypnotic Induction Profile in the assessment of psychopathology. (Submitted for publication.)

Stanton, H. E. 1975. Weight loss through hypnosis. *Amer. J. Clin. Hypn.* 18:34–38.

Stern, D. B. 1977. Handedness and the lateral distribution of conversion reactions. *J. Nerv. Ment. Dis.* 164:122–128.

Stuart, R. B. 1967. Behavioral control of overeating. *Behav. Res. Ther.* 5: 357–365.

Stunkard, A. J. 1975. Presidential Address 1974: From explanation to action in psychosomatic medicine: the case of obesity. *Psychosom. Med.* 37: 195–236.

———, and Mahoney, M. J. 1976. Behavioral treatment of the eating disorders. In *Handbook of Behavior Modification and Behavior Therapy,* ed. H. Leitenberg. Englewood Cliffs: Prentice-Hall.

Sullivan, H. S. 1949. *Conceptions of Modern Psychiatry.* The William Alanson White Institute. New York: W. W. Norton.

———. 1953. *The Interpersonal Theory of Psychiatry.* New York: W. W. Norton.

———. 1954. *The Psychiatric Interview.* New York: W. W. Norton.

Switras, J. E. 1974. A comparison of the eye-roll test for hypnotizability and the Stanford Hypnotic Susceptibility Scale, Form A. *Amer. J. Clin. Hypn.* 17:54–55.

Szent-Gyorgi A. 1972. Apollonians and Dionysians, Letter in *Science* 176: 996.

Tellegen, A., and Atkinson, G. 1974. Openness to absorbing and self-altering experiences ("absorption"), a trait related to hypnotic susceptibility. *J. Abnorm. Psychol.* 83:268–277.

Thompson, K. F. 1963. A rationale for suggestion in dentistry. *Amer. J. Clin. Hypn.* 5:181–186.

Travis, T. A., Kondo, M. A., and Knott, J. R. 1973. Interaction of hypnotic suggestion and alpha enhancement. *Am. J. Psychiatry* 130:1389–1391.

Vingoe, F. J. 1966. Hypnotic susceptibility of hospitalized psychotic patients: A pilot study. *Int. J. Clin. Exp. Hypn.* 14:47–54.

Wall, P. D. 1972. (July 20). An eye on the needle. *New Scientist.* 129–131.

Wallace, A. K. 1970. The physiological effects of transcendental meditation. *Science* 167:1751.

Watkins, H. H. 1976. Hypnosis and smoking: A five-session approach. *Int. J. Clin. Exp. Hypn.* 24:381–390.

Watzlawick, P., Weakland, J., and Fisch, R. 1974. *Change: Principles of Problem Formation and Problem Resolution.* New York: W. W. Norton.

Webb, R. A., and Nesmith, C. C. 1964. A normative study of suggestibility in a mental patient population. *Int. J. Clin. Exp. Hypn.* 12:181–183.

Wechsler, D. 1955. *Wechsler Adult Intelligence Scale.* New York: Psychological Corporation.

Weitzenhoffer, A. M. 1957. *General Techniques of Hypnosis.* New York: Grune & Stratton.

———, and Weitzenhoffer, G. B. 1958. Personality and hypnotic susceptibility. *Amer. J. Clin. Hypn.* 1:79–82.

———, and Hilgard, E. R. 1959. *Stanford Hypnotic Susceptibility Scale: Forms A and B.* Palo Alto, California: Consulting Psychologists Press.

———, and ———. 1963. *Standford Profile Scales of Hypnotic Susceptibility, Forms I and II.* Palo Alto, California: Consulting Psychologists Press.

Weldon, T. D. 1945. *Introduction to Kant's Critique of Pure Reason.* Oxford: Oxford University Press.

Wheeler, L., Reis, H. T., Wolff, E., Grupsmith, E., and Mordkoff, A. M. 1974. Eye-roll and hypnotic susceptibility. *Int. J. Clin. and Exp. Hypn.* 22:327–334.

White, H. C. 1961. Hypnosis in bronchial asthma. *J. Psychosom. Res.* 5: 272–279.

Wick, E., Sigman, R., and Erickson, M. V. 1971. Hypnotherapy, and therapeutic education in the treaatment: Differential treatment factors. *Psychiat. Quart.* 45:234–254.

Wilbur, S. 1907. *The Life of Mary Baker Eddy.* Boston: The Christian Science Publishing Society.

Wilcox, W. W., and Faw, V. 1959. Social and environmental perceptions of susceptible and unsusceptible hypnotic subjects. *Int. J. Clin. Exp. Hypn.* 7: 151–159.

Williams, D. T., Spiegel, H., and Mostofsky, D. I. 1978. Neurogenic and hysterical seizures in children and adolescents: differential diagnosis and therapeutic considerations. *Am. J. Psychiatry* 135:82–86.

Wilson, C. P., Cormen, H. H., and Cole, A. A. 1949. A preliminary study of the hypnotizability of psychotic patients. *Psychiat. Quart.* 23:657.

Wineburg, E. N., and Straker, N. 1973. An episode of acute, self-limiting depersonalization following a first session of hypnosis. *Am. J. Psychiatry* 130: 98–100.

Wolberg, L. R. 1948. *Medical Hypnosis,* 2 Vols. New York: Grune & Stratton.

Wolpe, J. 1958. *Psychotherapy by Reciprocal Inhibition.* Stanford, California: University Press.

———, and Lazarus, A. 1966. *Behavior Therapy Technique.* New York: Pergamon Press.

———. 1973. *The Practice of Behavior Therapy,* 2nd ed. New York: Pergamon Press.

Wright, E. A. 1970. A single-treatment method to stop smoking using ancillary self-hypnosis discussion. *Int. J. Clin. Exp. Hypn.* 18:261–267.

Zeig, J. K. 1974. Hypnotherapy techniques with psychotic in-patients. *Amer. J. Clin. Hypn.* 17:56–59.

Zuckerman, M., Persky, H., and Link, K. 1967. Relation of mood and hypnotizability: An illustration of the importance of the state versus trait distinction. *J. Consult. Clin. Psychol.* 31:464–470.

NAME INDEX

SUBJECT INDEX